E-COMMERCE LAW

E-COMMERCE LAW

Paul Todd

Reader in Law,
University of Wales Swansea

Cavendish
Publishing
Limited

London • Sydney • Portland, Oregon

First published in Great Britain 2005 by
Cavendish Publishing Limited, The Glass House,
Wharton Street, London WC1X 9PX, United Kingdom.
Telephone: +44 (0)20 278 8000   Facsimile: +44 (0)20 278 8080
Email: info@cavendishpublishing.com
Website: www.cavendishpublishing.com

Published in the United States by Cavendish Publishing
c/o International Specialized Book Services,
5824 NE Hassalo Street, Portland,
Oregon 97213–3644, USA

Published in Australia by Cavendish Publishing (Australia) Pty Ltd
45 Beach Street, Coogee, NSW 2034, Australia
Telephone: +61 (2)9664 0909   Facsimile: +61 (2)9664 5420

© Todd, P   2005

British Library Cataloguing in Publication Data

Todd, Paul
E-commerce law
1 Electronic commerce – Law and legislation – Great Britain
2 Electronic commerce – Law and legislation
3 Internet – Law and legislation – Great Britain
4 Internet – Law and legislation
I Title
343.4'109944

Library of Congress Cataloging in Publication Data
Data available

ISBN 1-85941-942-9
ISBN 978-1-859-41942-7

1 3 5 7 9 10 8 6 4 2

Printed and bound in Great Britain

PREFACE

This is a textbook on the law of e-commerce, intended primarily for students of law, or of schemes of study where law is an element, whether at undergraduate or postgraduate level. I teach e-commerce law, at undergraduate and postgraduate level, to students of law, business management and information technology, and I hope this book will be of use, at the very least, to my own students.

E-commerce is still a fairly new phenomenon, at least as we know it today, and when a new phenomenon arrives, the existing law has to apply to it as best it can. Often it does not apply very well, but there are still a number of areas where there is no legislation specifically to deal with e-commerce and the pre-existing law continues to apply. Sometimes the pre-existing law is statutory, as for example with trade marks, discussed in Chapter 3, but quite large areas remain covered only by common law. There is therefore quite a bit of material for case lawyers here, especially in the sections on contract formation, incorporation of terms, etc.

Yet though e-commerce as a phenomenon remains fairly new, the law is maturing and there has already been some development to deal with the new phenomenon; there is now quite a bit of legislation aimed at e-commerce in particular. Much of this legislation has EU origins, and is aimed at (at least) partial harmonisation of the law throughout the EU. All law students will know that the skills involved in interpreting EU legislation and cases are very different from those involved in studying domestic UK law.

Another consequence of e-commerce law having developed to a stage at least slightly above the embryonic is that there is less need to rely on cases from the US and other jurisdictions; for the most part, there is enough material from the UK and EU for us to be able, with reasonable certainty, to state the law on the basis of that material alone. There are some areas, however, for example ISP liability in Chapter 12, where reform is being actively considered. In such areas, cases and legislation from the US and elsewhere are discussed, not so much to help determine what the law is in the UK, but by way of comparison, since other jurisdictions may have desirable features, which the UK might consider adopting.

It is also clear that e-commerce practices and techniques continue to develop, and indeed to develop quickly, and the law should ideally continue to react to these new developments. A good example is the discussion in Chapter 4 of deep linking and peer-to-peer distribution systems, where technology has developed to assist copyright holders, and the focus of the law has moved from copyright infringement itself to protecting the technological devices used to protect the copyright. No doubt we can expect to see other changes in focus in other areas of e-commerce law over the next few years.

On an issue of language convention, many of the actors in this book are companies. A company has legal personality, and therefore cannot be 'it', but there are not two types, so 'he or she' would also be entirely inappropriate. A company is therefore 'he', in line with what I take to be conventional English usage, just as conventionally (I think), ships and countries are female. Nothing should be read into these conventions, any more than into the convention in French that a cat is male and a car is female – it is just language convention.

The law is stated as at 31 January 2005.

Paul Todd

CONTENTS

TABLE OF CASES

TABLE OF LEGISLATION

EUROPEAN LEGISLATION

DIRECTIVES

PART 1

INTRODUCTION

1

INTRODUCTION

1.1 WHAT IS E-COMMERCE?

1.1.1 The medium

At the core of e-commerce is the Internet, but it is certainly possible to define the activity more widely than this. The following, for example, is taken from a description of the role in e-commerce of the World Trade Organisation (WTO):[1]

> ... electronic commerce is broadly defined as referring to six instruments, namely: 'the telephone, the fax, television, electronic payment and money transfer systems, Electronic Data Interchange and the Internet.'

Another example of a wide definition of e-commerce is:[2]

> Any business transaction concerning goods and services, where participants are not in the same physical location and communicate through electronic means.

It can be seen that these definitions include, for example, contracting over the telephone, or by telex or fax. However, these do not raise issues which differ from any other kind of contract and, therefore, I do not propose to cover them in this book. Definitions can in any case vary, depending on the use to which they will be put. If a wide role is argued for the WTO, then a wide definition of e-commerce may well be appropriate. Conversely, the United Nations Commission on International Trade (UNCITRAL) refers to e-commerce as involving 'the use of alternatives to paper-based methods of communication and storage of information'.[3] This clearly excludes communicating by telex or fax and, indeed, as we will see, the EU concept of the Information Society is confined to communications and transactions that take place online.[4]

It is clear, then, that there are no generally accepted definitions of e-commerce. For the purposes of this book, it seems sensible to exclude anything that does not raise special issues that are particular to e-commerce. My own working definition, therefore, is narrow, as follows:

> Any transaction involving goods or services where digital electronic communication performs an essential function.

This is a commercial law book, so we shall also assume the existence of a commercial party, at least on one side of the transaction. The other party may also be a commercial party ('B2B e-commerce'), or a consumer ('B2C e-commerce').

---

1   Barchetta, M, Low, P, Mattoo, A, Schuknecht, L, Wager, H and Wehrens, M, *Electronic Commerce and the Role of the WTO*, 1998, Geneva: World Trade Organisation, p 5, quoted by Brownsword, R and Howells, G, 'When surfers start to shop: Internet commerce and contract law' (1999) 19 LS 287, p 288, note 1.

2   Lodder, A and Kaspersen, H (eds), *eDirectives: Guide to European Union Law on E-Commerce*, 2002, The Hague: Kluwer Law International, p 3.

3   Preamble to UNCITRAL's *Model Law on Electronic Commerce (1996)*, referred to in Lodder and Kaspersen, *ibid*, p 3. UNCITRAL's English frame is at www.uncitral.org/en-index.htm (then link to adopted texts and e-commerce).

4   See the E-commerce Directive, discussed in section 10.1.5.

The reference to digital communication is intended to exclude telephone conversations (since these are often analogue) and, for the same reason, telex and fax communications. It is not confined to Internet communications, however. In principle, this definition could include short message service (SMS) and local area network (LAN) communications and any other connection between computers. It also includes commerce within a closed electronic system, such as CompuServe, and also electronic data interchange (EDI) systems between businesses. All these raise issues which are peculiar to the method of communication. Future developments are also covered, insofar as they can be predicted – for example, the use of television and mobile phones, the last of which, in particular, may give rise to interesting issues.

To this extent, therefore, e-commerce law is wider than Internet law. In practice, of course, e-commerce will nearly always involve the Internet, at least part of the communication being either by e-mail or the World Wide Web, and to this extent there is an overlap between the two fields. E-commerce is narrower than Internet law, however, in that we are concerned only with commercial activity, and not (except peripherally) with criminal issues, such as pornography. Defamation is covered, however, because it can arise in a commercial context (for example, electronic newspapers), and also because much of the material on ISP liability, considered in Chapter 12, relates to defamation.

1.1.2   The transactions

There is no doubt that the real impetus to e-commerce has been the development, since about 1994, of the World Wide Web (WWW). Certainly, this was the impetus for the consumer-based e-commerce, around which quite a large proportion of this book is based. However, e-commerce includes more than just the obvious example of Internet shopping. Commercial activity includes not only sales, but also matters such as advertising and the provision of information (price lists, timetables, etc) to assist a commercial transaction. E-commerce includes reading an e-newspaper like the *Shetland Times* (on which there is a well known case, considered in Chapter 4 of this book),[5] the purchase of information products such as music, or database information such as LexisNexis or Westlaw.[6] Some of these activities are impossible in the paper-based world.

Ultimately, however, this book is concerned with commercial transactions, involving goods or services, including the provision of online services, and delivery of electronic goods.[7] Transactions can be purely commercial, between businesses, for example with EDI, or can involve consumers, dealing either with businesses or with other consumers. The book is also concerned with the support infrastructure for electronic trading, for example the allocation of domain names for business websites.

---

5   Section 4.4.3.
6   The legal databases respectively of Butterworths and Sweet & Maxwell.
7   This may not be the same as goods and services as defined in UK statute law. Indeed, the classification of these contracts itself raises issues: see further the discussion in section 10.1.1. There are also taxation implications, which are beyond the scope of this book, but see Basu, S, 'To tax or not to tax? That is the question? Overview of options in consumption taxation of e-commerce' at http://www2.warwick.ac.uk/fac/soc/law/elj/jilt/2004_1/basu.

1.2   SOME FEATURES OF THE INTERNET AND THE WWW

However e-commerce is defined, most of it is currently Internet-based[8] and, as we will see, it has been transformed by the emergence as a major force, in the mid-1990s, of the WWW. It is impossible to understand e-commerce law without at least some understanding of how it all works and, since most e-commerce is Internet-based, how the Internet works; some of the unique features of the Internet need to be grasped.

There was no inevitability about e-commerce being Internet-based, and indeed books on electronic data interchange, written around 1990, assumed that private 'Value Added Networks' ('VANs') would be set up.[9] The Internet, if mentioned at all, was dismissed as being hopelessly insecure for business purposes, and really only of use as a plaything for academics. It is also true that the Internet is not, at least at first sight, particularly suitable as a medium for commercial dealings. Its traditions are almost militantly democratic (albeit somewhat elitist), and there is no central control, except as to the communication protocols to be used (see further below at sections 1.2.1, 1.3.1 and 1.3.3.1). Control is certainly not generally exercised over the content of information available, or the use to which the medium is put. There is no certainty as to who you are dealing with. There is also a tradition of freedom of information, 'copyleft' not copyright, even to the extent that computer operating systems are simply given away.[10] It is not obviously a medium from which money can be made.

Yet the Internet is central to e-commerce today. The marriage of two apparently incompatible cultures is probably largely an accident of timing. Digital communications between computers became publicly accessible only with the development, around the mid-1990s, of the WWW and graphical browsers, such as Mosaic and Netscape. From the start, the WWW used the protocols then used on NSFNET,[11] the backbone of the Internet, funded ultimately by the American government. This was partly, no doubt, because NSFNET was by then a mature and high-capacity network, operating reliably, and connecting a wide range of people from all over the world. The WWW, no more than the Internet itself, however, was intended to be a vehicle for commerce.

To some extent, e-commerce has overcome the shortcomings of the Internet through technological means. Encryption and digital signatures, described in Chapter 5, allow parties to deal with each other, reasonably secure as to the identity of the other party. Information, even on the WWW, need not be free, but can be protected by password or other means. Reliable payment systems have been developed. By these means, the Internet has been moulded to suit the needs of commerce. Not everything can be resolved by technological means, however, and the law also has a role to play, as we will see.

---

8   Or Intranet or Extranet, to which the observations here also apply.
9   Eg, Emmelhainz, MA, *Electronic Data Interchange: A Total Management Guide*, 1990, New York: Van Nostrand Reinhold. VANs are described at pp 111 *et seq*. I can find no reference to the Internet at all.
10   See, eg, Naughton, J, *A Brief History of the Future: The Origins of the Internet*, 2000, London: Phoenix, Chapter 13.
11   National Science Foundation.

1.2.1   Connecting computers together

The principle of telephone networks, at any rate prior to cellular and Internet phones, was to set up for each call an end-to-end communication line, exclusively for that particular conversation, for the entire duration of the conversation. If the call was long-distance, it might have to be connected via a number of exchanges and amplified to counter signal deterioration over distance, but the principle was to set up an end-to-end link every time a call was made for the duration of the call. Since most conversations do not involve long silences but make use of the line for most of the time, this did not seem inherently wasteful.

When, around 35 years ago, computers were first connected together to transfer information, it was discovered that it was not generally efficient to set up end-to-end connections for the duration of the communication, as with a telephone conversation. Computer communications are inherently bursty, the time a computer takes to send and receive data being very small, relative to its other activities.[12] For computers to communicate as telephones do would entail long silences on the line, and be extremely wasteful. You have only to think of communicating by e-mail: most of the time is spent composing the mail, and only a short burst is needed to send it. Users of dial-up Internet connections often store all their outgoing mail in an outbox on their hard disk, connecting to their Internet Service Provider (ISP) for just long enough to send it all and then hanging up, in order to economise on phone usage. Even so, the time taken to connect is often significant, compared with the time actually spent online. Telephone exchange switches are simply not fast enough, so that even if computers batched outgoing communications (to the same destination) to send in a single burst, this would be a very slow method of communication.

Another problem with the end-to-end telephone link is that it is designed to be used exclusively for a single communication. A mainframe computer, however, or today a web server, will frequently be sending data to, and receiving it from, many destinations simultaneously.

It proved far more efficient to use permanent lines connecting each computer to its immediate neighbours, data being sent out in small packets via routers.[13] There was no need to set up end-to-end connections in order to do this, and it was found to be more efficient to send each packet to the best available router in the direction of the destination. The router would copy and forward the packet (but not store it) to the next router, and so on until the packet arrived at its destination. Each packet would take its own best route, traffic on the network being continuously and automatically monitored, and the data would be reassembled on arrival at the destination computer. This is the essence of a packet-switched network, the basis today of nearly all communications between computers.

---

12   At least this was true 35 years ago. With the large downloads facilitated, and indeed required, by the WWW, connection times can be both lengthy and busy.

13   With early networks, such as the ARPANET, the routers connected each (mainframe) computer directly to the network. Routers are nowadays used to transmit packets over the Internet, and to connect other networks (and ultimately the computers themselves) to the Internet.

For a history of early networks, see, eg, Hafner, K and Lyon, M, *Where Wizards Stay Up Late: The Origins of the Internet*, 1996, New York: Touchstone.

The earliest working network of computers was the ARPANET, set up in 1969 by the American Department of Defense Advanced Research Projects Agency (DARPA). Not long afterwards, other packet-switched networks appeared not just in the US, but all over the world. From the start, ARPANET spanned America and its fast connections could be used as a backbone to which other networks could be connected. The basic idea of many computer networks all over the world, connected by a very high-capacity network, operating as a backbone and funded by the US government, formed the basis of what eventually became the Internet. In 1983, DARPA decided that TCP/IP (on which more later at sections 1.3.1 and 1.3.3.1) would be the standard set of protocols used by computers connecting to ARPANET.[14] This meant that any smaller networks that wanted to connect to ARPANET also had to use TCP/IP. Hence TCP/IP became, effectively, the compulsory protocol of the Internet.

In 1986, the National Science Foundation (NSF) connected America's six supercomputing centres together, the network being called the NSFNET, or NSFNET backbone. This was connected to ARPANET, and hence also used TCP/IP. This very high-speed backbone, which was originally funded by the American government, eventually replaced the ARPANET as the backbone of the Internet. NSFNET was thus a network of networks, originally of US universities, but later expanded to academic institutions generally, and later still to businesses and other users. This is essentially the basis of the modern Internet.

There are a number of points that can be made about the resultant structure. First, the network is distributed with no central command or, indeed, central points. Nobody is in overall control, and nobody can shut it down. Indeed, it is even said to be proof against nuclear attack, though this was probably a by-product of, rather than the reason for, its structure. It has certainly survived large-scale power outages, with little interruption to traffic.[15] It is probably partly for this reason that the Internet has been seen as lawless and uncontrolled, but it does not follow at all that merely because there is no central authority, there is no control. It is probably true to say that the Internet is, in principle at least, the most controlled phenomenon on earth.

Packet switching also requires routers to copy and forward data. It is necessary to make copies of the data, albeit only for transmission purposes. There is no need to store it once it has been transmitted to the next router or to its destination. However, all copying has potential copyright implications, which are discussed in Chapter 4 of this book.

---

14 The TCP (Transfer Control Protocol) governs transfer of data, while IP (Internet Protocol) governs addresses, each computer connected to the Internet having a unique IP address. There is further discussion of IP addresses in section 2.1.1.

15 Eg, 'Chaos as massive power cuts hit US cities', *Electronic Telegraph*, 15 Aug 2003, www.telegraph.co.uk/news/main.jhtml?xml=/news/2003/08/15/wcut15.xml (registration needed to access).

1.2.2   The World Wide Web (WWW)

It has already been observed that much modern e-commerce is conducted on the WWW.[16] The WWW was originally conceived by Tim Berners-Lee, a British inventor who worked for CERN, the European Particle Physics Laboratory in Geneva, as a non-hierarchical system for storing and retrieving information, users linking the information using whatever association they wished regardless of any kind of hierarchy or organisation, in much the same way that mind association games work. The method used to create the links was (and still is) hypertext. It was, no doubt, a very good idea, but the Web was not a runaway success until graphical browsers, such as Mosaic, Netscape and, later, Windows Explorer made it (and the Internet) easily accessible to the general public.

Nowadays, the WWW can be used as a publishing medium, attracting all the legal consequences of publishing. Those who host web servers can, in principle at least, be liable for their content in the same way that newspapers and magazines may be liable for contributions. The Internet is also the method by which web pages are requested and transmitted, so that all the above statements about copying also apply. A web page need not be like a page from a newspaper or magazine, though. It does not have to exist as a single page, but can be assembled from material elsewhere on the web, anywhere in the world, material that is either the author's own or not. There might be thought to be obvious copyright problems where another's material is incorporated into the page, but there need not be any direct copying across from one page to the other (though there will necessarily be copying to the recipient's computer).

Another problem is deep linking (that is, linking to the inside pages of another site), thereby possibly avoiding advertising, terms of access or even password protection on the visited site. This may be another example of the commercial world having foisted on it a medium which, like the Internet itself, is possibly not appropriate to its needs. From the beginning, the conception of the Web was anti-hierarchical. Tim Berners-Lee, the inventor of the Web, says that:[17]

> The vision I have for the Web is about anything being potentially connected with anything. It is a vision that provides us with new freedom, and allows us to grow faster than we ever could when we were fettered by the hierarchical classification systems into which we bound ourselves.

The model was probably the child browsing through an encyclopaedia or a dictionary, jumping from word to word just by association. The idea of having to go to a top-level

---

16 Footnote 6 in the judgment in *Blumenthal v Drudge*, United States District Court for the District of Columbia, Civil Action No 97-1968 (PLF), is as follows:

> The term 'Internet' means the international computer network of both Federal and non-Federal interoperable packet switched data networks. ... The Internet is 'not a physical or tangible entity, but rather a giant network which interconnects innumerable smaller groups of linked computer networks'. ... The 'web' is a 'vast decentralized collection of documents containing text, visual images, and even audio clips' ... The web is designed to be inherently accessible from every Internet site in the world ...

The full text of this judgment can be found at www.techlawjournal.com/courts/drudge/80423opin.htm.

17 Berners-Lee, T, *Weaving the Web*, 2000, New York: HarperCollins, p 1.

(or home) page and then down a hierarchical structure was precisely what the Web was designed to avoid. But while it may well be true that people look for information on an association basis which has nothing to do with hierarchy,[18] businesses do not necessarily wish to provide information on that basis. They generally prefer something more structured, giving them more control over its presentation, but that is exactly what the Web was designed not to provide.[19]

That commerce was forced to use the Web, which was therefore not well suited to its purpose, was largely accidental and matters could easily have turned out differently. At around the same time as the Web developed, the University of Minnesota developed Gopher, which was a hierarchical, menu-based method for providing and locating information on the Internet. This would probably have been far more satisfactory for business use, and early indications were that Gopher would be far more successful than the then fledgling Web, but graphical browsers were written for the Web, not for Gopher, and so it is the Web, rather than Gopher, which survives today. Tim Berners-Lee postulates that this was because the University of Minnesota reserved the right to ask business users for a licence fee, whereas:[20]

> CERN agreed to allow anybody to use the Web protocol and code free of charge, to create a server or a browser, to give it away without any royalty of other constraint.

Deep linking problems arise, then, ultimately because for CERN the Web was a sideline and its business was not to make money from it.

As with the Internet itself, however, business has bent the Web to suit its needs. Technologies exist to impose the hierarchy that the Web was designed to counter and force users to go through the site's home page. It may well be that technological rather than legal means will be the way in which deep linking problems are solved. Deep linking has potential legal implications, however, but just as with incorporation discussed above, there is no copying between the sites, though there is to the recipient computer.

The fact that a web page can be constructed from material in many places also complicates questions as to where things happen. Physical and logical locations do not necessarily match. For example, because a web page may be assembled from many different locations, what appears to be a single web site may in fact be distributed around servers all over the world. This has obvious implications for the law to be applied, and to jurisdiction.[21] It is also true of the Internet in general that routing is dynamic, so the packets could go anywhere, again posing similar issues.

---

18 This may not always be true. Tim Berners-Lee also observes (*ibid*, p 72) that 'some people, when they saw the Web, thought hypertext was confusing, or worried that somehow they would get lost in hyperspace when following a link'. Nonetheless, from the user's viewpoint, hierarchies can be a nuisance, and deep links very useful. I often bookmark, and indeed reference in this book, law reports of particular cases within Bailii, AOL or Nominet sites, for example, to avoid the hassle of having to go through the home page each time I want to find them. Presenters of information, however, often prefer to force hierarchy on the user.

19 Not all commercial sites object to deep linking. The BBC, for example, frequently broadcasts the addresses of pages within its sites, for example particular programmes such as *Top Gear* or *Click Online*.

20 Berners-Lee, *Weaving the Web*, op cit fn 17, p 74.

21 See sections 10.2.2 and 10.2.3.

In order to decrease total traffic, and hence to improve overall performance, frequently used web pages are routinely copied to temporary caches, or even relatively permanent mirror sites. It is obvious that the routine copying of information, possibly to numerous jurisdictions, has copyright implications.[22]

The WWW can only work if every computer connected to it has a unique address. The Internet Protocol addressing system, which is part of TCP/IP, is discussed more fully in Chapter 2.[23]

1.3   E-COMMERCE AND THE LAW

1.3.1   Effect of the WWW on B2B commerce

If you adopt a wide definition of e-commerce as including telephone and fax communications, it is quite an old activity but most of the e-commerce described in this book is relatively new. It is true that e-commerce existed, to a limited extent, before the invention and development of the WWW, mostly on a B2B (business to business) basis. Before the WWW, however, it was necessary to agree everything in advance, including low-level protocols as to how to communicate.[24] After all, computers cannot talk to each other meaningfully. All they can do is transfer strings of ones and zeros, and some method has to be found of making these comprehensible. The Web, however, uses the Internet-based protocols, TCP/IP,[25] which are universal, and deal with all low-level communication issues. Because web interfaces are now universal, there is no need for the participants to deal with these issues any more. All they need to do is to ensure that their equipment can connect to the Web, so even B2B e-commerce has been transformed by the now ubiquitous WWW.[26] Universal application of TCP/IP removes the need for prior agreement as to how to communicate, at least at lower levels of abstraction.[27] There may still, however, be the need to agree other matters – for example, not to challenge electronic signatures and with regard to encryption systems. If such an agreement is necessary, it requires a closed system adopted by all participants.[28]

In any case, B2B developments continue, including a good deal of automation, with regard to ordering, invoicing, paying, etc. Communication protocols in this regard are still not standardised, so low-level agreements remain necessary. Another likely future development is electronic agents scouring the web with authority to make

---

22 See further Chapter 4.
23 Section 2.1.1
24 See, eg, Emmelhainz, *Electronic Data Interchange: A Total Management Guide, op cit* fn 9, Chapter 4.
25 See further section 2.1.1.
26 Eg, Bolero, a B2B scheme currently being piloted for electronic bills of lading, uses web communication exclusively.
27 In essence, the communication, as opposed to application levels, TCP/IP being simpler than the OSI model, with its seven levels. See, eg, www.stevenblack.com/PTN-Layers.asp.
28 Bolero is an interesting real-life example: www.boleroassociation.org. See also section 5.1.

purchases.[29] Here, too, software is not yet standardised, so agreements on how to agree will remain necessary.[30]

1.3.2   Effect of the WWW on B2C commerce

Particularly for consumers, however, it was not until use of the WWW became widespread that modern e-commerce could develop. The WWW, invented for a wholly unrelated purpose in 1989, was not released to the public until 1991, and it developed very slowly at first. It was not until at least 1994 that the introduction of graphical browsers, such as Mosaic and Netscape, made it accessible to the general public. Tim Berners-Lee, the inventor of the WWW, writing of early 1994, observes that:[31]

> O'Reilly had just published Ed Krol's book *Whole Earth Internet Catalog*, which was really the first book that made all this Internet stuff accessible to the public. When I had proofread it ... the World Wide Web occupied just one chapter; the rest was about how to use all the various Internet protocols such as FTP and Telnet and so on.

This accords with my own experience. I became interested in the Internet at about that time, and purchased the then up to date *Internet: The Complete Reference*.[32] Only Chapter 24 (of 25 chapters, or 15 pages of 815) is devoted to the WWW. There is no sense at all that it is to become the dominant medium of the Internet. For example:[33]

> Thus, we can characterize the Web a little more precisely. The Web is an attempt to organize all the information on the Internet (plus any local information that you would like to add on your own) as a set of hypertext documents. *Although this dream is somewhat unrealistic*, the Web does allow you to access all kinds of Internet resources, just be using a browser to 'read' the appropriate document.

Then:[34]

> The Web isn't perfect. There will be times when you would be better off using a tool that was designed specifically for a particular type of data.

This is only just over 10 years ago, but the Web was still competing at that time with Gophers and other tools. Most of the chapter describes line browsers, Mosaic being mentioned only right at the end of the chapter.[35] At that time, it could only be used with X Windows, a UNIX program which would hardly have been enjoyed by the general public. Amazon.com opened in 1995 and, by about 1996, consumer-based e-commerce was beginning to flourish. So the phenomenon of e-commerce, as we know it today, at least B2C (business to consumer), is no more than 10 years old.

---

29 See further section 9.7.
30 The W3C Consortium, by developing extended markup language (XML), and thereby forcing structure on data, will facilitate the standardisation needed at higher levels of abstraction for EDI applications: see further www.w3schools.com/xml/default.asp. Bolero is also (among others) interested in developing XML. See further, eg, www.computerweekly.com/Article22704.htm.
31 Berners-Lee, *Weaving the Web, op cit* fn 17, p 76.
32 Hahn, H and Stout, R, *Internet: The Complete Reference*, 1994, Berkeley: Osborne.
33 *Ibid*, p 497. The emphasis is mine.
34 *Ibid*, p 498.
35 *Ibid*, p 510.

1.3.3   The WWW and the law

1.3.3.1   An anarchic Internet?

It was also almost certainly the development of the WWW, which has always been (and remains) Internet-based, that led to the predomination of the TCP/IP protocol, which had been the basis of the NSFNET, the precursor to the Internet. Indeed, it was not until about 10 years ago that it became clear that the Internet would form the basis of e-commerce. It seemed possible that, at least in Europe, an alternative system, based on OSI (Open Systems Interconnection) developed by the ISO (International Standards Organisation), would predominate. OSI is now essentially history. Apart from the development of the WWW, other reasons for its demise were the earlier development of UNIX, the operating system used on most mainframe computers, greater availability of software, and the convenience of the NSFNET backbone.

There were major differences in the ideologies between the two systems. OSI would have been a theoretical standard, imposed from above, top down, whereas TCP/IP, the Internet protocols, even if conceptually inferior, had been working in real networks for many years. Thus, TCP/IP had been developed by the users of the system, bottom up. Moreover, until about 10 years ago, the Internet was mainly the preserve of a fairly small community of academics, especially American academics, the ethos of TCP/IP being essentially driven by them. TCP/IP came to predominate because users wanted it, not because authority decreed, and its eventual predominance probably exacerbated the distrust of a central authority. This anarchic ethos survives to this day, at least in terms of the Internet's structure, and to some extent its traditions also. This also stems partly from the nature of the beast. It is, for example, very easy (for anyone) to publish on the Internet. Anyone with Internet access can e-mail to large mailing lists, post messages to newsgroups, and most ISPs will also allow subscribers to create their own websites. Unlike other media, such as newspapers, radio or television, no permission is required from an editor or anybody else.[36] Drawing attention to your material and persuading others to read it is, of course, another matter entirely. This forms the substance of the next chapter, and most of Chapter 3, but even here, many of the steps that are taken generally require nobody's permission. There is no doubt that, at any rate compared with previous media, the Internet is a relatively anarchic place.

Not only was there, among the early users of the Internet, a general distrust of authority, but also a strong tradition of free and robust speech, to the extent that flaming was a wholly acceptable application of this freedom; this was, after all, a small community composed primarily of American academics. No doubt also, because of the way in which the Internet had developed without central control, there developed an anarchic culture which suggested that it was in some sense incapable of being controlled by law. For example:[37]

---

36   Academic and journalist John Naughton describes how he once timed creating a web page from scratch in 17 minutes: Naughton, *A Brief History of the Future: The Origins of the Internet, op cit* fn 10, p 22.

37   Hahn and Stout, *Internet: The Complete Reference, op cit* fn 32, p 3.

As unbelievable as it sounds, nobody actually 'runs' the Internet. Nobody is 'in charge' and no single organisation pays the cost. The Internet has no laws, no police, and no army. There are no real ways to hurt another person, but there are many ways to be kind.

This may have been acceptable when the Internet was primarily a tool for a small community of academics, but the anarchic culture and free speech tradition are simply incompatible with the widespread public use of the WWW and its evolution for commerce. We have only to look at some of the defamation cases in Chapter 12 to see how misplaced today is the view that the Internet cannot hurt anyone (in one of the American cases, a wholly innocent party was subjected to death threats because of Internet publications).[38] The Internet can also be used for blasphemy and sedition, for obscene publications, as an instrument of fraud or blackmail, and as a means of passing off one's own goods and services as those of another. The idea that it is merely a playground for academics, and harmless, is just nonsense. The Internet can also be used to create contracts, and to perform transactions, such as the transfer of money and even the electronic equivalent of goods and services. There is no reason why those contracts and transactions should not be given legal effect, just as they would have been had they been made or performed using traditional physical media.

There is no doubt that the informal structure of the Internet and the lack of central controls can make it difficult in practice for the law of any jurisdiction to control it.[39] It is possible to send mail and newsgroup postings anonymously, and a website that is under legal threat can easily move, if necessary, to a different jurisdiction. If an American citizen or company uses a website on a US server to defame a British citizen with a reputation to protect in the UK, the victim may well be able to sue in the UK courts, but the redress that he or she will obtain may in practice be limited.[40]

It does not follow at all, however, that the (undeniable) lack of central control over the running and evolution of the infrastructure implies total lawlessness. Far from it, indeed, though as a matter of practice the laws are not always easy to enforce. Though the Internet is sometimes referred to as cyberspace, as if it were in some magical space 'out there', the people who operate it and its physical means of operation are grounded firmly within existing jurisdictions. Publication and damage occurs within existing jurisdictions and can be controlled by the law of those jurisdictions. There is no such lawless place as cyberspace and, indeed, it is arguable that the Internet is, at least in theory, one of the most controlled places on earth.[41]

The problems of using the law to control the Internet are therefore practical rather than theoretical. This can be illustrated by examining the difficulties encountered by a government, in this case Singapore, which is worried by the potential of the Internet to

---

38 See section 12.2.1.2.
39 It can be quite difficult to keep track of Internet sources even where there is no attempt to hide them. In 1999, I gave a talk at the Help Institute in Kuala Lumpur on the Internet and the Law. I made use of a 1997 text, the footnotes of which contained URLs. About half of them no longer worked, after two years. Readers of this book may experience the same phenomenon, though all links were checked prior to publication.
40 See further the discussion on enforcement in section 12.1.6.
41 In passing, we might also observe that there are some crimes (eg, hacking) that can only be committed using computers, and even perhaps some that can only be committed using the Internet (distributing viruses in Java applets on the web, or Word macros via email).

intrude into the affairs of its citizens, and wishes to exercise control. So-called repressive Asian regimes are often looked on askance by western democracies, but there can be good reasons for censorship, and American free speech traditions are not accepted all over the world. This is an extract from an article by Dr Peng Hwa Ang and Ms Berlinda Nadarajan:[42]

> From a Western, especially American, perspective, censorship is difficult if not impossible to defend. But the position of the Singapore government and indeed even the citizenry is that there are good reasons for censorship. First, as there is anecdotal evidence to suggest that media can have negative effects on their consumers, it is therefore wiser to err on the side of caution through censorship. Second, there have been incidents in the past where media reports have caused racial riots and the shedding of blood. These are the 1950 Maria Hertogh riots, the 1964 riots during Prophet Muhammad's birthday, and the 1969 riot spillover from Malaysia. These riots have been blamed partly on uninhibited reporting and are often cited as examples of how the press can incite racial and ethnic violence.[43]

> In the Maria Hertogh case, the Malay press played up the angle (in its words and pictures) that the Dutch girl brought up as a Muslim by a Malay family was now forced to take up the Christian religion. The story was read by the Muslim community as a case of religious injustice and a riot broke out – leaving 18 dead and 173 wounded.[44] Most recently, the execution of a Filipino domestic help in Singapore has sparked off anti-Singapore sentiments in the Philippines. Again, uninhibited and erroneous reporting have been blamed for the demonstrations and protests against Singapore.[45]

> Events like these are used to justify the need for tight censorship in a multiracial/multireligious society, where the unimpeded flow of ideas instead of leading to enlightenment can sometimes have negative effects.[46]

> Censorship also survives because of the widespread support of Singaporeans, as a recent survey by the first author found. On a censorship scale of 1 to 7, the three areas where Singaporeans wanted most censorship were materials for the young, news leading to race conflict and racially offensive public expression in that order.[47]

> Thus, censorship in Singapore is justified on historical as well as socio-political grounds, favouring caution and prevention over liberalism. This position has been systematically articulated by the government and accepted by the people as one of the boundaries within which Singapore society must function.

The way in which censorship was imposed was to require Singapore citizens to use Singapore ISPs, and then to license and control the ISPs. This is an extract from the

---

42 Peng Hwa Ang and Berlinda Nadarajan, 'Censorship on the Internet – a Singapore perspective', at http://ad.informatik.uni-freiburg.de/hyperwave/goid/0x84e6983c_0x00033d60.html.

43 'B. Nair, in A. Mehra (Ed.), *Press systems in ASEAN states, Singapore: Asian Mass Communication Research and Information Centre*, 85-90, 1989.' [Original footnote]

44 'ibid.' [Original footnote]

45 'Jimmy Yap, *Internet abuzz with 'talk' of maid's hanging*, The Straits Times, 20, April 5 1995.' [Original footnote]

46 'Ministry of Information and the Arts, *Censorship Review Committee Report*, Singapore 1992.' [Original footnote]

47 'Peng Hwa Ang, Albert Gunther and Eddie Kuo, *Public Opinion and Censorship in Singapore*, (in press).' [Original footnote]

Electronic Telegraph archives for 3 September 1996, an article by Robert Uhlig, Technology Correspondent:[48]

> Singapore has become the first country to attempt to use technology to stop its citizens viewing violent and pornographic material on the Internet.
>
> From Sept 15, Singapore's 120,000 Internet users must adjust their software so that requests for images and text from the global computer network are routed via government-controlled computers known as 'proxy servers'. Failure to make the adjustments will lead to prosecution and a heavy fine.
>
> The servers hold a limited database of frequently accessed 'approved' material, and will check every Internet site a subscriber tries to access against the government's list of banned sites. If the site is banned, the proxy server will deny access.
>
> George Yeo, the Information Minister, said yesterday: 'If you are able to collect taxes, and if you are able to protect intellectual property rights on the Internet, then you can also censor it.' He called the move an 'anti-pollution measure in cyberspace'. Mr Yeo has set up a panel of 19 members, headed by Bernard Tan, dean of the faculty of science at the National University of Singapore, to advise the Singapore Broadcasting Authority on regulating the Internet.

There is no doubt that control is possible in theory, then, although even measures as draconian as this may encounter practical difficulties of policing. One problem is that many sites outside Singapore might well be generally entirely respectable – for example, newspaper or television news sites – but contain a small amount of material considered offensive to the government of Singapore. Placing the entire site on a banned list may be the only practical censorship option, but it will deny access also to much 'legitimate' material. The other problem is that a banned site can simply move. Given the sheer size of the WWW, even if one is as determined as the government of Singapore is to control its citizens' access to undesirable Internet content, to do so effectively may be a difficult and expensive task; one has to consider whether the gains are worth the costs.

Obviously, the government of Singapore is aware of the difficulties. It knows that if some of its citizens are really determined to access prohibited material, they will do so. In practice, however, control of ISPs operating within the nation's borders is likely to be fairly effective, since a citizen of Singapore would have to be fairly determined to pay the international call rates to dial outside. To achieve a fairly high level of compliance would no doubt be regarded by the Singapore government as better than nothing.

To conclude this section, the Internet can be controlled by the law, but control can pose practical difficulties. Some forms of control can also restrict the usefulness of the media and hence, in the context of this book, the development of e-commerce.[49]

---

48 Available at: www.telegraph.co.uk/htmlContent.jhtml?html=%2Farchive%2F1996%2F09%2F03%2Fwnet03.html&secureRefresh=true&_requestid=77022 (registration needed to access the site).

49 We continue aspects of this debate in Chapter 8.

1.3.3.2   Application of existing (pre-Internet) law

The issue is, though, what is the applicable law? Of course, like any new technology, the Internet was initially governed by existing legal structures. The extent to which the existing law can adapt to the new technology depends, to some extent at least, on the level of generality at which the law is expressed, and also whether the judges have the necessary freedom to develop it. In some areas, such as trade marks and (perhaps) passing off (both considered in Chapter 3), the existing law seems capable of adapting to the new way of doing business; the same could also be true of contract formation and incorporation of terms, if the judges adopt a sufficiently flexible approach and consider what fundamentally they are trying to do. By contrast, the existing law of copyright (see Chapter 4) did not deal well with either deep linking or the temporary copies which form the backbone of the Internet. Sometimes, the pre-existing law is so well established that it is impossible to change it in the absence of legislation. A good example of this is the innocent dissemination defence to defamation (considered in Chapter 12), which could not be changed without legislation and which (arguably at least) did not work at all well in an Internet context.

1.3.3.3   Technological responses to supposed shortcomings in existing law

Where disputes occur between two private parties and there is no direct state interest, but where the law is perceived not adequately to protect one or both parties, often the best approach is simply self-help, that is, for the traders to provide the protection themselves. In the case of contracts made over the Internet, for example, the parties may agree, by an express term, whose law is to apply to the contract, and the offeror can expressly exclude the application of the postal rule, should he or she so wish. Choice of law clauses are not entirely unproblematic, but, in the UK at any rate, will usually be effective.[50]

In Chapter 4, we consider the issue of deep linking, and examine the UK copyright infringement case, *Shetland Times v Wills*.[51] A competing newspaper (*Shetland News*) was prevented by interim interdict from deep linking to *Shetland Times'* stories, but the decision probably depended on the use by the *Shetland News* of *Shetland Times'* headlines (the copying of literary works); had *Shetland News* used its own headlines, the copyright infringement would have failed, since it had copied none of *Shetland Times'* text.[52] Not only (it was alleged) had *Shetland News* in effect passed off *Shetland Times'* stories as its own, but also, because readers avoided going through the *Shetland Times* home page, they also avoided the advertisements, and *Shetland Times* was worried about diminution in its advertising revenue.

Since the *Shetland Times* case, the law has possibly improved protection against deep linking, but most newspapers have helped themselves, and appear no longer to

---

50 See further sections 9.2.5 and 10.2.1.

51 [1997] FSR 604.

52 The pursuer also succeeded on the grounds that it was providing a cable broadcast, parts of which had been incorporated into the defendant's site. This reasoning (which does not survive later legislative change) was generally regarded as unsatisfactory and wrong. See further the discussion in section 4.4.3.

be open to this kind of attack. The stories are no longer stored as .html files, to which links from elsewhere can easily be made, but are generated from the home page, for example using a common gateway interface (CGI) program, or .asp (active server pages) script. Because the content of the program or script cannot be accessed by the user, there is no possibility of linking directly to the story without accessing the home page where, of course, all the advertising revenue is to be earned. This is nowadays a very common technique: with most sites now, the user simply accesses a framed front page containing an index and perhaps a search tool, and all other pages are brought up using programs; they do not actually exist as pages on the server.[53]

One of the effects of technological self-help is to change the nature of the disputes that arise. For example, *Shetland Times* has made some use of these techniques, but there is nothing to prevent *Shetland News*, should it so desire, from generating, and then downloading to its own site, *Shetland Times* story pages. However, to incorporate the stories directly into its own site would be a clear breach of copyright, without the need to argue over whether there is any literary merit in a headline.[54] It should not be possible to access the inside pages of a secure site whose designer intends to ensure that access is only through the front page, but it is possible that a hacker could find a way to do it. The dispute would then, however, be as to the lawfulness of the hacking.[55]

A slightly different type of self-help may eventually resolve another issue, that of top-level domain names (discussed in detail in Chapters 2 and 3).[56] By contrast with domain names, there have been few disputes about allocation of telephone numbers, because there are excellent telephone directories. Similarly with the Internet, top-level domain names should become less of a problem as search engines become more efficient and comprehensive, since users will simply work from the search engine, rather than laboriously typing in the URL. A new type of dispute is already beginning to emerge as businesses attempt to maximise their visibility to the search engines.

Obviously, self-help is not a solution where the criminal law is concerned, or where outside parties are affected (as, for example, with defamation) or where there is a state interest in the content of the Internet. Here, legislation is the only solution, with pressures to harmonise because of the international nature of the Internet.

1.3.3.4   *Legislative responses to supposed shortcomings in existing law*

Not everything can be achieved through technology, and pressure has quite quickly built up for Internet-specific legislation. We are now very much in this second phase of e-commerce law development and there is a considerable amount of legislation dealing, in particular, with the Internet.

---

53   This also prevented me, a number of years ago, from adopting the useful technique of deep linking from my own home page directly to particular *Times Law Reports*; the best I can do now is to link to *The Times* front page for that day.
     See also generally sections 4.4.3, and the protection given to such technology in 4.5.1. It is also important to ensure that the program used to generate the pages cannot be read by the user.
54   Or indeed whether websites are really cable broadcasts (an argument that has no relevance since the amendments to the law discussed in section 4.4.3).
55   See section 4.5.
56   An interesting, and civilised, idea can be found at www.reed.com.

Since we now seem to live in an era where piecemeal legislation is commonplace, it might be thought unnecessary to justify legislation applying specifically to a single area of trading, but I would suggest that it is necessary to justify the according of special treatment for this particular activity. One possible justification is the desire, on the part of many countries, to promote e-commerce. Another is that the legal infrastructure needs to adapt, simply to allow the system to work.[57] If these justifications for legislative intervention are accepted, it also follows that any legislation should not impede the growth of the Internet or the development of e-commerce.

We have seen that the WWW and modern forms of e-commerce are both still relatively new, and pressures to legislate quickly can lead to ill-considered or poor quality legislation. In this book, there are examples of legislation that arguably falls into this category.[58] Because of the inevitable globalisation, especially of Web-based e-commerce, legislation is often also affected by pressures to harmonise the law. Indeed, some degree of co-operation between states may be necessary even for effective enforcement of the law. Edwards and Waelde observe:[59]

> It is certainly false to regard the Internet as a 'lawless place'. It is much truer to say that the Internet is regulated by a hotch-potch of national laws. But it is more true still to acknowledge that very often, states have little or no ability to enforce observation of their laws in relation to Internet activity.

There is also, within the EU, the policy of developing a single market.

It is certainly arguable that international legislation, whereby individual states adopt international conventions, may be the best way to deal with what are essentially international problems. After all, other international problems are dealt with in this way, for example, oil pollution at sea. However, as Edwards and Waelde observe:[60]

> Multinational treaties require copious investment of time and money to draft, and political will to force through, as each state has significant interests in retaining complete control over its own law which it will be reluctant to surrender. They are particularly difficult to bring to successful fruition where there are substantial differences between the laws of the different states ..., or where the issue is one which is close to the domestic interests of a state and its people, as with the criminal law, especially that relating to obscenity and pornography.

---

57 There have been precursors. Edwards, L and Waelde, C (eds), *Law and the Internet: A Framework for Electronic Commerce*, 2nd edn, 2000, Oxford: Hart, p 5, uses the analogy of 17th century commercial law. There is also no doubt that the development of international trade, and especially the cif contract, required a legal as well as a technical infrastructure in order to work satisfactorily; the cif contract was only able to develop after the enactment of the Bills of Lading Act 1855. Legislation intended to promote a particular type of activity is, therefore, not new.

58 Eg, section 10.1.2. Another example, though not strictly within the boundaries of e-commerce, is discussed by Yaman Akdeniz in Edwards, L and Waelde, C (eds), *Law and the Internet: Regulating Cyberspace*, 1st edn, 1997, Oxford: Hart, pp 229 *et seq*. The problem is that it is a serious offence for a person to have an indecent photograph or pseudo-photograph of a child in his or her possession. Section 160 of the Criminal Justice Act 1988 was amended specifically, by the Criminal Justice and Public Order Act 1994, to cover Internet pornography downloaded on to hard disks, but in such a way that would probably catch someone who innocently came across such material and whose browser automatically cached the file without the knowledge of the disgusted user.

59 Edwards, L and Waelde, C, *ibid*, in the introduction at p 9. This introduction is not repeated in the 2nd edition.

60 *Ibid*, p 7.

Another problem is that it is far more difficult to alter bad or ill-considered legislation, where such legislation has had to be agreed across several jurisdictions.

In any case, harmonisation necessarily leads to the predominance of one set of values over another, and is not unreservedly a good thing. There are some areas, such as those considered in Chapter 12, where harmonisation will probably be impossible because of the diversity of values between countries. Thus, for example, Professor Samtani Anil, speaking only of a uniform ASEAN regulatory framework to apply to content regulation of the Internet, says:[61]

> It is this author's view that, at the present moment, such an initiative is unlikely to succeed. Despite sharing some common goals and, to a certain extent, a shared heritage, the different Asean [sic] member countries have very different outlooks on issues pertaining to censorship. What is permissible in say, the Philippines, could potentially flout Singapore's censorship laws. Moreover, the censorship laws of many countries are based, to a large extent, on the social mores and values of the people in those countries. These laws would, therefore, differ from country to country.

If this is true within the relatively narrow confines of South East Asia, then how much more so on a truly global scale? In Chapter 12, we consider, for comparative purposes, the positions taken in Singapore and the US on control of content on the Internet. Though both are advanced countries, intent on promoting the Internet and e-commerce, in other respects their social mores and values are poles apart. It is difficult to see that there could be the remotest prospect of harmonising these very different regimes. Indeed, even where the issue is, in principle, one upon which one might expect all countries to agree (for example, child pornography), the US might have difficulty in coming into line because of constitutional freedom of speech issues.[62] Given that even with oil pollution at sea, the US opted out of international conventions and went its own way with its own set of laws, it seems unlikely that harmonisation of e-commerce law is likely to have significant impact in practice, except perhaps within the EU or other local regions.

B2C e-commerce, of course, raises consumer protection issues, which are largely harmonised, at least within the EU.[63]

1.4   THE FUTURE OF E-COMMERCE?

The nature of e-commerce seems likely to change, and it is to be expected that this will also affect the law applying to it.

Although the WWW is still fairly new, it has evolved quite considerably since its inception, for example with the introduction of frames, javascript, XML, etc. As the Internet evolves, the nature of legal disputes alters, and this is partly because the technology can itself help to resolve issues. Some of the deep linking issues of the mid-1990s, which we look at in detail in Chapter 4, have been largely resolved in practice by use of CGI (or .asp) programming and the development of frame technology in browsers. Technology provided a better solution than the law could, effectively

---

61 http://www2.warwick.ac.uk/fac/soc/law/elj/jilt/2001_2/anil.
62 Witness the fate of the Communication Decency Act 1996, discussed in section 12.2.1.2.
63 See generally section 10.1.

preventing deep linking. Arguably, it is the technology itself which now needs to be protected, and the law has indeed moved in this direction.[64]

It seems likely that changing technology will also affect the nature of domain name disputes, where better search engines and directories will make the choice of domain name less important. The focus of legal dispute will then shift to control of search engine optimisation techniques. This is discussed further in Chapters 2 and 3.

Changing technology will also change the nature of e-commerce itself. For example, the acceptance of standards on structured data, for example XML, should make easier the development of e-business (EDI, or electronic data interchange). Another possibility, which will also demand standardisation, this time of the software used, is the formation of contracts by electronic agents, which could roam the web with instructions, but which would contract without further human intervention. Obviously, this could raise quite interesting challenges for the normal law of contract formation.[65]

On the consumer side, some items might seem inherently ill-suited to e-commerce, but experience does not fully bear this out. For some items, such as fresh vegetables, it might be predicted that buyers prefer to see, handle and even smell them, which is impossible electronically. In reality, however, even that wholly reasonable preference can be outweighed by the convenience of e-commerce, as, for example, the success of Tesco Online testifies.[66] Nonetheless, e-commerce is obviously better suited to standardised products (for example, airline tickets, CDs and washing machines), where there is no need to see or feel the product physically before deciding to buy, or books where it is possible to sample pages online before buying.

It might be objected that this is doing little more than using digital means of communication where mail and telephone ordering were used before. Delivery is still by traditional methods, a point hammered home in a recent television advertisement for the Royal Mail, featuring the well-known musician, Elton John. While this is no doubt true, it is nonetheless worth observing that there are advantages in using digital media, even if only for communication. Where there is a menu of choices, e-commerce has advantages over both mail and telephone. It is also well suited to the purchase of rare goods, since it is easier to search online: it is probably easier, for example, to obtain rare or out-of-print books from Amazon than through an offline supplier. E-commerce price savings can also facilitate the provision of services at exceptionally good value, for example, the very cheap bus fares provided by megabus.com. Moreover, while credit and debit cards (with very high transaction costs for small transactions) are still the usual form of payment, more flexible electronic payment systems are already developing, such as eBay's PayPal,[67] and eventually perhaps other types of digital

---

64 See section 4.5.

65 See section 9.7.

66 www.tesco.com.

67 Described at http://pages.ebay.co.uk/paypal/index.html?ssPageName=Paypal_88x31. While PayPal is far more flexible and convenient than traditional payment by credit or debit card, or indeed digital cash from the seller's viewpoint, it nonetheless remains credit or debit card-based. Hence transaction costs remain quite high: free for buyers but 2.7% of transaction value plus £0.20 for high-volume sellers, 3.4% of transaction value plus £0.20 for all other sellers.
eBay is a well known online auction site.

cash, better suited to micro sales.[68] With sales of tangible products, however, better delivery systems might also be necessary before e-commerce really takes off.

The greatest growth industry will surely be in electronic products, however, where the Internet (or perhaps the cable TV network) is used as a delivery, as well as a communication system. Obvious examples might be such products as music files, maps, newspapers, and online databases, the provision of which is impossible without e-commerce. There are also less obvious possibilities. Tickets really contain only information, and hotel reservations, for example, are often delivered electronically. Even where proof of payment is required, as for example with a coach ticket, it is often sufficient simply to deliver a code number to show the driver and, of course, this can also be done electronically.

South Korea has recently experienced a boom in multi-media online gaming (MMOG), fuelled by the highest take-up rate of broadband in the world, and this will no doubt be replicated elsewhere.[69] Somewhat bizarrely, weapons and other attributes acquired in online gaming can be traded in the real world, electronically at eBay for example, to be used again by the acquiring player in the online gaming world. This goes beyond mere weapons used in fighting games:[70]

> The wide availability of broadband has clearly made it easier for the South Korean firms to attract more than just hard-core gamers. Young men are a big audience, but the South Korean firms are also attracting women, who seem especially fond of virtual avatars. One online firm, Plenus, runs a popular web portal called NetMarble which does a good business selling everything from virtual hats and handbags to virtual plastic surgery for computer avatars.

So the possibilities for consumer e-commerce are far wider than groceries from Tesco or books from Amazon, and include entirely novel products. Perhaps, eventually, reality and fantasy will become entirely blurred!

Other developments we might expect to see include pay for view, with payment systems better suited to small-scale transactions,[71] mobile phone and 'instantaneous' SMS commerce, and e-commerce using cable television channels.

It is certainly a mistake, therefore, to regard any part of the present structure as set in stone. In particular, it seems likely that cable TV and mobile phones will significantly impact on the methods of communication on the Internet. There will also be knock-on legal consequences: for example, mobile phones in particular raise problems for the incorporation of contractual terms, an issue considered in section 9.4.

---

68   See generally section 11.7.
69   See, eg, www.findarticles.com/cf_dls/m0PJQ/18_1/111363304/p1/article.jhtml.
70   From 'Invaders from the land of broadband', www.economist.com/business/ displayStory.cfm?story_id=2287063, a story in *The Economist*, 11 December 2003. Plenus is at www.plenus.co.kr, and NetMarble at www.netmarble.net, but language on both sites is primarily Korean.
71   See, eg, the discussion of digital cash in section 11.7.

PART 2

INTELLECTUAL PROPERTY AND RELATED ISSUES

ESTABLISHING A WEB PRESENCE

2.1 INTERNET ADDRESSES AND THE CHANGING NATURE OF DISPUTES

This chapter was originally entitled 'Domain name allocation', but technology moves on. Domain names continue to be of importance, but perhaps less so than four or five years ago. There are other ways, apart from the domain name, by which a business can establish a presence on the World Wide Web (WWW). From a legal perspective, however, the nature of the disputes arising is similar to that of domain name disputes. It therefore seems sensible to group together all disputes arising from attempts by companies to establish a presence on the Web. This chapter describes how the system works, and the relationships between the parties. Chapters 3 and 4 cover the intellectual property issues arising therefrom.

It is very easy for any company, or indeed individual, to set up a website. There is little point in setting one up, however, unless people can be persuaded to visit it. Yet there are countless millions of sites, and merely to add one more is akin to placing a needle into a haystack. Somebody might find it but it is unlikely to attract attention. The site must advertise its presence. To have an attractive domain name is one way of doing this. Another is to make the site more visible to the search engines, such as Google, which increasingly are being used to locate pages on the WWW.

2.1.1 Domain names

A user of the WWW requests a web page from a server,[1] which then has to be sent back to the user's computer. This requires both the server and the user's computer to be uniquely identifiable, to have a unique address. Obviously, the user needs to know the address of the server, and the server needs to know to which computer to send web pages. In practice, the server's address is likely to be relatively permanent; the user's, on the other hand, might be set up just for the session by the Internet Service Provider (ISP).[2] Nonetheless, both computers will have a uniquely assigned address. These addresses are required by the system to work.

It is the IP part of TCP/IP (Transfer Control Protocol/Internet Protocol) which deals with addresses. IP assigns numbers uniquely to identify each computer connected to the Internet. The numbers are in the form of four octets, separated by full stops.[3] Because these numbers are difficult to remember, domain names are mapped

---

1   As we saw in section 1.2.2, this can be composed from material from many sites.

2   Computers connected to workplace Local Area Networks (LANs), such as the computer in my university office, will usually have permanent IP addresses assigned to them, but when I connect to the Internet from home, via my ISP, I will be assigned an address for the session; this reduces the number of addresses that need to be allocated.

3   Eg, 137.44.42.18 (this is actually the address of my university mail server when I access it from the WWW). An octet is a number in the range 0–255, there being 2^8 such numbers (hence the term octet). If you type in the number, the browser will find the site; you do not need the name as well.

on to them, which make them relatively easy to remember.[4] This was done initially by IANA (Internet Assigned Numbers Authority),[5] and later by ICANN (Internet Corporation for Assigned Names and Numbers, set up in 1998), which sub-contracts the allocation of domain names for individual countries. Nominet registers domain names in the UK.[6]

There are two important points to make about domain names. First, though some form of unique identification is necessary to allow the Web to work, domain names are a matter of convenience and are not essential to the free running of the WWW.[7] In *Pitman Training Ltd v Nominet (UK)*,[8] considered below, the Vice Chancellor (Sir Richard Scott) began his judgment with the following description:

> The Internet is a network of computer networks. A computer which is attached to an appropriate network can use appropriate software to communicate and exchange information quickly with any other computer on the network. In order to receive or to make available information on the Internet a domain name is needed. A domain name can be likened to an address. It identifies a particular Internet site. A particular domain name will only be allocated to one company or individual. It represents that company's computer site and is the means by which that company's customers can find it on the Internet. Electronic messages (e-mail) can be transmitted and received on the Internet. These messages are directed to e-mail addresses, which will include the domain names of the addressees. A web site address, too, will include the main name of the owner of the web site. A web site is a series of files on a computer on the Internet that can be accessed by anyone via the Internet.
>
> It will be apparent, therefore, that in order to receive e-mail on the Internet and in order to establish a web site on the Internet a domain name is needed. Domain names appear as words. The name in issue in the present case, for example, is 'pitman.co.uk'. However, when a domain name is used on the Internet it is translated into numbers known as IP numbers. The translation is carried out by a series of computer software packages known as domain name servers. An IP number is required both to send and to receive e-mail. Besides translating domain names into IP numbers the name servers provide services to the software on clients' computers.

Though this is an accurate description of the way the system operates in the UK,[9] it is in fact only the numbers, and not the names, which are essential for the operation of both e-mail and the WWW.

The second point to note is that it is not necessary for domain names to be assigned by any particular body – it is quite possible, in principle, to provide for competing systems of domain names. The domain name system (DNS) works by allowing ICANN and subsidiary bodies to have access to root servers, which maintain

4   Eg, http://exchange.swansea.ac.uk, the name that maps to the IP address in the previous footnote.

5   At www.iana.org; this was an arm of the US Government.

6   There is quite a good description in Edwards, L and Waelde, C (eds), *Law and the Internet*, 2nd edn, 2000, Oxford: Hart, Chapter 6. See also further below.

7   If you type in the IP number in note 3, above, it will connect to the mail server, just as the name will.

8   The full judgment is set out on Nominet's website, at www.nic.uk/ReferenceDocuments/CaseLaw/ThePitmanCase.html. The case is considered further in section 2.1.4.

9   The judgment then describes the bodies responsible for allocating domain names, but this is now out of date. See further section 2.1.3.

databases of addresses. This information is, in principle, capable of being copied, and alternative registers also exist.[10]

Nonetheless, the commercial reality is that domain names are centrally allocated. Generic Top-Level Domain names (gTLD), such as the coveted .com, are allocated by ICANN,[11] which was set up as a not-for-profit organisation in 1998. Country Code Top-Level Domain names (ccTLD), such as .co.uk, are contracted to organisations within the particular countries: Nominet (UK) in the UK.[12] The gTLD and ccTLD names are fiercely fought over and have given rise to a number of legal disputes.

However, it has also been argued that the nature of these disputes is changing. Increasingly, web users are using search engines, such as Google,[13] rather than simply typing in domain names. There are thought to be ways of improving the ranking on a search engine, using metatags that are not intended to be visible except to the search engine. Arrangements can also be made with search engine providers to provide banner advertising on stipulated search words. It has been suggested that disputes will move away from domain name allocation and become centred instead on search engine optimisation techniques.[14]

2.1.2   Types of domain name dispute

A common way for users to find companies on the Internet is simply to type in likely possibilities. Not surprisingly, therefore, companies like to register domain names likely to be typed in by a casual user looking for the site. Thus, for example, Microsoft has www.microsoft.com, and Marks & Spencer has www.marksandspencer.com.

However, since the name must be unique and the range of top-level domains is limited, the names can be fought over. It is possible to categorise types of disputes into a list such as the following:

* domain name hijacking;

* reverse domain name hijacking;

* cybersquatting;

* typosquatting;

* parody; and

* sucks.com disputes.[15]

---

10 Eg, www.opennic.unrated.net/ and www.igoldrush.com/links2-2.htm.
   However, Nominet took proceedings, which were eventually settled, against Domain Registrar Services Ltd for passing themselves off as Nominet itself: www.nominet. org.uk/drs-statement.html. The story is also reported at http://news.zdnet.co.uk/ 0,39020330,39117247,00.htm.
11 Internet Corporation for Assigned Names and Numbers, whose website is at www.icann.org/index.html.
12 At www.nominet.org.uk/index.html. Nominet (UK) was set up in 1996 and, like ICANN, operates as a not-for-profit organisation.
13 www.google.com.
14 See, eg, Murray, A, at www.bileta.ac.uk/00papers/murray.html. See also section 3.9 on some of the legal issues arising therefrom.
15 These are just generic descriptions, not legal terms of art. See also, eg, Colston, C, 'Passing off: the right solution to domain name disputes' [2000] LMCLQ 523, p 526.

Domain name envy is where two or more companies with similar names quite reasonably covet the same domain name. It would not be surprising, for example, if www.aa.com were coveted by the Automobile Association or Alcoholics Anonymous, but it is in fact the site of American Airlines.[16] Similarly, neither www.times.com nor www.times.co.uk are the sites of *The Times* newspaper, but respectively *The New York Times* and (somewhat curiously) the Name-Shop.[17] Domain name hijacking involves the use of an attractive domain name, involving another company name, to attract visitors to the business site of the hijacker. Reverse domain name hijacking is where a trading company buys up all the possible domain names that it could ever want, including (for example) top-level country domains in countries other than its principal location. Cybersquatting was an activity that took place primarily in the early days of the WWW, where far-sighted individuals (usually) registered domain names with resemblances to large companies, with a view to selling them to those companies when they realised the need for a web presence. Typosquatting is similar to domain name hijacking, but with the name misspelt, again with a view to attracting custom to the site. Parody and sucks.com sites are not official sites of a company, but are instead run by individuals with a view to parodying or rubbishing the company concerned.

From the perspective of the likely legal disputes to which these forms of activity can give rise, the first three are likely to involve use in the course of business of a domain name identical with a company trade mark. Cybersquatting will involve an identical or similar name, but may not involve its use. The last three may involve use, but not necessarily in the course of business, and the domain name will usually differ from the mark. In the last two cases, there will also usually be no risk of confusion.

2.1.3   The domain name allocation system

The Internet is said to be a network of networks and, in the early days, the backbone connecting the networks was funded ultimately by the US government.[18] There were relatively few users and both IP numbers and domain names could be allocated, on an *ad hoc* basis, by individuals or other entities without any particular legal basis or accountability. Even as the Internet expanded into the 1990s, and after 1992 was opened up to commercial traffic, allocation was still performed by what were ultimately arms of the US government. By the mid-1990s, allocation of IP addresses was performed by IANA. Domain name registration was the province of Network Solutions, Inc (NSI), under a contract with the National Science Foundation (NSF), which by then had US statutory authority to maintain and manage the 'backbone' to which other networks were connected. Domain names within countries were allocated by separate agencies, with either the authority or at least the acquiescence of the government concerned. In the UK, this function was performed by the UK Naming

---

16   www.aa.co.uk has not been allocated. The two other sites have respectively www.theaa.com and www.alcoholics-anonymous.org.

17   The Name-Shop is, however, a member of Nominet, the UK Internet names organisation. *The Times* newspaper has www.the-times.co.uk and www.timesonline.co.uk.

18   Originally the Department of Defense's Advanced Research Projects Agency (DARPA).

Committee,[19] which evolved into Nominet (UK) in 1996. There were no formal rules at all but, in practice, first-come first-served principles were adopted.

By 1998, the US government had decided to withdraw from its role in domain name allocation, and there were pressures to change, for example:[20]

* There is widespread dissatisfaction about the absence of competition in domain name registration.

* Conflicts between trademark holders and domain name holders are becoming more common. Mechanisms for resolving these conflicts are expensive and cumbersome.

* Many commercial interests, staking their future on the successful growth of the Internet, are calling for a more formal and robust management structure.

* An increasing percentage of Internet users reside outside of the US, and those stakeholders want to participate in Internet coordination.

* As Internet names increasingly have commercial value, the decision to add new top-level domains cannot be made on an *ad hoc* basis by entities or individuals that are not formally accountable to the Internet community.

* As the Internet becomes commercial, it becomes less appropriate for US research agencies to direct and fund these functions.

Accordingly, in 1998, allocation of domain names was granted to the Internet Corporation for Assigned Names and Numbers (ICANN), a not-for-profit corporation incorporated in the US, on a more formal basis than previously. Although the first-come first-served principle is retained as a basis, there is a recognition that some companies might have the right to a particular domain name, even if someone else has registered it first. There is therefore provision for reallocation of domain names, and a dispute resolution procedure.[21]

Domain names within countries outside the US continue to be allocated as before; those in the UK continue to be allocated by Nominet (UK) Ltd. The allocation has been put on a formal basis, however, and there are also dispute resolution procedures. As we will see, the dispute resolution procedures are influenced by the trade mark and related laws of the countries concerned although, for both ICANN and Nominet, except possibly for cybersquatting cases,[22] trade mark owners are generally less well protected than they are by the courts.

2.1.4   Relationships between the parties

Disputes about domain names are likely to arise either when one party wants to stop another from using a domain name, or when objection is taken to removal of a domain name by a domain name provider. Obviously, there is no remedy without a cause of

---

19 An offshoot of the United Kingdom Education and Research Networking Association (UKERNA), which had been authorised by IANA to administer the domain name system for the United Kingdom under the .uk top-level domain.

20 United States Department of Commerce, policy statement on 'Management of Internet Names and Addresses', available at www.ntia.doc.gov/ntiahome/domainname/6_5_98dns.htm.

21 See section 2.2.

22 Some of the legal difficulties in pursuing cybersquatters through the courts are considered in section 3.7.4.

action, but not all disputes about domain names involve intellectual property issues. It is, after all, ICANN who actually allocates top-level domain names (gTLDs), or in the UK the ccTLDs are allocated by Nominet, and in many cases they are party to the resolution of the dispute. The request for a domain name will also usually be made through an ISP, so it is important to examine the nature of the relationship between applicants for domain names, ISPs and (in the UK at least) Nominet.

Usually there will, of course, be a contract between the applicant and the ISP. The ISP will then make an arrangement with ICANN or, in the UK, Nominet. In pre-ICANN times, when top-level domain names were allocated by IANA, there was probably no contract between the applicant and Nominet's precursor (the UK Naming Committee). In *Diane Wraith v Nominet UK*,[23] Nominet suspended the domain name psinet.co.uk, registered by Diane Wraith's company, Psinet Ltd, following a complaint by PSINet (UK) Ltd. Diane Wraith sued for breach of contract. The domain name had, however, been registered, not by Nominet, but in 1995 by its precursor, the UK Naming Committee. In the Dewsbury County Court, His Honour Judge Hickinbottom decided that Ms Wraith had no cause of action: the Naming Committee had effected the registration without charging a fee and no consideration had thus moved from Ms Wraith; therefore, there was no contract between Ms Wraith and the Naming Committee and, consequently, no contract between Ms Wraith and Nominet UK. No doubt, she had a contract with her ISP (Demon) for hosting services because she had paid a £200 fee at the time of registration, but that gave her no cause of action against the Naming Committee, as a third party.

In principle, the contract between the applicant and the ISP can also affect Nominet, but in reality this is unlikely. In *Pitman Training Ltd and Another v Nominet UK and Another*,[24] I-Way (an ISP) had a contract with the second plaintiff, PTC Oxford Ltd (PTC), and had (apparently through an oversight on the part of the UK Naming Committee) secured the domain name pitman.co.uk. Pitman Publishing (PP), who had previously registered pitman.co.uk, threatened legal proceedings against Nominet (who had, by then, taken over from the UK Naming Committee the responsibility for allocating UK domain names) if the domain name was not re-transferred to them. The domain name was accordingly re-transferred by Nominet to PP, and PTC sued PP, among other things, for interference with contract (that is, the contract between PTC and I-Way). In order for PTC to succeed, they would have had to show that there was a term in the contract between PTC and I-Way, which was broken as the result of the re-transfer procured by PP. There was no breach of any express term, however, and the court refused to imply a term: 'that once delegated to [PTC] the domain name "pitman.co.uk" would not be withdrawn from the [PTC] or transferred to another without the consent of [PTC]', observing that:

---

23 A county court case, not fully reported, but summarised at www.nic.uk/ ReferenceDocuments/CaseLaw/DianeWraith-v-NominetUk.html.

24 Full text at Nominet's website at www.nominet.org.uk/ReferenceDocuments/ CaseLaw/ThePitmanCase.html. This case, which raises several issues, is also considered at section 3.8.

The control of domain names is not in the hands of I-Way but of Nominet UK. Formerly it was in the hands of the UK Naming Committee. For I-Way, in effect, to guarantee to a client what the Naming Committee, or now Nominet, would or would not do with a particular domain name would seem to me a very improbable obligation for I-Way to assume. I can see no basis upon which such an obligation could be introduced into the agreement between PTC and I-Way as an implied term. It is not a term necessary for the business efficacy of the alleged agreement. It is certainly not a term to which the parties, if asked by the officious bystander, would have given the testy answer, 'Of course'.

In the absence of an express term to that effect, there was therefore no basis for any contention that Pitman Publishing had interfered with the contract between PTC and I-Way. In any case, even were there such a term, there is a defence of justification. It would not be tortious for:

> Pitman Publishing, to whom after all the domain name had first been allocated, [to] make representations in its own interests and for its own legitimate trading reasons in order to recover for itself the domain name of which it had been in error deprived ...

Pitman Publishing was simply pursuing its own legitimate interests, and that is not tortious.[25]

Though the interference with contract action was brought against Pitman Publishing, it could also presumably have been brought against Nominet. The action would have failed, but only on the first ground, that there was no breach of contract procured between PTC and I-Way.

Ultimately, PTC failed for want of a cause of action (they also failed in passing off and abuse of process actions). The case does not decide that Pitman Publishing could have had the domain name restored to them, had they sued Nominet: indeed, this was left open, although again, it is not easy to see what cause of action there would have been.

As will appear below, the position of both ICANN and Nominet has now been put on a contractual footing, but the *Pitman* case remains an authority on the relationship between the ISP and its customer. Nevertheless, clearly I-Way had undertaken some obligation towards PTC. After all, ISPs typically charge for their services. Presumably, it was simply to set the procedure in motion, or perhaps to use best endeavours, rather than guarantee any particular outcome.

While it may have been acceptable, prior to the commercialisation of the Internet, for domain names to have been allocated on a first-come first-served basis without contractual protection for the parties, with the effective privatisation by the US government of the allocation of domain names in 1998, it was necessary to place matters on a more regular footing. ICANN and Nominet now charge fees for their services,[26] and this necessitates a contract between themselves and the domain name applicant. In any case, these are not-for-profit organisations and, for their own

25 The House of Lords decision in *Stratford & Son Ltd v Lindley* [1965] AC 269 was distinguished because 'the facts of that case were miles away from the facts of the present case'. In the earlier case, however, the defendants, who were trade union officers, were unable to rely on a defence of legitimate interest, where one union was effectively competing with another.
26 Nominet charges a biannual fee of £80 plus VAT: www.nominet.org.uk/ RegisteringYourDomainName/RegistrationFees.

protection, would wish, by contract, to limit their liability,[27] and also put the dispute resolution procedure on to a contractual footing. A dispute such as that in the *Pitman* case would probably today be resolved under the dispute resolution procedure (the result being the same, since Pitman Publishing's initial registration of the name would not be an abusive registration which, as we will see, is required before the domain name is transferred).

2.2   DOMAIN NAME DISPUTE RESOLUTION

For both ICANN and Nominet, a dispute resolution procedure is incorporated into the contract, binding the owner of the registered domain name. ICANN's procedure is the Uniform Domain Name Dispute Resolution Policy (UDRP), Nominet's is the Dispute Resolution Service Policy (DRS).

2.2.1   Relationship between dispute resolution policy and court action

It has already been observed that the relationship between an applicant for registration and Nominet or ICANN is now on a contractual footing, and disputes can now be compulsorily resolved under the provisions of this contract.[28] However, unlike commercial arbitration, it is not compulsory for the claimant, who is free to take court action if he prefers. Thus, for example, para 4(k) of ICANN's UDRP states:

> The mandatory administrative proceeding requirements set forth in Paragraph 4 shall not prevent either you or the complainant from submitting the dispute to a court of competent jurisdiction for independent resolution before such mandatory administrative proceeding is commenced or after such proceeding is concluded.

Nominet say in the general description of their DRS:[29]

> The DRS does not replace the role of the courts; it is however open to all and the decisions are binding on the parties involved. As a result of a DRS decision, Nominet has the power to transfer, cancel or suspend the Domain Name registration.

Clause 10(d) of their recently revised procedure provides:

> The operation of the Dispute Resolution Service will not prevent either the Complainant or the Respondent from submitting the dispute to a court of competent jurisdiction.

Because it is recognised that claimants may prefer to take court action, it is necessary to protect ICANN and Nominet from the consequences of such action. Thus, para 2 of

---

27 See, eg, Nominet's rule 4, and in particular 4.1 and 4.5:
> 4.1. Nominet does not carry out any investigation as to whether you are entitled to register or have any rights in the Domain Name. By registering the Domain Name we are not acknowledging that you have any rights in the name comprised in the Domain Name, and we are not authorising you to use the Domain Name in the course of trade.
> ...
> 4.5. Our aggregate liability to you whether under these terms and conditions or otherwise (including liability for negligence) shall not exceed £5,000.

www.nominet.org.uk/ReferenceDocuments/TermsAndConditions/TermsAndConditions.html.

28 Eg, ICANN UDRP, para 1; Nominet terms and conditions, cl 7.

29 www.nominet.org.uk/ref/drs.html.

ICANN's UDRP places requirements on representations made by applicants when they register, and also provides: 'It is your responsibility to determine whether your domain name registration infringes or violates someone else's rights.' Para 3(b) also allows cancellation of a domain name on 'our receipt of an order from a court or arbitral tribunal, in each case of competent jurisdiction, requiring such action', which would protect ICANN from any action in contract should they simply be carrying out the order of a court. There is also in para 3 an 'or other legal requirements' catchall. Nominet protects itself by exempting liability in their terms and conditions for 'loss of registration and/or use (for whatever reason and whether temporary or otherwise) of the Domain Name'.[30]

Nominet's procedure is influenced by (but probably does not exactly mirror) UK trade mark law, which is considered in detail in Chapter 3. Nevertheless, the dispute resolution procedures are not simply quick ways of allowing trade mark holders to assert their legal rights, and ICANN's procedure, in particular, affords narrower protection than the law to holders of trade marks.

2.2.2 Pros and cons of dispute resolution

The dispute resolution procedures are a quick, expedient and cheap method of reallocating the domain name,[31] based usually on correspondence alone, and are independent of the jurisdiction of the parties, whereas asserting jurisdiction over a foreign defendant can be difficult.[32] Moreover, trade mark law is jurisdictional, and varies between jurisdictions. Neither of these is true of the dispute resolution procedures.

However, reallocation is the only remedy offered. If the claimant wants, for example, financial damages, he or she needs to look to the courts. Thus, para 4(i) of ICANN's UDRP provides that: 'The remedies available to a complainant pursuant to any proceeding before an Administrative Panel shall be limited to requiring the cancellation of your domain name or the transfer of your domain name registration to the complainant.' We have also already seen, from the passage from Nominet's general description, that Nominet has the power 'to transfer, cancel or suspend the Domain Name registration', but no other powers are mentioned.

2.2.3 ICANN's policy

ICANN's UDRP has been adopted by all accredited domain name registrars for domain names ending in .com, .net and .org.[33] It has also been adopted by certain

---

30 Para 4.3.6. Note, however, that para 4 does not apply against consumers, and it must surely be doubtful whether, given the width of this particular term, it would be enforceable anyway.
31 Actual transfer, as opposed to simply preventing use, was new under ICANN's rules.
32 However, *in rem* cybersquatting jurisdiction has been provided for in the US Anticybersquatting Consumer Protection Act 1999.
33 ICANN's rules are at www.icann.org/dndr/udrp/uniform-rules.htm (this is essentially procedural), and the substantive UDRP is at www.icann.org/dndr/udrp/policy.htm. For a recent description of ICANN's resolution policy, see http://www2.warwick.ac.uk/fac/soc/law/elj/jilt/2002_2/mcmahon. See also www.internic.net/faqs/udrp.html. There is commentary on ICANN's UDRP by Abby R Michels in [2002] Ent L Rev 8, where reform proposals are also made. See also Colston, 'Passing off: the right solution to domain name disputes', *op cit* fn 15, pp 533 *et seq.*

managers of country code top-level domains (for example, .nu, .tv, .ws). The rules are aimed primarily at cybersquatting, and what might be termed illegitimate business use. Clause 4(a) of the policy provides that:

a.   **Applicable Disputes.** You are required to submit to a mandatory administrative proceeding in the event that a third party (a 'complainant') asserts to the applicable Provider, in compliance with the Rules of Procedure, that

(i)   your domain name is identical or confusingly similar to a trademark or service mark in which the complainant has rights; and

(ii)   you have no rights or legitimate interests in respect of the domain name; and

(iii)   your domain name has been registered and is being used in bad faith.

In the administrative proceeding, the complainant must prove that each of these three elements is present.

This is limited to trade or service marks, and hence not to persons (celebrities, for example). In the US (but not the UK), persons are protected under the law by the Anticybersquatting Consumer Protection Act 1999.

'Confusingly similar' (in para 4(a)(i)) was added to the earlier NSI grounds, which worked only for identical marks, but para (iii), the bad faith requirement, limits the application of the procedure effectively to deliberate hijacking, cybersquatting,[34] typosquatting and (maybe) sucks.com disputes. Note also that there is a usage requirement (it is not clear whether this could include a cybersquatter's threats of use). No provision is made for dilution, without the need to prove confusing similarity, though this is provided for in US trade mark legislation.[35] However, McMahon suggests that the threshold for confusion is not high in the actual operation of the ICANN UDRP.[36]

A non-exhaustive list of evidence of bad faith is set out in cl 4(b), and can include:

(i)   circumstances indicating that you have registered or you have acquired the domain name primarily for the purpose of selling, renting, or otherwise transferring the domain name registration to the complainant who is the owner of the trademark or service mark or to a competitor of that complainant, for valuable consideration in excess of your documented out-of-pocket costs directly related to the domain name; or

(ii)   you have registered the domain name in order to prevent the owner of the trademark or service mark from reflecting the mark in a corresponding domain name, provided that you have engaged in a pattern of such conduct; or

(iii)   you have registered the domain name primarily for the purpose of disrupting the business of a competitor; or

(iv)   by using the domain name, you have intentionally attempted to attract, for commercial gain, Internet users to your web site or other on-line location, by creating a likelihood of confusion with the complainant's mark as to the source, sponsorship, affiliation, or endorsement of your web site or location or of a product or service on your web site or location.

---

34   Note also that there is a usage requirement, but this could presumably include threats. Like passing off and trade mark law, this procedure does not protect persons.

35   See section 3.6.

36   http://www2.warwick.ac.uk/fac/soc/law/elj/jilt/2002_2/mcmahon.

Paras (i) and (ii) are aimed at cybersquatting; paras (iii) and (iv) at domain name hijacking.

Clause 4(c) sets out another non-exhaustive list, this time of rights to, and legitimate interests in, the domain name registered:

(i) before any notice to you of the dispute, your use of, or demonstrable preparations to use, the domain name or a name corresponding to the domain name in connection with a *bona fide* offering of goods or services; or

(ii) you (as an individual, business, or other organization) have been commonly known by the domain name, even if you have acquired no trademark or service mark rights; or

(iii) you are making a legitimate noncommercial or fair use of the domain name, without intent for commercial gain to misleadingly divert consumers or to tarnish the trademark or service mark at issue.

2.2.4 Nominet's policy

Nominet has its own dispute resolution policy (Dispute Resolution Service (DRS)), and there are also associated rules of procedure.[37] It is the policy that sets out the grounds of objection. It is clearly influenced by trade mark law in the UK and, for this reason, Nominet's rules are wider than those of ICANN. Clause 2 of the policy provides that:[38]

a. A Respondent must submit to proceedings under the Dispute Resolution Service if a Complainant asserts to us, according to the Procedure, that:

   i. The Complainant has Rights in respect of a name or mark which is identical or similar to the Domain Name; and

   ii. The Domain Name, in the hands of the Respondent, is an Abusive Registration.

b. The Complainant is required to prove to the Expert that both elements are present on the balance of probabilities.

An 'abusive registration' is defined in the definition section, cl 1:

Abusive Registration means a Domain Name which either:

   i. was registered or otherwise acquired in a manner which, at the time when the registration or acquisition took place, took unfair advantage of or was unfairly detrimental to the Complainant's Rights; OR

   ii. has been used in a manner which took unfair advantage of or was unfairly detrimental to the Complainant's Rights.

The wording is clearly influenced by s 10(3) of the Trade Marks Act 1994, considered in the next chapter, potentially covering dilution, blurring and tarnishment.[39] Thus, unlike ICANN, there is no requirement for confusing similarity. However, unlike the 1994 Act, the DRS policy does not require a reputation in the UK. However, cl 2(a)(i) probably requires the complainant to have rights in respect of a trade mark.

---

37 Nominet's dispute resolution policy is described at www.nominet.org.uk/ref/drs.html. The detailed terms are set out at www.nominet.org.uk/DisputeResolution/ DrsPolicy/DrsPolicy.html; the associated procedure at www.nominet.org.uk/ DisputeResolution/DrsProcedure/DrsProcedure.html.

38 The policy was recently revised, as to its details, with the new version applying to all disputes filed on or after 25 October 2004.

39 Section 3.6.

As with ICANN, there are then set out non-exhaustive lists of evidence of good and bad faith. These are not exactly the same as ICANN's, again being apparently influenced by UK trade mark law. Thus, cl 3 (Evidence of Abusive Registration) provides:

a.   A non-exhaustive list of factors which may be evidence that the Domain Name is an Abusive Registration is as follows:

i.   Circumstances indicating that the Respondent has registered or otherwise acquired the Domain Name primarily:

A.   for the purposes of selling, renting or otherwise transferring the Domain Name to the Complainant or to a competitor of the Complainant, for valuable consideration in excess of the Respondent's documented out-of-pocket costs directly associated with acquiring or using the Domain Name;

B.   as a blocking registration against a name or mark in which the Complainant has Rights; or

C.   for the purpose of unfairly disrupting the business of the Complainant;

ii.   Circumstances indicating that the Respondent is using the Domain Name in a way which has confused people or businesses into believing that the Domain Name is registered to, operated or authorised by, or otherwise connected with the Complainant;

iii.   The Complainant can demonstrate that the Respondent is engaged in a pattern of registrations where the Respondent is the registrant of domain names (under .uk or otherwise) which correspond to well known names or trade marks in which the Respondent has no apparent rights, and the Domain Name is part of that pattern;

iv.   It is independently verified that the Respondent has given false contact details to us; or

v.   The domain name was registered as a result of a relationship between the Complainant and the Respondent, and the Complainant:

A.   has been using the domain name registration exclusively; and

B.   paid for the registration and/or renewal of the domain name registration.

b.   Failure on the Respondent's part to use the Domain Name for the purposes of e-mail or a web-site is not in itself evidence that the Domain Name is an Abusive Registration.

c.   There shall be a presumption of Abusive Registration if the Complainant proves that the Respondent has been found to have made an Abusive Registration in three (3) or more Dispute Resolution Service cases in the two (2) years before the Complaint was filed. This presumption can be rebutted (see paragraph 4 (c)).

Paragraph (i) is primarily aimed at cybersquatting and (maybe) hijacking. Paragraph (ii) is similar to s 10(2) of the Trade Marks Act 1994, considered in the following chapter.[40] There is nothing explicitly on dilution, blurring, tarnishment, etc, but this is, of course, a non-exhaustive list.

Conversely, cl 4 ('How the Respondent may demonstrate in its response that the Domain Name is not an Abusive Registration') provides:

---

40   Section 3.5.

a. A non-exhaustive list of factors which may be evidence that the Domain Name is not an Abusive Registration is as follows:

   i. Before being aware of the Complainant's cause for complaint (not necessarily the 'complaint' under the DRS), the Respondent has

      A. used or made demonstrable preparations to use the Domain Name or a Domain Name which is similar to the Domain Name in connection with a genuine offering of goods or services;

      B. been commonly known by the name or legitimately connected with a mark which is identical or similar to the Domain Name;

      C. made legitimate non-commercial or fair use of the Domain Name; or

   ii. The Domain Name is generic or descriptive and the Respondent is making fair use of it;

   iii. In relation to paragraph 3(a)(v); that the Registrant's holding of the Domain Name is consistent with an express term of a written agreement entered into by the Parties; or

   iv. In relation to paragraphs 3(a)(iii) and/or 3(c); that the Domain Name is not part of a wider pattern or series of registrations because the Domain Name is of a significantly different type or character to the other domain names registered by the Respondent.

b. Fair use may include sites operated solely in tribute to or in criticism of a person or business.

c. If paragraph 3(c) applies, to succeed the Respondent must rebut the presumption by proving in the Response that the registration of the Domain Name is not an Abusive Registration.

It is probably fair to say that, although these provisions are influenced by trade mark law, they aim to retain essentially a first-come first-served principle, as long as the registration has not been effected in bad faith, bad faith being defined generally in terms of legitimate business practice. As will become apparent in the following chapter, Nominet's dispute resolution jurisdiction is narrower than substantive trade mark law.

TRADE MARKS AND PASSING OFF

Though many disputes about domain names are no doubt dealt with by the procedures discussed in the previous chapter, there is nothing in ICANN's dispute resolution procedure that prevents the parties litigating. Most of the cases on domain names are allegations of trade mark infringement or passing off. Passing off is considered in detail later in the chapter.[1] Domain name disputes seem to be receding, and are being overtaken by disputes about metatags and other forms of search engine optimisation. These are also considered in detail later in the chapter.[2]

3.1   INTRODUCTION TO TRADE MARKS AND PASSING OFF

It has long been tortious for a business to deceive customers by passing itself off as someone else. It is possible for a choice of domain name to amount to passing off. The tort of passing off is entirely common law based.

The use of a domain name can also amount to a trade mark infringement. By contrast with passing off, trade marks jurisdiction is entirely statutory. Its origin, however, was effectively as a registration system to protect owners of distinctive marks. Without trade mark protection they could still prevent other traders from using their distinctive marks to pass themselves off as the owner of the mark. However, they would have to bring a multiplicity of passing off actions, and would have to lead similar evidence to prove each claim. They would also have to show, in each action, an established reputation, whereas trade marks can be protected in advance of a reputation being established.[3] It was to avoid this that trade marks jurisdiction was developed in the UK in the 19th century. All that was necessary was to show that the defendant was infringing the rights of the owner of the mark, by using the mark in an unauthorised manner.

Trade marks are registered into categories of use, it being necessary to show the relevant usage at registration. It is also possible to challenge a registration on the ground of lack of use.[4]

Because trade mark law developed from passing off, English trade mark law has traditionally been characterised by a number of features:

(a) it is (or at least was) based on the idea of confusing other trading parties and consumers;

---

1   Section 3.7.
2   Section 3.9.
3   A point made by Jacob LJ in *Reed Executive plc v Reed Business Information Ltd* [2004] RPC 40, at paras 79 and 80. This case is discussed extensively later in the chapter.
4   Trade Marks Act 1994, s 46. Categories of use are considered further below, section 3.2, fns 16 and 17.

(b) accordingly, it requires trade usage by the defendant, and only protects traders, not, for example, famous persons. .

Passing off is a tort and is therefore based on the conduct of the defendant, rather than any idea of a property right in the claimant. English trade mark law has traditionally remained close to this idea, and has been reluctant to develop the concept of a trade mark as a property right in itself. English judges have been reluctant to extend the monopoly granted to trade mark owners and have always allowed traders to use their own names, for example, and to describe their products in a reasonable way, even if to do so involves using words which are someone else's trade mark. Mr MacDonald can (or at least could) use his own name to trade as a butcher in Aberdeen, whatever the views of the multinational food company which trades under the same name.

However, the EU required Member States to implement Council Directive 89/104/EC of 21 December 1988, the purpose of which was:[5]

> ... to approximate the trade mark laws of the member states in order to remove disparities which may impede the free movement of goods and freedom to provide services or distort competition within the common market; however, the intervention of the Community legislature, not being intended to achieve full scale approximation of those laws, remains limited to certain aspects concerning trade marks acquired by registration.

The Directive was implemented in the UK by the Trade Marks Act 1994 (TMA 1994), which is the relevant legislation for present purposes. The Directive is aimed at partial harmonisation:[6]

> It restricts its operation to trade marks acquired by registration ... It is, to a certain extent, a de minimis provision, which does not prevent, in certain situations, the member states from granting more extensive protection than that afforded by the Community provision.

However, a potential problem with any kind of harmonisation of law is the forcing together of what are very different traditions. Trade mark protection in other EU states has traditionally been much wider than in English law, and the European Court of Justice treats the trade mark, to a far greater extent than was traditional in English law, as a property right arising from investment. To a great extent, it is entitled to protection in its own right, and there is far less insistence on showing confusion.

It is therefore not surprising that the latest UK statute, the TMA 1994, which was intended to implement the EC Directive, also increased the protection afforded to trade mark owners. The new legislation saw a change in emphasis in UK trade mark law, which is no longer confined to the same ethos as a passing off action. There is, for example, the new dilution remedy in s 10(3), which really protects a property right per se and does not depend on an idea of confusion. The trade mark definition was also widened (see further below, especially section 3.6).

---

5   *Sieckmann v Deutsches Patent-und Markenamt* (Case C-273/00) [2003] 3 WLR 424, para 3, also
     cited in *Arsenal Football Club plc v Reed* [2003] Ch 454, p 457, para 13, both in the speech of the
     Advocate General. A text version of the Directive can be found at http://europa.eu.int/
     smartapi/cgi/sga_doc?smartapi!celexapi!prod!CELEXnumdoc&lg=EN&numdoc=31989L010
     4&model=guichett, and a PDF file at http://europa.eu.int/eur-lex/en/consleg/pdf/1989/
     en_1989L0104_do_001.pdf.
6   *Arsenal Football Club plc v Reed* [2003] Ch 454, para 21.

In the meantime, as we will see, the boundaries of passing off have also been extended.[7] Passing off is considered in detail later in the chapter (see section 3.7), but it may be noted that the combined effect of this and the extension of trade mark law has been considerably to increase the protection afforded to owners of marks, and, in particular, well known marks – that is, in relation to big business. By the same token, intellectual property law has a greater control over the activities of traders than before and, in the present context, in relation to allocation of domain names and some other web-related activities.

3.2   THE RELEVANT TRADE MARK LEGISLATION IN OUTLINE

Trade mark infringements are defined in Art 5 of the Directive, with the defences in Art 6. The implementation of these provisions into UK law is respectively by ss 10 and 11 of the TMA 1994.[8] In *Bravado Merchandising Services Ltd v Mainstream Publishing (Edinburgh) Ltd*, Lord McCluskey observed that:[9]

> The express purpose of the Act, as is clear both from the long title and the wording of its provisions, was to change the existing law by making new provision for registered trade marks, certain of the changes being derived from a harmonisation Directive of the Council of the European Union.

Its purpose, as we have seen then, was to implement Council Directive 89/104/EC of 21 December 1988 to approximate the laws of the Member States relating to trade marks.

Trade mark infringements are provided for in s 10 of the 1994 Act.[10] Section 10(1) to (3) provides that:

(1) A person infringes a registered trade mark if he uses in the course of trade a sign which is identical with the trade mark in relation to goods or services which are identical with those for which it is registered.

(2) A person infringes a registered trade mark if he uses in the course of trade a sign where because—

(a) the sign is identical with the trade mark and is used in relation to goods or services similar to those for which the trade mark is registered, or

(b) the sign is similar to the trade mark and is used in relation to goods or services identical with or similar to those for which the trade mark is registered,

there exists a likelihood of confusion on the part of the public, which includes the likelihood of association with the trade mark.

---

7   See, eg, the *Advocaat* and *One in a Million* cases, respectively at [1979] AC 731 and [1999] 1 WLR 903, considered in detail below.

8   The full text can be found at www.opsi.gov.uk/acts/acts1994/Ukpga_19940026_en_1.htm.

9   [1996] FSR 205, p 212.

10 Section 9(1) provides generally that:

> The proprietor of a registered trade mark has exclusive rights in the trade mark which are infringed by use of the trade mark in the United Kingdom without his consent. The acts amounting to infringement, if done without the consent of the proprietor, are specified in section 10.

> However, it has twice been held that this is just a chatty introduction, adding nothing: *British Sugar plc v James Robertson & Sons Ltd* [1996] RPC 281, p 291; *Euromarket Designs Inc v Peters and Crate & Barrel Ltd* [2001] FSR 20, para 18.

(3) A person infringes a registered trade mark if he uses in the course of trade a sign which—

(a) is identical with or similar to the trade mark, and

(b) is used in relation to goods or services which are not similar to those for which the trade mark is registered,

where the trade mark has a reputation in the United Kingdom and the use of the sign, being without due cause, takes unfair advantage of, or is detrimental to, the distinctive character or the repute of the trade mark.

Section 10(1) and (2) implements Art 5(1)(a) and (b) of the Directive, and s 10(3) implements Art 5(2). In summary, the three forms of infringement in s 10 are essentially as follows:

- **10(1)**: Using a sign which is identical to the mark, in relation to identical goods or services.

- **10(2)**: Using a sign which is either identical to the mark, in relation to similar goods or services, or a sign which is similar to the mark, in relation to identical or similar goods or services. However, now there has to exist a likelihood of confusion on the part of the public (including association).

- **10(3)**: This requires a sign which is identical or similar to the trade mark, but dissimilar goods or services. Use of the sign is required to take unfair advantage of, or to be detrimental to, the distinctive character or the repute of the trade mark.

Section 10(1) and (2) is about confusion. In s 10(2), it is an explicit requirement, but it is assumed in s 10(1) and so there is no added confusion requirement.[11] Section 10(3) was added in 1994. It does not depend on confusion, and was added to give proper protection to very well known marks.[12] Neuberger J observed in *Premier Brands UK Ltd v Typhoon Europe Ltd* that:[13]

> According to Recital 9 of the Directive, the purpose of Article 5(2) is to provide 'extensive protection to those trade marks which have a reputation', and such protection is clearly intended to be over and above that available to marks without a reputation. As already mentioned, section 10(3) represents a significant extension to the protection hitherto accorded to proprietors of registered trade marks in this country.

The main protection is against what are sometimes described as diluting or tarnishing famous marks. Section 10(3), which is most likely to affect parody and sucks.com sites, and perhaps cybersquatters, is considered later in the chapter.[14]

There are a number of general points to note. Trade marks are jurisdictional, so that a UK trade mark will only be protected in the UK.[15] They are also granted for

---

11 See, eg, *Reed Executive plc v Reed Business Information Ltd* [2004] RPC 40, [2004] EWCA Civ 159 CA, para 28 (full text at www.bailii.org/ew/cases/EWCA/Civ/2004/159.html, and at first instance, [2002] EWHC 2772 (Ch), para 132 (full text at www.bailii.org/ew/cases/EWHC/Ch/2002/2772.html).

12 See, eg, *Arsenal Football Club plc v Reed* [2003] Ch 454, p 461, para 33.

13 [2000] FSR 767, p 786.

14 Section 3.6.

15 There is also, however, a Community Trade Mark, which can be protected throughout the EU. Relevant provisions are Council Regulation (EC) No 40/94 of 20 December 1993 on the Community Trade Mark, implemented by Part II of the TMA 1994. Infringements are defined similarly to those for UK marks.

particular categories of goods and services, the 45 categories being derived from the eighth edition of the Nice Agreement, brought into force in the UK by the Trade Marks (Amendment) Rules 2001. Schedule 4 sets out the categories,[16] and is relevant to the question whether goods or services are identical.[17] Use is defined in s 10(4) of the TMA 1994:

(4) For the purposes of this section a person uses a sign if, in particular, he—

   (a) affixes it to goods or the packaging thereof;[18]

   (b) offers or exposes goods for sale, puts them on the market or stocks them for those purposes under the sign, or offers or supplies services under the sign;

   (c) imports or exports goods under the sign; or

   (d) uses the sign on business papers or in advertising.

The alleged infringing use must be in the course of trade. (In a domain name context, this could be problematic in parody sites, which may not be trading, and possibly in some cybersquatting disputes. Indeed, in the latter case, there may not even be use of the sign.)

There are also defences in s 11, the most important of which are set out in s 11(2):

(2) A registered trade mark is not infringed by—

   (a) the use by a person of his own name or address,

   (b) the use of indications concerning the kind, quality, quantity, intended purpose, value, geographical origin, the time of production of goods or of rendering of services, or other characteristics of goods or services, or

   (c) the use of the trade mark where it is necessary to indicate the intended purpose of a product or service (in particular, as accessories or spare parts),

provided the use is in accordance with honest practices in industrial or commercial matters.

Of these, s 11(2)(a) is most likely to be applicable in relation to the Internet domain name disputes considered in this chapter. However, any of the defences could be relevant to metatag use and the other matters considered in section 3.9. The defences in general are dealt with in section 3.10.

Many of the cases are argued alternatively, as s 10(1) or 10(2), or s 10(2) or 10(3), and a passing off claim may be made as well. There is a degree of overlap, and claimants will obviously advance all plausible arguments.[19]

3.3   DOMAIN NAMES AND TRADE MARKS

It is not obvious why domain names have anything to do with trade marks. They are just addresses, and arguably say no more about the origin of goods or services than an

---

16 The full text of the Rules can be found at www.opsi.gov.uk/si/si2001/20013832.htm.

17 However, in *British Sugar plc v James Robertson & Sons Ltd* [1996] RPC 281, Jacobs J observed at p 289 that 'The main purpose of the classes is to enable trade mark searching to be carried out'. In other words, the classes are not necessarily intended to determine identicality.

18 See the discussion of *Bravado*, in section 3.4.

19 It used to be thought, however, that s 10(2) and (3) are mutually exclusive, since 10(2) requires similarity and 10(3) dissimilarity of goods or services. However, the ECJ has now ruled that this reasoning is incorrect: see section 3.6.2.

address would.[20] If I call my house (or indeed business premises) Microsoft House, that connotes nothing, I would suggest. It is true that domain names, unlike house names, are unique, but surely the same would hold if I were to buy the personal number plate MSN 1 for my car. People do not generally go to court over telephone numbers, but businesses have been very exercised over the allocation of domain names.

A few years ago it might have been common for people to search for a business simply by typing a likely domain name (for example, www.microsoft.com), but that was always going to be a hit and miss affair, and it is difficult to believe that users were really confused if the site they arrived at was not what they expected. Everyone knows that domain names are unique, whereas company names are not. If I type in www.apple.com, hoping to get a list of fruit suppliers, I might be disappointed at getting instead the site of the famous computer company, but surely not confused.

The reason for the disputes probably has nothing to do with the confusion of web users. Any company wants to maximise the number of hits to its site and, if having a domain name similar to a company name achieves that, then they will fight for that.[21] As web users and search engines get more sophisticated, however, domain names are likely to take on less significance and we can expect to see the nature of disputes change. This is dealt with later in the chapter, at section 3.9.[22]

Nonetheless, as we will see, the courts have treated domain names as being capable of infringing company trade marks, but because a domain name is unique, the problem is far more acute with domain names than it would be with choice of a company name. There are 45 recognised classifications of goods and services, for example, and no reason, at least in principle, why companies with identical names should not compete in dissimilar categories, but only one can use its name in a domain name. Moreover, whereas trade marks are still essentially jurisdiction based, only one company can use its own name as a gTLD, such as the much-coveted .com.

3.4   DOMAIN NAMES AND SECTION 10(1)

To use a sign as a domain name which is identical to a registered trade mark for identical goods or services, is (subject to the defences in s 11) an infringement, whether or not either there is a likelihood of confusion (as required by s 10(2)), or the defendant acts without due cause, unfairly to take advantage of, or to be detrimental to, the

---

20 See also Azmi, IM, 'Domain names and cyberspace: the application of old norms to new problems', *International Journal of Law and Information Technology* [2000] 8(2) 193, p 194. Full text (PDF format) is available at www3.oup.co.uk/inttec/hdb/Volume_08/Issue_02/pdf/080193.pdf.

21 As recognised explicitly by Jacob J in *Avnet Inc v Isoact Ltd* [1998] FSR 16: see further section 3.5.3.

22 By contrast with domain names, there is relatively little argument over telephone numbers in the UK, presumably because directories or directory services are universally used. *800 Flowers Trade Mark*, in section 3.4.3 below, is probably atypical, and probably arose in any case because telephone handset technology was more advanced in the US than the UK at the time the dispute arose (1993).

distinctive character or the repute of the trade mark (as required by s 10(3)).[23] It is clearly to the claimant's advantage, then, to establish a s 10(1) claim, if he can.

It is not obvious, though, that a domain name can be identical to a registered trade mark, since it can only be text, without shapes, logos, etc, where indeed even the significance of upper and lower case letters is lost:[24]

> Domain names do not allow for distinctiveness, so 'Nike loses its swish, Coca-Cola its distinctive typeface, Guinness its harp'.

Nonetheless, the courts seem prepared to regard www.nike.com and www.guinness.com as equivalent to the 'Nike' and 'Guinness' marks respectively:[25]

> [The] Domain name system could not support the distinctive character of a mark such as capitalizations, stylized formats, graphical designs that are normally adopted in the real world. Because of this, we find that the court has adapted the normal trade marks rules and taken into consideration only the word itself.

The issue whether text could be considered identical to a graphical mark first arose in a non-Internet context, in *Bravado Merchandising v Mainstream Publishing (Edinburgh)*.[26] The petitioner was the registered owner of the trade mark 'Wet Wet Wet', the name of a well known band. A book entitled 'A Sweet Little Mystery – Wet Wet Wet – The Inside Story' appeared, the typeface for the words 'Wet Wet Wet', however, being quite different from the graphic representation of the registered mark. The book appears to have been an unauthorised story of the band, the name of the band appearing in the title of the book. This was held, in principle (by the Scottish Court of Session), to constitute a breach of s 10(1), by affixing the sign to the goods within s 10(4)(a), the typeface being regarded as incidental to the words when considering identicality to the mark. The judgment does not make clear whether, as the petitioner argued, this would also have been the position under the old law,[27] but there could be no doubt in the light of the changes to the wording in the 1994 Act:[28]

> The feature of a trade mark under the old law was that you could recognise a trade mark by looking at it, ie, it has a graphic representation. One effect of the 1994 Act had been to change that. The definition was now that contained in s 1(1) of the 1994 Act:
>
> > 'In this Act a "trade mark" means any sign capable of being represented graphically which is capable of distinguishing goods or services of one undertaking from those of other undertakings. A trade mark may, in particular, consist of words (including personal names), designs, letters, numerals or the shape of goods or their packaging.'
>
> This new definition introduced the concept of a 'sign' and the qualification '*capable* of being represented graphically'; thus, although a trade mark might be recognised by looking at it, it was not necessarily itself a graphic representation: it could be in an

---

23 See section 3.6 for the courts' interpretation of these requirements.

24 McMahon: http://www2.warwick.ac.uk/fac/soc/law/elj/jilt/2002_2/mcmahon.

25 Azmi, 'Domain names and cyberspace: the application of old norms to new problems', *op cit* fn 20, p 200.

26 [1996] FSR 205, Scottish Court of Session. There is commentary (by the Trade Marks Registry) on *Bravado*, and some of the other cases considered here, at www.info.gov.hk/ipd/eng/newtrade/work_manual/pdf/Relative%20grounds%20for%20refusal.PDF.

27 See the petitioner's argument, *ibid*, p 209.

28 *Ibid*, p 208.

electronic or digital, but non-graphic form. Section 103(2) provided that references to 'use' 'including use ... otherwise than by means of a graphic representation'. Accordingly it was possible to infringe a trade mark other than by using a graphic representation of the trade mark.

Thus, the sign needs only to be capable of a graphic representation. This could apply, for example, to digital photographs or, by an extension of the reasoning, to plain text representations of domain names.

In the case itself there was, however, a defence under s 11(2)(b), since the sign was used merely to describe the characteristic of the book.[29] The importance of *Bravado* for present purposes, however, is that by an extension of the reasoning there, use of text in a domain name could be held capable of infringing a trade mark under s 10(1),[30] even though the trade mark has a graphic character.[31]

3.4.1   What is an identical mark?

Even once it is accepted that the use of a domain name can infringe a registered trade mark, for a case to come within s 10(1) the domain name has to be identical to the mark, and also to be used in the course of trade for identical goods or services. Domain name envy disputes will normally involve a domain name identical to the mark, used in the course of trade, but (subject to what is said below, section 3.4.3, about globalisation) surely not for identical goods or services? Of course, there may be two companies trading as, for example, Xerxes in the same line of business, where the registration of www.xerxes.com infringes the other's registered mark, but (subject to what is said below, section 3.4.3, about globalisation) there would be problems in such a case, even in the absence of a domain name. The *Reed* case, considered below,[32] was argued (ultimately unsuccessfully) as a s 10(1) case but, although it is an e-commerce case involving the use of a website, there was no issue about the domain name itself, and the issues could equally well have arisen in a non-Internet context. So it would seem unlikely that s 10(1) would apply often to domain name envy disputes, unless a very wide view is taken of identical goods or services.

Cybersquatting will usually involve identical signs to the mark. Cybersquatters will not necessarily trade, however, and even if they do,[33] will not normally trade in similar goods or services, and therefore will be unlikely to fall within s 10(1), in spite of using an identical sign to the mark. Sucks.com and parody sites will also not generally trade, and in any case the domain name will not be precisely identical to the mark. Fan clubs might choose a domain name identical to the mark, but will usually trade (if at

---

29   The defences are considered further in section 3.10.

30   For surely it is used 'in relation to goods or services', and affixed to the goods, to satisfy s 10(4), just as the cover title was in *Bravado* itself.

31   For a similar (but Internet-related) US decision, see *Jews for Jesus v Brodsky*, DC NJ Civil Action No 98-274 (AJL) 3/6/98, also described in Edwards, L and Waelde, C (eds), *Law and the Internet*, 2nd edn, 2000, Oxford: Hart, p 139 (no stylised O in domain name).

32   *Reed Executive v Reed Business Information Ltd* [2004] RPC 40.

33   See *One in a Million*, below, section 3.7.4, where the possibility was discussed (inconclusively) of a s 10(3) argument succeeding in this context.

all) in dissimilar goods or services.[34] Typosquatters might well trade in identical goods or services, especially if their motive is to take trade away from the owner of the registered mark,[35] but the domain name will not be precisely identical. So in that case the question is, when are the words in the domain name considered identical to the mark?

As to what is regarded as identical text to the mark, quite a wide view was taken in the early first instance cases of *Decon Laboratories Ltd v Fred Baker Scientific Ltd* and *Reed Executive v Reed Business Information Ltd*.[36] These decisions would certainly have had serious consequences for parody sites and sucks.com sites. In *Decon*, Pumfrey J thought that an action succeeded under s 10(1) (although he thought it would have succeeded anyway under s 10(2), were he wrong on s 10(1)). This case concerned, in essence, variations on the word 'Decon', with different suffixes being added,[37] both parties producing cleaning fluids. In para 8, Pumfrey J said:

> Matter added to the sign used by the defendant is to be discounted. This widely stated principle is not absolute, but must be judged on the facts of the case. If for example a word mark is buried in the defendant's sign so that in Jacob J's phrase only a crossword fanatic could find it then the sign used by the defendant does not comprise the mark at all. In the *Treat* case,[38] Jacob J gave the example of the presence of the word in the phrase 'theatre atmosphere'.

In *Reed*, another decision of Pumfrey J, the test adopted at first instance[39] was 'whether the defendant's sign differs from the claimant's mark only by additional matter which does not change the identity of the sign to the mark'. In other words, in Pumfrey J's opinion, a sign which reproduces the mark and adds text to it would almost always have been regarded as identical to the mark[40] and, indeed, he held that the signs ('Reed Elsevier' and 'Reed Business Information' logos, used as part of the content of a website) were identical to the registered mark, 'Reed'.

However, given that a successful application of s 10(1) relieves the trade mark owner of the need to prove confusing similarity, there is a case for a narrower test and, indeed, in later cases, the courts have been more reluctant to find identicality. The issue of identicality was considered by the ECJ in *LTJ Diffusion v Sadas Vertbaudet*,[41] which concluded that:[42]

> ... Art 5(1)(a) of the Directive[43] must be interpreted as meaning that a sign is identical with the trade mark where it reproduces, without any modification or addition, all the

---

34 Not necessarily, however, as the trade mark owner may itself sell promotional items: eg, *Arsenal Football Club plc v Reed* [2003] Ch 454, where the football club also sold clothing.

35 Compare the *Yahooindia* case, in section 3.7.4, which was argued as passing off because trade mark protection in India did not extend to services.

36 Respectively [2001] RPC 17 and [2003] RPC 12, [2002] EWHC 1015 (Ch).

37 Eg, 'Decon-Ahol'.

38 *British Sugar plc v James Robertson & Sons Ltd* [1996] RPC 281.

39 [2003] RPC 12, para 99.

40 However, there is also the suggestion, at para 101, that 'a change of type to one noticeably different from that registered would be sufficient to render the mark and the sign merely similar, as would the addition of another name'.

41 Case C-291/00, [2003] ECR I-2799.

42 *Ibid*, para 54.

43 Which is identical to s 10(1)(a) of the UK TMA 1994.

elements constituting the trade mark or where, viewed as a whole, it contains differences so insignificant that they may go unnoticed by an average consumer.

The ECJ test was applied by the UK Court of Appeal in *Reed Executive v Reed Business Information Ltd*.[44] The latter case, though Internet-related, was not a dispute over a domain name, but rather over the content of the website. 'Reed' was registered to Reed Executive, who complained about the use, on a website, of logos, 'Reed Business Information' and 'Reed Elsevier'. The Court of Appeal held that there was no infringement of s 10(1), because of the additions. Though Jacob LJ described the ECJ guidance as 'opaque', he said that the ECJ did not intend to soften the edges of 'strict identity' very far. Moreover, the ECJ had prefaced the test with: 'The criterion of identity of the sign and the trade mark must be interpreted strictly. The very definition of identity implies that the two elements compared should be the same in all respects.' This is obviously a narrow test of identicality, and Jacobs LJ, reversing Pumfrey J, took the view that neither 'Reed Business Information' nor 'Reed Elsevier' were identical to the registered mark, 'Reed'.

However, no doubt was cast in *Reed* on Pumfrey J's *decision* in the *Decon Laboratories* case,[45] where the claimants, who had registered 'Decon', successfully claimed under s 10(1), against a company which had used 'Decon-Ahol' and various other composite marks beginning with 'Decon'. The suffixes there really added nothing; thus it could reasonably be said that the addition did not change the identity of the sign to the mark. In *Reed*, Jacobs LJ thought 'Palmolive Soap' would have added nothing of significance to 'Palmolive'. The issue can depend on how the sign is used, purely descriptive additions being less likely to be of significance than those which actually suggest a different name:[46]

> It was over 'Reed Business Information' that battle was joined. The composite is not the same as, for instance, use of the word 'Reed' in the sentence: 'Get business information from Reed.' In the latter case the only 'trade-marky' bit would be 'Reed'. In the former, the name as a whole is 'Reed Business Information'. The use of capital letters is of some visual significance – it conveys to the average user that 'Business Information' is part of the name. If the added words had been wholly and specifically descriptive – really adding nothing at all (eg 'Palmolive Soap' compared with 'Palmolive') the position might have been different. But 'Business Information' is not so descriptive – it is too general for that.

A narrow test was also adopted by Laddie J in *Compass Publishing v Compass Logistics*:[47]

> It seems to me that the advantage to the trade mark proprietor of Article 9.1(a) [of the EC Directive] is that it releases him from having to address the issue of confusing similarity. That advantage is only to be secured in cases where the mark and sign are so close that one could be considered a counterfeit of the other. However identity still exists where the marks look and sound identical save to the eye or ear of an expert. Differences which ordinary members of the public will not notice, save by close side-by-side comparison or

---

44 [2004] RPC 40; [2004] EWCA Civ 159; also at www.bailii.org/ew/cases/EWCA/Civ/2004/159.html, paras 20 *et seq*.
45 [2001] RPC 17. It is, however, fair to point out that neither was the decision expressly approved.
46 [2004] RPC 40, para 37. Another issue in *Reed* was whether the services provided by the claimants and the defendants were the same (the Court of Appeal, again reversing Pumfrey J, held not).
47 [2004] EWHC 520 (Ch), www.bailii.org/ew/cases/EWHC/Ch/2004/520.html, para 20.

the pronunciation of a 1940s BBC news reader, can be ignored. Where such small differences exist, in the market place the mark and sign are identical.

It must be so similar that there should be no need to prove confusion. He held that 'Compass Logistics' was not the same as 'Compass' (although, in the event, a s 10(2) claim succeeded).

Nonetheless, as we saw in *Reed*, purely descriptive additions are less likely to be of significance. In a domain name context, therefore, it seems likely that typosquats, parody and sucks.com sites might be regarded as using signs identical to the marks. On the above tests, 'micorsoft' and 'microsoftsucks' will probably be regarded as being identical to 'microsoft'. Typosquatters will often also satisfy the other requirements of s 10(1). Parody and sucks.com sites will often not trade, and even if they do, for example by selling 'microsoftsucks' tee-shirts and mugs, will usually not trade in the same line of business.[48] Section 10(1), then, will probably be confined in practice (subject to what is said below, section 3.4.2) to domain name envy and typosquatting disputes.

3.4.2   What are identical goods or services?

Section 10(1) requires not only use of an identical sign to the mark, but also identical goods or services. Merely similar goods or services will not do (although they could still come within s 10(2)).

Avnet Inc v Isoact Ltd was a dispute over the domain name avnet.co.uk.[49] The plaintiffs chose to put their case only under s 10(1). But though the domain name was identical to the registered mark, it was for services in a different trade mark category. The plaintiffs, an American company, were in the business of selling goods through catalogues, and had the AVNET trade mark registered in the UK for 'advertising and promotional services, included in class 35'. In addition to their physical catalogues, they also had a web page, which did no more than support their catalogue business. The catalogues carried advertisements for the goods of a variety of suppliers, for which a charge was made to the supplier.

The defendants were an ISP, specifically for aviation. They called themselves Aviation Network, or Avnet, and had registered avnet.co.uk. The services provided included provision of space to allow its customers to advertise on their own web pages by displaying their own advertisements. However, it offered no advice or editorial facilities.

The plaintiff's infringement action failed, and the defendants retained the domain name.[50] Although the domain name was identical to the mark, the defendants' services were not considered to be identical. Jacob J decided this partly by a direct comparison of services. The defendants provided advertising only in the indirect sense

---

48   They are also unlikely to meet the confusion requirement of s 10(2), but might fall foul of s 10(3): see further section 3.6.

49   [1998] FSR 16, also described in Edwards and Waelde, *Law and the Internet, op cit* fn 31, p 138.

50   The site still exists, and clearly still belongs to the defendants, now called Aviators Network. Note that this was an application for summary judgment, so the issues were not finally decided.

that they allowed customers to put whatever they wanted on to their own websites, but 'a man who provides a facility for building a library is not a librarian'. Nor did the defendants assist their customers to write their copy, as an advertising agent would, nor provide advice on how to advertise, where to advertise and where best to advertise at a given price, and, of course, there was neither a requirement nor expectation that their customers would use their websites for advertising. Jacob J also thought it relevant, however, that the defendants' services would have been considered, under Trade Mark Registry practice at the time of registration, to come under class 42,[51] rather than 35.[52] He therefore regarded Trade Mark Registry practice as relevant to this issue.

Jacob J also prefaced his reasoning by a reluctance to take a wide view of identicality of services:

> In my view, specifications for services should be scrutinised carefully and they should not be given a wide construction covering a vast range of activities. They should be confined to the substance, as it were, the core of the possible meanings attributable to the rather general phrase.

As Jacob LJ, he adopted the same view in *Reed Executive v Reed Business Information Ltd*.[53] Here the claimants, Reed Employment, had registered 'Reed' for 'employment agency services'. They were in fact an employment agency, with a website. The defendants sold magazines, many of which advertised jobs, and later set up a website of their own, totaljobs.com, a site which at the time of writing continues to exist. They did not use 'Reed' in the domain name, but had used logos and wanted to use copyright notices in the main body of the site. As we have seen, the Court of Appeal held that their sign was not identical to the claimants' mark, but even if it had been, it was not being used in respect of identical services. Crucial for Jacob LJ was that the claimants, but not the defendants, vetted candidates, and only put forward to employers those who they thought suitable:[54]

> ... the core meaning adopted here involves a vetting for suitability by the agency – which does not happen with totaljobs.

The defendants were providing only a publishing service, not an agency. Indeed, the defendants certainly did not act as an agent for the job-seeker.[55]

In *Reed*, evidence of Trade Mark Registry practice was not called and the court drew its conclusions, based simply on factual differences between the services provided. There was also a clear reluctance to embrace a wide view of the activities claimed by the claimants.

An identical mark in relation to non-identical goods also does not bring you within s 10(1). In the non-Internet case of *British Sugar plc v James Robertson & Sons Ltd*,[56]

---

51 'Scientific and technological services and research and design relating thereto; industrial analysis and research services; design and development of computer hardware and software; legal services.'
52 In taking into account Trade Mark Registry practice, he followed *GE Trade Mark* [1969] RPC 414.
53 [2004] RPC 40; [2004] EWCA (Civ) 159, para 43.
54 *Ibid*, para 61.
55 *Ibid*, para 62.
56 [1996] RPC 281.

Jacob J thought it relevant that the defendants' goods would have been registered in a different class; the claimants had registered the word 'Treat' for 'Dessert sauces and syrups; all included in Class 30'. The defendants described their jam or spread as a 'Toffee Treat'. Jacob J regarded the goods as non-identical, partly because it simply was not, in his view, a dessert sauce, but also because the evidence suggested that they would have been registered under Class 29, covering jellies and jams, not Class 30.

It must be concluded that, even where the defendant uses a domain name which is identical to the claimant's mark, successful actions under s 10(1)(a) will be quite rare,[57] confined to typosquatters, rare fan club cases (like *Arsenal*, where the trade is in goods identical to those produced by the owner of the mark) and, to the extent that the discussion in the following section applies, domain name envy disputes.

3.4.3 Globalisation issues

Trade marks are jurisdictional, so that Xerxes trading as a florist in France will not, in general, infringe the trade mark of another company, Xerxes, trading as a florist in England. Websites, however, can potentially be accessed and viewed from anywhere in the world, so for the French company to register www.xerxes.com, even if used only on a server in France, could in principle lead to an infringement in England. This is a problem caused by the global nature of the Internet.[58]

The UK courts have, however, taken the view that, even if a web page is capable of being accessed globally, the courts should have regard to the target audience. They will not necessarily assume that it is intended to be a global publication so that even if it is directed primarily at a trade within a particular jurisdiction it might infringe trade marks elsewhere in the world. In *800 Flowers Trade Mark*,[59] an American company, 1-800 Flowers Inc, which used the telephone number 1-800-FLOWERS in the US, applied to register '800-FLOWERS' as a trade mark in the UK. Objection was successfully taken by a UK franchiser of telephone numbers, which had 0800-FLOWERS in the UK. One of the grounds of objection was that the applicants had no intention of using the number to trade in the UK, the applicant's business (flower delivery services) being based entirely in New York. The applicants' argument that the publication of their US trade mark on the Internet necessarily constituted use in the UK was rejected by Jacobs J:[60]

> Reliance is also placed on Internet use of 1-800 FLOWERS. This name (with the addition of Inc) is used for a website. Mr Hobbs [for the applicants] submitted that any use of a trade mark on any website, wherever the owner of the site was, was potentially a trade mark infringement anywhere in the world because website use is in an omnipresent cyberspace; that placing a trade mark on a website was 'putting a tentacle' into the computer user's premises. I questioned this with an example: a fishmonger in Bootle who put his wares and prices on his own website, for instance, for local delivery can

---

57 *Prince v Prince* [1998] FSR 21 is another case where the domain name was identical to a registered trade mark, but the companies operated in different areas (computer services as against sports goods). Though it was not explicitly found that there was no trade mark infringement, this is the clear implication of the decision.

58 See generally Bainbridge, http://www2.warwick.ac.uk/fac/soc/law/elj/jilt/2003_1/ bainbridge.

59 [2001] EWCA Civ 721; [2000] ETMR 369; [2000] FSR 697.

60 [2000] FSR 697, p 705.

hardly be said to be trying to sell the fish to the whole world or even the whole country. And if any web surfer in some other country happens upon that website he will simply say 'this is not for me' and move on. For trade mark laws to intrude where a website owner is not intending to address the world but only a local clientele and where anyone seeing the site would so understand him would be absurd. So I think that the mere fact that websites can be accessed anywhere in the world does not mean, for trade mark purposes, that the law should regard them as being used everywhere in the world. It all depends upon the circumstances, particularly the intention of the website owner and what the reader will understand if he accesses the site. In other fields of law, publication on a website may well amount to a universal publication, but I am not concerned with that.

A similar view was taken in *Euromarket Designs Inc v Peters and Crate & Barrel Ltd*,[61] where Jacobs J held that merely putting up a website is not doing business throughout the world, if the site is aimed simply at a local market. This was a dispute between an American company, with a UK trade mark for 'Crate & Barrel' for household goods and furniture, and an Irish company, with one store called Crate & Barrel, which had registered the domain name www.crateandbarrel-ie.com, and later crateandbarrel.ie, for its own similar business (also household goods and furniture).[62] However, the Irish company did not aim its advertising outside the local market, and was held not to have infringed the claimant's trade mark.[63] (Indeed, neither company had any substantial trade in the UK.) Jacobs J reasoned as follows:[64]

> Whether one gets there by a search or by direct use of the address, is it rational to say that the defendants are using the words 'Crate & Barrel' in the United Kingdom in the course of trade in goods? If it is, it must follow that the defendants are using the words in every other country of the world. Miss Vitoria [for the American company] says that the Internet is accessible to the whole world. So it follows that any user will regard any website as being 'for him' absent a reason to doubt the same. She accepted that my Bootle fishmonger example in *800 Flowers* is that sort of case but no more. I think it is not as simple as that. In *800 Flowers* I rejected the suggestion that the website owner should be regarded as putting a tentacle onto the user's screen. Mr Miller [for the Irish company] here used another analogy. He said using the Internet was more like the user focusing a super-telescope into the site concerned; he asked me to imagine such a telescope set up on the Welsh hills overlooking the Irish Sea. I think Mr Miller's analogy is apt in this case. Via the web you can look into the defendant's shop in Dublin. Indeed the very language and the Internet conveys the idea of the user *going to* the site – 'visit' is the word. Other cases would be different – a well-known example, for instance, is Amazon.com. Based in the US it has actively gone out to seek world-wide trade, not just by use of the name on the Internet but by advertising its business here, and offering and operating a real service of supply of books to this country. These defendants have done none of that.

---

61   [2001] FSR 20.
62   The case was brought only under s 10(1), for identical goods, no reliance being placed on s 10(2).
63   Indeed, it even successfully applied for the trade mark to be revoked, on the basis of non-use in the UK.
64   [2001] FSR 20, para 24.

In *Crate & Barrel*, a s 11(2) own name defence also succeeded, in spite of the defendant being a company, and in spite also of the removal of 'Ltd' from the domain name.[65] The application of the own name defence to company names has now been approved by the Court of Appeal in *Reed*.[66]

The effect of Jacob J's views in these two cases, if correct, combined with the application of the own name defence, makes it less likely that domain name envy disputes will be affected by the necessarily global nature of the Internet. It is also clear from the above passage quoted, however, that a site like www.amazon.com would be different, where the company clearly intends to address a global market.

3.5   DOMAIN NAMES AND SECTION 10(2)

Section 10(2) does not require either the domain name to be identical to the mark, or for the sign to be used in relation to goods or services which are identical to those for which the trade mark is registered. Similarity is enough, as long as the use of the sign creates 'a likelihood of confusion on the part of the public, which includes the likelihood of association with the trade mark'. If typosquatting does not come within s 10(1), it will surely normally fall within s 10(2), since it is likely that the goods or services will be identical, and confusion is the purpose of the typosquat. Conversely, parody and sucks.com sites would not normally fall under s 10(2), in spite of the similarity between the sign and the mark, because even if the sign is used in the course of trade at all, it is unlikely to be used in relation to similar goods or services, and it is also unlikely that any confusion will be generated.

In general, the courts have taken a narrow view of confusing similarity in relation to goods and services in an Internet context. It seems likely that they would take a similarly narrow view, in relation to similarity between domain name and mark. The general test is exactly the same. In *Premier Brands UK Ltd v Typhoon Europe Ltd*,[67] Neuberger J found no confusing similarity between 'Typhoo', the well known tea trade mark, and 'Typhoon', the name under which the defendants traded, in spite of their aural similarity. It is true that one is a dictionary, the other an invented word, and that the decision was based on lack of evidence of confusion, but it is also difficult to detect in Neuberger J's judgment any enthusiasm to extend the effect of s 10(2).

---

65 Note that the proviso will prevent making up new company names to defeat existing marks, since use of the mark must be in accordance with honest practices in industrial or commercial matters.

66 See generally section 3.10 on the defences.
    Curiously, both www.crateandbarrel-ie.com, and crateandbarrel.ie appear now to have reverted to the US company. Perhaps the explanation is that this was only an application for summary judgment, and different facts might have come to light at the full trial. There is the suggestion, at para 5, that the Irish company had got the idea of their store (and the name 'Crate & Barrel') from seeing one of the claimant's stores in the US. The case, however, proceeded on the basis that this allegation, which was not proved at the application for summary judgment, was not true. Another possible explanation is that a commercial arrangement was made after the hearing of the case.

67 [2000] FSR 767. Typhoon was a kitchenware product. This case is more fully discussed in section 3.6.3.

3.5.1   Identical names and similar goods or services

Most of the litigation has arisen over domain name envy, where two companies are trading under identical names and similar goods or services. In *British Sugar plc v James Robertson & Sons Ltd*,[68] Jacob J said that the class of 'similar goods' in s 10(2) was a narrow one, which approximated to the test of 'goods of the same description' under s 12(1) of the Trade Marks Act 1938 (that is, the old law). He also treated the similarity of the goods (dessert sauce compared with spread) separately from the issue of confusion. The similarity of goods is an objective test, depending only on factors relating to the goods themselves, and in *British Sugar*, because the goods were dissimilar, the issue of likelihood of confusion never arose. Were one to elide the tests of similarity and confusion, in Jacob J's view, a '"strong" mark would get protection for a greater range of goods than a "weak" mark'.[69]

The ECJ has, however, taken a different interpretation, a global assessment. Likelihood of confusion depends not only on the similarity of the goods, but also 'the recognition of the trade mark on the market'. In other words, it takes precisely the view that Jacob J had rejected, that the more distinctive the mark, the greater the range of goods and services that could be considered similar.[70] In *Reed*, Jacob LJ (as he had then become) observed that:[71]

> The court has laid down the 'global assessment' test (*Sabel* para 22, *Lloyd* para 18). This requires the court to take all the circumstances into account.

At first instance, Pumfrey J had observed, in summarising the effect of the ECJ decisions, that they decided that:[72]

> There is a greater likelihood of confusion with very distinctive marks.[73] This is a very surprising proposition (and perhaps only a presumption of fact, since this cannot be a legal issue), since normally it is easier to distinguish a well-known word mark from others close to it. But it seems to me to make more sense when one comes to consider device marks. I have difficulty understanding how it can affect the similarity of goods, but that is the law.

In the Court of Appeal, Jacobs LJ was prepared to accept, not so much that there is a greater likelihood of confusion with very distinctive marks, or that it will be easier to establish confusion with a famous mark, as the converse proposition:[74]

---

68   [1996] RPC 281. The case is also reported (partially) at [1997] ETMR 118.

69   The quote is from *DaimlerChrysler AG v Javid Alavi (T/A Merc)* [2001] RPC 42, para 78. This case is considered in detail in section 3.6.3.

70   Expressed most clearly in *Canon Kabushika Kaisha v Metro-Goldwyn-Mayer Inc* [1999] RPC 117 (in Edwards and Waelde, *Law and the Internet, op cit* fn 31, p 141), the reasoning expanding on the earlier decision of *Sabel BV v Puma AG* [1998] RPC 199. The quote is from the 10th recital of the preamble to the Directive, quoted in para 39 of the Opinion of Advocate General Jacobs in *Canon*, and para 15 of the judgment.

71   [2004] RPC 40, para 79. The *Lloyd* case referred to is *Lloyd Schuhfabrik Meyer & Co GmbH v Klijsen Handel BV* [1999] ECR I-3819; [1999] ETMR 690.

72   At first instance, [2002] EWCA 1015 (Ch), [2003] RPC 12, para 103. His views were also adopted in the CA, [2004] EWCA (Civ) 159, para 78. See also *DaimlerChrysler AG v Javid Alavi (T/A Merc)* [2001] RPC 42, para 80 (also Pumfrey J).

73   He cites *Sabel v Puma* [1997] ECR I-6191, *Canon v MGM* [1998] ECR I-5507; [1999] RPC 117 and *Lloyd v Klijsen* [1999] ECR I-3819; [1999] ETMR 690.

74   [2004] RPC 40, para 83.

... although I agree with the judge's questioning of the court's proposition of fact that 'there is a greater likelihood of confusion with very distinctive marks' there is some truth with the opposite proposition.

In other words, there is a lesser likelihood of confusion with less well-known marks (such as 'Reed', presumably).

From a purely factual perspective, the idea that confusion is easier to establish with a well known mark is difficult to justify; indeed, one might well think that the opposite were the case. The ECJ's approach to s 10(2) seems not so much to be based on a reasonable factual inference,[75] as simply to be motivated by a desire to protect famous marks, in which there has probably been significant investment over a long period of time. It seems to be a purposive, rather than literal interpretation.

'Reed' was not a famous mark. Moreover, in *Reed*, Jacobs LJ observed that it had long been recognised, at any rate as a matter of fact, that there was less likelihood of confusion with a mark that was mostly descriptive.[76] The same was true for common surnames, such as Reed. The test was whether there was a risk of confusion for 'the average consumer'. This was not unlike the test of confusion used in passing off cases and, looking at the evidence as a whole, Jacob LJ did not think a s 10(2) infringement had been established in *Reed*.

3.5.2 The test

The following approach, taken by Pumfrey J in *Reed*,[77] was accepted as correct in the Court of Appeal:[78]

> If this is a subsection 10(2) case the nature of the comparison, and the factors to be taken into account, have been considered by the ECJ in a number of cases. The cases on the corresponding provisions of the Directive, that is, Art 5(1) and 5(2) are ... [79] From these cases I derive the following propositions:
>
> 1) Under Art 5(1)(b) the comparison is not a straightforward mark for sign comparison. On the contrary, it involves a global assessment of the likelihood of confusion as to origin of the goods or services concerned. This involves an assessment of the distinctiveness of the mark, and involves the assessment of many factors familiar in passing-off cases (*Sabel, Lloyd*).
>
> 2) The person to be considered in considering the likelihood of confusion is the ordinary consumer, neither too careful nor too careless, but reasonably circumspect, well-informed and observant. There must be allowance for defective recollection, which will of course vary with the goods in question (a fifty pence purchase in the station kiosk will involve different considerations from a once-in-a-lifetime expenditure of £50,000).

---

75   Or, more accurately, Art 5(1)(b) of the Convention, which is in almost identical terms, and has been held to have the same effect: *Pfizer Ltd v Eurofood Link (UK) Ltd* [2001] FSR 3, para 20.

76   [2004] RPC 40, paras 83–86.

77   [2003] RPC 12, at para 103.

78   [2004] RPC 40, paras 78–79. There is a virtually identical passage, also by Pumfrey J, in *DaimlerChrysler AG v Javid Alavi (T/A Merc)* [2001] RPC 42, para 80.

79   Pumfrey J cites Case C-251/95 *Sabel v Puma* [1997] ECR I-6191, Case C-39/1997 *Canon v MGM* [1998] ECR I-5507, [1999] RPC 117, Case C-342/97 *Lloyd Schuhfabrik Meyer & Co GmbH v Klijsen Handel BV* [1999] ECR I-3819, [1999] ETMR 690 and Case C-425/98 *Marca Mode CV v Adidas AG* [2000] 2 CMLR 1061.

3) The mark is to be considered as a whole. All relevant similarities (visual, aural, conceptual) must be assessed having regard to the fact that some aspects of the mark and sign will be more distinctive and dominant than others.

4) The phrase likelihood of association is an explanation of the kind of confusion as to origin with which the provision is concerned. It is not a different type of infringement from confusion as to origin (*Sabel, Canon, Marca Mode*).

5) There is a greater likelihood of confusion with very distinctive marks (*Sabel, Canon, Lloyd*). ...[80]

6) A mere association between the mark and the sign created in the mind of the public will not amount to an infringement unless it also entails deception as to the economic source of the goods bearing the sign (*Marca Mode, Canon*).

In the Court of Appeal, Jacob LJ observed that the test was similar to that in passing off, discussed in section 3.7.

3.5.3   Low risk of confusion in Internet cases

In reality, the UK courts seem reluctant to apply s 10(2) in cases where a domain name is identical to a registered mark, but where the goods or services are not identical, on the ground that, in Internet cases, the risk of confusion is very low. It is fair to point out, however, that the cases have not concerned really strong marks, such as 'Coca-Cola', where it is possible that a different result would be reached.

In *Reed*, the defendants, as we have seen, were publishers of magazines which advertised jobs. When they expanded their business, by setting up their website, www.totaljobs.com, their business became similar to that of the claimants, an employment agency, which had registered the trade mark 'Reed'. The defendants' website contained logos for 'Reed Business Information' and 'Reed Elsevier' but, as we have seen, the Court of Appeal did not accept that these were identical to the claimants' mark, nor that the services provided were precisely similar. The claimants also argued an infringement under s 10(2), however, in that the sign was similar to the mark and was being used in respect of similar services. At first instance, Pumfrey J had taken the view that:[81]

> ... when two traders with confusingly similar marks operate in fields which are sufficiently different that neither substantially affects the other (or shows up on the other's radar, to use a metaphor employed by one of the witnesses) it goes without saying that if one of them expands its activities with the result that there could be a risk that what was previously mere confusion becomes deception causing damage to goodwill there is a positive duty upon that trader to take such steps as may be necessary to reduce that risk to zero. That is what the greater part of this case is about.

He found an infringement of s 10(2). If this view were correct, it would make life difficult for any trader expanding his activities by creating a website, the name of which was similar to that of another trader with a similar business, but in the Court of Appeal Jacob LJ emphatically disagreed with Pumfrey J's view.[82]

---

80 Here, Pumfrey J makes the comments on this 'surprising proposition', quoted above.

81 [2003] RPC 12, para 22.

82 [2004] RPC 40, para 90. www.totaljobs.com now has no reference to 'Reed', including in the metatags. Even the copyright notice is to The Potential Job Board Company Ltd 2004. www.reed.co.uk is owned by the claimants, Reed Executive.

In *Avnet*, as we have seen in section 3.4.2, the domain name was identical to the mark and the services were similar, but not identical. Surprisingly, only a s 10(1) infringement was argued, no reliance being placed on s 10(2), but Jacob J commented on it nonetheless. He did not think that any confusion would arise in practice, given the nature of search engine searches and the sophistication of Internet users:[83]

> The plaintiffs' real concern is not that the defendants are going to compete with them in any way. The defendants do not. The concern is that there will be confusion over the word 'Avnet', that search engines and the like will produce the wrong Avnet and the man looking for them might either give up or somehow get himself into some other sort of muddle. It is difficult to see how the latter could occur, because he would see immediately that he is not getting advertisements for semiconductor chips and the like and things to do with aviation instead.

> It is a general problem of the Internet that it works on words and not words in relation to goods or services. So, whenever anyone searches for that word, even if the searcher is looking for the word in one context, he will, or may, find Web pages or data in a wholly different context.

> That is the reason why the plaintiffs bring these proceedings. Of course, users of the Internet also know that that is a feature of the Internet and their search may produce an altogether wrong Web page or the like. This may be an important matter for the courts to take into account in considering trade mark and like problems ...

This implies a clear judicial reluctance to apply s 10(2) in cases such as this, where there is no suggestion of passing off, and indeed the Court of Appeal found no s 10(2) infringement in *Reed* either. In any case, even if there had been an infringement, there would have been a defence under s 11(2), because the defendants had done no more than use their own name.[84]

It probably follows that s 10(2) will have limited application in domain name envy cases. Of course, the sub-section would apply more clearly in typosquatting and cases such as 'yahooindia',[85] where there is an intention to confuse, and perhaps in parody and sucks.com sites, at any rate where the sign is used in course of trade (although these last are perhaps more likely to fall under s 10(3)).

3.6   DOMAIN NAMES AND SECTION 10(3)

Like s 10(2), s 10(3) (bringing into force Art 5(2) of the Directive) requires the sign to be identical or similar to the mark, but to be used for goods or services which are dissimilar. There is no explicit requirement for confusion, but the trade mark must have a reputation in the UK, and the use of the sign has, without due cause, to take unfair advantage of, or act in a manner detrimental to the distinctive character or the repute of the trade mark. The first could be established where the defendant unfairly uses the mark to increase his own sales; the second by what is described in US law as

---

83 See, eg, Edwards and Waelde, *Law and the Internet, op cit* fn 31, p 141. It was also assumed that no confusion arose in *Prince v Prince* [1998] FSR 21 (see further fn 57 above). Both these are identical mark, similar goods/services cases.

84 It was accepted in *Reed* that the own name defence would normally apply in passing off cases. Defences are discussed in section 3.10.

85 *Yahoo! Inc v Akash Arora* [1999] FSR 931, discussed in section 3.7.4.

blurring the mark, either by tarnishing (in effect rubbishing it), or diluting (in effect watering down the mark). Section 10(3) was added by the 1994 Act, and is in the European rather than the UK tradition of trade mark protection.

It seems that part of the purpose of s 10(3) was to provide for what had been the law for some time in the US and, at least, some parts of the EU.[86] The following explanation is taken from the opinion of the Advocate General in *Adidas-Salomon AG v Fitnessworld Trading Ltd*:[86a]

37. The concept of detriment to the distinctive character of a trade mark reflects what is generally referred to as dilution. That notion was first articulated by Frank I Schechter in 'The rational basis of trademark protection' (1927) 40 Harvard Law Review 813 – he advocated protection against injury to a trade mark owner going beyond the injury caused by use of an identical or similar mark in relation to identical or similar goods or services causing confusion as to origin. Schechter described the type of injury with which he was concerned as the 'gradual whittling away or dispersion of the identity and hold on the public mind' of certain marks. (He considered, however, that only 'arbitrary, coined or fanciful marks' should benefit from such protection.) The courts in the United States, where owners of certain marks have been protected against dilution for some time, have added richly to the lexicon of dilution, describing it in terms of lessening, watering down, debilitating, weakening, undermining, blurring, eroding and insidious gnawing away at a trade mark. ... At federal level, the Federal Trademark Dilution Act of 1995 created a federal cause of action for the dilution of famous trademarks. That Act defines dilution as 'the lessening of the capacity of a famous mark to identify and distinguish goods or services'. ... The essence of dilution in this classic sense is that the blurring of the distinctiveness of the mark means that it is no longer capable of arousing immediate association with the goods for which it is registered and used ... Thus, to quote Schechter again, ... 'for instance, if you allow Rolls Royce restaurants and Rolls Royce cafeterias, and Rolls Royce pants, and Rolls Royce candy, in ten years you will not have the Rolls Royce mark any more'.

38. In contrast, the concept of detriment to the repute of a trade mark, often referred to as degradation or tarnishment of the mark, describes the situation where – as it was put in the well known *Claeryn/Klarein* decision of the Benelux Court of Justice ...[87] – the goods for which the infringing sign is used appeal to the public's senses in such a way that the trade mark's power of attraction is affected. That case concerned the identically pronounced marks 'Claeryn' for a Dutch gin and 'Klarein' for a liquid detergent. Since it was found that the similarity between the two marks might cause consumers to think of detergent when drinking Claeryn gin, the 'Klarein' mark was held to infringe the 'Claeryn' mark. ...

39. The concepts of taking unfair advantage of the distinctive character or repute of the mark in contrast must be intended to encompass 'instances where there is clear exploitation and free-riding on the coat tails of a famous mark or an attempt to trade upon its reputation' ... Thus, by way of example, Rolls Royce would be entitled to prevent a manufacturer of whisky from exploiting the reputation of the Rolls Royce mark in order to promote his brand ...

In the US, dilution is defined in s 145 of the Lanham Act as:

---

86   See, eg, *Premier Brands UK Ltd v Typhoon Europe Ltd* [2000] FSR 767, p 787.

86a C-408/01 *Adidas-Salomon AG v Fitnessworld Trading Ltd* [2004] Ch 120.

87   Case A 74/1, judgment of 1 March 1975, Jurisprudence of the Benelux Court of Justice 1975, at p 472.

... the lessening of the capacity of a famous mark to identify and distinguish goods or services, regardless of the presence or absence of—

(1) competition between the owner of the famous mark and other parties, or

(2) likelihood of confusion, mistake or deception.

While the UK courts have been reasonably willing to extend the notions of tarnishing and (to a lesser extent) free riding, they have been very reluctant to embrace the concept of dilution. It seems that UK and ECJ views are divergent, however, and that the UK courts will eventually have to extend protection for famous marks. This could have significant implications, in the context of this chapter, for parody sites, fan clubs, etc, which trade in dissimilar goods or services from those of the holder of the mark.

3.6.1 No need for confusion

Originally the UK courts were reluctant to apply s 10(3),[88] in particular taking the view that if confusion was required for s 10(2), it was illogical not to do so for s 10(3), given that the goods or services were not even similar. In *BT v One in a Million*, neither Jonathan Sumption QC, sitting as a Deputy Judge of the High Court, nor the Court of Appeal needed to decide the issue, because confusion was clearly established (the case is dealt with in detail later in the chapter, section 3.7.4 below).[89] The matter was left open, in the absence (at that time) of a clear reference to the European Court.[90]

There was some logic to the position adopted in the early UK decisions if s 10(3) can *only* apply where the goods or services are not similar to those protected by the mark, and this appears literally to be the meaning of s 10(3)(b). In other words, where goods and/or services are similar, it is necessary only to establish a likelihood of confusion. Where they are dissimilar, the additional requirements of s 10(3) need to be satisfied as well.

The ECJ has subsequently and clearly taken the view that the section was intended to accord additional protection to marks with a very high reputation, whether or not there is likelihood of confusion. In the judgment in *Sabel v Puma*, there is a passage in the following terms:[91]

Article 5(2) of the Directive ... [permits] the proprietor of a trade mark which has a reputation to prohibit the use without due cause of signs identical with or similar to his mark and do not require proof of likelihood of confusion, even where there is no similarity between the goods in question.

---

88 See *Oasis Stores Ltd's Trade Mark Application* [1998] RPC 631 and *Audi-Med Trade Mark* [1998] RPC 863, under the similarly worded s 5(3) (which allows registration of marks to be opposed on similar grounds).

89 The Court of Appeal held that there had been a threat to infringe under s 10(3) in *BT v One in a Million Ltd* [1999] 1 WLR 903 (see below, section 3.7.4), but there was confusion in that case, and this point was expressly left open, Aldous LJ adopting the position, at p 926, that: 'I am not satisfied that section 10(3) does require the use to be trade mark use nor that it must be confusing use, but I am prepared to assume that it does.'

90 At the time of *One in A Million*, there had been only a passing dictum in *Sabel BV v Puma AG* [1998] RPC 199.

91 [1998] RPC 199, p 223. See also *Premier Brands UK Ltd v Typhoon Europe Ltd* [2000] FSR 767, p 785, but cf *Pfizer Ltd v Eurofood Link (UK) Ltd* [2001] FSR 3, paras 54 and 59, where s 10(2) and 10(3) were regarded as being mutually exclusive.

This, however, was merely a passing *dictum*, the discussion being primarily on Art 5(1)(b), the equivalent of s 10(2).

After *One in a Million*, the ECJ returned to the confusion issue, in *General Motors Corp v Yplon SA*,[92] the first case where Art 5(2) was considered directly by that court. The ECJ appeared to accept without argument that there is no need for confusion. The case involved the use of the 'Chevy' name for detergents, and it could hardly be contended that there was any likelihood of confusion with 'Chevy', the registered mark for cars and vans. In the view of Advocate General Jacobs:[93]

> It may be noted at the outset that, in contrast to art 5(1)(b), there is no requirement under art 5(2) of a likelihood of confusion on the part of the public. It had been thought in some quarters that a requirement of confusion was implicit in art 5(2) since it seemed paradoxical that confusion should be required under art 5(1)(b) where the respective goods or services were identical or similar, but not required under art 5(2) in relation to dissimilar goods or services. However the issue was resolved by the Court in its judgment in *Sabel*[94] which made it clear, when ruling on art 5(1)(b), that art 5(2) did not require confusion.

Later decisions have entrenched this view. There is no doubt that likelihood of confusion is not required.[95]

3.6.2 Can apply where there is similarity as well

Once the confusion requirement is removed, there is also no logical reason to limit the application of s 10(3) to cases where there is no similarity of goods and/or services. Note in the quote above from *Sabel* the use of the word 'even', not 'only', suggesting that the provision provides additional protection for strong marks, whether or not there is similarity. Certainly, there is no logic in extending that protection only to cases where goods and/or services are dissimilar, and according lesser protection where they are similar.

In any case, the matter has now been put beyond doubt in *Adidas-Salomon AG v Fitnessworld Trading Ltd*, with Advocate General Jacobs observing that Art 5(2):[96]

> cannot be given an interpretation which would lead to marks with a reputation having less protection where a sign is used for identical or similar goods or services than where a sign is used for non-similar goods or services.

This matter at least, therefore, has now been put beyond doubt. Like the ECJ's interpretation of Art 5(1)(b), however, it is an entirely purposive interpretation, and does not accord with the literal wording of the legislation.

---

92 [2000] RPC 572; [1999] 3 CMLR 427.
93 [1999] 3 CMLR 427, para 26. See also [1999] All ER (EC) 865, p 870. Note that Advocate General Jacobs' view does not appear in the RPC reports.
94 Case C-251/95 *Sabel v Puma* [1997] ECR I-6191.
95 C-292/00 *Davidoff & Cie SA v Gofkid Ltd* [2003] 1 WLR 1714; [2003] ECR I-389; C-408/01 *Adidas-Salomon AG v Fitnessworld Trading Ltd* [2004] Ch 120.
96 [2004] Ch 120, para 30, referring to *Davidoff & Cie SA v Gofkid Ltd* (Case C-292/00) [2003] 1 WLR 1714, 1734, para 25.

3.6.3 Scope of s 10(3)

In the *Chevy* case, the main issue was in how to determine whether a trade mark has a reputation, a famous mark test effectively being adopted:[97]

> a registered trade mark must be known by a significant part of the public concerned by the products or services which it covers.

The *Chevy* decision therefore protects well known marks, whether or not there is confusing similarity. In the context of this book, well known (but not other) marks might be protected against parody sites and other forms of dilution or tarnishment. They might also be protected against use of a domain name similar to the mark, even by a wholly different trade, if the trader was intending to benefit in some way from the famous mark. However, the ECJ in *Chevy* laid down no useful guidelines as to what is meant by 'without due cause, takes unfair advantage of, or is detrimental to, the distinctive character or the repute of the trade mark', except to the extent (in *Chevy*) that the stronger the distinctive character and reputation of a particular mark, the easier it would be to establish detriment to it. (In *Chevy* itself, dilution of the mark was successfully argued.) The scope of s 10(3) is clearly going to depend on the readiness of the courts to adopt a wide view of these requirements.

Turning our attention to the UK, following the *Chevy* decision, s 10(3) has been successfully applied in the UK courts, but only in fairly clear cases of tarnishing. The UK courts do not appear willing to accord s 10(3) a wide scope and, in particular, seem unwilling to embrace the concept of dilution. It seems also to have been accepted in the UK that the burden of proof on due cause is with the defendant; on the other points it is with the claimant.[98]

The requirements for s 10(3) were met in the UK courts in *CA Sheimer (M) Sdn Bhd's Trade Mark Application*,[99] and *Pfizer Ltd v Eurofood Link (UK) Ltd*.[100] *Pfizer* is not a very strong case, however, since there was in any case a s 10(2) infringement, and the defendants' actions also amounted to passing off. Eurofood were attempting to benefit from Pfizer's famous 'Viagra' mark by calling a beverage that they marketed 'Viagrene', intending to imply that the product would enhance the consumer's love life. The metatag key words for the Viagrene site were 'beverages, viagra, impotence, sex, sex stimulants, elderly sex, Viagra, Beverages, Pfizer, Impotence, Damiana, Cocktails, Vodka, Gin, Teguila [*sic*], Barcadi [*sic*], Smirnoff'. Simon Thorley QC held that Eurofood had both taken unfair advantage of and caused undue detriment to the claimants' mark,[101] the former by using it to enhance sales of their product,[102] and the latter effectively by tarnishing, since Viagra was marketed as a medical, rather than

---

97 *General Motors Corp v Yplon SA* [2000] RPC 572, at para 31 of the judgment.
98 *Pfizer Ltd v Eurofood Link (UK) Ltd* [2001] FSR 3, paras 31–32.
99 [2000] RPC 484 ('VISA' for condoms and contraceptive devices). To be accurate, this case involved the similarly worded s 5(3), an objection being taken to an application to register a trade mark.
100 [2001] FSR 3 ('Viagrene' beverage). However, the court took the view that s 10(2) and 10(3) were mutually exclusive and, therefore, because the requirements of s 10(2) were satisfied, there could be no room for the application of s 10(3). As we have seen, it is now clear that this interpretation is incorrect.
101 [2001] FSR 3, para 59.
102 *Ibid*, para 58.

recreational product. However, since there was both confusing similarity and passing off, s 10(3) could have accorded the claimants no additional protection.

The earlier *Sheimer* decision involved the use of the 'VISA' mark, well known for financial services, for condoms. This time there was no real possibility of confusion and the elements of passing off were not established, but a claim based on the similarly worded s 5(3) succeeded.[103] Mr Geoffrey Hobbs QC found detriment (tarnishing) but no unfair advantage. He adopted a narrow view of unfair advantage, taking the view that it was not sufficient for Sheimer merely to 'gain attention for its products by feeding on the fame of the earlier trade mark'.[104] Something much more substantial was required to increase marketability than a mere marketing advantage. He was also generally reluctant to extend s 10(3):[105]

> The provisions of ... [section 10(3)] are clearly not intended to have the sweeping effect of preventing the registration of any mark which is the same as or similar to a trade mark with a reputation, nor are they intended to make it automatically objectionable for the use of one trade mark to remind people of another, so the importance of [the additional requirements of the section] should not be underestimated.

He was also reluctant to use the concept of dilution, regarding it:[106]

> as a word of uncertain meaning which may overstate the purpose and effect of the language used in ... the Act and in parallel Community legislation.

However, it seems to have been the nature of Sheimer's goods that was decisive, making it easy to establish tarnishing.[107]

Neither of these cases therefore suggest that s 10(3) is likely to be applied widely in the UK. By contrast, in *Premier Brands UK Ltd v Typhoon Europe Ltd*,[108] Neuberger J did not think the requirements of s 10(3) were satisfied. The claimants, who had registered 'Typhoo' for a famous brand of tea, objected to the defendants' use of the sign 'Typhoon' for kitchenware. There was no suggestion that the defendants had taken unfair advantage of the mark and, having held that there was no confusion so as to bring the case within s 10(2), Neuberger J adopted a narrow view of the detriment requirements of s 10(3). He did not accept that mere dilution was sufficient, and held that there was neither tarnishing nor blurring. Unlike the earlier cases, association with the Typhoon product itself was not particularly detrimental to the mark; Premier Brands had instead to argue tarnishing from association with the sign itself and, in particular, the destructive power of typhoons. This was clearly always going to be an uphill struggle. Clearly, tarnishing suggests some kind of association, which is not necessarily the same as confusion, but nonetheless Neuberger J's definitions of both tarnishing and blurring seemed to be sufficiently narrow as, in practice, to require a likelihood of confusion, except perhaps in the case of tarnishing by ridicule.

---

103 Section 5(3) because this was an opposed application for a trade mark. The wording of the two sections is the same, however.
104 [2000] RPC 484, p 505.
105 *Ibid*, p 505.
106 *Ibid*, p 506.
107 See also *DaimlerChrysler AG v Javid Alavi (t/a MERC)* [2001] RPC 42, paras 87–88, where Pumfrey J considered the nature of the goods in *Sheimer* to have been a decisive factor, and the case to have been one of tarnishing: 'The case could be viewed as one involving ridicule.'
108 [2000] FSR 767.

In *DaimlerChrysler AG v Javid Alavi (t/a MERC)*,[109] the defendant had marketed clothing under the name 'MERC', which DaimlerChrysler claimed infringed their trade mark in Mercedes Benz cars, for which Merc was a commonly used abbreviation. No confusion was shown, however, to bring the case within s 10(2); there was no question of cashing in on the Merc name. Indeed, it was simply:[110]

> a short catchy name which would be registrable as a business name, and MERC was made up of the initial names of four countries, Mexico, England, Russia and Canada supplied by members of his staff.

Thus, there was no question of gaining an unfair advantage. He seemed to limit the detriment head to tarnishing, which seems to imply almost ridicule, and clearly cannot occur, in practice, in the absence of confusion, or at least association:[111]

> I consider that in order to succeed under Art 5(2) and s 10(3) it must be shown that there is established in the mind of the relevant public a connection between the mark with which they are familiar and the disparaging use. Thus, it is not sufficient to see the word MERC, note that this is the word which one uses to refer to Mercedes cars, see the disagreeable web-site and register it as disagreeable, if nothing actually rubs off on the sign MERC itself or on MERCEDES, or on DaimlerChrysler.

Note that s 10(3) also requires a reputation in the UK. Pumfrey J summed up the requirements for a s 10(3) infringement as follows:[112]

> The enquiry is as follows. (1) Does the proprietor's mark have a reputation? If so, (2) is the defendant's sign sufficiently similar to it that the public are either deceived into the belief that the goods are associated with the proprietor so that the use of the sign takes unfair advantage of the mark, or alternatively causes detriment in their minds to either (a) the repute or (b) the distinctive character of the mark, or (3) even if they are not confused, does the use of the sign nonetheless have this effect, and (4) is the use complained of nonetheless with due cause. Detriment can take the form either of making the mark less attractive (tarnishing, to use Neuberger J's word [from *Typhoon*]) or less distinctive (blurring). On this analysis, 'VISA' is of course a case of tarnishing.

In practice, the UK courts seem happier to develop the idea of tarnishing (as in VISA) than blurring, blurring being similar to the US concept of dilution.

To sum up, then, in the context of this book, s 10(3) could clearly apply where a trader uses a domain name identical or similar to a famous mark in order unfairly to increase sales, or where the goods are of a nature to tarnish the image of the mark. Otherwise, the section is likely to be limited to parody sites, since the UK courts have been reluctant to develop the concepts of blurring or dilution. The section does not, however (at least explicitly), require proof of confusion, and with parody sites there is at least the possibility of tarnishing.

---

109 [2001] RPC 42.
110 *Ibid*, para 32.
111 *Ibid*, para 94.
112 *Ibid*, para 88.

3.7 DOMAIN NAMES AND PASSING OFF

3.7.1 Definition of passing off

Passing off is a tort developed at common law, with no statutory provisions or EU harmonisation initiatives.[113] No doubt, the principles of passing off informed the original trade mark legislation but, as we have seen, EU harmonisation initiatives have, to some extent, moved trade mark law away from its original historic basis, at least in the UK.

Deception misleading customers is the essence of the tort, rather than protection of the claimant's mark. So passing off can be used even where there is no trade mark infringement and, of course, does not require registration of any mark. Moreover, the deception does not have to lead customers to believe that the defendant's goods and/or services are those of a rival trader (though this used to be the test): it is enough that the public be generally deceived as to the nature of the goods/services. In *Erven Warnink Besloten Vennootschap v J Townend & Sons (Hull) Ltd*,[114] the misrepresentation was as to the manufacturing process, a drink being marketed described as 'Keeling's Old English Advocaat', with ingredients quite different from the liquor called 'Advocaat', which had for many years been manufactured in Holland. In the earlier decision of *J Bollinger v Costa Brava Wine Co Ltd*,[115] it was about the geographical location of the vineyards used to describe champagne; sparkling wines not made by the *champenois* process from grapes produced in the Champagne district of France could not be called champagne without passing themselves off as something they were not.

Passing off applies to both goods and services.[116]

However, dilution is not passing off, nor is parody. There must be confusion, at least in the *Advocaat* sense. The claimant must also have goodwill which the defendant is damaging, or proposing to damage.

There are many definitions of passing off,[117] but detailed analysis of the tort is beyond the scope of this book. In summary, it is possible to identify the following requirements for a passing off action:

(a) The defendant is making a misrepresentation, in the course of business, to potential customers.

---

113 See generally Bainbridge, DI, *Intellectual Property*, 5th edn, 2002, Harlow: Longman, Chapter 23; Cornish, WR and Llewelyn, D, *Intellectual Property*, 5th edn, 2003, London: Sweet & Maxwell, Chapter 16.

114 [1979] AC 731.

115 [1960] Ch 262.

116 This was also accepted by Buckley LJ in *HP Bulmer v J Bollinger* [1978] RPC 79 at 93 (also cited in Bainbridge, *Intellectual Property*, *op cit* fn 113, p 640).

117 Lord Diplock in *Ervin Warnink v Townend* [1979] AC 731, p 742 (basing himself on *Spalding v Gamage* (1915) 84 LJ Ch 449), a definition which concentrates on the activities of the defendant; Lord Fraser, at p 755 in the same case, but concentrating on the characteristics of the plaintiff; see also Colston, C, 'Passing off: the right solution to domain name disputes' [2000] *LMCLQ* 523, p 527; *Anheuser-Busch Inc v Budejovicky Budvar NP* [1984] FSR 413 (combining both tests); Lord Oliver in *Reckitt & Colman v Borden* [1990] 1 WLR 491, p 499; see also Colston, *op cit* above, p 528.

(b) Damage (or likely damage) to the claimant's trade reputation and goodwill within the UK.[118] Note that personal reputations are excluded, being limited to defamation actions (discussed in Chapter 12).

We have also seen that passing off requires confusion in the sense that there is no protection against dilution as such. However, it does not require confusion in that the defendant is passing his or her goods or services off as those of the claimant in particular, since there was no such confusion in *Advocaat* itself, nor indeed in *One in a Million*, considered below in section 3.7.4.[119]

3.7.2   Not set in stone

In *Advocaat*, Lord Diplock also said:[120]

> Nevertheless, the increasing recognition by Parliament of the need for more rigorous standards of commercial honesty is a factor which should not be overlooked by a judge confronted by the choice whether or not to extend by analogy, to circumstances in which it has not previously been applied, a principle which has been applied in previous cases where the circumstances, although different, had some features in common with those of the case which he has to decide. Where, over a period of years, there can be discerned a steady trend in legislation which reflects the view of successive Parliaments as to what the public interest demands in a particular field of law, development of the common law in that part of the same field which has been left to it ought to proceed upon a parallel rather than a diverging course.

This perhaps justified *One in a Million*, considered below (section 3.7.4), since it suggests that the tort is not set in stone, but can evolve over time. *Advocaat* itself represented an extension of passing off to protect shared commercial reputation.

3.7.3   Injunctions

It is not necessary for damage actually to have occurred. In *Glaxo plc v Glaxowellcome Ltd*,[121] an injunction was granted to prevent company registration in advance of merger. This principle was applied in *One in a Million*.

3.7.4   Passing off in the domain name context

Obviously, for a trader to design a website, or to make representations therein, taking advantage of another's goodwill can amount to passing off just as surely as similar representations in a non-Internet context. Domain name hijacking would also often amount to passing off, unless the claimant and the defendant had the same name (and

---

118 In *Anheuser-Busch Inc v Budejovicky Budvar NP*, the plaintiffs (the US manufacturers of Budweiser beer) failed to establish a reputation (or at any rate goodwill) within the UK, the defendants being Czechoslovakian brewers of a beer of the same name. Also *DaimlerChrysler AG v Javid Alavi (t/a MERC)* [2001] RPC 42, where the claimants were unable to establish any UK goodwill for 'MERC' clothing.

119 *BT v One in a Million* [1999] 1 WLR 903, considered in detail in section 3.7.4. See also Colston, 'Passing off: the right solution to domain name disputes', *op cit* fn 117, p 531.

120 *Ervin Warnink v Townend* [1979] AC 731, p 743.

121 [1996] FSR 388.

quite often even then).[122] In *Yahoo! Inc v Akash Arora*,[123] the defendants used the domain name 'yahooindia' and also adopted Yahoo!'s website appearance, including the format, contents, lay out, colour scheme, and source code of another Yahoo! site,[124] apparently to make their site appear to be a Yahoo! search engine. Search engine services were also offered. The case was brought in the High Court of Delhi but, in deciding in favour of Yahoo!, the court applied *One in a Million* and other UK decisions, and there is little doubt that an action for passing off would also have succeeded in the UK. Of course, there would almost certainly have been a trade mark infringement had similar facts occurred in the UK; there was no trade mark infringement under Indian law, whose trade mark laws apply only to goods, not services.[125] In any case, Yahoo! had no trade mark in India (though an application was pending). Thus, if Yahoo! were to succeed, it had to be in a passing off action.

The domain name in the *'yahooindia'* case was not identical to Yahoo!'s mark, but was sufficiently similar to cause confusion. Indeed, the plaintiffs' argument, which seems to have been accepted by the court, was that:[126]

> it would not be unusual for someone looking for an authorised 'Yahoo!' site with India-specific content to type in 'Yahooindia.com', ie, the defendants' domain name and thereby instead of reaching the Internet site of the plaintiff, the said person would reach the Internet site of the defendants.

On the basis of similar reasoning, typosquatting would also usually amount to passing off, since there the intention is to confuse, in precisely the same way. Sucks.com sites do not normally give rise to confusion, however, and to parody is also not normally to pass off.

Cybersquatting is not so clear cut, however. In *BT v One in a Million*,[127] the defendant cybersquatters registered, among others, the domain names ladbrokes.com, sainsbury.com, sainsburys.com, j-sainsbury.com, marksandspencer.com, cellnet.net, bt.org, virgin.org, marksandspencer.co.uk, britishtelecom.co.uk, britishtelecom.net, and britishtelecom.com. They made no use of the names as active sites, but instead tried to sell them to the companies who would most obviously be interested in them, threatening to sell them elsewhere in default of such a purchase. It was by no means self-evident that this was passing off. The defendants argued that there was no use, nor even threatened use of the domain names, and that they never intended to use the domain names in the course of business. The last point was relatively easily dealt with, since the defendants were effectively trading in domain names and, in the view of Jonathan Sumption QC, at first instance:[128]

---

122 See further the discussion of *Pitman v Nominet*, in section 3.8, where the passing off claim failed. See also the discussion of defences in section 3.10.

123 [1999] FSR 931 (in the High Court of Delhi).

124 *Ibid*, para 2.

125 An unsuccessful argument on behalf of the defendants was that passing off should also therefore not apply to services: *ibid*, para 7.

126 *Ibid*, para 2.

127 [1999] 1 WLR 903 (CA), on appeal from [1998] FSR 265, noted in [1998] EIPR 468. Aldous LJ's full judgment can be found at www.nominet.org.uk/ReferenceDocuments/CaseLaw/OneInAMillionAppealJudgement.html.

128 See www.nominet.org.uk/ReferenceDocuments/CaseLaw/OneInAMillionAppeal Judgment.html. Jonathan Sumption QC's decision was upheld in the Court of Appeal.

Use 'in the course of trade' means use by way of business. It does not mean use as a trade mark: *British Sugar plc v James Robertson & Sons Ltd*.[129] The use of a trade mark in the course of the business of a professional dealer for the purpose of making domain names more valuable and extracting money from the trade mark owner is a use in the course of trade.

It was also enough, for an injunction to be granted, for the defendants to threaten to pass off. They did not actually have to make use of the domain name themselves.

The case involving Marks & Spencer was more straightforward than the others. To return again to the first instance judgment:

In the case of Marks & Spencer, it is in my judgment beyond dispute that what is going on is calculated to infringe the plaintiff's rights in future. The name marksandspencer could not have been chosen for any other reason than that it was associated with the well known retailing group. There is only one possible reason why anyone who was not part of the Marks & Spencer plc group should wish to use such a domain address, and that is to pass himself off as part of that group or his products off as theirs. Where the value of a name consists solely in its resemblance to the name or trade mark of another enterprise, the court will normally assume that the public is likely to be deceived, for why else would the defendants choose it? In the present case, the assumption is plainly justified. As a matter of common sense, these names were registered and are available for sale for eventual use. Someone seeking or coming upon a website called http://marksandspencer.co.uk would naturally assume that it was that of the plaintiffs.

The only point made by the defendants which is worthy of any attention is that there are uses to which they can put the domain name which would not involve passing off by them or any one else, namely (i) the sale of the domain name to Marks & Spencer themselves, and (ii) its simple retention with a view to blocking the use of the same name by Marks & Spencer in order to induce them to pay. I would accept that neither of these activities in themselves constitutes passing off. But that is not the point. The point is that the names are only saleable to Marks & Spencer and blocking their use by Marks & Spencer is only a useful negotiating tactic on the footing that they are names which it is dangerous for Marks & Spencer to allow to remain out of their control. The danger arises from the risk of deception which their existence necessarily presents. The allegation that this was the defendants' object in this case is fairly made, supported by overwhelming evidence, and is left wholly unanswered by the defendants' affidavits. Any person who deliberately registers a domain name on account of its similarity to the name, brand name or trade mark of an unconnected commercial organisation must expect to find himself on the receiving end of an injunction to restrain the threat of passing off, and the injunction will be in terms which will make the name commercially useless to the dealer.

In other words, the only people who would be interested in buying a Marks & Spencer domain name would be either Marks & Spencer themselves, or someone wishing to pass themselves off as Marks & Spencer. Since the defendants had threatened to sell the name elsewhere if Marks & Spencer did not buy it, this could only be construed as a threat to sell an instrument of deception to a third party. The uniqueness of the Marks & Spencer name made this an undeniable conclusion.

It was also noted that Nominet offered (and still offers) a 'whois' service,[130] where the identity and details of the person registering the name are set out for anyone to

---

129 [1996] RPC 281, 290–92 (not, however, a passing off case).
130 The service is offered at www.nominet.org.uk/whois.html.

inspect. Mere registration of the Marks & Spencer names was therefore held to amount to passing off, even in the absence of any use of the name, since anyone checking the domain name using 'whois' would assume One in a Million to be associated with Marks & Spencer.[131]

The position was less straightforward in the case of the other names, since (continuing with the first instance judgment) these names 'may be sold to someone with a distinct interest of his own in the name, for example a solicitor by the name of John Sainsbury or the government of the British Virgin Islands, with a view to its use by him'. Thus, the 'whois' reasoning would no longer necessarily apply, and even the threat to sell would no longer necessarily amount to a threat to sell an instrument of fraud. However, as Jonathan Sumption QC observed:

> In the four other cases, the facts relevant to both causes of action are substantially the same in all relevant respects save one. The difference is that in the other four cases, it is somewhat less absurd for the defendants to suggest the names which they have registered have an innocent use. It is impossible to imagine any unconnected party using the phrase 'Marks and Spencer' in his name or address if not to deceive, and the same may well be true of Cellnet. But the possibility is not so far-fetched in the case of the words 'Sainsbury', 'Ladbroke', 'Virgin' or 'BT'. The defendants also say that in some cases the suffix (for example .org in the case of BT), serves to differentiate them from the trade marks. The defendants make much of this point, but I am not impressed by it for the simple reason that although the words are probably capable of an innocent use, that is not the use that these defendants intend. The history of the defendants' activities shows a deliberate practice followed over a substantial period of time of registering domain names which are chosen to resemble the names and marks of other people and are plainly intended to deceive. The threat of passing off and trade mark infringement, and the likelihood of confusion arising from the infringement of the mark are made out beyond argument in this case, even in which it is possible to imagine other cases in which the issue would be more nicely balanced.

In other words, evidence outside the registration of these names was taken into account, including the defendants' activities over a long period of time, their registration of the Marks & Spencer domain names, and threat to sell them elsewhere, which clearly showed a fraudulent intent.

Though *One in a Million* is sometimes portrayed as a general case against cybersquatters, much of the reasoning depends on the particular facts before the court. For example, an individual with a grudge could register a company's name with no risk of passing off, since he or she would not be a trader. In any case, whoever registered the name, if the registration were used merely as a blocking device with no threat to sell, none of the *One in a Million* reasoning would apply, apart from the 'whois' service, which can only apply to unique names such as Marks & Spencer. It might even be possible, were the name still available, for an individual to register a name such as ladbrokes.com, offer it for sale to Ladbrokes, and threaten to sell elsewhere otherwise. It seems unlikely that offering to sell one name would amount to a use in the course of business, and the threat to sell the name elsewhere need not be unlawful, as it necessarily would, for example, with marksandspencer.co.uk.

---

131 A 'whois' search against marksandspencer.co.uk today reveals the name and address of Marks & Spencer plc.

It should also be remembered that passing off protects only traders. Registering the name of an individual will not be actionable unless, as is the case with many celebrities today, the individual also uses the name to trade.

Cybersquatting is, however, a ground for complaint within both ICANN's and Nominet's dispute resolution procedures, considered in section 2.2. The remedy, the transfer of the domain name to the complainant, will often be a suitable remedy, so for any complainant the dispute resolution procedure may be a better route to redress than a court action, given the limits of passing off in some cybersquatting situations.

It seems likely that the cybersquatting era is passing, since all businesses, whether old or new, must by now appreciate the importance of a presence on the Web. Where they arise, however, it is perhaps more likely that they will be of the Marks & Spencer type, since new businesses often use imaginary names, where the Marks & Spencer reasoning in *One in a Million* will apply.

3.8 WHERE NO CAUSE OF ACTION, NO REASON TO INTERFERE WITH FIRST-COME FIRST-SERVED

To sue in a court successfully obviously requires a cause of action and, if none can be found, there will be no redress, however much the claimant objects to the defendant's conduct. In the absence of a cause of action, matters will simply remain as they are.

In *Pitman v Nominet*,[132] considered in another context in section 2.1.4, Nominet's first-come first-served rule was upheld, because Pitman Training were left without a cause of action. We have already seen that they failed to show interference with contract by Pitman Publishing, the relevant contract being between Pitman Training and I-Way, their ISP. They also failed in an abuse of process action and to show passing off by Pitman Publishing, the Vice-Chancellor observing that:[133]

> It is said that the use by Pitman Publishing of the domain name 'pitman.co.uk' would constitute passing off. This strikes me as a strange proposition, bearing in mind that Pitman Publishing has traded under the style Pitman for nearly 150 years and that in 1985 when the Pitman businesses were sold off separately it was agreed that the purchaser of the publishing business would continue to trade under the style Pitman. Indeed, it was agreed that the purchaser of the training business would not trade under that style unless the name 'Pitman' was accompanied by the word 'training'. ... PTC contends that its, PTC's, use of the domain name in the period March 1996 to date has led the public to associate that domain name (as opposed to the style Pitman *per se*) with it, PTC. So the use of the domain name 'pitman.co.uk' by Pitman Publishing would, it is contended, constitute passing off by Pitman Publishing. The evidence does not even begin to support the contention that the public associates the domain name 'pitman.co.uk' with PTC. PTC has had only two e-mail responses to the advertisements it has put out. During the time PTC has been using the 'pitman.co.uk' domain name in its advertisements so too has Pitman Publishing been using the domain name in its

---

132 [1997] FSR 797 (described rather briefly in Edwards and Waelde, *Law and the Internet, op cit* fn 31, p 136, and in slightly more detail by Colston, 'Passing off: the right solution to domain name disputes', *op cit* fn 117, p 533).

133 The full transcript is at www.nominet.org.uk/ReferenceDocuments/CaseLaw/ThePitmanCase.html.

advertisements. Both have been using the domain name in their respective advertisements. Not only is there no evidence that the public has come to associate the domain name exclusively with PTC, but it is in my opinion highly improbable that that could have happened. That there may be some confusion experienced by some members of the public is undoubtedly so. But that confusion results from the use by both companies, PTC and Pitman Publishing, of the style Pitman for their respective trading purposes. No viable passing off claim against Pitman Publishing arising out of the future or past use by Pitman Publishing of the 'pitman.co.uk' domain name has, in my judgement, been shown.

Since there was no cause of action, the domain name remained where it was, with the publishers.

It does not necessarily follow that in all cases where a company uses its own name as a domain name there will be no passing off. In *Pitman*, a new company was suing one which was old, established and well known, and it is not surprising that the case was pretty hopeless. Suppose the old company had, instead, been suing the new, or indeed the general case where an established company sues one which has only recently started to trade. In such a case, the public may well be deceived, and it is accepted that application of the own name defence is very limited in passing off actions. (On the defences in general, see section 3.10.) Passing off is therefore a possible action in a domain name envy case.

3.9   METATAGS AND SEARCH ENGINE OPTIMISATION

With the increasing sophistication of Internet users, it is reasonable to suppose that the role of the search engine will be enhanced, whereas fewer Internet users will expect to find a company simply by typing into file-open a similarly sounding domain name. It seems likely, therefore, that domain name disputes will lessen in importance, and that new disputes will be generated by search engine optimisation, and other means of drawing a company to the attention of a more Internet-savvy public.

There have already been disputes about metatags. Metatags are written into the head of an HTML page. They describe the page, but are not normally visible to someone accessing that page. They are, however, picked up by the search engines and, indeed, the original reason for them was to enable a text search to find files consisting entirely of non-textual content, such as pictures. A description metatag can become visible, but only when the search engine displays a result. For completeness, it should be added that all metatags can be viewed by anyone who chooses deliberately to view the HTML source code, but most web users would not do this.[134] It is also important to observe that the content of metatags lies entirely within the control of the writer of the web page; there is no third party involved, as there is with domain names.

Search engines do not disclose how the ordering of their listings is arrived at, but a company may well suppose that if a search matches a word in a metatag that will increase the likelihood of the search engine finding a page, and placing it high in the

---

134 In Internet Explorer, the user chooses view source; in Netscape it is view page source. Most users would not do this, since it is generally only of value for creators of sites, who wish to modify the HTML source.

listings. Obviously, a company would prefer its page to appear as number three or four than number 1,987,456, for example. It may therefore be possible to increase the likelihood of exposure by, for example, including competitors' trade marks in your metatags. (There is, however, evidence that search engines are wisening up to this, and that the importance of metatags in determining the order of listings is lessening.)[135]

Search engines also offer services whereby a banner advertisement is displayed when a particular search term is entered. Indeed, this typically generates the overwhelming majority of a search engine's income.[136] It is done by agreement between the search engine and the advertiser, but obviously it can be to the advantage of a business, for example, to trigger a banner advertisement on a search for the trade mark of a competitor, as well as its own.

The question here is whether the use of metatags or other forms of search engine optimisation can give rise to intellectual property issues. The logical way to approach this is to consider, first, whether the use of a metatag can be a trade mark use at all; if so, secondly, whether it falls within s 10(1), (2) and (3); and if so, thirdly, whether defences such as the own name defence apply.

3.9.1 Are these trade mark infringements at all?

Metatags are in principle visible only to search engines, although description metatags can become visible in the search engine results, and it must, therefore, first be asked whether an invisible usage can constitute a trade mark infringement.

Until recently, there appeared to be no doubt about this, either in the US (where there has been a greater wealth of litigation) or in the UK. One of the better known cases in the US is *Playboy Enterprises Inc v Terri Welles Inc*.[137] Terri Welles was Playboy Playmate of the Year for 1981, and included in the metatags on her business page the following:[138]

<META NAME="description" CONTENT="Playboy Playmate Of The Year 1981 Terri Welles website featuring erotic nude photos, semi-nude photos, softcore and exclusive Members Club">

---

135 See, eg, http://answers.google.com/answers/threadview?id=210902, an address that was discovered by one of my e-commerce law students. There are, however, other methods of using words that are invisible to users to improve search engine rankings: see http://en.wikipedia.org/wiki/Spamdexing for examples. These methods raise similar issues to metatags themselves.

136 'Google relies on adword sales for around 98 per cent of its income': www.theregister.co.uk/2005/01/21/google_adword. An interesting development is the so-called 'click fraud', since banner advertisement payments can depend on the number of click-throughs (*Financial Times*, 6 December 2004: http://news.ft.com/cms/s/f606ccac-472b-11d9-b099-00000e2511c8.html):

A rival company, for example, can programme a network of computers to automatically click on these links.

This increases the amount a company has to pay Google, and in some cases causes the advert to stop being displayed, as the company burns through its agreed advertising budget with Google.

It is not at all clear that the victim would have a cause of action under UK law.

137 United States Court of Appeals for the Ninth Circuit. The full judgment can be found at http://caselaw.lp.findlaw.com/data2/circs/9th/0055009p.pdf. There are also notes at www.phillipsnizer.com/library/cases/lib_case264.cfm, and www.phillipsnizer.com/library/cases/lib_case197.cfm.

138 The site is at www.terriwelles.com.

<META NAME="keywords" CONTENT="terri, welles, playmate, playboy, model, models, nude, naked, breast, breasts, tit, tits, nipple, nipples, ass, butt,">

The nature of the site is fairly obvious from the metatags, as was presumably intended by Terri Welles. Objection was taken by Playboy, among other things, to the use of their trade mark in her metatags. It was clearly assumed by the court that this could in principle be a trade mark infringement.[139] The assumption is weakened by two factors: first, Playboy's trade mark was used in the body of the site as well, so that the case could not be said to turn on the metatag use, and secondly, the mark appeared in a description metatag which was therefore made visible by the search engine. In the result, Playboy's action did not succeed, at least as far as the metatags were concerned, because Terri Welles was using the mark legitimately to identify herself,[140] and in the metatags accurately to describe the contents of her website.

In the UK, metatag use was also assumed to constitute trade mark infringement in *Roadtech Computer Systems Ltd v Mandata (Management and Data Services) Ltd*.[141] In *Pfizer*, as we have seen, the defendants used the claimants' mark, 'Viagra', in their metatags, but *Pfizer* clearly did not turn on this, and the metatags were mentioned mostly as evidence of the defendants' intention to confuse.[142] However, the whole assumption that metatag use can constitute trade mark infringement has been brought into question in *Reed Executive v Reed Business Information Ltd*.[143] Here, a similar sign to the claimants' mark was used in the metatags, and to trigger banner advertisements, in relation to similar but not identical services. Jacob LJ held that there was no infringement under s 10(2), because the use did not create any confusion (this aspect of the case is considered further below in section 3.9.2). But he also said this (though wishing to reserve his opinion):[144]

> First, does metatag use count as use of a trade mark at all? In this context it must be remembered that use is important not only for infringement but also for saving a mark from non-use. In the latter context it would at least be odd that a wholly invisible use could defeat a non-use attack. Mr Hobbs [for the claimants] suggested that metatag use should be treated in the same way as uses of a trade mark which ultimately are read by people, such as uses on a DVD. But in those cases the ultimate function of a trade mark is achieved – an indication to someone of trade origin. Uses read only by computers may not count – they never convey a message to anyone.

The argument is, then, that metatag use cannot be use for infringement purposes, because it cannot be use as a defence to a non-use claim. It is not clear whether the same reasoning would apply to agreements for banner advertisements to be displayed on a search by the claimants' mark – perhaps these would fall into the same category as uses on a DVD. It is also not clear that it would apply to a description metatag, which can be made visible in the search engine results.

---

139 There are a number of US cases, some involving Playboy (referred to in Bainbridge, *Intellectual Property, op cit* fn 113), who seem to be very litigious, suggesting that metatags can infringe trade marks.

140 US nomenclature is 'permissible, nominative uses'. This appears to be similar to the own name defence in the UK.

141 [2000] ETMR 970. Mandata used a competitor's trade mark in their metatags.

142 See section 3.6.3.

143 [2004] RPC 40.

144 *Ibid*, para 149(a).

The view of Jacob LJ in the above paragraph was not necessary for the decision in the case, since there was in any case no confusion as required under s 10(2). It seems also to be counter to the trend of the 1994 Act to expand the notion of a mark, and indeed Jacob LJ's own view, earlier in the same case, that oral use could possibly infringe.[145] Moreover, s 10 merely requires use of the sign in the course of trade, whereas s 46 allows revocation of a mark if there has been no 'genuine use' in the UK for five years. It is surely possible in principle for metatag use to count for the purposes of s 10, while nonetheless not amounting to 'genuine use' for the purposes of defending a s 46 non-revocation action. Nevertheless, in the light of the view of Jacob LJ, it cannot be assumed that metatag use can ever give rise to trade mark infringement in the UK.

3.9.2   If use, is it a s 10 infringement?

If, however, metatag use (whether description or otherwise) can amount to use for the purposes of trade mark infringement, *Reed* tells us (as part of the *ratio*) that it will not give rise to a breach of s 10(2), because of the lack of the necessary element of confusion:[146] 'causing a site to appear in a search result, without more, does not suggest any connection with anyone else.' He clearly took a view, not dissimilar to that in *Avnet* (in section 3.5.3) that Internet users are generally reasonably sophisticated and unlikely to be confused over the origin of goods or services by search engine results. He observed that 'when you conduct a search, some of the results appear to have nothing to do with your search term'.[147] The reasoning seems quite general, and not limited to the particular facts before him. If he is right, metatag use will never give rise to a s 10(2) infringement, and nor, for the same reason, to an action for passing off. 'This is equally so whether the search engine itself rendered visible the metatag or not.'[148] He adopted a similar view of banner usage:[149]

> The web-using member of the public knows that all sorts of banners appear when he or she does a search and they are or may be triggered by something in the search. He or she also knows that searches produce fuzzy results – results with much rubbish thrown in. The idea that a search under the name Reed would make anyone think there was a trade connection between a totaljobs banner making no reference to the word 'Reed' and Reed Employment is fanciful. No likelihood of confusion was established.

Confusion is only required, of course, for s 10(2) and for passing off, so it remains possible, assuming that metatag use is trade mark use at all, that it can give rise to an infringement of s 10(1) or 10(3). Jacob LJ left open the s 10(1) issue, but observed that:[150]

> If metatag use does count as use, is there infringement if the marks and goods or services are identical? This is important: one way of competing with another is to use his

---

145 *Ibid*, para 31.
146 *Ibid*, para 148. Although this is an issue of fact, not law, the reasoning is in very general terms, applying in principle to any search engine optimisation technique.
147 *Ibid*, para 145.
148 *Ibid*, para 147.
149 *Ibid*, para 140. The UK position appears to be similar to that in the US but not France: www.theregister.co.uk/2004/12/16/google_adwords and www.theregister.co.uk/2005/01/21/google_adword.
150 [2004] RPC 40, para 149(b).

trade mark in your metatag – so that a search for him will also produce you in the search results. Some might think this unfair – but others that this is good competition provided that no one is misled.

He also left open banner use and s 10(1):[151]

> If this had been an Art 5.1(a) [that is, s 10(1)] case then the position might have been different. For then there would have been no requirement to prove a likelihood of confusion. The question would appear to turn on whether the use of the word 'Reed' by Yahoo at the instance of RBI properly amounted to a 'use in the course of trade' as to which, as I say, I reserve my opinion. It may be that an invisible use of this sort is not use at all for the purposes of this trade mark legislation – the computers who 'read' sets of letters merely 'look for' patterns of 0s and 1s – there is no meaning being conveyed to anyone – no 'sign'.

This is of course a policy argument for not extending trade mark protection. From a purely legal perspective, however, if metatag or banner use can infringe at all, then use of a sign identical to a mark, for identical goods or services, necessarily breaches s 10(1), subject only to the defences considered below. Similarly, if metatag or banner use can infringe at all, then in principle s 10(3) ought also to apply, since it does not depend on a likelihood of confusion. So, for example, it might be an infringement to use another's mark in a metatag to boost the exposure of a webpage, thereby unfairly taking advantage, even if the sign were used in connection with dissimilar goods or services.

In the UK, therefore, we have Court of Appeal authority on metatags, banner use and s 10(2), and also by inference passing off, but the issue whether metatag use counts at all has been left open. Given the growing importance of this type of dispute, it seems unlikely that this will remain the position for long.

If there has been a s 10 infringement, it is subject to the s 11 defences, which are considered in the next section.

3.10 DEFENCES

As we saw in section 3.2, it is a defence to an infringement action that the sign is used to describe the goods or services, or their intended purpose, subject to the proviso that 'the use is in accordance with honest practices in industrial or commercial matters'.[152] It seems unlikely that this defence could have significant application in terms of domain names, but, of course, it could for web content, and also perhaps for metatags. For example, it would not be unreasonable to place in a metatag 'A book about Wet Wet Wet', or 'High quality models of famous cars, Ferrari, Rolls Royce and Aston Martin'.

Section 11(1)(a) allows the use by a person of his own name or address, but subject to the same proviso. One of the issues in *Reed Executive v Reed Business Information Ltd*[153] was whether this defence could apply to company names:[154] 'It has been

---

151 *Ibid*, para 142; the services provided would have had to be identical, of course.
152 This is a paraphrase of s 11(2)(b) and (c) of the 1994 Act.
153 [2004] RPC 40.
154 *Euromarket v Peters* [2001] FSR 20, *per* Jacob J at para 30.

suggested that companies are different from people because a company name can be chosen at will whereas the name of a person is pretty well fixed at birth and by usage.' However, in *Reed*, Jacob LJ thought that the issue had already been decided in UK law, but added that:[155]

> It would be very strange if no company could avail itself of the defence. Think, for instance, of a company formed to take over a business established under an individual's name and having his name. It would be outrageous if the defence were lost upon incorporation.
>
> ... Any fear that dishonest people might form companies with misleading names so as to take advantage of the defence is easily removed by the use of the proviso – such a deliberate attempt to avail oneself of another's mark would not be an honest practice.

He had previously taken a similar view to the second paragraph in the *Crate & Barrel* case:[156]

> ... anyone who chooses a new company name knowing of an existing reputation in a registered mark, or indeed just knowing that the mark was registered and having no reason to suppose the registration as invalid, would be likely to be caught by the proviso. They would not be using the mark in accordance with honest practices in industrial or commercial matters.

Jacob LJ also thought in *Reed* that if 'the defendant in fact caused significant deception, albeit innocently, there is no defence'.[157] This would in practice prevent use of the own name defence in many passing off, or indeed, s 10(2) actions. However, Reed did not set out to deceive, the confusion (if any) which they caused being on the other side of the line. It was of the sort:[158] 'I wonder if there is a connection'. That is not sufficient to trigger the proviso.

Passing off, of course, involves a deception and, in contrast to trade mark infringement, there is no statutory own name defence. To use one's own name can be a defence to a passing off action, but it is a limited defence. As Jacob LJ observed in *Reed*, where (as we have seen) the defendants had recently expanded into a line of business similar to that of the claimants:[159]

> 109. It is long and well settled that it is no defence to passing off that the defendant has or had no intention to deceive. It is also settled that there is only a very limited own name defence. It was put this way by Romer J in *Rodgers v Rodgers*,[160] a passage approved by the majority of the House of Lords in *Parker-Knoll v Knoll International*:[161]
>
> > To the proposition of law that no man is entitled to carry on his business in such a way as to represent that it is the business of another, or is in any way connected with the business of another, there is an exception, that a man is entitled to carry on his business in his own name so long as he does not do anything more than that to cause confusion with the business of another, and so long as he does it honestly. To the proposition of law that no man is entitled so to describe his goods as to represent that the goods are the goods of another, there is no exception.

---

155 [2004] RPC 40, para 116.
156 *Euromarket v Peters* [2001] FSR 20, *per* Jacob J at para 30.
157 In *Reed*, paras 131–32.
158 *Ibid*, para 111.
159 *Ibid*, beginning at para 109.
160 (1924) 41 RPC 277.
161 [1962] RPC 265.

110. Thus the English law of passing off abounds with cases where people have been prevented from using their own name. ...

111. I have already observed that the difference between mere confusion and deception is elusive. ... Once the position strays into misleading a substantial number of people (going from 'I wonder if there is a connection' to 'I assume there is a connection') there will be passing off, whether the use is as a business name or a trade mark on goods.

112. The Judge rightly observed that the passing off defence is narrow. Actually no case comes to mind in which it has succeeded. Because the test is honesty, I do not see how any man who is in fact causing deception and knows that to be so, can possibly have a defence to passing off.

In the case itself, he concluded that there was, at best, no more than some minimal degree of confusion, and therefore Reed Business Executive were entitled to use their own name.

COPYRIGHT ISSUES

4.1   COPYRIGHT AND THE INTERNET

Copyright protects copyright holders, among other things, against unauthorised copying of their work. It is worth beginning, therefore, by examining where copying occurs in an e-commerce environment and, in particular, on the Internet.

Copyright protection extends to the Internet in the same way as everywhere else. For a web author, for example, to copy on to his or her website, and thence to make public, someone else's text or graphics can amount to a breach of copyright just as surely as if the same text or graphics were published in a newspaper. Similarly, a website offering for sale digital copies of pirated music files is breaching copyright just as surely as a shop in the physical world selling the same music on tape or CD. The same is true of a commercial site offering, in digital form, articles, comments, newspaper stories, etc. The copyright implications are exactly the same as for physical newspapers, magazines, etc.

The Internet also attracts the law of copyright, however, in ways which have no real counterpart in the physical world. Probably more than any other medium, the Internet works by making copies of material and, in general, copying of material is allowed only by, or with the permission of, the copyright holder. It is not surprising, therefore, that the law of copyright has enormous significance for e-commerce.

It is important, however, to be aware of the nature of the copying process, since it is unlike the processes that occur in other media. The precise manner of application of copyright law is therefore unusual, and perhaps counter-intuitive.

The Internet is a packet-switched network, and every communication over the Internet involves the copying and forwarding of each packet by the routers. This copying is essential to the Internet process, but the copies are not retained once it is clear that a packet has reached the next router or its ultimate destination. Access to the World Wide Web (WWW) also requires the web page at least to be copied into the Random Access Memory (RAM) of the user's computer. This is necessary to allow the user to view the page.

Other forms of copying are also common, although not strictly necessary to the operation of the Internet (though they usually improve its speed of operation). Sites which are very popular are often mirrored elsewhere to spread traffic load, and US sites are often mirrored in the UK to reduce the flow of traffic across the Atlantic. These mirror sites are often maintained on a fairly permanent basis. Additionally, browsers often cache recently used pages on the user's hard disk, again to speed up access time, and also give the option of a permanent download, should this be required.

A web page itself can incorporate text or pictures, which will then appear to the user to be part of the page being accessed. They can, however, be incorporated from any site, anywhere in the world. The copyright in the material may therefore not belong to the owner of the web page being accessed. However, nothing is copied to the site of the incorporating page, only to the user's computer. Any primary copyright infringement will therefore be committed by the user, not by the owner of the incorporating website. If the owner of the incorporating website is to be liable, it will be on the basis of secondary infringement only, or possibly the rights management provisions introduced into UK law in 2003 (see section 4.5.2 below).

Raising similar issues is the practice of deep linking, where a link is made not to the home page but to the inside page of another site. Again, clicking on the link copies material only to the user's computer, and the issues are similar, but not identical to those considered in the previous paragraph.

Secondary liability is also relevant to the activities of music sharing enterprises, such as those at one time conducted by Napster; the enterprise does not itself copy files, but facilitates the copying of files between users, who are connected to the Web. The enterprise therefore commits no primary breach of copyright.[1]

Copyright owners can use technology to protect themselves against unwanted deep linking and, to some extent, also against peer-to-peer music distribution of the type pioneered by Napster. The emphasis of the law is moving to reflect this away from the infringement itself, and towards protection of the technology employed by copyright owners to protect their rights.[2]

4.2   HOW COPYRIGHT WORKS IN OUTLINE

Copyright is a species of intellectual property and, as that description implies, is a form of property. It is, however, not property in anything tangible, and nor indeed (unlike, for example, property in a lease of land) need it even relate to anything tangible.[3]

Property concepts in tangible goods, such as a piece of machinery, are relatively uncomplicated. Property protects possession, or the right to possess, and it is protected by the tort of conversion. The tort of negligence also protects the property against damage or destruction, in some circumstances.

Property rights can be asserted against anybody and property can be bought and sold. It is also possible to attach conditions to a sale, for example to prevent the purchaser of machinery using it to compete with the seller. The conditions operate by way of contract, however, and the privity of contract doctrine puts difficulties in the way of binding third parties. The condition would not, of itself for example, bind a subsequent purchaser of the machinery. It is true that there are devices that can be used, such as a chain of indemnities, and the tort of interference with contract can also affect third parties to a limited extent,[4] and these probably give sufficient protection in most cases, where the number of subsequent purchasers is likely to be one, or a small number.

---

1   These are also called peer-to-peer systems, and are considered in section 4.4.5. Unfortunately, judgment was still awaited in the ongoing American dispute, between MGM and Grokster, at the time of publication of this book.
2   See section 4.5.
3   For a fuller introduction to the nature of copyright, see (eg) Cornish, WR and Llewelyn, D, *Intellectual Property*, 5th edn, 2003, London: Sweet & Maxwell, Chapter 9.
4   As in, eg, *British Motor Trade Association v Salvadori* [1949] Ch 556.

With the development of printing presses in the 16th century, however, the third party problem became considerable, and still more is this true today with the ease of copying possible with digital technology. It is, no doubt, possible to sell a book, a CD, or even a music file transmitted over the Internet, on condition that it will not be copied, and this condition is, in principle at least, enforceable against the purchaser, but if many copies are made, it will be very difficult indeed to enforce contractual conditions against all the recipients.

If contractual remedies were all that were available, therefore (or so it is argued), there would be no incentive for creative writers of books or music, for example, or producers of pictures, to work. This argument prevailed in the UK as long ago as 1710, when the Copyright Act of that year introduced the idea of a property right, not merely in the underlying physical medium (in those days, most probably a book or pamphlet), but in the copy of the creative medium itself. As a property, rather than merely a contractual right, copyright could be asserted not only against the purchaser of the book or pamphlet, but also against recipients of any copies made.

Copyright protection remains to this day entirely statutory, the relevant provision in the UK now being the Copyright, Designs and Patents Act 1988 (CDPA 1988), as subsequently amended, most significantly by the Copyright and Related Rights Regulations 2003 ('the 2003 regulations'), bringing into force in the UK the EC Council Directive (2001/29/EC) on the harmonisation of certain aspects of copyright and related rights in the information society.[5]

Whereas with tangible goods there is no difficulty in determining the subject matter of the property right, with copyright the subject matter itself has to be defined. Copyright does not protect mere ideas, but rather the manifestation of those ideas once they have been worked into a definable form. The law accordingly allows copyright to be owned by the creator of various types of work defined in the Act. The law also has to define precisely what is protected, since there is nothing akin to the possession of a tangible object, whose protection is relatively straightforward. The law works by permitting only the copyright holder to perform various acts with the work, again defined in the Act, but most significantly including making copies of the work. Anybody else who performs these acts, without the permission of the copyright holder, in principle acts in breach of copyright. However, uses with the permission of the copyright holder are lawful. The law allows a number of permitted uses, such as disclosure in the public interest, fair dealing for the purposes of research or private study, etc.[6] These permitted uses operate similarly in an Internet context to any other context.

4.2.1   What is the property right protected?

In an Internet context, s 1(1) of the CDPA 1988, as subsequently amended, allows copyright to subsist as a property right in:

---

5   Full text of the Directive is at http://cryptome.org/eu-copyright.htm, and of the regulations at www.opsi.gov.uk/si/si2003/20032498.htm.
6   See ss 29 *et seq*, as amended by the 2003 regulations.

(a) original literary, dramatic, musical or artistic works,

(b) sound recordings, films or broadcasts and

(c) the typographical arrangement of published editions.

Most web material will come within s 1(1)(a), given that, as we will see, the requirement for originality is not stringent, or possibly s 1(1)(b) for multi-media material. Databases are also included within the category of literary, dramatic and musical works.[7]

4.2.2   Extent of the property right

All property creates a monopoly, in the sense that the owner has exclusive rights over the property in question. Where the property right protects ideas, albeit only indirectly, monopoly rights might be seen as undesirable, since societies evolve by developing the ideas of their forebears. No doubt, copyright is justified by the wrongness of allowing one person to take over and reap rewards from the intellectual activity or the marketing of another, but:[8]

> 'Reaping without sowing' declare those with a strong sense of injustice. 'But the sower's seed came from the crops of others before her', answer those who would preserve a sense of moral proportion in the matter.

It may be that this argument is overstated, given that it is only particular manifestations of ideas that are protected, rather than the ideas themselves. Nonetheless, the view appears to have taken hold that monopoly rights should be protected only as far as they can be justified and, in particular, that creative people are unlikely to be motivated by the existence of copyright into the very distant future. Copyright is time-limited, therefore, though the duration of the protection is considerable, especially in the context of ephemeral media, such as the Internet.

In the case of s 1(1)(a), copyright usually 'expires at the end of the period of 70 years from the end of the calendar year in which the author dies'.[9] For sound recordings, copyright usually expires:

(a) at the end of the period of 50 years from the end of the calendar year in which the recording is made, or

(b) if during that period the recording is published, 50 years from the end of the calendar year in which it is first published, or

(c) if during that period the recording is not published but is made available to the public by being played in public or communicated to the public, 50 years from the end of the calendar year in which it is first so made available.[10]

---

7   See further section 4.2.4 on protection of databases.
8   Cornish and Llewelyn, *Intellectual Property, op cit* fn 3, paras 1–38.
9   CDPA 1988, s 12(2), but there are minor qualifications in s 12(3). The period was harmonised in the EU around the German provision, which gave the longest protection.
10   CDPA 1988, s 13A(2), again with minor qualifications. There are currently proposals to extend the period.

4.2.3   How is the property right infringed?

Section 16(1)(a) of the 1988 Act gives the copyright owner the exclusive right to copy the work.[11] Section 16(2) defines infringement as follows:

> Copyright in a work is infringed by a person who without the licence of the copyright owner does, or authorises another to do, any of the acts restricted by the copyright.

It follows that if anyone else copies the work without the permission of the copyright holder that will involve a breach of copyright, unless it is a permitted use. As we will see, the law permits some copying, even without the permission of the copyright holder.[12] Alternatively, the copyright holder might himself or herself permit copies to be made.

It is reasonable to conclude from this rather short outline that almost all use of the WWW will infringe copyright, unless it is a permitted use, or unless the copyright holder consents to (or authorises) the use.

4.2.4   Protection of databases

Some commercial websites offer access to databases. For example, in my own field of the study and teaching of law, my university has purchased the right to access LexisNexis and Westlaw, which would, for example, allow me to view cases, statutes and perhaps articles matching my search criteria. There is no doubt that I can do this lawfully, but I am restricted in what else I can do with any information extracted.

Copyright in databases exists by virtue of s 3(1)(d) of the CDPA 1988. Databases are defined under s 3A:[13]

(1) In this Part 'database' means a collection of independent works, data or other materials which—

(a) are arranged in a systematic or methodical way, and

(b) are individually accessible by electronic or other means.

(2) For the purposes of this Part a literary work consisting of a database is original if, and only if, by reason of the selection or arrangement of the contents of the database the database constitutes the author's own intellectual creation.

---

11   The full list of exclusive rights under the unamended Act were to:
(a) copy the work;
(b) issue copies of the work to the public;
(c) rent or lend the work to the public;
(d) perform, show or play the work in public;
(e) broadcast the work or include it in a cable broadcast;
(f)   make an adaptation of the work or do any of the above in relation to an adaptation.
However, (a) is the most important for present purposes. Minor additions were made by the 2003 legislation, considered below.

12   Eg, fair use provisions, and temporary copies necessary for transmission of material over the Internet. The former do not present problems which are peculiar to e-commerce and are therefore not considered in detail. On the latter, see below, section 4.3.1.

13   Added by reg 6 of the Copyright and Rights in Databases Regulations 1997 SI 1997/3032, at www.opsi.gov.uk/si/si1997/1973032.htm. This Part in s 3A(2) refers only to the copyright section; s 3A(2) does not apply at all to the *sui generis* right, below, where there is no originality requirement.

Apart from making unauthorised copies, making an unauthorised adaptation of a database will also infringe copyright, an adaptation being defined in s 21 of the 1988 Act as 'an arrangement or altered version of the database or a translation of it'. Thus, I would infringe copyright, for example, if I were to compile material obtained from a database into another database, whether or not the second database was a copy of the first.

Copyright only exists, however, if 'the selection or arrangement of the contents of the database constitutes the author's own intellectual creation'. This may not seem to be a particularly appropriate limitation in a database context, and there is doubt over the position of databases compiled automatically by a computer.[14] However, implementing Council Directive (96/9/EC) on the legal protection of databases, the Copyright and Rights in Databases Regulations 1997 also provide for a *sui generis* database right, with a 15-year life,[15] for a database in respect of which 'there has been a substantial investment in obtaining, verifying or presenting the contents of the database'.[16] The *sui generis* right is therefore intended to protect investment as such, regardless of any element of creativity. Investment in creating the actual data, however, is irrelevant; it is the collection, rather than the data itself, which is protected.[17] Infringement is by extraction or re-utilisation of 'all or a substantial part of the contents of the database'.[18] Copyright and the *sui generis* right can co-exist.[19]

This is not a book on intellectual property, and a full discussion is beyond its scope. By virtue of reg 9, adding a new s 50D to the 1988 Act:

> It is not an infringement of copyright in a database for a person who has a right to use the database or any part of the database, (whether under a licence to do any of the acts restricted by the copyright in the database or otherwise) to do, in the exercise of that right, anything which is necessary for the purposes of access to and use of the contents of the database or of that part of the database.

To access the database is lawful, but creating an adaptation will infringe copyright, if the database qualifies for copyright protection, and extraction or re-utilisation (as long as sufficiently substantial) will infringe the *sui generis* right, as long as 'there has been a substantial investment in obtaining, verifying or presenting the contents of the database'.

---

14 Discussion of this issue is beyond the scope of this book, but see, eg, Cornish and Llewelyn, *Intellectual Property, op cit* fn 3, Chapter 19; Bainbridge, DI, *Intellectual Property*, 5th edn, 2002, Harlow: Longman, p 214 *et seq.*

15 Renewed, however, with any substantial change: reg 17(3). This could potentially create a perpetual monopoly, therefore, in what is essentially information.

16 Reg 13. A database, by reg 12, 'has the meaning given by section 3A(1) of the 1988 Act (as inserted by Regulation 6)', but s 3A(2) applies only to the copyright part of the regulations. There is therefore no requirement for the selection or arrangement of the contents of the database to constitute the author's own intellectual creation, for the *sui generis* right.

17 See *William Hill Organisation Ltd v British Horseracing Board* [2005] ECDR 1, paras 36 *et seq.*

18 Reg 16.

19 The ECJ has interpreted the investment aspect of the *sui generis* right quite restrictively in *William Hill Organisation Ltd v British Horseracing Board* [2005] ECDR 1, also at www.curia.eu.int/jurisp/cgibin/gettext.pl?lang=en&num=79958890C19020203&doc=T&ouv ert=T&seance=ARRET&where (the information on this site is subject to a disclaimer and a copyright notice). The dispute revolved around William Hill's use on its website, for its Internet betting service, of lists of runners which (though the information could be obtained elsewhere) had in fact come (albeit indirectly, through a third party) from BHB's database.

So far, I have assumed a database, such as Westlaw or Lexis, existing behind the scenes and accessed by a program. But the definition of a database in s 3A(1) is sufficiently wide to cover almost any searchable collection of materials, and it may be that many websites, or parts of websites, can themselves qualify as databases,[20] and therefore also adaptations of a database. To place information in a website, so organised, could also amount to re-utilisation.[21] Thus, to include information, derived from a database, in a website, could be to infringe the *sui generis* right, even if the database does not qualify for copyright protection.

There are also, of course, databases underlying the Web and e-commerce which are not normally accessible, for example customer addresses and details, which are often created automatically by traders in the process of trading with customers. Obviously, the same protection applies to them. Access itself will also be unlawful, however, and would not normally be possible in the absence of some form of hacking. The databases will usually be protected by technology, for example restricting access by password. Any hacking into these databases will also therefore attract the provisions considered in section 4.5.1. The same is also true, of course, of databases such as Westlaw or LexisNexis where the access is by someone unauthorised, who has avoided the technological password protection.

4.3   PRIMARY LIABILITY FOR BREACH OF COPYRIGHT

If, as we saw at the conclusion of section 4.2.3, most web usage involves a *prima facie* breach of copyright unless it is authorised by the copyright holder, the main issues usually revolve around what the copyright owner has authorised.[22] Authorisation may be express or implied, and many of the disputes will revolve around what is authorised use.

It is not uncommon for commercial sites expressly to state the terms upon which pages are accessed. For example, when I sign into Westlaw, I have explicitly to agree to a page of terms and conditions before I can search the databases, and my employer university will also have a contract with Sweet & Maxwell, the publishers of Westlaw. At this level, therefore, contract, rather than intellectual property law, will determine the extent of allowable use of the material.

Most web pages are accessible directly, however, there being no attempt to subject the user to express terms. It is also possible for a link to avoid terms and conditions pages. In those cases, the issue is what is impliedly authorised.

---

20 See, eg, Edwards, L and Waelde, C (eds), *Law and the Internet*, 2nd edn, 2000, Oxford: Hart, p 191.

21 This was certainly the view of the ECJ in *William Hill Organisation Ltd v British Horseracing Board* [2005] ECDR 1, para 65, in respect of William Hill's publicising everything on the Internet. The re-utilisation has to be of 'all or a substantial part of the contents of the database', of course. The ECJ held that this 'must be assessed in relation to the total volume of the contents of the database' (para 82). It is a test of proportion, not importance to the organisation of the owner of the database. William Hill had re-utilised only a very small proportion, and thus did not fall foul of the Directive.

22 As we will see below, the making of a temporary copy in the user's RAM does not amount to a copyright infringement, but only if the copying is otherwise 'lawful', implying that it has been consented to by the copyright holder.

4.3.1   Copying necessary for the efficient functioning of the WWW

It is surely reasonable to suppose that someone who puts material on the WWW, without protecting access to it by a password or other form of protection (and subject to what is said below about framing and deep linking), is consenting at least to the copying necessary for web users to access it. After all, the whole essence of the Web is that pages can be accessed from any computer connected to it. If this is correct, copying of packets by routers, and of the page into the user's RAM, must surely be authorised, since this copying is essential to the very running of the Web. It also seems reasonable to suppose authorisation of copying which, while not strictly necessary to the functioning of the Web, does no more than facilitate its operation, for example caching and mirroring.

To some extent, this position is now, in any case, provided for by statute. Thus, s 8 of the 2003 regulations provides (adding the following new s 28A to the 1988 Act) that:[23]

> Copyright in a literary work, other than a computer program or a database, or in a dramatic, musical or artistic work, the typographical arrangement of a published edition, a sound recording or a film, is not infringed by the making of a temporary copy which is transient or incidental, which is an integral and essential part of a technological process and the sole purpose of which is to enable
>
> (a)   a transmission of the work in a network between third parties by an intermediary; or
>
> (b)   a lawful use of the work;
>
> and which has no independent economic significance.

This section is clearly appropriate to cover the copying of packets by routers, which are temporary, an integral and essential part of the process and transmitted in a network between third parties by an intermediary.

It is also reasonably clear that the section covers caches, whether on the user's computer or elsewhere; caches are normally relatively temporary, of course. The section implements the EU Copyright Directive, of which para 33 of the explanatory notes assumes that caches would be covered:

> (33) The exclusive right of reproduction should be subject to an exception to allow certain acts of temporary reproduction, which are transient or incidental reproductions, forming an integral and essential part of a technological process and carried out for the sole purpose of enabling either efficient transmission in a network between third parties by an intermediary, or a lawful use of a work or other subject-matter to be made. The acts of reproduction concerned should have no separate economic value on their own. To the extent that they meet these conditions, this exception should include acts which enable browsing as well as acts of caching to take place, including those which enable transmission systems to function efficiently provided that the intermediary does not modify the information and does not interfere with the lawful use of technology, widely recognised and used by industry, to obtain data on the use of the information. A use should be considered lawful where it is authorised by the rightholder or not restricted by law.

---

23 Implementing Art 5(1) of the EC Council Directive (2001/29/EC) on the harmonisation of certain aspects of copyright and related rights in the information society.

Copying pages into the user's RAM can also satisfy the general requirements of s 28A, though whether it does so in fact will depend on the licensing reasoning considered below. Although it does not involve transmission between third parties by an intermediary, it can be a lawful use of the work, but only if it is considered to be authorised by the rightholder (see the last sentence of the explanatory notes set out above). It is difficult to see, therefore, that s 28A(b) provides any additional protection to that already granted by the law.

There is additional protection for 'mere conduits' and caches given by the E-commerce Directive considered in Chapter 12, but neither this section nor the E-commerce Directive appears appropriate to cover mirror sites, unless the material is mirrored on a temporary basis only.

Section 28A does not cover databases, but we have seen that provision has been made elsewhere for lawful access to databases.[24]

4.3.2 Other copying

It seems reasonable to suppose that anyone who places a page on the WWW authorises others to access it, and hence the copying required for that to be done. It also seems reasonable to assume authorisation of copying the purpose of which is to increase the efficiency of the Web.

Beyond that, however, the position is far less clear. It is less obvious that a web author authorises users to download the file on to the hard disk, as opposed temporarily to caching it. Still less obvious is an implication authorising copying on to another website, or copying parts of the page (for example, so as to pass off parts of the text as someone else's, or copying the photographs but not their context), or altering the page in any way. A freedom to view a page does not imply a freedom to do whatever you like with the page that is viewed.

Ultimately, the test for authorisation must be what the web author intended. In the absence, however, of a clearly expressed intention, such as might be found, for example, on the front page of a commercial password-protected site, inferences must be drawn. The test cannot therefore be what the author actually intended, because this is unknown and uncommunicated, but what a reasonable user would have thought authorised. This has similarities with the test for implying terms into contracts. Moreover, access to web pages is free, and some guidance might therefore be obtained from provision of other free services, such as (for example), in a slightly different context, licences to use shareware or freeware.

The terms upon which shareware was licensed were considered by the Federal Court of Australia in *Trumpet Software Pty Ltd v OzEmail Pty Ltd*.[25] Trumpet had produced a Winsock program, which at the time was one of the best methods of establishing connection with the Internet,[26] from a personal computer over a modem.

---

24 Section 4.2.4.
25 [1996] 34 IPR 481. Full text can be found at www.austlii.edu.au/au/cases/cth/federal_ct/1996/560.html.
26 The program was originally released in 1994.

The program was released as shareware, which is to say that it was freely available to anyone for evaluation prior to purchase. OzEmail, an Internet Service Provider (ISP), downloaded a copy of the software from a website, and caused some 60,000 copies to be distributed (on a disk) with an issue of Australian Personal Computer magazine. Though there had been correspondence with Trumpet, negotiations faltered and, ultimately, the distribution was without Trumpet's authority.[27] Moreover, various alterations were made to some of the files on the disk, effectively to remove Trumpet's copyright and disclaimer information, and to connect the user to OzEmail as an ISP, to the exclusion of any other ISP.[28] In spite of Trumpet's position by now being absolutely clear to OzEmail, OzEmail distributed further copies, similarly altered, in another magazine, Australian PC World.

OzEmail's main argument was that the shareware was freely distributed and that they had not broken the express conditions that the programs were not to be resold or distributed for sale with other programs which were for sale. Heerey J held that any licence that may have been granted was revoked by Trumpet's express objection to their distribution of a non-timelocked version of the software.[29] But he was also prepared to imply terms into any licence, in addition to the express conditions. Although no consideration moved from OzEmail, he adopted the same test for implication of terms as is used routinely in contracts:[30]

In particular two criteria are apposite, namely (i) whether the supposed condition is necessary to give business efficacy, in the light of the fundamental purpose of shareware, which is that of evaluation, and (ii) whether it is so obvious that it 'goes without saying'.

He continued:

Applying those criteria, I think it is essential that, in the case of a distributor dealing with shareware, it be distributed in its entirety and without modification, addition or deletion.

Heerey J also felt that OzEmail's use of the shareware was not for the purpose of shareware, that is to say evaluation by the potential user, but that its aim was to use the software as a give-away in the hope of encouraging subscribers to its ISP service.

Heerey J would also have been prepared to consider custom (trade usage being receivable as evidence of fact as to how custom is followed in a particular trade), were there sufficient evidence of a customary usage. He observed, however, that the evidence fell well short of that required to establish custom in the legal sense.

It would probably be a mistake to read too much into this case. Australian cases are at best persuasive in the UK and, in any case, most web pages are more akin to

---

27 One of the reasons for this was that Trumpet wanted to wait until a timelocked version of their software was available.

28 Trumpet was distributed in zipped (compressed) form, various installation files being packaged along with the program. It was the installation files that had been altered by OzEmail.

29 He had also to conclude that the program was protected by copyright. He held it to be a literary work and, as we have seen, this will be true of much material on the Web. It is less clear for programs, however. Detailed discussion is beyond the scope of this book, but see, eg, Cornish and Llewelyn, *Intellectual Property, op cit* fn 3, Chapter 19.

30 The criteria were adopted from *BP Refinery (Westernport) Pty Ltd v Shire of Hastings* (1977) 180 CLR 266, p 283 (a contractual licence case), full text of which can be found at www.austlii.edu.au/au/cases/cth/high_ct/180clr266.html.

freeware than shareware, in that they can usually be viewed freely and without condition. However, the reasoning is, I suggest, convincing and, if correct, suggests at least that:

(a) the mere fact that web pages are freely accessible does not mean that no conditions are attached to their use;

(b) whether or not there are express terms, terms will be implied on the same basis as for contractual licences;

(c) customary use may be relevant if a custom can be proved; and

(d) even though permission may be given to view the unaltered page, it does not follow that alterations to it are permissible.

The contractual test seems appropriate in that the test must be that of the author's intention, but objectively ascertained, which is similar to the test of what parties to contracts intend. It is only the intention of the author, and not that of the user, which is relevant, however, whereas the intention of both parties is relevant to the incorporation of contractual terms.

In the context of a web page, it may be that customary usages will develop, but it seems probable that they have not done so yet. Heerey J adopted the view of Jessel MR in *Nelson v Dahl*, who said that the existence of a trade custom was:[31]

> a question of fact, and, like all other customs, it must be strictly proved. It must be so notorious that everybody in the trade enters into a contract with that usage as an implied term. It must be uniform as well as reasonable, and it must have quite as much certainty as the written contract itself.

Though he was referring to a trade custom, it is clear that strict proof would apply to any custom involving web usage, whether in a particular trade or otherwise.

In the absence of a custom, it is by no means clear that any usage would be considered authorised, outside those already discussed. However, as all browsers have a download function, it seems that downloading a page to a hard disk would be permitted unless expressly prohibited. However, it is far less clear that any licence would extend to sending copies to others, or mounting the page on another website, and it seems likely that any licence would relate only to the page unaltered. Thus, for example, the mounting of pictures in a different page would probably not be permitted. By the same token, nor would the incorporation of pictures or text from another page into one's own page (framing), though in this case the copying would be done not by the web author but by the user. This raises problems considered in the next section.

4.4   INCORPORATION OF MATERIAL FROM ELSEWHERE, DEEP LINKING AND SECONDARY LIABILITY

4.4.1   Relevance of secondary liability

If I incorporate into a book somebody else's picture or text, I must necessarily copy that picture or text, and this could, in principle, amount to a primary breach of copyright. But I can create a web page incorporating someone else's pictures or text

---

31 (1979) 12 Ch D 568, p 575.

without copying anything at all. For example, on my university's home page there is (at time of writing) a picture of the graduation in 2004. I could incorporate this picture into a page of my own by copying it to my server and using the line:[32]

```
<p><img border="0" src="grad2095.jpg" width="100" height="133"></p>
```

If I did not have the permission of the university, that would amount to a breach of copyright, just as surely as copying a printed version of the picture into a book. But I do not have to do that. The following code will do just as well:[33]

```
<p><img border="0" src="http://www2.swan.ac.uk/resources/news/grad2095.jpg"
width="100" height="133"></p>
```

The difference is that in the second case I have not copied the picture at all. However, anybody accessing my page will see the picture, apparently incorporated. Indeed, it will look identical in all respects to the first version.[34]

I can do the same with text, or indeed entire web pages. The simplest way to do this is using frames, and the technique is often described as framing.[35] The 'borrowed' material will appear to be incorporated into my own page, and I can surround it with my own logos and advertising, if I wish. But again, I have copied nothing. As with the picture, the copying will be done by the user and the web author's liability, if any, will be secondary only.

An area that raises similar issues is deep linking, in other words linking to the inside page rather than the home page of a site. In this case again, any copying will be done by the user, and not by the author of the linking page. Again, therefore, the web author's liability, if any, will normally be secondary only.

Information sharing, or peer-to-peer systems,[36] also gives rise to issues of secondary liability. These systems encourage users to share information (or more accurately, copy it from one user to another), usually in the form of music files, and they took off when compression techniques, such as MP3, made it feasible to store large quantities of high quality music on home computer hard disks. One of the early sites was Napster, of which it was said in litigation in California:[37]

> Napster facilitates the transmission of MP3 files between and among its users. Through a process commonly called 'peer-to-peer' file sharing, Napster allows its users to: (1) make MP3 music files stored on individual computer hard drives available for copying by other Napster users; (2) search for MP3 music files stored on other users' computers; and (3) transfer exact copies of the contents of other users' MP3 files from one computer to another via the Internet. These functions are made possible by Napster's MusicShare software, available free of charge from Napster's Internet site, and Napster's network

---

32 For an excellent description of hypertext markup language, and all other aspects of the WWW, see www.w3schools.com. (This is an official W3C Consortium site.)

33 The location of the .jpg image file in Swansea's website (in the resources/news directory) can easily be determined by examining the source code for the home page.

34 I have copied nothing, but, of course, the web user will copy that picture, at least into the RAM of his or her computer.

35 See www.w3schools.com/html/html_frames.asp. Also Cornish and Llewelyn, *Intellectual Property, op cit* fn 3, paras 19–67.

36 Eg, Cornish and Llewelyn, *Intellectual Property, op cit* fn 3, paras 19–67.

37 *A & M Records Inc v Napster Inc* 239 F Supp 3d 1004 (9 Circ, 2001), para 5. The following paragraphs describe in greater detail how the system worked. These were interim proceedings, not the full trial. Full text can be found at www.law.cornell.edu/copyright/cases/239_F3d_1004.htm.

servers and server-side software. Napster provides technical support for the indexing and searching of MP3 files, as well as for its other functions, including a 'chat room,' where users can meet to discuss music, and a directory where participating artists can provide information about their music.

Napster no longer engages in these practices, but there are other organisations which do.[38] Of course, the copying of music files will normally involve a breach of copyright[39] but, as can be seen from the above description, Napster itself copied nothing. The liability, if any, of the organisers of the system, will therefore also be secondary only.[40]

Clearly, therefore, the basis of secondary liability needs to be considered.

4.4.2   Secondary liability in general

Section 16(2) of the 1988 Act provides that:

> Copyright in a work is infringed by a person who without the licence of the copyright owner does, or authorises another to do, any of the acts restricted by the copyright.

It is not necessary to copy the material oneself, therefore: it is sufficient to authorise another to do so. Note, however, that the word is 'authorise', not 'facilitate'. It is not enough simply to provide the means for another to copy.

The leading case on authorising is *CBS Songs Ltd v Amstrad Computer Electronics plc*,[41] where the claim did not succeed. The appeal, which was clearly intended to be a test case, was described by Lord Templeman as 'the climax of a conflict between the makers of records and the makers of recording equipment',[42] and was brought by a representative of the one against a representative of the other.

Amstrad produced a tape recorder with twin tape decks and a high-speed dubbing facility. They also advertised that their product:[43]

> now features 'hi-speed dubbing' enabling you to make duplicate recordings from one cassette to another, record direct from any source and then make a copy and you can even make a copy of your favourite cassette.

Clearly, such copying by the consumer would often involve an infringement of copyright, but a footnote warned:[44]

---

38 See, eg, on Gnutella, www.firstmonday.dk/issues/issue5_10/adar/, www.rixsoft.com/ Knowbuddy/gnutellafaq.html#resgnutela or http://capnbry.net/gnutella/protocol.php. Gnutella is less centralised than the original Napster, and for that reason may be less likely to commit a secondary breach. See further section 4.4.5.

39 In the *Napster* case itself, a fair use argument on the primary infringement issue was unsuccessfully advanced.

40 Napster was held to be liable, but the provisions on secondary liability were (of course) different from those in the UK. It is not clear whether, under US law, more decentralised systems would also attract liability; we must await the outcome of the ongoing Grokster litigation.

41 [1988] AC 1013, and see Bainbridge, *Intellectual Property, op cit* fn 14, p 240. The case was decided under the 1956 legislation, but s 1(2) of the 1956 Act is in the same terms as s 16(2) of the present legislation.
There is a similar US case, with a similar conclusion: *Sony Corp v Universal City Studios, Inc*, 464 US 417 (1984), concerning the manufacture and retail of video tape recorders.

42 [1988] AC 1013, p 1046.

43 *Ibid*, p 1050.

44 *Ibid*, p 1051.

The recording and playback of certain material may only be possible by permission. Please refer to the Copyright Act 1956, the Performers' Protection Acts 1958–1972.

The House of Lords held that Amstrad had not authorised a breach of copyright, though obviously the production and sale of this type of tape recorder facilitated it. Lord Templeman adopted the following definition of 'authorise' from the judgment of Atkin LJ in *Falcon v Famous Players Film Co*:[45]

to 'authorise' means to grant or purport to grant to a third person the right to do the act complained of, whether the intention is that the grantee shall do the act on his own account, or only on account of the grantor ...

In the same case, Bankes LJ had accepted that 'authorise' meant 'sanction, approve, and countenance',[46] and Lord Templeman observed that 'Amstrad did not sanction, approve or countenance an infringing use of their model'.[47] Amstrad did not ask anyone to use one of their models in a way that would amount to an infringement,[48] nor did they have any control over the copying process, or indeed over the use of their machines once sold.[49] The advertisement probably would have amounted to authorising, but for the copyright warning. In the end, it was held to draw attention but not to authorise.

The House therefore adopted quite a narrow definition of authorisation, which clearly requires far more than mere facilitation. The effect of the case appears at first sight significantly to reduce the scope of secondary liability. However, it was clearly a factor in *CBS v Amstrad* that the tape deck could be used for lawful copying, that an alternative lawful use could therefore be made of the equipment, so that the decision whether to copy unlawfully rested entirely with the user.[50] The House also emphasised Amstrad's lack of control over the equipment once sold, distinguishing *Moorhouse v University of New South Wales*,[51] a decision of the High Court of Australia, where a university had been held liable for secondary infringement for providing photocopying facilities in its library. Unlike Amstrad, the university had control over the photocopying machine at all times.

The issue is how the principles enunciated by the House of Lords in *Amstrad* apply to web usage.

4.4.3   Deep linking

Secondary liability only arises where there is a primary breach, and it may be wondered why deep linking, as such, should give rise to any breach of copyright at all. As we noted in Chapter 1, a distinguishing feature of the Web is that it is non-hierarchical, and that any page can be linked to any other page. There is no need to go

---

45   [1926] 2 KB 474, p 499.
46   *Ibid*, p 474.
47   [1988] AC 1013, p 1054.
48   *Ibid*, p 1056.
49   *Ibid*, p 1054.
50   *Ibid*, pp 1052–53.
51   [1976] RPC 151.

down from a top-level (or home) page.[52] Search engines do not discriminate, and are as likely to link to an inside page as to a home page. On the face of it, it seems odd, therefore, that anyone who posts a page on this medium can object to this essential feature of the medium. Moreover, many web authors positively encourage deep linking, and this can include commercial sites. The BBC, for example, has separate pages for its programmes, such as *Top Gear* or *Click Online*, and is quite happy for those pages to be bookmarked.[53] It does not insist that its home page is accessed first.

Nonetheless, there is a range of reasons why some commercial sites prefer to direct visitors through their home page. The home page may contain advertisements or logos, or the terms and conditions upon which the site may be accessed, or possibly password protection or a registration requirement. The owners of these sites naturally object to any means of circumventing the home page by accessing inside pages directly.

The first UK case involving deep linking was *Shetland Times Ltd v Wills*.[54] It is a well known case, much written about, but, for various reasons, too much should not be read into it. It is actually a case of primary, rather than secondary liability, but on facts which are probably atypical. The case was settled before full trial, and the law has been changed since the decision. Moreover, the facts occurred in the mid-1990s. Technology has changed since then, and it is possible today, using technology alone, to protect websites from unwanted secondary linking. Thus, the type of dispute that is likely to arise is different from that which arose in that era.

The essence of the complaint was that *Shetland News*, which was owned by a company of which Dr Jonathan Wills was the managing director, had linked to *Shetland Times* stories from its own site, in such a way as to make them appear as *Shetland News* stories. *Shetland Times* objected to this, partly because it hoped to sell advertising space on the home page on its web site, which readers would by-pass if they accessed the stories via *Shetland News*. Thus, *Shetland Times* was worried about diminution in its advertising revenue.

Shetland Times was able to get an interim interdict against the *Shetland News* on two grounds, the principal one of which depended on both websites being considered a cable programme, the infringement being inclusion of one cable programme within another.[55] This argument, which did not receive universal acclamation,[56] is now of historical interest only, in the light of the 2003 amendments. Cable programmes were provided for in the 1988 Act, at a time before modern e-commerce and, in particular, the WWW were even conceived, and it is at least clear, therefore, that the concept was never intended to apply to the Web. Regulation 4 of the 2003 amendments, amending

---

52 Gophers, by contrast, were arranged hierarchically, although even there it was possible to link to lower-level pages directly.

53 Indeed, *Top Gear* has its own 'home page' at www.bbc.co.uk/topgear. *Click Online*'s is at http://news.bbc.co.uk/1/hi/programmes/click_online/default.stm.

54 [1997] FSR 604; [1997] EMLR 277 (Scottish Court of Sessions). Full text can be found in Westlaw, and also www.linksandlaw.com/decisions-87.htm. See also Edwards and Waelde, *Law and the Internet, op cit* fn 20, p 185.

55 A cable programme was defined in s 7(1) of the Act, and infringement under s 20. Section 7 has since been repealed (by para 5 of the 2003 regulations).

56 Though it was accepted as being correct in *Sony v Easyinternetcafé* [2003] ECDR 297, p 305 (para 47). The issue did not arise directly, however. (The case is discussed in section 4.4.5.)

s 6 of the 1988 Act, replaced 'cable programme' with 'broadcast', which is defined in s 6(1A) in such a way as clearly to exclude websites of this type:[57]

(1A) Excepted from the definition of 'broadcast' is any internet transmission unless it is—

(a) a transmission taking place simultaneously on the internet and by other means,

(b) a concurrent transmission of a live event, or

(c) a transmission of recorded moving images or sounds forming part of a programme service offered by the person responsible for making the transmission, being a service in which programmes are transmitted at scheduled times determined by that person.

The notion of broadcast is, in any case, not really apposite to describe the WWW, where the user requests the information on an individual basis. It seems correct in principle not to treat the Internet as analogous to broadcasting.[58]

Though the main argument in the *Shetland* case is therefore of historical interest only, the second argument would still apply today, at any rate on identical facts. Though *Shetland News* merely linked to, and did not copy, *Shetland Times'* stories, it copied the headlines and reproduced them on its own site. This was held sufficient for a breach of copyright action. However, the case depended on this; had *Shetland News* used its own headlines, the copyright infringement would have failed (unless the URLs themselves could attract copyright protection), since it had copied none of *Shetland Times'* text. The case also depended on the headlines being regarded as original literary works, and this may well depend on the headline; Lord Hamilton said:[59]

I was not referred to any authority on this aspect. While literary merit is not a necessary element of a literary work, there may be a question whether headlines, which are essentially brief indicators of the subject matter of the items to which they relate, are protected by copyright. However, in light of the concession that a headline could be a literary work and since the headlines at issue (or at least some of them) involve eight or so words designedly put together for the purpose of imparting information, it appeared to me to be arguable that there was an infringement, at least in some instances, of section 17.

This is a case into which too much should not be read. It went only to the interlocutory injunction stage, not full trial, so the claimant had only to make a *prima facie* case. It does not necessarily follow that the decision would have been the same at a full trial.[60] It does, however, illustrate the difficulties in the way of holding that deep linking can amount to a primary breach of copyright. Here, there was a primary breach, but only because the headlines were copied, some at least of which, in the light of their length, could be regarded as literary works. Actually, the primary breach depended only on

---

57 The main purpose of the 2003 regulations was to implement the EC Copyright Directive, considered below (section 4.5). This, however, is purely a UK provision, the 'cable programme' having been a creature specifically of UK legislation.

58 See, however, the description of legislation in Singapore, in section 12.2.3, where (in a different context) a broadcasting model is adopted.

59 One of the headlines was 'Bid to save centre after council finding "cock up"'. Wills conceded that a headline could attract copyright, but argued that these did not, since they were not original literary works within the meaning of the Act.

60 The case was settled at the doors of the court – see Edwards and Waelde, *Law and the Internet, op cit* fn 20, p 185.

the copying of the headlines, and not on the deep linking at all (there would have been liability, even in the absence of any linking). Secondary liability was not argued at all.[61]

If the precise facts of *Shetland* occurred today, the decision would be the same, but suppose the headlines were not copied. Then liability, if any, would be secondary only. On the face of it, *Amstrad* would probably not protect the deep linker, since no alternative is offered but for the user to follow the link, and the link remains within the linker's control throughout.

A related issue is that search engines often access inside pages, and so a similar question could arise, whether there is a secondary breach of copyright. It would be an interesting question, though, whether what is effectively an automatic indexing system, operating without human intervention, could reasonably be said to authorise anything.

However, a secondary breach will arise only if the user, by copying the page into the RAM, commits a primary breach. Technology has moved on since *Shetland*, and there is no reason for disputes of this type to arise at all today. Most newspapers do not nowadays provide the text on accessible .html files, but generate them on each request using a common gateway interface (CGI) program, or an .asp script file.[62] Source code for a CGI or active server pages (ASP) program can be kept secret, because it can be made executable only, without read access either to it or to the directory structure of the site. Of .asp files, the W3C Consortium say that:[63]

> Because ASP scripts are executed on the server, you cannot view ASP code in a browser, you will only see the output from ASP which is plain HTML.

It is possible to hide from the command line any values sent to the program, so that all a user sees is the name of (for example) the .asp file. However, since the user cannot see the code, he or she does not have the information necessary to generate the .html page, except by using the link from the site's home page. Perhaps a hacker could get around the security, but, as we will see below, the law now has ample means of dealing with this problem. Of course, the eventual output will be in .html format, which could be copied and placed on another website. It would actually require copying, though, unlike *Shetland Times* itself, and would involve a clear breach of copyright (it would surely be impossible to argue that this was authorised, given the steps that had been taken to prevent it).

The *Shetland Times'* successor uses frames and .asp files,[64] and would no longer be vulnerable to the type of attack complained of in the case. Interestingly, *Shetland News* continues to use .htm files which are readily accessible (so that deep linking remains possible). Nonetheless, the point is that if a website owner wants to hide inside pages except through the home page, it is now possible to do so, as indeed *Shetland Times* have now done.

---

61 For summary and full text of a similar type of case in the USA, *Washington Post v TotalNews*, see http://legal.web.aol.com/decisions/dlip/wash.html.

62 *Times Law Reports* used to be directly accessible without registering on *The Times* newspaper's home page, and I used to deep link to them from my own website, but it has been impossible to avoid the home page since 1997.

63 www.w3schools.com/asp/default.asp.

64 www.shetlandtoday.co.uk.

The same technique should also prevent an inside page being accessed by a search engine, but even if a page is stored in simple .html format, search engines can be kept away from inside pages, either using a robots.txt file, or a metatag as follows:[65]

<META NAME="ROBOTS" CONTENT="NOINDEX, NOFOLLOW">

In the light of all this, I would tentatively suggest the following. It is well known that the Web allows links to be made from any page to any other page and that search engines will index all pages, regardless of where they are in the structure of any particular site. Indeed, many sites positively encourage deep linking. The technology, however, now exists, and is routinely used, to prevent access to inside pages, except through a home page, perhaps bounded by a frame. It is also possible to prevent search engines from accessing inside pages. Surely it is reasonable, then, to infer that a site which does not use this technology authorises access to its inside pages. If so, deep linking will not cause any primary breach of copyright by the user, and issues of secondary breach only arise if this argument is wrong.

In short, the debate has moved on since *Shetland Times*. The topical issue now is protecting the technology that protects the inside pages rather than concentrating on the infringement (if any) itself. This change in emphasis is examined further below.

4.4.4   Framing

Framing raises different considerations, because the page is now being viewed in a way that is not necessarily covered by any licence. We have seen that there is no reason to suppose that, for example, placing pictures or text in a page on website A authorises viewing them in a wholly different context, apparently within a page on website B. Thus, even copying into the user's RAM will not be lawful, and there will be a primary infringement.[66] Moreover, since the unlawful use is forced on the user, without any choice on his or her part, the framer will not be able to avoid secondary liability on the basis of *Amstrad*.

4.4.5   Music distribution issues

For a consumer to download music files from the Internet will (subject to a fair use defence discussed below) usually involve a breach of copyright. The same will be true if, for example, a licence is granted to listen to the song or tune once,[67] and the user saves the streamed music to a hard disk or CD.

Peer-to-peer systems, such as that originally set up by Napster, and subsequently operated by (for example) Gnutella, involve the organisers in no copying at all, so that any liability would be secondary only. Exceptionally, however, commercial concerns

---

65 See, generally, www.robotstxt.org/wc/exclusion.html#robots.txt, and linked pages. Not all robots implement the metatag instruction.

66 As we have seen, the 2003 regulations prevent copying into the RAM from being a copyright infringement, but only where it is for a lawful purpose, which surely implies within the terms of the implied licence.

67 Eg, with Internet 'radio', such as Yahoo! Launchcast.

can be liable for a primary infringement. If a commercial concern makes the copies on behalf of the consumer then that concern will itself commit a breach of copyright. In *Sony v Easyinternetcafé*,[68] an Internet café, whose founder was also the founder of EasyJet, Stelios Haji-Ioannou, provided CD copying facilities, the copying being done not by the customer directly but by an employee of the café, for a fee. The café was successfully sued for breach of copyright by Sony and other members of the British Phonographic Industry Limited (BPI), presumably in a test case.[69]

Easyinternetcafé argued that no breach of copyright had been proved, since the customers' private directories could have consisted of material uploaded from a user's disk rather than downloaded from the Internet. This was, however, rejected on the evidence on the normal balance of probabilities. There was simply no evidence of uploading. In any case, uploading from a floppy disk would have been wholly unrealistic given the size of the files, and uploading from a CD produced by the customer would have been absurd from an economic viewpoint, given that the customer would necessarily have his or her own CD burning facilities. Easyinternetcafé also unsuccessfully argued a private and domestic use defence, under s 70 of the 1988 Act, the wording of which then allowed copying for the purpose of listening or viewing at a more convenient time (time-shifting):[70]

> The making for private and domestic use of a recording of a broadcast or cable programme solely for the purpose of enabling it to be viewed or listened to at a more convenient time does not infringe any copyright in the broadcast or cable programme or in any work included in it.

Although this defence might have been available to customers, it was not to the café.

Sony v Easyinternetcafé is another case into which too much should not be read, since it depended on the cafe making the copies itself. If the customers had done their own copying, then of course Sony would have had to establish a secondary liability. Probably they would have been able to distinguish *Amstrad*, since the café retained control over the copying process and equipment, but Sony would also have had to argue that the customers' copying amounted to a primary breach; unlike the café, however, the customers might well have been able to invoke the s 70 time-shifting defence. If there were no primary liability, there would have been no secondary liability either. Since the case, however, the s 70 defence has been restricted to copies made 'in domestic premises', which obviously removes this particular problem.[71]

There are also peer-to-peer sites, such as the operation run by Gnutella, which facilitate the copying of music from one user to another. Gnutella copies nothing itself, nor does it allow copies of any material to be made from its own server. What it does is to put users in touch with each other to facilitate copying between themselves. Its liability, if any, must also therefore be secondary. Provision of a facility for copying music would appear, at first sight, to be doing no more than Amstrad were doing. Peer-to-peer music sites could, in principle, be used for both lawful and unlawful copying and, depending on how they are set up, the copying may not remain under

---

68 [2003] ECDR 27, Chancery Division.
69 It was an action for summary judgment, before Peter Smith J.
70 Changes have been made to this defence by the 2003 regulations: see fn 71.
71 Copyright and Related Rights Regulations 2003, reg 19.

the control of the organisation. However, whereas Amstrad warned customers against copyright breach, the entire *raison d'être* of peer-to-peer systems is surely for unlawful copying. That would probably be sufficient to distinguish *Amstrad*, in which case there probably is secondary liability, assuming that the copying itself is in breach of copyright.

So could the users argue the time-shifting defence, in which case there would be no primary, and hence no secondary liability either? But any recipient who realised that copyright was not in the sender could surely not argue this. In any case, the 2003 amendments to s 70 would certainly prevent the defence being argued for the outgoing copy, subsequent dealings with time-shifted material being treated as infringements by virtue of s 70(2), which was added to the 1988 Act by the 2003 legislation.[72]

It follows that both primary and secondary infringements could probably be established in most peer-to-peer systems. This is one area, however, where enforcement of the law in practice might prove difficult, because of the nature of the Internet.

4.4.6   Transmitting

Secondary liability can also be imposed for transmitting. This might, in principle at least, affect ISPs,[73] but, in reality, it is unlikely to do so in normal situations.

Liability for transmitting is provided for under s 24(2) of the 1988 Act. The section, as amended in 2003, is as follows:

> (2) Copyright in a work is infringed by a person who without the licence of the copyright owner transmits the work by means of a telecommunications system (otherwise than by communication to the public), knowing or having reason to believe that infringing copies of the work will be made by means of the reception of the transmission in the United Kingdom or elsewhere.

Section 24(2) requires knowledge or reason to believe that infringing copies will be made, so ISPs will probably normally be safe.[74]

4.5   EC COPYRIGHT DIRECTIVE

Copyright protection has been increased, both generally and specifically in an e-commerce context, by the Directive (2001/29/EC) on the harmonisation of certain aspects of copyright and related rights in the information society, which was brought into force in the UK by the Copyright and Related Rights Regulations 2003.[75]

---

72 Assuming that an MP3 compression is regarded as a copy of a CD at all, but it was held to be in the *Napster* case itself, at para 24. In *Napster*, the outgoing copying could also not be said to be a fair use: para 45. Of course, the American position does not mirror ours precisely (there is, for example, also a space-shifting defence, which has no counterpart in the UK).

73 See, eg, Bainbridge, *Intellectual Property*, *op cit* fn 14, pp 238 *et seq*.

74 There was previously an exception for 'broadcasting or inclusion in a cable programme service', but this has been removed by the 2003 regulations.

75 Full text of the Directive is at http://cryptome.org/eu-copyright.htm, and of the regulations at www.opsi.gov.uk/si/si2003/20032498.htm.

The Directive (which is based on earlier work by the World Intellectual Property Organisation (WIPO)) attempts partial harmonisation of copyright laws throughout the EU. Though the harmonisation is imperfect, it is likely at least to curtail states from going entirely their own way in the future. Regulations 9–23 of the legislation bringing the Directive into force in the UK amend the scope of lawful, or fair, uses, and though they are no doubt of great importance to the general law of copyright, contain little that has particular relevance to e-commerce.

As for Internet-specific provisions, we have already seen the operation of Art 5(1), providing immunity for copying necessary for its efficient functioning. Article 3 of the Directive provides a right to communicate to the public, and Art 4 provides a distribution right.

The right to communicate to the public has been implemented into UK law by a new section 16(d) of the 1988 Act, a new s 20(2) providing that:[76]

(2)   References in this Part to communication to the public are to communication to the public by electronic transmission, and in relation to a work include—

      ...

      (b)   the making available to the public of the work by electronic transmission in such a way that members of the public may access it from a place and at a time individually chosen by them.

Article 4 has not, however, been implemented in UK law; the UK has never recognised a distribution right as such.

Whereas implementation of Arts 3 and 4 may make a difference in states with relatively weak copyright protection, it is unlikely that either significantly extends protection under UK law. Article 3 makes clear, for example, that placing information on to a server to which members of the public have access is an infringement. However, it probably adds little to the pre-existing law, since copying would necessarily be involved, which would necessarily involve an infringement anyway.[77] Article 4, if implemented, would probably cover peer-to-peer operations, which, as we have seen, involve no copying by the organisation, but most of these will in any case involve secondary infringements, and so are covered by UK law in any event.

Of far greater consequence are the new provisions on protection of technological measures (Art 6) and rights management (Art 7). These have been implemented in the UK by regs 24 and 25 of the 2003 amendments, amending s 296 of the 1988 Act.

4.5.1   Circumvention of technological measures

Technological measures protection is aimed at hackers who circumvent password protection, encryption or other methods of controlling access. It would also cover matters such as date restrictions on software, restrictions on the number on copies made and alterations to CDs to make them playable only on audio players. This is clear from the definition of 'technological measures' in the new section 296ZF:[78]

---

76   Substituted respectively by regs 6(2) and 6(1).
77   This is clear from the *Shetland* case described in section 4.4.3.
78   Added by the 2003 regulations to the 1988 Act, to implement Art 6(3) of the Directive.

(1) ... 'technological measures' are any technology, device or component which is designed, in the normal course of its operation, to protect a copyright work other than a computer program.

(2) Such measures are 'effective' if the use of the work is controlled by the copyright owner through—

(a) an access control or protection process such as encryption, scrambling or other transformation of the work, or

(b) a copy control mechanism,

which achieves the intended protection.

Clearly, this covers access and copy control mechanisms. It is relevant to the deep linking debate in that, if a provider takes technological steps to hide an inside page, circumvention of that security will attract these provisions.

The basic effect of the provisions, in s 296ZA, is to give the copyright owner the same rights against the person who circumvents those measures as if he or she had infringed the copyright itself. The section applies where:[79]

(a) effective technological measures have been applied to a copyright work other than a computer program; and

(b) a person ... does anything which circumvents those measures knowing, or with reasonable grounds to know, that he is pursuing that objective.

In other words, there is a *mens rea* requirement, but it is objective.

There are also criminal offences for manufacturers, sellers, distributors, etc, of:[80]

any device, product or component which is primarily designed, produced, or adapted for the purpose of enabling or facilitating the circumvention of effective technological measures.

The regulations also make it an offence to provide, promote, advertise or market, in the course of business, 'a service the purpose of which is to enable or facilitate the circumvention of effective technological measures'.[81]

It is sometimes argued that provisions such as this accord too much protection to the copyright industry. Traditionally, copyright protection has not extended to fair use, but a technological device can prevent any access to material, whether the use would otherwise be lawful or not. However, s 296ZF goes on to provide that:

(3) In this section, the reference to—

(a) protection of a work is to the prevention or restriction of acts that are not authorised by the copyright owner of that work and are restricted by copyright; and

(b) use of a work does not extend to any use of the work that is outside the scope of the acts restricted by copyright.

This is intended to implement Art 6(4) of the Directive, and remove protection from devices restricting even fair dealing in the copyright work. It is very difficult to see how this might work in practice though, except perhaps where agreement is reached

---

79   Section 296ZA(1), added to the 1988 Act by the 2003 Regulations.
80   Section 296ZB.
81   This is a paraphrase of s 296ZB(2).

between the parties (since how can the technology know to what use the user intends to put the information?).

4.5.2   Rights management

The motivation for rights management protection came originally from the music industry, in an attempt to trace the origin of copied music and hence determine whether the copies were legitimate or not. The industry uses digital watermarking holders to trace illegitimate copies and wanted protection against removal of the watermarking by hackers.[82]

Rights management protection is provided by s 25 of the 2003 regulations, adding a new s 296ZG to the 1988 Act. The section begins:[83]

(1) This section applies where a person (D), knowingly and without authority, removes or alters electronic rights management information which—

    (a) is associated with a copy of a copyright work, or

    (b) appears in connection with the communication to the public of a copyright work, and

where D knows, or has reason to believe, that by so doing he is inducing, enabling, facilitating or concealing an infringement of copyright.

(2) This section also applies where a person (E), knowingly and without authority, distributes, imports for distribution or communicates to the public copies of a copyright work from which electronic rights management information—

    (a) associated with the copies, or

    (b) appearing in connection with the communication to the public of the work,

has been removed or altered without authority and where E knows, or has reason to believe, that by so doing he is inducing, enabling, facilitating or concealing an infringement of copyright.

(3) A person issuing to the public copies of, or communicating, the work to the public, has the same rights against D and E as a copyright owner has in respect of an infringement of copyright.

(4) The copyright owner or his exclusive licensee, if he is not the person issuing to the public copies of, or communicating, the work to the public, also has the same rights against D and E as he has in respect of an infringement of copyright.

In other words, the hacker (identified as (D)) is treated in the same way as the copyright infringer himself or herself. Note again the objective *mens rea* requirement: 'where D knows, or has reason to believe, that by so doing he is inducing, enabling, facilitating or concealing an infringement of copyright.' This is similar to the *mens rea* requirement for circumvention of technological devices, considered above at section 4.5.1. Distributors of copies are also caught by the regulations, with a similar *mens rea* requirement (identified as (E)).

Though the provisions may originally have been aimed primarily at removal of digital watermarks, the definition of rights management is quite wide:[84]

---

82   Eg, Cornish and Llewelyn, *Intellectual Property, op cit* fn 3, paras 19–81.
83   Implementing Art 7 of the Directive.
84   Section 296ZG(7)(b), implementing Art 7(2).

'rights management information' means any information provided by the copyright owner or the holder of any right under copyright which identifies the work, the author, the copyright owner or the holder of any intellectual property rights, or information about the terms and conditions of use of the work, and any numbers or codes that represent such information.

This would seem to apply, in principle, to any attempt to hide authorship, and could therefore apply to incorporation of material from others' websites into one's own web page, whether by framing or otherwise. It might also apply to the type of deep linking that occurred in *Shetland Times*, where again the authorship of the articles was hidden.[85] Similarly, deep links which are intended to circumvent password pages, or pages of terms and conditions, clearly fall within the last part of this definition, although of course, these would also normally be caught by the circumvention of technological measures protection described above.

Rights management provisions would not cover all deep linking or framing, however. If, for example, authorship were acknowledged, and by-passing of the home page merely affected potential advertising revenues, then that would not appear to fall within the provisions.

---

85 Cornish and Llewelyn (*op cit* fns 3 and 82) do not make this link, but the definition seems wide enough in principle.

PART 3

ENCRYPTION

ENCRYPTION, ELECTRONIC AND DIGITAL SIGNATURES IN PRINCIPLE

5.1   WHY ENCRYPTION?

Parts of the Internet are not particularly secure. Satellite transmissions in particular can be intercepted, in principle by anyone. E-mail is stored on the servers of Internet Service Providers (ISPs) into which unauthorised persons might gain access, or there might even be cases where the ISP itself monitors content.[1] For e-commerce (or indeed personal) purposes, there can therefore be value in using encryption to hide content. Some information is sensitive, for example trade secrets, confidential references and, in a consumer context, credit card details.

Encryption can also be used to determine identity. Some websites are password protected, and sometimes it is very important to keep out intruders. For example, I have an Internet bank account, and would be very unhappy if it could be accessed by anyone other than myself. Passwords have to be stored somewhere, since otherwise there would be no means of checking that they have been correctly entered, but for security reasons they are always stored in their encrypted form.

Identity can be important for other reasons. A common Internet banking fraud is to send an e-mail to customers, purporting to come from the bank, giving a spurious reason for requesting password details. For example, this one was recently directed at Lloyds TSB customers:

> Please read this important message about security. We are working very hard to protect our customers against fraud. Your account has been randomly chosen for verification. This is requested to us to verify that you are the real owner of this account. All you need to do is to click on the link below. You will see a verification page. Please complete all fields that you will see and submit the form. You will be redirected to Lloyds TSB home page after verification. Please note that if you don't verify your ownership of account in 24 hours we will block it to protect your money ... [link] ... Lloyds TSB Bank plc and Lloyds TSB Scotland plc are authorised and regulated by the Financial Services Authority.

Of course, the intention was to capture customers' passwords, the sender not being authorised by Lloyds TSB. Needless to say, scams like this are not by any means directed only to customers of Lloyds TSB. Some fraudsters go further, even to the extent of setting up sham websites, posing as legitimate traders. In principle at least, the technology described in this chapter could be used to verify identities, although to date at least, it has not been used to anything like the full extent possible.

The point is that it is easy for anybody to pretend to be somebody else on the Internet. Anybody can set up an e-mail account, for example with Hotmail or Yahoo!, giving details which are completely false, enabling them to pose as anybody they wish. An e-mail address 'paultodd@hotmail.com' could be anyone's; it need not be (and indeed is not) mine. Encryption can be used to determine identity and, in a trading

---

1   Eg, Akdeniz, Y, 'UK government policy on encryption', http://webjcli.ncl.ac.uk/1997/issue1/akdeniz1.html, the ISP instanced being America On-line.

context, the identity of the other party may matter for reasons other than fraud: contracts with a minor are void; some traders might be entitled to a discount; some people may not be creditworthy, etc. Some trades might be illegal with individuals or companies from a particular nation. Some pornography sites might be adult only. Only students enrolled in a particular university might be licensed to use certain databases (for example, Justis, Westlaw).

Where documents are sent over the Internet, it might be important to know not only the identity of the sender, but also that the document has not been subsequently altered by anybody else. A document in which there is much interest in developing is the electronic bill of lading.[2] There are good reasons for wishing to dematerialise this document. Typically, buyers of goods imported by sea are required to pay against tender of the bill of lading. If the buyer pays, then he acquires the bill of lading, and hence the right to delivery of the goods when the ship arrives. Conversely, if he does not pay, the seller retains the bill of lading, so the document is also an important form of security for the seller in the event of non-payment by the buyer. It follows that the buyer is required to pay for goods which he has had no opportunity physically to inspect.[3] In the physical world, he can do this confidently, since the bill has been signed by the ship's master, usually on behalf of the shipowner, certifying that goods of the contractual description have been loaded,[4] and that when loaded they were in apparent good order and condition.[5] If these statements are false, then, in principle at least, the shipowner can be liable to the buyer in damages, so it is not in the interests of the master to lie. Obviously, it is important to know that the document has in fact been signed by the master, rather than (for example) the seller, and also that it has not been altered. In the physical world, identity can be determined by the handwritten signature and alterations to a paper document are reasonably easy to spot. In the electronic world, the digital signature technology described later in this chapter (see section 5.4) can perform both functions, far more securely, if desired, than is possible in the physical world, but only through the use of encryption.

It is clear, then, that the ability to use encryption is extremely important in e-commerce. Security costs, however, and the greater the degree of security required, the greater the cost. Strong encryption requires a minimum infrastructure, simply in order to work. Public key cryptography, as described in section 5.4 below, can be very secure but, as we will see, the infrastructure required can be both complex and costly. An advantage of electronic technology is that levels of security can be varied, depending on sensitivity. Some information is not particularly sensitive and risks of fraud are not very high, in which case it is perfectly rational to dispense with high degrees of security. Thus, for example, in consumer sales, customers are generally identified only by credit card details. Many people will trust, even in a trading context, the e-mail address of the other party, more elaborate cryptographic systems in each case not having caught on. The risks of impersonation are small and it is not cost-effective to

---

2   There is indeed a pilot scheme, operated by Bolero (Bill of Lading Electronic Registry Organisation). Bolero has a comprehensive website at www.boleroassociation.org.

3   For the system to work effectively, it is important the tender of the document, and payment against it, occurs before the goods arrive. This is, however, often problematic and is one of the reasons for the interest in developing an electronic version of the document.

4   The buyer ought to be protected by insurance, should they have been lost or damaged at sea.

5   The master cannot, of course, certify that they were in actual good order and condition.

use high levels of security. Similarly, if you make a cheap purchase, such as a coach ticket, over the Internet, the only proof of identity that the driver is likely to require is the ticket number which is presented on boarding.[6] The chances of a fraudulent impostor stealing a bus ticket are, no doubt, sufficiently low as to require no greater security.

5.2   A TERMINOLOGICAL NOTE

At this point, a terminological note is appropriate. I shall follow what I shall take to be the usual custom of using the term 'digital signature' to refer to the process, described in section 5.4 below, involving public key cryptography, with the associated public key infrastructure, or PKI. The term 'digital signature' is technology-specific, therefore. (This appears to be pretty well universal usage.) Conversely, the term 'electronic signature' is technology-neutral, including any variety of electronic signature. For example, the name at the bottom of an e-mail would be an electronic, but not a digital signature. Of course, an electronic signature, unlike a digital signature, will often not conclusively prove either the identity of the signer or the integrity of the document signed but, as we have seen, such conclusive proof is not always needed.

5.3   LEGAL ISSUES RELATING TO ENCRYPTION (OUTLINE)

For any country to encourage the development of e-commerce requires a recognition of the desirability, indeed necessity, of strong encryption. However, to allow free encryption of content can pose problems for law enforcement agencies, given that the technology is freely available to terrorists and other criminals. On the other hand, control over encryption of content raises civil liberties issues, as well as tending to impede promotion of e-commerce. There is therefore a delicate balance to be struck. The issues (which do not appear to be capable of an entirely satisfactory solution) are discussed in Chapter 8.

It seems now to be appreciated, however, that encryption of content (or at least messages) raises different issues from the other uses of encryption discussed above. Moreover, whereas many states would wish to control encryption of content, promotion of e-commerce requires states to encourage the use of digital and electronic signatures. There is no real pressure for state control over digital and electronic signatures alone.

As far as electronic signatures are concerned, there are two main types of legal issue.[7] First, there may be formal writing or signature requirements for a document to be regarded as legally valid. These are usually statutory, but they need not be: for example, the common law imposes requirements for a bill of lading to be valid as a document of title, and putting a signature onto a contractual document has clear legal consequences.[8] Whether the requirements are statutory or not, they can obviously pose

---

6   National Express, for example, provides an eight-figure alphanumeric code: www.nationalexpress.com.

7   Using the term 'electronic signature' broadly, as defined in section 5.2, above.

8   On the latter, see section 9.4.1.

problems for electronic documents and signatures. There may also be requirements before a document may be used in evidence. Secondly, there are liability issues when things go wrong, for example where a digital or other form of electronic signature fails correctly to identify the author of a document, or where unauthorised alterations are hidden. These issues are considered in the next chapter.

5.4   PRINCIPLES OF ENCRYPTION

This section introduces the principles of encryption.[9] It is necessary to understand at least a little of its workings to understand digital signatures, their associated infrastructure and the law.[10]

5.4.1   Keys: symmetric and asymmetric encryption

Digital signatures, and other forms of encryption used in e-commerce, are a development of ciphers that have been around for millennia.[11] All ciphers rely upon a key. Keys are used to encrypt plaintext and to decrypt ciphertext.[12] The sender needs to know to encrypt the message and the recipient how to decrypt it. Otherwise, the method must be kept secret. To take a very simple example, I could substitute each character in my name with one two further on in the alphabet, to produce the ciphertext, Rcwn Vqff.[13] This is gobbledegook to anybody who does not know the method for decrypting it, in this case the opposite process to encryption (that is, substituting each character in the ciphertext with one two further back in the alphabet).

It is important that only the recipient knows the decryption method, but with a cipher as simple as this and given enough text to work on, it is very easy for a cryptanalyst to deduce it from the ciphertext alone.[14] To thwart cryptanalysts, ciphers of great complexity were developed. A simple variant was to use letters a varying number further on in the alphabet. Now the sender and recipient need to know not only the encryption method, in this case substituting each letter in the plaintext with a letter some number further on in the alphabet, but also the number of letters to add.[15]

---

9   An excellent, and very readable introduction is Singh, S, *The Code Book*, 1999, London: Fourth Estate, which informed much of the discussion in this section.

10 Reed, C, *Internet Law: Text and Materials*, 2nd edn, 2004, Cambridge: CUP, Chapter 5 and section 6.1.2 are a good introduction. There is also Edwards, L and Waelde, C (eds), *Law and the Internet*, 2nd edn, 2000, Oxford: Hart, Chapter 3, but it is less detailed.

11 Ciphers are traditionally distinguished from codes in that individual characters are altered, or their order changed, or both. Codes usually substitute entire words or phrases, by reference to a code book. It is ciphers, rather than codes, that are relevant for present purposes.

12 This is a very basic review. See further, eg, Akdeniz, 'UK government policy on encryption', *op cit* fn 1, and references therein.

13 It is not necessary in this example, but after z you go round again, the next letter being a, and so on.

14 Cryptanalysis is also called codebreaking, incorrectly in the present context because we are not dealing with a code.

15 This is basically the idea of the Caesar alphabet, which as its name suggests, is millennia old.

A later (and far more sophisticated) variant was the polyalphabetic cipher, where each letter was substituted by another letter, a different number further on. In this case, a key was used, determining how many to add to each letter.[16] Methods for breaking polyalphabetic ciphers were discovered in the 19th century, and still more complicated substitution methods had to be devised. By the Second World War, electro-mechanical encryption devices were being used – the use, for example, of the German Enigma machine to encrypt messages transmitted by radio is well known. Cryptanalytcal techniques had also advanced, however, and it is also well known that many German secret messages were decrypted in Bletchley Park in England.[17]

With the more complex ciphers, it is only the key that needs to be kept secret – the encryption algorithm is usually in the public domain. So, for example, in the Second World War, capture of an Enigma machine (obviously a risk in battle) did not of itself compromise German ciphers. By taking apart an Enigma machine, it was possible to determine the encryption algorithm, but without the key this was useless. The keys were, of course, closely guarded, and British and other allied forces had to rely on difficult cryptanalytic techniques, which often took weeks or even months.

Since the Second World War, the increasing power of computers has enabled ciphers of far greater complexity to be developed. This does not of itself guarantee security, since powerful computers are also used by the cryptanalysts. AES (Advanced Encryption Standard) is replacing DES (Data Encryption Standard) as the current industry standard.[18] Both the AES and DES algorithms are in the public domain; like all modern ciphers, security lies in the key being kept secret.

Until quite recently, encryption algorithms always worked just as well one way as the other. They were always two-way functions, the decryption process being just as easy as that used for encryption, usually a simple reversal. Moreover, the same key was always used for decryption as for encryption. With an Enigma machine, for example, the process for decryption was exactly the same as for encryption, that is to say, if the ciphertext was encrypted using the same key on the same machine, the plaintext would reappear. DES and AES are also two-way functions. The problem is that sender and recipient have to agree the key in advance and, since it can be used for decryption as well, keep it secret. In a military environment this is possible – for example, Enigma machines had daily key settings, which were used for one day only and distributed in advance.[19] Even so, communication with submarines at sea, for example, for key distribution, could be problematic. In the 1960s, banks used to distribute keys physically, in very high security operations using couriers. Obviously, this would have been wholly impracticable in an e-commerce environment, with

---

16 Eg, using a Viginère tableau.
17 Cryptanalysis is not always successful on its own, however. The German Naval ciphers were initially beyond the competence of the British cryptanalysts, but the Royal Navy was able to capture keys from weather ships and crippled submarines.
18 The DES standard key length was crippled by the US government to ensure that they could break DES-encrypted messages. AES supports longer key lengths, and should be more secure. See generally the RSA Laboratories site at www.rsasecurity.com/rsalabs, Crypto FAQ, Chapter 3, 'Techniques in cryptography'.
19 The daily key was used to encrypt a message key, which the sender used for each message – using the daily key directly would have made cryptanalysis much easier.

hundreds of millions of traders and customers, often trading on a one-off basis. Key distribution became the single most important problem for cryptographers:[20]

> For military purposes – or for banks, the diplomatic service, or any situation where all the correspondents are known in advance – the secret key can be physically transported by armed guards to its destination. Obviously, this isn't possible for those using encryption over the Internet to pass secure messages to people in different countries whom they might never meet in real life. The issue of how to achieve this is termed the 'key exchange problem' and it was solved using a clever mechanism that was developed by three American cryptographers, Rivest, Shamir and Adleman. Their initials give us the name of the scheme: RSA.

The essence of the RSA scheme, the essential workings of which are fundamental to the operation of e-commerce, is to use one-way functions, not two-way functions such as Enigma and DES. A one-way function is easy to work one way, but reversing the process is very difficult. In the present context, reversing the process, even with powerful computers, takes an infeasibly long time, perhaps many years.

The idea of one-way functions was only developed (or at least made publicly available) by Diffie, Hellman and Merkle in around 1976, just in time for the development of e-commerce. Diffie, in particular, foresaw the development of e-commerce and the difficulties of key distribution.[21] There are many such operations in ordinary life (try unmixing a mixture of paint from two tins, back into their original colours), but it was not so easy to find mathematical one-way functions. Modular arithmetic and factorising large numbers provides the basis, for the time being at least.[22]

For encryption of content, the problem is how to communicate securely without having previously met to agree a key. This problem was only solved in the late 1970s, by developing the idea of one-way functions into a workable system of private and public key (asymmetric) encryption. The two keys are mathematically interrelated, but using one-way functions. Thus, whereas it is easy to derive the public from the private key, deriving the private from the public key, though possible, would take even a powerful computer an infeasibly long time (for example, hundreds of years). The breakthrough was the RSA algorithm,[23] alluded to in the above quote. Public keys can be distributed all over the world in the confidence that it is infeasible to derive the private key from the public.

Unlike conventional 'symmetric' cryptography, different keys are used for encryption and decryption. A message encrypted with Bob's public key can only be

---

20 Barrett, N, *Traces of Guilt*, 2004, London: Bantam Press, p 52. This is a book about discovering, preventing and prosecuting computer crime.

21 See generally, eg, Singh, *The Code Book*, op cit fn 9, Chapter 6. Singh also considers the possibility that asymmetric encryption might have been independently invented, over a decade earlier, by an employee of GCHQ.

22 A commonly used public key/private key technique is to derive the private key from two or more very large prime numbers, and the public key from the product of those numbers. Obtaining the public key from the private key is easy (just multiply the numbers), but if the numbers are sufficiently large (eg, numbers of 200 digits), the reverse process (finding prime factors of very large numbers) can be computationally infeasible. Exhaustive search (division of the public key by all known prime numbers up to its square root) is the only known method for very large numbers and, so long as the numbers are sufficiently large, this can take even a fast computer many years.

23 Rivest, Shamir and Adleman, the discoverers of the process.

decrypted using his private key. Thus, if Alice wants to send a message to Bob, she encrypts it using Bob's public key, which everybody knows. Unlike 'symmetric' cryptography, the message cannot be decrypted using Bob's public key, but only using Bob's private key, which only he knows. Obviously, this can effectively hide the message contents from everyone except Bob.[24]

Public/private key encryption can also be used for digital signatures since, conversely, a message encrypted using Alice's private key can only be decrypted using her public key. Even Alice cannot decrypt it using her private key. This is useless to hide the contents of the message since everyone knows Alice's public key, but it proves that the message must have come from Alice. It also proves that *that particular message* came from Alice, since the decryption (with her public key) will reveal what she said. This technique can be used not only to identify the sender, but also to establish that the message has not been altered.

Encryption and digital signature techniques can be combined, if desired. Thus, messages encrypted with Alice's private key and Bob's public key can only be decrypted with Bob's private key and Alice's public key. Only Bob can read the message, and he knows that it must have come from Alice.[25]

Where encryption of content is used (that is, the message itself is encrypted), asymmetric encryption (which is expensive in computer time) is often used just for the key, symmetric encryption using (for example) DES being used for the message itself. This was really the breakthrough of Phil Zimmermann's PGP (Pretty Good Privacy), which could (because of this technique) run asymmetric encryption on ordinary personal computers. PGP does not really affect the debate on digital signatures, or indeed e-commerce in general,[26] but its development fuelled the more general encryption debate in the early 1990s (which is considered further in Chapter 8). Because it allowed ordinary people to send strongly encrypted messages, the authorities were (and are) worried about its possible use by terrorists and other criminals, because it would defeat any kind of wire-tapping or equivalent surveillance.

5.4.2   How digital signatures work

Let us assume that the content of the message is not particularly sensitive. The message can be sent to Bob in the clear, but Alice wants Bob to know that it came from her, and also that its content has not been altered. A ship's master's certificate that goods were loaded in apparent good order and condition would be a good example. It does not really matter if the whole world knows the content – what does matter is that the master certified it, and certified that particular content.

---

24 Communications between an innocent Alice (or somebody purporting to be her) and an equally innocent Bob, with attempts at interception by the evil Eve, seem to be conventional in discussions involving cryptography, having originated with the original discussions of the RSA asymmetric encryption system in 1977: Levy, S, *Crypto*, 2000, London: Allen Lane, p 102. Certification authorities are usually identified, in such discussions, as Carol.

25 Note that the order of decryption matters.

26 Though SET (Secure Electronic Transaction) in section 5.5.2 uses the same technique.

A summary of the process can be described as follows:[27]

(a) Alice passes the message through an algorithm, called a 'digest' or 'hash' function. This function carries out a mathematical operation on the original message, creating a unique and concise version of the original text – the 'message digest'. This is not essential, but asymmetric encryption is expensive in computer resource, and it is easier to work with a compressed version of the message.

(b) Alice encrypts the digest with her private key.

(c) Alice sends the original message, unencrypted, and the encrypted message digest, to Bob. (Note that if she wanted only Bob to read it, she could also encrypt both with Bob's public key. On receipt, Bob would decrypt both with his private key. That is not necessary for a digital signature, however.)

(d) Bob uses the same hash function on the original message, to obtain the message digest. He also decrypts the encrypted digest, using Alice's public key. That should also reveal the original digest.

(e) If both versions of the digest are the same, Bob knows that Alice sent the message, and that it has not been tampered with.

5.4.3   Certification authorities

The major weakness of public/private key encryption, in an e-commerce environment at any rate, is in matching private keys to people.

The digital signature only works if Bob can be sure that Alice's public key really is Alice's. To return to the ship's master's signature, suppose Eve, who has shipped rotten goods, pretends to be Alice, the ship's master, signing a clean bill of lading for them. She tells Bob that she is Alice, and also that the public key she is using belongs to Alice. Bob has to have some means of knowing whether this public key really belongs to Alice. Where public key encryption is used by people who are known to each other, as with groups of friends or a criminal gang, this is not really a problem. For other small groups, such as freedom fighters in Burma, where not all members are known to everyone else, Phil Zimmermann (who has a distrust of authority) suggests that a web of trust be built up. For example, I may not know Sarah but I know Harry who knows Sarah. I would therefore be prepared to trust Sarah's public key, if it were certified as being hers by Harry. In an e-commerce environment, with millions of traders, a web of trust is unlikely to be effective on its own, but there is nonetheless a place for it, as we will see.

In the commercial context, however, it is the role of certification authorities (CAs) to match public keys to people, for example by signing Alice's public key with their own private key. Bob decrypts the thereby-encrypted (that is, Alice's) public key with the CA's public key, in order to obtain Alice's public key. The CA should obviously have taken some steps to ensure that the person claiming to be Alice really is Alice.[28]

---

27 On how digital signatures work, there is a useful downloadable .pdf file at http://bolero.codecircus.co.uk/assets/31/digital%20signatures%20in%20the%20Bolero%20 System1092161527.pdf. See also Reed, *Internet Law: Text and Materials*, *op cit* fn 10, section 6.1.2. Also Steffen Hindelang [2002] 1 JILT, http://www2.warwick.ac.uk/fac/soc/law/elj/ jilt/2002_1/hindelang (but this is mostly about the liability of certification authorities).

28 In reality, they tend to offer various levels of security – see Reed, *Internet Law: Text and Materials*, *op cit* fn 10, pp 148–49.

CAs can also certify each other so that chains of trust can be built up, rather in the manner of the freedom fighters considered above.[29] This time, however, the chain of trust is of CAs themselves, rather than individual people or traders. For example, if I am importing goods on a Malaysian vessel, I may be unwilling to trust a master's signature certified by a Malaysian CA, but would be prepared to do so if the Malaysian CA's public key had itself been certified by a CA in my own jurisdiction, with whom I had had dealings in the past.

Another possibility is accreditation of CAs, perhaps combined with some form of supervision. Accreditation may or may not be by the state, and may be voluntary or compulsory. Along with, or as an alternative to accreditation might be requirements for CAs, such as financial stability and audits as to their operation, concerning both the issue and revocation of certificates, requirements as to software, etc.

It seems more likely that accreditation will predominate, rather than chains of trust, although there is no reason why both systems cannot co-exist. Whatever system is used it is clear that public key encryption requires an infrastructure of CAs, which can either be certified by other CAs in an identity chain, or accredited, or both, the term public key infrastructure, or PKI, often being used. Obviously, an accreditation structure requires a greater degree of bureaucracy than an identity chain.

5.5   ENCRYPTION IN E-COMMERCE TODAY

Apart from the uses of digital signatures discussed so far, there are two vital uses of encryption in e-commerce, without which e-commerce probably would not survive at all.

5.5.1   Passwords

For security reasons, passwords are always stored in an encrypted form, never as plaintext. When the user types in the password it is encrypted and then tested against the stored encrypted password. Obviously, this has to be done quickly. However, the encrypted password file has to be stored somewhere, and so is in principle capable of being hacked into. The encryption algorithm must also (obviously) be stored on the computer. In fact, encryption algorithms are usually in the public domain and, until about 10 years ago, encrypted passwords were also often stored on a public file that was available to all users.[30] This was thought not to matter, because though encryption of a password is fast using the algorithm, it takes what is usually described as 'a computationally infeasible time' to reverse the process, even knowing the encryption algorithm. In an extreme case, this process could take even a powerful computer thousands of years. At a time when the Internet was used mainly by academics and the information was probably not particularly sensitive, this was thought to be sufficient security.

---

29   *Ibid*, pp 150–52.
30   Eg, on the UNIX mainframe system on which I was registered about 12 years ago, the etc/passwd file was available for all users to see. My entry was:
      slapnt:paKzoNvwFzb3o:2182:52:Mr P N Todd 92:/pub5/slapnt:/bin/csh
      The encrypted password is in the second field.

This is fine as long as passwords are chosen with care, but users are lazy and often use dictionary words, or other passwords that are relatively easy to guess. That is not as unreasonable as it might sound as they have to be easy enough for the user to remember without having to be written down. The problem with a publicly available file, even of encrypted passwords, is that it can be downloaded, allowing a hacker as much time as he or she pleases to discover the plaintext. For example, if passwords are dictionary words, a hacker with an electronic dictionary and the algorithm can download the password file and simply run the algorithm on all the dictionary words. It is then easy to check whether any match the encrypted password. Decrypting the encrypted password might be difficult, but the hacker is not doing that. The hacker is using the encryption algorithm to encrypt, which is, of course, very fast.

Nowadays, therefore, access even to the file of encrypted passwords is usually restricted to privileged users. The hacker, therefore, has to obtain the privileged user's password before being able to use the encrypted passwords file to attack the others.

5.5.2   Encryption of credit card details

Credit and debit cards are still the mainstay of e-commerce payment systems, especially in B2C commerce. Though digital cash may eventually push them aside, there is little sign as yet of that happening and, in any case, secure transmission of digital cash depends, at least to some extent, on encryption.[31]

With public key encryption, it is possible to encrypt a customer's credit card details, even in a one-off trade. The trader's public key, which can be sent out with the order form, is used for encryption. Only the trader, using his private key, can decrypt the details. This is, in essence at least, how SSL (Secure Sockets Layer), recently succeeded by TLS (Transport Layer Security), works.[32] These protocols are supported by browsers, such as Explorer and Netscape.

Mastercard and Visa also support SET (Secure Electronic Transaction), where the customer also receives a public key (on opening the account). Though the merchant can read the order information, he cannot read the credit card details, which are encrypted using the bank's public key and forwarded to the bank for authorisation of the transaction.[33] An advantage of SET is that it prevents fraudsters setting up sham trading sites to obtain credit card details. However, not all banks support SET.

5.6   HOW GOOD ARE ELECTRONIC SIGNATURES?

A question that obviously needs to be asked is whether electronic signed documentation can replace its traditional paper counterpart. In order to answer this question, we have to appreciate that paper signatures perform different functions in different circumstances. We should therefore expect the ideal electronic equivalent to

---

31   On digital cash, see further section 11.7.

32   See generally RSA Laboratories at www.rsasecurity.com/rsalabs, Chapter 5, 'Cryptography in the real world'.

33   See generally http://whatis.techtarget.com/definition/0,289893,sid9_gci214194,00.html, and also the discussion in section 11.2.

be different in different contexts. This discussion is also relevant to the value the law should accord an electronic signature.

Professor Reed observes that an electronic signature can provide evidence of:[34]

- the identity of the signatory;
- his intention to sign; and
- his intention to adopt the contents of the document as his own.

This may be all that a signature is needed for, for example if an intending purchaser needs to know that a ship's master has certified that goods of the contractual description have been loaded on board the vessel, on the stated date, in apparent good order and condition. As we have seen, a digital signature can do this with as much security as the parties desire, and it can also guard against later alteration of the document.[35] Digital signatures, in short, are very good at proving the identity of the signer and the integrity of the message.

Another value of a signature can be to ensure that the signer has attended to the document personally, as opposed to delegating it. A digital signature can also ensure this, if the private/public key pair is personal, at any rate as long as the signer has not disclosed his private key to a subordinate.

Sometimes, however, the identity of the signatory may be relatively unimportant. For example, the Law of Property (Miscellaneous Provisions) Act 1989 tightened up the formality requirements for contracts for the sale of land. A contract for the sale of land is usually the culmination of an extended bargaining process. The identity of the contracting parties is not normally in doubt, nor indeed the contents of the document, which both parties will check carefully before signing.

It may be objected that there is no call for contracts for the sale of land to be electronically signed, but given that the Land Registration Act 2002 paves the way for electronic conveyancing, it would surely be perverse to rule out electronic possibilities at the contracting stage. But it is important to appreciate that the signature is performing a function entirely different from that of the ship's master considered above.

For the 1989 Act, there appear to have been two mischiefs.[36] The signed document determines, first, at what stage, in what are normally lengthy negotiations, a binding contract is concluded and, secondly, what are its terms. It should be remembered that, in transactions involving land, there are likely to have been many communications between the parties during the negotiation process, some of which will have been written but some typically by telephone. Moreover, disputes could arise many years after the transaction has been concluded, when recollection is likely to be unreliable. One rationale for the Law of Property (Miscellaneous Provisions) Act 1989 was to

---

34   Reed, C, 'What is a signature?', 2000 (3) JILT, http://www2.warwick.ac.uk/fac/soc/law/elj/jilt/2000_3/reed/. This article also describes the mechanics of the digital signature, and use of biometric data as an alternative.

35   Note that only asymmetric encryption can do this; with symmetric encryption the recipient, as well as the sender, has the key, so you cannot know which of the two sent and/or altered it.

36   See generally the Law Commission, *Transfer of Land: Formalities for Contracts of Sale etc of Land*, Law Com 164, 1987, London: HMSO; also *Firstpost Homes Ltd v Johnson* [1995] 1 WLR 1567, pp 1571 and 1576.

ensure that all the terms were recorded in one document, obviating the need for (or indeed relevance of) external evidence. Given the protracted nature of negotiations, and the fact that only the parties to them will typically be aware of the details, it is probably important to ensure that all the details are properly certified.[37] In principle, of course, this could be achieved using a single, digitally signed electronic document. Proving the identity of the parties may not be particularly important, but a digital signature can, of course, also prove the integrity of the document, and that it has not been subsequently altered.

However, this is not the only reason for this type of formality requirement. It is also necessary to guard against the parties becoming bound without fully intending to. This aspect of formality is also relevant in some consumer contracts (an attempt to ensure informed consent),[38] and even more so with formal transactions where, for example, a deed is required. Yet a framework for electronic conveyancing has been set up by the Land Registration Act 2002, so it must be envisaged that there could be an electronic equivalent. What is important here is that there is a prescribed form and, in the case of a conveyance, perhaps an element of publicity as well. The form is important, in order to achieve the function.

Whereas a digital signature is very capable of establishing identity, and proving the integrity of a document, it is far less capable of establishing seriousness of intention, or of showing (for example, in a consumer context) informed consent. The encryption software may involve complex mathematical algorithms, but these are invisible to the user; as far as the user is concerned, a document can be digitally signed with no more than a mouse click. This aspect of the paper signature is less easy to replicate electronically, but it would be possible to require, for example, two signatures a requisite interval apart, to ensure that the intention was more than merely spontaneous.

It is clear, then, that different types of electronic signature might be appropriate in different situations. Any legal regulation of electronic formalities should also take account of this. Yet whereas, as we will see, many legal systems are now adopting two tiers of legislation, none has really addressed the problem of informed consent. Legislation throughout the world has tended to concentrate on the digital signature, which on its own does not prove informed consent.

---

37 This function is also of great importance for wills, where external evidence is unlikely to be available. It is of the utmost importance, for testamentary dispositions, that the details can all be gleaned from the face of the one document.

38 Eg, s 64 of the Consumer Credit Act 1974, which can require cancellation rights 'in the prescribed form' to be sent to the debtor by post. These formality requirements have nothing to do with identity, but are intended to ensure that the consumer truly has informed consent. These requirements might be difficult to replicate electronically.

VALIDITY OF ELECTRONIC AND DIGITAL SIGNATURES

6.1   OUTLINE OF LEGAL ISSUES

The legal control and debate over encryption of content is considered in Chapter 8. However, although many states in the world would like to place controls on encrypted content, electronic signatures for identification purposes are generally regarded differently for the purposes of this debate. There is no suggestion that they should be regulated by the state.

On electronic and digital signatures, in particular,[1] there are really four main issues. First, is the signature secure enough for the parties to the transaction? Secondly, what, if any, is its evidential value in a court? Thirdly, where the law requires writing and a signature, will a digitally signed electronic document or other form of electronic signature suffice? All of these issues are dealt with in this chapter.

Fourthly, however, there is the issue of liabilities when things go wrong and, in particular, where a digital signature fails correctly to identify the signer. This could occur in a number of ways, for example:

(a) The certification authority misidentifies the holder of the private key.

(b) The encryption algorithm is defective, allowing a fraudster to impersonate the signer.

(c) A fraudster is able to substitute his or her own version of encryption software (a Trojan horse attack). If, for example, the software is supplied by CD, the fraudster substitutes his or her own. If it is downloaded from the Web, the fraudster impersonates the legitimate website.

(d) The private key of a CA (certification authority) or a trader is compromised. Private keys are too long to be easily remembered and would often be stored on a hard disk or physical card. If it is stored on the hard disk then, obviously, it should be protected by a password or pass phrase, but since this word or phrase ought to be memorable (to avoid having to write it down), it will usually be the weakest link in the security.[2] Hacking a hard disk, or loss or theft of a card, obviously present security risks. This is probably the most likely cause of error, apart perhaps from the first.

Liability issues when things go wrong are the subject of Chapter 7.

6.2   EVIDENTIAL VALUE OF A SIGNATURE

The reasons for requiring an electronic signature are either that the parties themselves want the evidential security it offers, or that the document might later be used as

---

1   See section 5.2 for the terminological difference between electronic and digital signatures.

2   Eg, Barrett, N, *Traces of Guilt*, 2004, London: Bantam Press, p 85, in the context of seizure of a suspected criminal's computer, all files on the computer being encrypted, and e-mails encrypted using PGP (Phil Zimmermann's Pretty Good Privacy).

evidence in court. Where the issues are only evidential (as opposed to the formal requirements considered below), there is no reason why a digital or other electronic signature should be treated differently from its paper and ink equivalent, if it performs the same function.

6.2.1   Security as between the parties

Sometimes a digital signature will be required by one of the parties to the transaction. This would be rational, for example, in the case of the purchaser paying against an electronic bill of lading, as described in the previous chapter.[3] In such a case, the main concern is as to the security of the signature. It would be logical to demand a digital, rather than other form of electronic signature, and to specify CA and (perhaps) encryption standards. This would be done by contract, in which case the only concern of the courts is to interpret the contract. In international sales contracts, there would be much for standardisation of contractual requirements, but this would have to be a matter essentially of private business initiative.

6.2.2   Electronic signatures as evidence in the courts

The UK common law has nothing to say, explicitly at least, on the evidential value of electronic signatures in a court of law.

Many signatures in the physical world (for example, a handwritten signature at the bottom of a letter) are not, strictly speaking, necessary, in the sense that there is no legal requirement for them. But if the letter is called in evidence, the handwritten signature creates evidential presumptions, for example of the identity of the signatory, the adoption by him or her of the contents of the document and perhaps also of an appreciation by the signer of the seriousness of the transaction. The signature can evidence commitment. The evidence of the signature is not conclusive, however, and can be rebutted, for example by other evidence that suggests it is a forgery.[4]

There is no reason why an electronic signature should not be used in exactly the same way. It does not need to be a digital signature, certified by a CA, with a public key infrastructure in place.[5] A name at the bottom of an e-mail, or a scanned handwritten signature inserted into an electronic document, also has evidential value, for example, if electronic correspondence is being examined to determine the terms of a contract. Of course, its evidential value is lower than that of a digital signature, since it is easier to forge, but that does not mean that it has no evidential value at all. No doubt, its value could be rebutted by, for example, evidence that the e-mail account was not that of the alleged author, or that somebody else wrote or scanned the name, but in most cases there will be no contrary evidence and no reason against taking the electronic communication, however insecure, at its face value.

---

3   Sections 5.4.2 and 5.4.3.
4   Eg, a wife's signature on a legal charge on the house in favour of a bank is evidence that she has executed the charge, but can be rebutted by counter evidence that her husband forged it: eg, *First National Securities Ltd v Hegerty* [1985] QB 850.
5   See the definitions of electronic and digital signatures in section 5.2.

Ideally, therefore, an electronic signature should be capable of creating the same evidential presumptions as its conventional physical counterpart. It is unclear whether this principle would have been accepted by the English common law. This issue is, however, now covered by the Electronic Communications Act 2000.[6] Section 7(1) provides that:

In any legal proceedings—

(a) an electronic signature incorporated into or logically associated with a particular electronic communication or particular electronic data, and

(b)   the certification by any person of such a signature,

shall each be admissible in evidence in relation to any question as to the authenticity of the communication or data or as to the integrity of the communication or data.

There is a general discussion of legislation on electronic and digital signatures below.

6.3   FORMAL VALUE OF A SIGNATURE

The law requires formality for some transactions. The reasons for formality requirements vary, but it should (at least in principle) be possible for an electronic signature to satisfy them. It may be that the common law is sufficiently flexible to allow this, but this is an area in which legislation might ideally be required.

It is possible for parties to a transaction to agree not to take formality issues. For example, the Bolero electronic bill of lading operates only as between members, all of whom agree to be bound by Bolero's Rule Book.[7] The effect of this is to create contractual relationships between all the members. Para 2.2.2 of the Rule Book states:

2.2.2. *Validity and Enforceability*

(1) *Writing Requirements.* Any applicable requirement of law, contract, custom or practice that any transaction, document or communication shall be made or evidenced in writing, signed or sealed shall be satisfied by a Signed Message.

(2) *Signature Requirements.* The contents of a Message Signed by a User, or a portion drawn from a Signed Message, are binding upon that User to the same extent, and shall have the same effect at law, as if the Message or portion thereof had existed in a manually signed form.

(3) *Undertaking not to Challenge Validity.* No User shall contest the validity of any transaction, statement or communication made by means of a Signed Message, or a portion drawn from a Signed Message, on the grounds that it was made in electronic form instead of by paper and/or signed or sealed.

It would, of course, also be possible for any parties in a contractual relationship with each other to enter into a similar arrangement.

There are, however, two problems with relying on contracts to resolve formality issues. First, because of the privity of contract doctrine, only parties to the agreement will be bound by this. In the event that a Bolero bill of lading affected anybody outside

---

6   The full text of the Electronic Communications Act 2000 can be found at www.opsi.gov.uk/acts/acts2000/20000007.htm.

7   See also section 5.1.

Bolero, they would be perfectly entitled to challenge its validity. Secondly, some contracts, for example a contract for the sale of land, are completely void unless quite stringent formality requirements are satisfied. The law surely cannot allow the parties to avoid this consequence by entering into what is, after all, an agreement that does not satisfy the same formality requirements.

6.3.1   Form v function

A recurring issue in the debate is whether the law should concern itself with the form or function of a signature. Let us take the requirement, for example, that a contract of guarantee is required to be evidenced in writing.[8] If the courts concern themselves only with the form of the signature, then clearly an electronic signature cannot be considered equivalent to its physical counterpart. Conversely, if all that matters is that it performs the same function, then at least some electronic signatures ought to be regarded as equivalent, depending of course on what the function of the signature is seen to be.

In a similar vein, where legislation is required, one of the issues is whether it should be technology-specific or technology-neutral. Technology-specific legislation looks to the form of the signature, whereas technology-neutral legislation essentially asks: 'Is the signature good enough?' It does not require a particular form of signature.

Technology-specific legislation always requires public key asymmetric encryption, as described in Chapter 5.[9] This is thought to be very secure today, but today's technology might be rendered useless in the future by mathematical advances (for example, a faster method of finding prime factors). On the other hand, new cryptographic techniques are also being developed, for example using cryptosystems relying on elliptic curves, which are expected to allow significantly reduced key lengths.[10] There are also emerging, even now, methods that may become better, at least of certifying identity, than asymmetric cryptography. Techniques involving the use of biometric data are developing, and their reliability is improving. These will also require a similar infrastructure, however, probably with CAs again tying in the measurements to the signatory. Reed observes that data:[11]

> can be checked against the signatory's known biometric data, either in the possession of the recipient of a document or held by a trusted third party.

Moreover, encryption techniques will continue to be needed to prevent fraudsters transmitting other people's biometrics (which must inevitably be, to some extent at least, public). Reed also alludes to encryption,[12] so asymmetric encryption would not necessarily be displaced by biometric data.

---

8   Statute of Frauds 1677, s 4. See also generally, Bradgate, R, *Commercial Law*, 3rd edn, 2000, London: Butterworths, p 545 *et seq*.

9   Section 5.4.

10   There is a description in the explanatory notes to the United Nations Commission on International Trade Law (UNCITRAL) *Model Law on Electronic Signatures*, 2001, para 39. See also the RSA Laboratories site at www.rsasecurity.com/rsalabs, Crypto FAQ, section 3.5.1: 'What are elliptic curve cryptosystems?' Like RSA, they rely on one-way functions, and there would still be a PKI; the main advantage is shorter key lengths.

11   Reed, C, *Internet Law: Text and Materials*, 2nd edn, 2004, Cambridge: CUP, p 187.

12   *Ibid*, p 188.

The possibility clearly exists, at least in theory, however, that better methods will emerge, where public key cryptography has no role at all to play. The main problem of technology-specific legislation is precisely that technology does not stand still. To deal with possible future advances, there is a case for providing for functional equivalence, rather than using technology-specific legislation. In other words, the legislation should make provision for signatures that are as good as their paper equivalents, whatever method they use to perform that function.

There are, however, formidable counter-arguments. With conventional formality requirements, it is possible for the parties to the transaction to be certain that a document which complies will be valid. There is no need for them to litigate in order to decide this. On the other hand, if the law did no more than provide that an electronic signature that was as good as a paper signature would be valid, there would be no similar certainty. The law has to provide that a signature that complies with its requirements will be valid in any event, without the need to prove that it is as good as its paper equivalent. It is only really possible to provide this certainty by stipulating clear requirements, and these will necessarily be technology-specific.

There is a case, then, for two types of legislation. If all we are concerned about is the evidential value of a signature, I suggested earlier in the chapter that an electronic signature should be capable of creating the same evidential presumptions as its conventional physical counterpart. Clearly this implies that we look at the function, rather than the form. Moreover, bearing in mind that the signature creates only a presumption, a relatively low threshold is appropriate. Some electronic (as opposed to digital) signatures may provide little or no security in the sense that they are easy to forge, but it does not follow that they have no evidential value at all. There is no need for the law to demand a signature in a particular form, or using a specific technology, such as public key encryption (PKI).

We have seen that, in the UK, the evidential validity of an electronic signature is covered by the Electronic Communications Act 2000. Section 7(1) defines an electronic signature in functional terms; there is no formal requirement, nor any need for a digital signature, PKI infrastructure, etc. Obviously, the strength of the evidential presumption will depend on the precise type of signature used.

On the other hand, if I wish to enter into a contract that I cannot enforce unless it is signed, for example a contract of guarantee, I need to be sure now that if its validity is later challenged, I can rely upon that signature. In an electronic context, I must be able to be certain that, as long as I have used a signature of a certain form, the law will recognise it. That requires a test of form, not function.

It follows, then, that both types of legislation have their merits, but for different purposes. This seems now to be widely recognised, with many states adopting two-tier legislation, probably for precisely the reasons rehearsed here. Evidential value is provided for (as in the UK) by a test of functional equivalence. However, when it comes to formal requirements, states usually require a digital signature, certified by an accredited CA. This provides the requisite degree of certainty required by commerce.

Such a signature should also be very secure but, as we have seen, security is not the only, nor even the most usual reason for a legal requirement that a document be signed. It may be wondered whether the other justifications for a signed document have been adequately thought out in the context of electronic formality requirements.

6.4   ELECTRONIC SIGNATURES AND UK COMMON LAW

It should be remembered that there are no formality requirements for most commercial transactions and obviously if, for example, oral contracts can validly be made, there is no reason why a contract cannot be concluded using electronic documentation. It follows that e-commerce, like its physical counterpart, is not significantly affected by formality requirements.

Sometimes, however, formality requirements are imposed by statute, which can cause problems, at least in principle, for electronic communications and signatures. For example, contracts of guarantee are unenforceable unless they are evidenced by a written memorandum, and (as we have seen) contracts for the sale of land are valid only if in writing and signed.[13] Bills of exchange are only valid if they are written and signed. Bills of exchange are defined in s 3 of the Bills of Exchange Act 1882, which begins:

(1)   A bill of exchange is an unconditional order in writing, addressed by one person to another, signed by the person giving it, requiring the person to whom it is addressed to pay on demand or at a fixed or determinable future time a sum certain in money to or to the order of a specified person, or to bearer.

(2)   An instrument which does not comply with these conditions, or which orders any act to be done in addition to the payment of money, is not a bill of exchange.

Similarly, arbitration clauses are valid only if in writing. There are, in addition, consumer protection provisions requiring writing and signatures. Their purpose appears to be to ensure that a consumer has thought seriously about the transaction (informed consent). See, for example, the discussion at the end of section 5.6.[14]

Sometimes, formality requirements are imposed by the common law. A bill of lading, for example, is probably only recognised as a document of title at common law if it is written and signed. There is also a principle, discussed in Chapter 9, that a signature on a contractual document binds the signer to its terms.[15] Since this conclusion is drawn regardless of whether he or she had actually read them, this is clearly a formal rather than an evidential rule.

Where signed writing is required for validity, if the common law allows electronic signed documents to satisfy the requirements, then there is no problem. To click 'I agree' on a website page of terms should have exactly the same effect as signing a page of terms. If the common law is insufficiently flexible to recognise the electronic signature, legislation is needed to allow e-commerce to flourish.

Formality requirements are, however, many and diverse, and the wording and purpose of formality legislation varies widely. It is, therefore, not possible to generalise about the validity of electronic writing and signatures, merely to state the principles that seem likely to apply.

---

13   Law of Property (Miscellaneous Provisions) Act 1989.
14   These are but a few (of many possible) examples of statutory signature requirements. Reed provides many more examples: Reed, C, 'What is a signature?' [2000] 3 JILT, http://www2.warwick.ac.uk/fac/soc/law/elj/jilt/2000_3/reed/.
15   Section 9.4.1.

6.4.1 Writing

Schedule 1 of the Interpretation Act 1978 contains the following definition:

> 'Writing' includes typing, printing, lithography, photography and other modes of representing or reproducing words in a visible form, and expressions referring to writing are construed accordingly.

This would appear, in principle, to be wide enough to include a page visible on a computer screen, in which case writing requirements should not present any particular difficulty. Professor Reed is more pessimistic, however, on the grounds that:

> digital information, held either as on/off states of switches in a processing chip or as magnetic or optical variations on the surface of some recording medium, is not in fact a representation or reproduction of words in a visible form.

But the same is true of a digital photograph. Both are, however, a mode of producing a visible form, whether connected to a printer or to a screen. It is difficult to see why these outputs should be treated differently. In *Lockheed-Arabia v Owen*, Mann LJ said (of this very section) that an 'ongoing statute ought to be read so as to accommodate technological change'.[16] The Law Commission also takes the view that both e-mail and web pages can satisfy the writing requirement in the 1978 Act.[17] EDI (electronic data interchange) messages, however, which are not intended to be read by anyone (but which will probably become more common with greater automation of the contracting process), do not.

6.4.2 Signature

There is no general statutory definition of a signature, nor is there usually a definition in the specific formality statutes, although some statutes expressly allow facsimiles (for example, photocopied signatures).[18]

Where (as is usual) the formalities legislation is silent, there are a number of cases suggesting that functional equivalence will suffice. In *Goodman v J Eban Ltd*,[19] the majority held that a facsimile rubber stamp, applied personally, sufficed as a signature, under s 65(2) of the Solicitors Act 1932,[20] because it authenticated the document. Romer LJ adopted a dictionary definition of a signature:[21]

> speaking generally a signature is the writing, or otherwise affixing, a person's name, or a mark to represent his name, by himself or by his authority with the intention of authenticating a document as being that of, or as binding on, the person whose name or mark is so written or affixed.

---

16 [1993] 3 All ER 641, p 646.
17 Law Commission, *Electronic Commerce: Formal Requirements in Commercial Transactions (Advice from the Law Commission)*, 2001, London: HMSO, paras 3.9 *et seq*, available at www.lawcom.gov.uk. This particular file (which can be downloaded in .pdf format) is at www.lawcom.gov.uk/files/e-commerce.pdf.
18 Professor Reed provides examples: Reed, C, 'What is a signature?', *op cit* fn 14, section 2.1.
19 [1954] 1 QB 550.
20 The section required a signature, but there were no specific requirements, and it ought to be possible to generalise to other statutes requiring a signature without more. The solicitor's handwritten signature was personally impressed on the stamp.
21 [1954] 1 QB 550, p 563, quoting from *Stroud's Judicial Dictionary*, 3rd edn, now 6th edn, 2001, London: Sweet & Maxwell.

This definition is wholly functional, and does not depend at all on the form of the signature.

Evershed MR expressed personal doubt whether the statutory requirement ought to be satisfied by a rubber stamp, but in the end was prepared to accept the reasoning of Sir William Bovill CJ in the earlier but generally similar case of *Bennett v Brumfitt*:[22]

> The ordinary mode of affixing a signature to a document is not by the hand alone, but by the hand coupled with some instrument, such as a pen or a pencil. I see no distinction between using a pen or a pencil and using a stamp, where the impression is put upon the paper by the proper hand of the party signing. In each case it is the personal act of the party, and to all intents and purposes a signing of the document by him. If the objector here had used a pencil or a paintbrush, it would hardly have been contended that he had not signed the notice.

This statement also emphasises the function rather than the form of the signature (in effect, what difference can it make what instrument he had used to sign the document?). Evershed MR, persuaded by this and other authorities, concluded that:[23]

> ... it must be taken as established ... that where an Act of Parliament requires that any particular document be 'signed' by a person, then, *prima facie*, the requirement of the Act is satisfied if the person himself places upon the document an engraved representation of his signature by means of a rubber stamp.

6.4.3   Personal signature

Denning LJ dissented in *Goodman v Eban* but, like his brethren, his reasoning was in functional, not formal terms; his dissent was on the ground that a rubber stamp did not perform the same function as a handwritten signature:[24]

> The virtue of a signature lies in the fact that no two persons write exactly alike, and so it carries on the face of it a guarantee that the person who signs has given his personal attention to the document. A rubber stamp carries with it no such guarantee: because it can be affixed by anyone. The affixing of it depends on the internal office arrangements with which the recipient has nothing to do. This is such common knowledge that a 'rubber stamp' is contemptuously used to denote the thoughtless impress of an automaton, in contrast to the reasoned attention of a sensible person.

He also observed that 'anyone can affix a rubber stamp'. The main issue in the case was thus whether a *personal* signature was required (the majority thinking not).

There may well be some statutes which require a personal signature, but in principle, on a functional test at least, a digital signature could satisfy this requirement, as long as the private key has not been disclosed to a subordinate. The automaton argument is less easy to address, and would perhaps require a requisite form.

---

22   (1867) LR 3 CP 28, at 30, quoted with approval by Evershed MR at p 556.

23   [1954] 1 QB 550, p 557.

24   *Ibid*, p 561.

6.4.4 Extensions to electronic signatures

It is not clear whether the majority reasoning in *Goodman v Eban* would extend to an e-mail with a scanned signature attachment, but Laddie J thought in *Re A Debtor*, a case involving a faxed proxy form which the relevant legislation required to be signed, that a scanned signature, sent remotely to a fax machine over telephone lines, would suffice. His reasoning is wholly in terms of function:[25]

> It seems to me that the function of the signature is to indicate, but not necessarily prove, that the document has been considered personally by the creditor and is approved of by him. It may be said that a qualifying proxy form consists of two ingredients. First, it contains the information required to identify the creditor and his voting instructions and, secondly, the signature performing the function set out above. When the chairman receives a proxy form bearing what purports to be a signature, he is entitled to treat it as authentic unless there are surrounding circumstances which indicate otherwise. Once it is accepted that the close physical linkage of hand, pen and paper is not necessary for the form to be signed, it is difficult to see why some forms of non-human agency for impressing the mark on the paper should be acceptable while others are not.
>
> For example, it is possible to instruct a printing machine to print a signature by electronic signal sent over a network or via a modem. Similarly, it is now possible with standard personal computer equipment and readily available popular word processing software to compose, say, a letter on a computer screen, incorporate within it the author's signature which has been scanned into the computer and is stored in electronic form, and to send the whole document including the signature by fax modem to a remote fax. The fax received at the remote station may well be the only hard copy of the document. It seems to me that such a document has been 'signed' by the author.

If he was prepared to go this far, it is difficult to see why the remote fax should be needed at all, as long as the electronic document including the signature could be displayed on the recipient's computer screen.

6.4.5 Distinctions between statutes

Although in *Goodman v J Eban*, Evershed MR expressed reluctance to 'open the way to arguments for creating fine distinctions between one statute and another',[26] there is no doubt that statutory requirements can differ, so that it is impossible to state *generally* whether electronic signatures will suffice. This is also to be expected of a functional equivalence view, since the purpose of each statutory provision differs.

For example, in *Firstpost Homes v Johnson*, a stricter view was taken of the Law of Property (Miscellaneous Provisions) Act 1989, which strengthened the formality requirements for contracts for the sale of land, than of the previous legislation which was based on the Statute of Frauds 1677.[27] Peter Gibson LJ refused to accept that:[28]

---

25 [1996] 2 All ER 345, p 350.
26 [1954] 1 QB 550, pp 558–59.
27 Law of Property Act 1925, s 40.
28 [1995] 1 WLR 1567, p 1575.

... authorities on what was a sufficient signature for the purposes of the Statute of Frauds 1677 and s 40 of the Act of 1925 should continue to govern the interpretation of the word 'signed' in s 2 of the Act of 1989. Prior to the Act of 1989 the courts viewed with some disfavour those who made oral contracts but did not abide by them. The courts were prepared to interpret the statutory requirements generously to enable contracts to be enforced and in relation to the question whether there was a sufficient memorandum evidencing an agreement extrinsic evidence was admissible.

... The Act of 1989 seems to me to have a new and different philosophy from that which the Statute of Frauds 1677 and s 40 of the Act of 1925 had. Oral contracts are no longer permitted. To my mind it is clear that Parliament intended that questions as to whether there was a contract, and what were the terms of the contract, should be readily ascertained by looking at the single document said to constitute the contract.

Any interpretation must be statute-specific, in other words. It is also clear that the 1989 Act, unlike its 1677 precursor, is intended to exclude entirely the admissibility of evidence outside the written contract. As Balcombe LJ observed:[29]

I am not prepared to construe the word 'signed' in section 2(3) of the Law of Property (Miscellaneous Provisions) Act 1989 by reference to the old learning on what amounted to a signature of a note or memorandum sufficient for the purposes of the Statute of Frauds 1677 or section 40 of the Law of Property Act 1925. To do so would, as Peter Gibson LJ has said, defeat the obvious intention of section 2 of the Act of 1989, which is to ensure that a contract for the sale of land must be made in writing, in one document, leaving aside the position where contracts are exchanged, and with the document being signed by or on behalf of each party obviously so as to authenticate the document: see *Goodman v J Eban Ltd*.[30] The clear policy of the section is to avoid the possibility that one or other party may be able to go behind the document and introduce extrinsic evidence to establish a contract, which was undoubtedly a problem under the old law.

Special considerations no doubt apply to the 1989 Act, as we have seen above. The passages from this case remain clearly purposive, however, not therefore ruling out the possibility that a single electronic document, containing all the terms, could suffice.

6.4.6   Requirement for a mark?

Having said that, it remains arguable that the common law requires some form of mark, in which case the validity at any rate of digital signatures would be doubtful. Even in the above passage from *Re A Debtor*, Laddie J assumes eventual printing of the document. Moreover, some legislation specifically requires a mark. Thus, s 1(4) of the Law of Property (Miscellaneous Provisions) Act 1989 provides that:

In subsections (2) and (3) above 'sign', in relation to an instrument, includes making one's mark on the instrument and 'signature' is to be construed accordingly.

It is difficult to see how a digital signature could ever satisfy this requirement as in no sense does it make a mark. Even where the statute itself makes no such provision, all the members of the court in *Goodman v Eban* refer to the making of a mark, but, of course, these remarks predated the possibility of digital signatures and are not, I

---

29 *Ibid,* p 1577. In *Firstpost Homes v Johnson,* there were two related documents, only one of which was signed by both parties. Though the requirements of the earlier legislation would have been satisfied, those of the later legislation were not.

30 [1954] 1 QB 550.

would suggest, good authority for the proposition that a mark is always required.[31] Moreover, it is difficult to see why printing a fax on a printer should be treated differently from displaying it on a screen. Both devices convert strings of bits into a visible form. The Law Commission says, discussing the view of Laddie J:[32]

> We do not believe that the position is any different if an alternative form of electronic transmission is used. A document incorporating a scanned manuscript signature is capable of indicating to the recipient that the signatory had the necessary authenticating intention, in the same way an original manuscript signature would.

If functional equivalence is the test, a digital signature ought to be regarded as functionally equivalent to an ink signature, at least where the purpose of the legislation is essentially evidential.[33] The same ought also to be true of clicking on a website button.[34]

Sometimes, however, the legislation requires a particular form, which clearly envisages a physical document, or (as with the Consumer Credit Act 1974, referred to in section 5.6) the use of the postal service. Clearly, this could not be satisfied by an electronic communication, in the absence of further legislation.

6.4.7   Conclusion

It is at least arguable that even at common law, electronic signatures can satisfy many statutory formality requirements, given the functional approach adopted by the courts. However, this cannot be stated with any certainty, and it certainly does not apply to all formalities legislation. Moreover, if a formal definition is adopted, or a physical mark is required on a document, then electronic signatures are unlikely to suffice, in which case legislation is needed.

In any case, even a purposive interpretation might lead to different results where the purpose of the signature requirement is to ensure that a consumer has informed consent to a transaction, or that there is a clear intention to be bound, for example with a contract for the sale of land. In such cases, the form is arguably more important. Certainly, it would be difficult to argue that a single mouse click should suffice.

6.4.8   Contractual possibilities

For example, in closed trading systems (such as the Bolero electronic bill of lading considered in section 6.3), the parties can agree not to take formality issues, but only parties to the agreement are bound by this. There are also problems with statutes such

---

31 See also Law Commission, *Electronic Commerce: Formal Requirements in Commercial Transactions, op cit* fn 17, at para 3.38(3): 'Some old authorities did suggest that a signature was required to be a "mark" which would, by definition, be visible. We believe it is unlikely that the courts would regard such authorities as binding in modern conditions.' In the footnote they observe that 'The effect of the technology previously available was that the signature had to be visible: that is no longer the case'.

32 *Ibid*, para 3.33.

33 Leaving aside non-evidential aspects, Reed suggests that the process of applying the private key (often a physical card) makes it equivalent to a rubber stamp: Reed, C, 'What is a signature?', *op cit* fn 14, section 4.4.

34 As the Law Commission accept, *op cit* fn 17, para 3.38.

as the Law of Property (Miscellaneous Provisions) Act 1989, which makes *void* unwritten contracts for the sale of land, or of an interest in land. Since there is a public policy requirement that all the terms can be determined from one document, it seems unlikely that such a provision could be avoided by agreement.

6.5   LEGISLATIVE SOLUTIONS

If the common law adopts a functional approach to the definition of a signature, then a digital (or other electronic) signature might satisfy the definition. If not, we have to look to legislation.

There is legislation in the UK, which is relatively weak. The UK is also required to implement the EC Directive (1999/93/EC) on Electronic Signatures, but the implementation to date has been partial only. It is not possible to understand the UK position in a vacuum, however, and we should start by looking at legislative solutions in general, throughout the world.[35]

6.5.1   Legislative solutions (in general)

The first legislation on electronic and digital signatures was enacted around 10 years ago and there have been three basic approaches adopted. A fairly clear trend appears to be emerging, however, and it is probably safe to predict how most legislation will eventually work. As will appear, I am not convinced that the trend takes account of all the functions to which a signature can be put.

Even today, many states have enacted nothing, although there has been acceleration in the pace of legislation. As we have seen, legislation can be either technology-specific, or provide for a functional equivalence approach, or adopt a mixture of the two, since there are arguments for and against both individual approaches. Much of the early legislation was technology-specific, covering only 'digital signatures', which were defined strictly in terms of asymmetric cryptography. This is no longer the trend, and little of this early legislation remains in force. Some later legislation, following the trend of the UNCITRAL Model Law of 1996,[36] adopted a functionally equivalent definition of 'electronic signature'. Such definitions look to what the signature does, and do not assume asymmetric cryptography. Today, however, the main trend is towards two-tier legislation.

6.5.2   Early form-based technology-specific legislation

The first legislation on digital signatures was the Utah Digital Signature Act 1996.[37] It was a strong piece of legislation,[38] providing for digital signatures to be the equivalent

---

35   For a survey of legislation throughout the world, see www.ilpf.org/groups/survey.htm. See also www.qmw.ac.uk/~tl6345/.

36   UNCITRAL *Model Law on Electronic Commerce* (1996) – see further, section 6.5.4 below.

37   Available at www.le.state.ut.us/~code/TITLE46/46_02.htm. This was an amended version of an earlier draft (1995): www.jus.unitn.it/USERS/PASCUZZI/privcomp9798/documento/firma/utah/udsa.html.

38   It has now been superseded by the US Federal Electronic Signatures in Global and National Commerce Act 2000.

in all respects of handwritten signatures. In other words, it provided both for evidential value and formality. It was, however, technology-specific, s 401(1) providing that:[39]

(1) Where a rule of law requires a signature, or provides for certain consequences in the absence of a signature, that rule is satisfied by a digital signature if:

    (a) that digital signature is verified by reference to the public key listed in a valid certificate issued by a licensed certification authority;

    (b) that digital signature was affixed by the signer with the intention of signing the message; and

    (c) the recipient has no knowledge or notice that the signer either:

        (i) breached a duty as a subscriber; or

        (ii) does not rightfully hold the private key used to affix the digital signature.

Validity was provided for all purposes, but the conditions presupposed public key encryption. Thus, for example, in the definition section:[40]

'Digital signature' means a transformation of a message using an asymmetric cryptosystem such that a person having the initial message and the signer's public key can accurately determine whether:

(a) the transformation was created using the private key that corresponds to the signer's public key; and

(b) the message has been altered since the transformation was made.

'Asymmetric cryptosystem' and 'certification authority' were also defined, clearly envisaging the use of a 'key pair', which was defined in terms of a public and private key. No other technology was catered for at all, whether or not it performed the same function as public key encryption, or indeed of the physical signature that it was intended to replace.

The Act also required a state-licensed CA,[41] making no provision at all for unlicensed CAs even where a chain of identity checking was used to establish a trust relationship.[42] The Utah structure was essentially hierarchical, with the state providing the root of trust. It is effectively therefore an accreditation scheme,[43] accreditation being by the state. There were also stringent qualification requirements for CAs in s 201, and there were rigorous audit and record-keeping requirements. Thus, very close control was exercised over the licensed CAs.[44]

Clearly, then, the Utah approach was very form-specific, indeed a triumph of form over function. Moreover, no distinction was made in s 401 between the requirements

---

39 Utah Digital Signature Act 1996 (Utah Code § 46-3), 46-3-401 (Satisfaction of Signature Requirements).

40 *Ibid*, (10).

41 Under the definition section, '"Licensed certification authority" means a certification authority to whom a license has been issued by the division and whose license is in effect', and '"Division" means the Division of Corporations and Commercial Code within the Utah Department of Commerce'.

42 As described in Chapter 5, and by Reed, *Internet Law: Text and Materials*, op cit fn 11, pp 150 *et seq*.

43 As described by Reed, *ibid*, pp 153 *et seq*.

44 This was, however, enacted at a time when the US was keen to license CAs, with a view to controlling encryption (see the discussion in Chapter 8).

for the factual presumptions created by a signature and its legal validity. Just one kind of signature was recognised, which was valid for all purposes. A similar approach was adopted in Germany and Italy in 1997.[45] The German legislation, for example, also provided only for digital signatures which 'shall mean a seal affixed to digital data which is generated by a private signature key and establishes the owner of the signature key and the integrity of the data with the help of an associated public key provided with a signature key certificate of a certification authority', and CAs had to be licensed by a competent authority.

6.5.3   Advantages and disadvantages of Utah approach

There is no doubt that the detailed technology-specific approach adopted by Utah, concentrating on the form of the signature, make for certainty in the law. Traders and consumers can be certain, in advance of litigation, that a signature that conforms to the requirements of the Utah statute is valid for all purposes for which a signature is required.

There are also good arguments in favour of licensing CAs, enforcing strict qualification requirements and supervising their operation. A chain of identity, by contrast, does not necessarily attest to the reliability of a CA, merely its identity.

On the other hand, insisting on strict formal requirements can impede the development of e-commerce, as well as new technology (since the legislation is technology-specific). Also, the idea of state accreditation is repugnant to open free market ideals and, in particular (in the context of a book on English law), the development of a single market within the EU.

It is also not easy to operate e-commerce globally, if states require CAs to be licensed in their own jurisdiction. Utah was very much a state-based system, for example requiring CAs to 'maintain an office in Utah or have established a registered agent for service of process in Utah'.[46] It was also extremely bureaucratic and there would be significant start-up costs for CAs.

6.5.4   UNCITRAL *Model Law on Electronic Commerce* (1996)

The approach adopted in UNCITRAL's *Model Law on Electronic Commerce* (1996) was very different.[47] UNCITRAL appears to have feared that development of state laws,

---

45 The original German Digital Signature Act 1997 (Signaturgesetz, SiG) can be found at www.iuscomp.org/gla/statutes/SiG.htm. See also Lodder, A and Kaspersen, H (eds), *eDirectives: Guide to European Union Law on E-Commerce*, 2002, The Hague: Kluwer Law International, p 36. Note that there is a later version of the German legislation: see further, section 6.5.8 below.

46 Utah Digital Signature Act 1996, section 46-3-201(1)(g). 46-3 is simply the Utah code for the Act – the reference is therefore to s 201.

47 UNCITRAL *Model Law on Electronic Commerce* (1996) and *Model Law on Electronic Signatures* (2001) can be found by going through UNCITRAL's home page: www.uncitral.org/en-index.htm, following links for adopted texts, on e-commerce. The 2001 document is a downloadable .pdf file.
   The Model Law on Electronic Commerce deals with matters other than just writing and signatures; indeed, it was intended primarily to deal with issues that were arising, at the time, about EDI. There was clearly a concern that the laws of states should not stifle the use of EDI.

such as those in Utah, Germany and Italy, might impede the development of e-commerce. The main features of the Model Law are:[48]

(a) technological neutrality;

(b) functional equivalence as the test;

(c) lack of formal or bureaucratic requirements.

All of these are very much a contrast with the Utah approach.

Paragraph 16 of the Guide to Enactment expressly argues for a functional equivalence approach. It also recognises the need for flexibility, in that the functions of writing and signatures can vary in different circumstances. In other words, it allows for context-specific requirements. Specifically, in relation to signatures, para 53 provides:[49]

> It was noted that, in addition, a signature could perform a variety of functions, depending on the nature of the document that was signed. For example, a signature might attest to the intent of a party to be bound by the content of a signed contract; the intent of a person to endorse authorship of a text; the intent of a person to associate itself with the content of a document written by someone else; the fact that, and the time when, a person had been at a given place.

For present purposes, the relevant substantive provisions are Arts 7 (signature) and 8 (original). Article 7 provides:

(1) Where the law requires a signature of a person, that requirement is met in relation to a data message if:

(a) a method is used to identify that person and to indicate that person's approval of the information contained in the data message; and

(b) that method is as reliable as was appropriate for the purpose for which the data message was generated or communicated, in the light of all the circumstances, including any relevant agreement.

(2) Paragraph (1) applies whether the requirement therein is in the form of an obligation or whether the law simply provides consequences for the absence of a signature.

Clearly, Art 7(1)(b) allows the use of any appropriate technology. The problem is that it is extremely vague, and would be difficult to use on its own as the basis for legislation. It does little more than state the general principle to be applied. However, para 58 of the Guide to Enactment fills out criteria:

> 58. In determining whether the method used under paragraph (1) is appropriate, legal, technical and commercial factors that may be taken into account include the following: (1) the sophistication of the equipment used by each of the parties; (2) the nature of their trade activity; (3) the frequency at which commercial transactions take place between the parties; (4) the kind and size of the transaction; (5) the function of signature requirements in a given statutory and regulatory environment; (6) the capability of communication systems; (7) compliance with authentication procedures set forth by intermediaries; (8) the range of authentication procedures made available by any intermediary; (9) compliance with trade customs and practice; (10) the existence of insurance coverage mechanisms against unauthorized

---

48 Note the legislative technique of the Model Law, which is inherently more flexible that an international convention.

49 See also paras 48–50, in relation to writing.

messages; (11) the importance and the value of the information contained in the data message; (12) the availability of alternative methods of identification and the cost of implementation; (13) the degree of acceptance or non-acceptance of the method of identification in the relevant industry or field both at the time the method was agreed upon and the time when the data message was communicated; and (14) any other relevant factor.

Article 8 of the Model Law, defining the requirements for originality, provides:

(1) Where the law requires information to be presented or retained in its original form, that requirement is met by a data message if:

   (a) there exists a reliable assurance as to the integrity of the information from the time when it was first generated in its final form, as a data message or otherwise; and

   (b) where it is required that information be presented, that information is capable of being displayed to the person to whom it is to be presented.

(2) Paragraph (1) applies whether the requirement therein is in the form of an obligation or whether the law simply provides consequences for the information not being presented or retained in its original form.

(3) For the purposes of subparagraph (a) of paragraph (1):

   (a) the criteria for assessing integrity shall be whether the information has remained complete and unaltered, apart from the addition of any endorsement and any change which arises in the normal course of communication, storage and display; and

   (b) the standard of reliability required shall be assessed in the light of the purpose for which the information was generated and in the light of all the relevant circumstances.

Similar comments can be made about Art 8(1)(a) as apply to Art 7(1)(b). Both are too vague to allow a trader or consumer to know, with certainty, that they have been satisfied.

The UNCITRAL Model Law also does not insist on certification authorities, or any kind of hierarchical structure.

6.5.5   Similar legislation

Following the publication of the UNCITRAL Model Law, a number of jurisdictions enacted their own legislation, purely in terms of functional equivalence. As we have seen, the UK is itself an example. Another is Australia. Section 10(1) of the Australian Electronic Transactions Act 1999 provides:[50]

Requirement for signature

(1) If, under a law of the Commonwealth, the signature of a person is required, that requirement is taken to have been met in relation to an electronic communication if:

   (a) in all cases – a method is used to identify the person and to indicate the person's approval of the information communicated; and

---

50 At http://scaleplus.law.gov.au/html/pasteact/3/3328/0/PA000170.htm. Section 13 sets out exemptions from this section.

(b) in all cases – having regard to all the relevant circumstances at the time the method was used, the method was as reliable as was appropriate for the purposes for which the information was communicated; and

(c) if the signature is required to be given to a Commonwealth entity, or to a person acting on behalf of a Commonwealth entity, and the entity requires that the method used as mentioned in paragraph (a) be in accordance with particular information technology requirements – the entity's requirement has been met; and

(d) if the signature is required to be given to a person who is neither a Commonwealth entity nor a person acting on behalf of a Commonwealth entity – the person to whom the signature is required to be given consents to that requirement being met by way of the use of the method mentioned in paragraph (a).

Sub-sections (a) and (b) do not prescribe a form, and (b) is purely in terms of functional equivalence. The requirements of the section are cumulative, but presumably (c), which could be technology-specific, would not often apply. There is also a consent requirement in (d).

Another example of pure functional equivalence is the US Federal Electronic Signatures in Global and National Commerce Act 2000.[51]

There are, however, good arguments in favour of technology-specific legislation. Essentially, technology-specific legislation promotes certainty; functional equivalence promotes flexibility. The modern trend is to attempt to harness the advantages of both using two-tier legislation, according differing weights to differing types of signature. This is the position adopted by the EC Directive.

6.5.6 Approach of the EC Directive: the two tiers

EU legislation in this area was delayed by an unwillingness of states to discuss cryptography policy, which was seen as a matter of state security and national defence, and also by a lack of technical standards. In the end, as we saw in section 6.5.2, individual states started to enact their own legislation, technology-specific in both Germany and Italy (that is, along Utah lines), and the EU responded quickly to try to achieve a common legal framework within the Single Market.[52] The Directive is intended to be facilitative, and there was also a concern to promote e-commerce in Europe, seen at that time to be lagging behind the US.[53]

The EC Directive adopts a two-tier approach, defining two different types of electronic signature in Art 2:[54]

---

51 See Reed, *Internet Law: Text and Materials, op cit* fn 11, p 195. This legislation renders obsolete the Utah legislation, which remains of historical interest only.

52 The initiative has enjoyed some success; Germany replaced its original legislation in 2001 with technology-neutral legislation, essentially along EU lines.

53 See, generally, Lodder and Kaspersen, *eDirectives: Guide to European Union Law on E-Commerce, op cit* fn 45, pp 34 *et seq.*

54 The full text of the EC Directive can be found at http://europa.eu.int/eur-lex/pri/en/oj/dat/2000/l_013/l_01320000119en00120020.pdf, or if preferred, www.minstrel.org.uk/papers/1999-93-ec/1999-93-ec-directive.txt (ASCII format).

1. 'electronic signature' means data in electronic form which are attached to or logically associated with other electronic data and which serve as a method of authentication;

2. 'advanced electronic signature' means an electronic signature which meets the following requirements:

   (a) it is uniquely linked to the signatory;

   (b) it is capable of identifying the signatory;

   (c) it is created using means that the signatory can maintain under his sole control; and

   (d) it is linked to the data to which it relates in such a manner that any subsequent change of the data is detectable.

Article 2(1) covers almost any electronic signature. The definition is in terms of functional equivalence and is very much along the lines of the UNCITRAL Model Law. Further provision is then made in Art 5(2):

2. Member States shall ensure that an electronic signature is not denied legal effectiveness and admissibility as evidence in legal proceedings solely on the grounds that it is:

   – in electronic form, or

   – not based upon a qualified certificate, or

   – not based upon a qualified certificate issued by an accredited certification-service-provider, or

   – not created by a secure signature-creation device.

This provides for evidential validity, and is essentially what the UK legislation has brought into force. It does not provide for formal validity.

Article 2(2) is also, in principle at least, a technologically-neutral definition. Further provision is then made in Art 5(1):

1. Member States shall ensure that advanced electronic signatures which are based on a qualified certificate and which are created by a secure-signature-creation device:

   (a) satisfy the legal requirements of a signature in relation to data in electronic form in the same manner as a handwritten signature satisfies those requirements in relation to paper-based data; and

   (b) are admissible as evidence in legal proceedings.

This provides for formal, as well as evidential validity. Indeed, it provides for equivalence to a paper and ink signature.

However, although the advanced electronic signature itself is defined in a technology-neutral way, it must also be based on a qualified certificate and created by a secure signature-creation device. These are themselves further defined, also in Art 2:

'qualified certificate' means a certificate which meets the requirements laid down in Annex I and is provided by a certification-service-provider who fulfils the requirements laid down in Annex II

and

'secure-signature-creation device' means a signature-creation device which meets the requirements laid down in Annex III.

Annex I lays down formal requirements for what a qualified certificate must contain, and Annex II sets out requirements for certification authorities.[55] Annex III sets out requirements for secure signature-creation devices. The annexes are quite detailed. Thus, although Art 2(2), like Art 2(1), appears to be a functionally equivalent definition, the uncertainty problems inherent in the UNCITRAL Model Law are effectively negated by the detailed requirements in the annexes. In any case, for the present at least, the certification requirement effectively ties the advanced electronic signature into a PKI infrastructure.

6.5.7 EC Directive and accreditation

A peculiar characteristic of the EU is its demand for a level playing field among Member States, allowing free competition within the internal market, including free competition for certification service providers. This is wholly antithetical to any idea of prior authorisation, and indeed Art 3(1) provides:

1. Member States shall not make the provision of certification services subject to prior authorisation.

However, there is nothing inherently anti-competitive about a voluntary accreditation scheme, so Art 3(2) continues:

2. Without prejudice to the provisions of paragraph 1, Member States may introduce or maintain voluntary accreditation schemes aiming at enhanced levels of certification-service provision. All conditions related to such schemes must be objective, transparent, proportionate and non-discriminatory. Member States may not limit the number of accredited certification-service-providers for reasons which fall within the scope of this Directive.

The explanation for these provisions can be found in recitals 10–12 of the Directive:

(10) The internal market enables certification-service-providers to develop their cross-border activities with a view to increasing their competitiveness, and thus to offer consumers and businesses new opportunities to exchange information and trade electronically in a secure way, regardless of frontiers; in order to stimulate the Community-wide provision of certification services over open networks, certification-service-providers should be free to provide their services without prior authorisation; prior authorisation means not only any permission whereby the certification-service-provider concerned has to obtain a decision by national authorities before being allowed to provide its certification services, but also any other measures having the same effect;

(11) Voluntary accreditation schemes aiming at an enhanced level of service-provision may offer certification-service-providers the appropriate framework for developing further their services towards the levels of trust, security and quality demanded by the evolving market; such schemes should encourage the development of best practice among certification-service-providers; certification-service-providers should be left free to adhere to and benefit from such accreditation schemes;

(12) Certification services can be offered either by a public entity or a legal or natural person, when it is established in accordance with the national law; whereas Member States should not prohibit certification-service-providers from operating outside

---

55 Or, in EU-speak, 'certification-service-providers'.

voluntary accreditation schemes; it should be ensured that such accreditation schemes do not reduce competition for certification services.

The UK legislation is generally in accord with these provisions, the mechanism for setting up a voluntary accreditation scheme being found in ss 1–6 of the Electronic Communications Act 2000.

In any case, for the advanced electronic signature falling within Art 5(2), the parties need the certainty of knowing that the requirements of the annexes have been met without having to litigate to discover this. There needs to be some method of certifying this, and accordingly Art 3(4) provides:[56]

4.   The conformity of secure signature-creation-devices with the requirements laid down in Annex III shall be determined by appropriate public or private bodies designated by Member States. The Commission shall, pursuant to the procedure laid down in Article 9, establish criteria for Member States to determine whether a body should be designated.

Thus, though there is an ideological problem with compulsory state accreditation requirements, given the free market imperative, in practice the Directive promotes at any rate the intervention of some kind of official body, at least to determine whether the requirements for secure signature-creation devices have been met. There is also a supervision provision in Art 3(3):

3.   Each Member State shall ensure the establishment of an appropriate system that allows for supervision of certification-service-providers which are established on its territory and issue qualified certificates to the public.

The likelihood is, surely, that certification authorities wishing to issue 'advanced electronic signatures which are based on a qualified certificate and which are created by a secure-signature-creation device' will need to be accredited, and their proceedings supervised.

6.5.8   Other two-tier systems

Following the EU lead, after initially enacting a technology-specific provision, Germany has replaced its *Signaturgesetz* with two-tier.[57]

Singapore's Electronic Transactions Act 1998 is also two-tier,[58] though different in some respects from the EU legislation. It provides for electronic signatures and secure electronic signatures, both of which are defined in terms of functional equivalence.[59] Section 8 provides for the electronic signature:

8. (1) Where a rule of law requires a signature, or provides for certain consequences if a document is not signed, an electronic signature satisfies that rule of law.

(2)   An electronic signature may be proved in any manner, including by showing that a procedure existed by which it is necessary for a party, in order to proceed further

---

56   Article 9 sets up an 'Electronic-Signature Committee'.
57   Law Governing Framework Conditions for Electronic Signatures and Amending Other Regulations, 2001, s 2. For an English language version, see www.regtp.de/ imperia/md/content/tech_reg_t/digisign/119.pdf.
58   Singapore statutes, including the ETA, can be found at http://agcvldb4.agc.gov.sg.
59   The electronic signature is so defined in s 2, the interpretation section.

with a transaction, to have executed a symbol or security procedure for the purpose of verifying that an electronic record is that of such party.

This is a functionally equivalent, technologically neutral definition, which appears, however, to cover both evidential and formal requirements.

A secure electronic signature is provided for in s 17, and these enjoy certain factual (rebuttable) presumptions in s 18:

17. If, through the application of a prescribed security procedure or a commercially reasonable security procedure agreed to by the parties involved, it can be verified that an electronic signature was, at the time it was made—

(a) unique to the person using it;

(b) capable of identifying such person;

(c) created in a manner or using a means under the sole control of the person using it; and

(d) linked to the electronic record to which it relates in a manner such that if the record was changed the electronic signature would be invalidated,

such signature shall be treated as a secure electronic signature.

18. (1) In any proceedings involving a secure electronic record, it shall be presumed, unless evidence to the contrary is adduced, that the secure electronic record has not been altered since the specific point in time to which the secure status relates.

(2) In any proceedings involving a secure electronic signature, it shall be presumed, unless evidence to the contrary is adduced, that—

(a) the secure electronic signature is the signature of the person to whom it correlates; and

(b) the secure electronic signature was affixed by that person with the intention of signing or approving the electronic record.

(3) In the absence of a secure electronic record or a secure electronic signature, nothing in this Part shall create any presumption relating to the authenticity and integrity of the electronic record or electronic signature.

Neither s 17 or 18 is technology-specific. However, a digital signature can also be a secure electronic signature, by virtue of s 20:

20. When any portion of an electronic record is signed with a digital signature, the digital signature shall be treated as a secure electronic signature with respect to such portion of the record, if—

(a) the digital signature was created during the operational period of a valid certificate and is verified by reference to the public key listed in such certificate; and

(b) the certificate is considered trustworthy, in that it is an accurate binding of a public key to a person's identity because—

(i) the certificate was issued by a licensed certification authority operating in compliance with the regulations made under section 42;

(ii) the certificate was issued by a certification authority outside Singapore recognised for this purpose by the Controller pursuant to regulations made under section 43;

(iii) the certificate was issued by a department or ministry of the Government, an organ of State or a statutory corporation approved by the Minister to act

> as a certification authority on such conditions as he may by regulations
> impose or specify; or
>
> (iv) the parties have expressly agreed between themselves (sender and
> recipient) to use digital signatures as a security procedure, and the digital
> signature was properly verified by reference to the sender's public key.

This is an alternative method of creating a 'secure electronic signature', allowing the
parties certainty, should they so desire. It is, however, technology-specific, requiring a
digital signature and PKI,[60] and one method is to use a state-licensed CA. There are
then fairly stringent provisions for the control of licensed CAs, and also a liability
regime, which is considered in Chapter 7.

In 2001, UNCITRAL followed up its *Model Law on Electronic Commerce* (1996) with
Model Law on Electronic Signatures (2001).[61] While remaining true to its views on
functional equivalence, UNCITRAL has filled out its earlier text, the new text
promoting certainty to a greater extent than before. Thus, para 4 of the Guide to
Enactment states:

> In a modest but significant addition to the UNCITRAL Model Law on Electronic
> Commerce, the new Model Law offers practical standards against which the technical
> reliability of electronic signatures may be measured.

Article 6(1) and (2) continue to provide for functional equivalence:

1.   Where the law requires a signature of a person, that requirement is met in relation to
     a data message if an electronic signature is used that is as reliable as was
     appropriate for the purpose for which the data message was generated or
     communicated, in the light of all the circumstances, including any relevant
     agreement.

2.   Paragraph 1 applies whether the requirement referred to therein is in the form of an
     obligation or whether the law simply provides consequences for the absence of a
     signature.

Recognising, however, that Art 6(1) might be difficult to operate in practice, Art 6(3)
and (4) provides:

3.   An electronic signature is considered to be reliable for the purpose of satisfying the
     requirement referred to in paragraph 1 if:

     (a) The signature creation data are, within the context in which they are used,
          linked to the signatory and to no other person;

     (b) The signature creation data were, at the time of signing, under the control of the
          signatory and of no other person;

     (c) Any alteration to the electronic signature, made after the time of signing, is
          detectable; and

     (d) Where a purpose of the legal requirement for a signature is to provide assurance
          as to the integrity of the information to which it relates, any alteration made to
          that information after the time of signing is detectable.

---

60   The digital signature is also defined in s 2, the interpretation section, but in a way that is
     technology-specific.
61   Like UNCITRAL *Model Law on Electronic Commerce* (1996), the law on *Electronic Signatures*
     (2001) can be found by going through UNCITRAL's home page (no deep linking possible):
     www.uncitral.org/en-index.htm – they are adopted texts, on e-commerce. The 2001
     document is a downloadable .pdf file.

4. Paragraph 3 does not limit the ability of any person:

   (a) To establish in any other way, for the purpose of satisfying the requirement referred to in paragraph 1, the reliability of an electronic signature; or

   (b) To adduce evidence of the non-reliability of an electronic signature.

This does not quite operate in the manner of the EU legislation, providing one test for evidential and another for formal validity, but instead provides a general test, of which one method to satisfy is then filled out in more certain terms. This is similar in principle to the way in which the Singapore legislation operates.

There are also liability provisions, discussed in the next chapter.

UNCITRAL continues to recognise that writing and signatures can perform different functions in different contexts, and continues to maintain a more flexible position than most of the states.

6.5.9 Further comments on two-tier systems

The EU legislation has a functionally equivalent definition for evidential purposes and a more formal definition for purposes of formal validity. The issue of a qualified certificate by a CA also triggers a liability regime, considered further in the next chapter.

Singapore and UNCITRAL (2001) adopt what appears to be a different approach. Functional equivalence will suffice for all purposes, but if the parties want certainty, there are also ways of ensuring validity without needing to litigate to determine this. In this latter regard, Singapore appears to be far more robust than UNCITRAL; traders in Singapore have methods of ensuring that their signatures will be regarded as 'secure electronic signatures'.

In all cases, however, the actual requirements for the advanced or secure signature are, in effect, that it is better at verifying the identity of the signer and the integrity of the data than the ordinary electronic signature. But as we saw at the end of the last chapter, this will not always be the issue.[62] No real thought appears to have gone into the type of signature which says 'I am very serious' or 'I am giving my informed consent'. It may be, however, that no general provision can be appropriate to apply such a test and that each situation requiring such a signature should be considered on its own merits.

6.5.10 Legislative position in UK

The UK Electronic Communications Act 2000 provides the machinery for setting up voluntary accreditation systems,[63] and provides for evidential validity.[64] It therefore brings partially into force the EC Directive on a Community framework for electronic

---

62 Section 5.6.

63 www.opsi.gov.uk/acts/acts2000/20000007.htm, ss 1–6.

64 *Ibid*, s 7.

signatures. It also gives power to the minister further to change the law,[65] but there is no equivalent of Art 5(1) of the EC Directive, nor, as we will see in the next chapter, is there a liability regime.

Though s 7(1), the validity provision, looks weak, Reed suggests that, in fact,[66] it provides equivalence to a traditional physical signature, and thus satisfies the requirements of the Directive, noting that:

> under current English law, hand-written signatures do not benefit from any particular presumptions of validity, and are simply assessed case-by-case for their evidential effectiveness in authenticating the signed document.

This might be true of evidential, but not of formal issues, where surely the UK law is weak. Section 7 does not address formal validity at all. As the Law Commission observes:[67]

> Whilst section 7 deals with admissibility, it does not provide that electronic signatures will satisfy a statutory signature requirement. It does not, therefore, assist in determining to what extent existing statutory signature requirements are capable of being satisfied electronically.

However, the Law Commission also takes the view that, in general, electronic signatures do satisfy existing formality requirements,[68] and that, therefore, the UK is in line with the EC Directive. No doubt, where formalities are intended to resolve evidential difficulties, a digital signature might suffice, even under existing law, if (but only if) the courts are prepared to adopt a functional approach. There are, however, two problems. First, the English law is itself uncertain, so that it cannot be said with certainty that any digital signature will satisfy formality provisions. Secondly, even if it might, the certainty accorded to the parties by Art 5(1) that if the requirements are met the signature will certainly be valid, is not present in English law. Somebody prepared to lend money, for example, only against a valid guarantee, needs to know, *in advance of parting with the money*, whether the contract of guarantee satisfies the formality requirements of the Statute of Frauds 1677, s 4.[69] It is not enough to discover only at the litigation stage. It follows that legislation is needed to provide the parties with protection equivalent to that in the Directive.

Where the intention is to ensure informed consent, or a genuine intention to be bound, or that all terms are recorded in one document, then no digital signature is likely to suffice under existing law.[70] In such cases, for example with contracts for the sale of land, the Law Commission takes the view that it would be very difficult, indeed risky, to provide appropriate general legislation and that each situation should be

---

65 *Ibid*, s 8.

66 Reed, 'What is a signature?', *op cit* fn 14, section 5.2.

67 Law Commission, *Electronic Commerce: Formal Requirements in Commercial Transactions (Advice from the Law Commission)*, *op cit* fn 17, para 3.27. There are also guidelines, issued by the Judicial Studies Board, introducing digital signatures to judges at www.jsboard.co.uk/publications/digisigs/index.htm.

68 There is quite a detailed discussion at *ibid*, paras 3.24 *et seq*, where the Law Commission reviews (among others) the cases that we considered earlier in this chapter.

69 Section 4 requires a guarantee contract to be evidenced by a memorandum in writing, and signed by the guarantor. See also section 6.3.1, above.

70 For the sort of situation we are considering, see section 5.6.

considered on its own merits.[71] Indeed, if its conclusion is correct, it might even be desirable sometimes to impose greater formality requirements to prevent electronic signatures being valid in some circumstances. Certainly, in such cases, any legislation needs to address the form of the digital signature; functional equivalence is not enough.

The UK government concedes, incidentally, that its legislation is out of line with the requirements of the Directive for a liability regime. This is the subject of the next chapter.

---

71 Law Commission, *Electronic Commerce: Formal Requirements in Commercial Transactions (Advice from the Law Commission)*, *op cit* fn 17, para 3.43.

LIABILITY OF CERTIFICATION AUTHORITIES

The issue we are going to consider in this chapter is this:[1]

> Carol, a CA, mistakenly certifies that impostor Eve is Alice. Consequently, Bob, believing the electronic message has come from the truthful and trustworthy Alice, suffers loss. Consider the basis, if any, upon which Carol can be liable to Bob (under current UK law). Is there any possibility that Alice might be liable to Bob? If so, in what circumstances?

There is no legislation in force in the UK, so we will begin by examining the English common law. Then we will examine legislation in the EU and elsewhere.

Let us perhaps make the issues more concrete. At the beginning of Chapter 5, we considered an electronic bill of lading. Suppose Bob has contracted to purchase 100 bales of rubber from Eve, paying against the electronic bill of lading tendered. He is happy to do this, even though he has had no chance to inspect the bales, knowing that Alice, the ship's master, has signed the electronic bill of lading showing that 100 bales have been loaded on board the ship. In fact, only 10 bales have been loaded, but Eve, by posing as Alice, has had her own public key certified (by Carol) as Alice's. She has therefore been able to sign the bill of lading herself, showing 100 bales to have been loaded. Bob would never have paid had he known that the bill of lading had been signed by Eve, rather than Alice. Eve disappears with the purchase price and Bob, having relied on Carol's certification, has lost the value of 90 bales of rubber.

There are many other scenarios which could be conceived. Eve might be a competitor with whom Bob would never trade, or even perhaps an enemy in wartime. Alice, but not Eve, might be entitled to trade discounts. Eve might be a child, not entitled to purchase Bob's adult merchandise. All the scenarios have in common, however, that Carol has made an incorrect statement of fact (the identity of the signatory), which Bob has relied upon and that, if Bob has suffered loss as a result, it will be economic loss, not damage to person or property.[2]

It is also worth noting that Carol might issue various classes of certificate, offering different levels of security. It seems likely that these levels of security will be published, so that anyone relying on a certificate will be aware of the degree of security it purports to offer.[3]

---

1   See, in general, Hindelang, S, 'No remedy for disappointed trust? The liability regime for certification authorities towards third parties outwith the EC Directive in England and Germany compared' [2002] 1 JILT, www2.warwick.ac.uk/fac/soc/law/elj/jilt/2002_1/hindelang (there is also a description here of the mechanics of a digital signature). Note that the identities of personae in any discussion of cryptography is conventional, dating from discussions of the original RSA algorithm in 1977.

2   In the bales of rubber example, Bob never obtained property in the missing 90 bales, if indeed they have ever existed at all, the loss he has suffered being their value.

3   For an example, see the various classes of certificate offered by GlobalSign: www.globalsign.net/digital_certificate/index.cfm and links therefrom. Note that with the personal certificate at www.globalsign.net/digital_certificate/personalsign/index.cfm, GlobalSign say what steps they take to verify identity and also place a cap on liability, these varying with the class of certificate.

There are only two possibilities under English common law: an action in contract, or an action in tort.

Professor Reed has observed that there 'is no physical world activity which corresponds to that of a CA, and thus the obligations of CAs and the extent of their liability under existing law are difficult to determine'.[4] There are, however, physical world activities that are analogous to the operation of a CA. There are real world cases where X certifies facts to Y, being aware of the possibility that they might be communicated to, and relied upon by Z, who will suffer loss if the facts are incorrect. There are also real world cases where X publishes information generally, which is relied upon by Z. It is therefore possible to deduce at least the general principles upon which Carol (X) will incur liability to Bob (Z).

7.1   CAROL'S LIABILITY TO BOB IN CONTRACT

7.1.1   The problem in outline

The basic problem is that it is unlikely that there will be a direct communication, and hence an express contract, between Carol and Bob.[5] Carol's only direct communication is likely to be with Eve, although, of course, she knows that Eve will circulate her ID certificate, and that it might be relied upon by other parties. If repositories are set up,[6] which will hold ID Certificates for CAs, there may be a direct relationship between a repository and an enquirer, but this cannot necessarily be predicted. Another possibility might be for Carol to publish public keys, for example on a website. In that case, communication is to the world rather than to Bob in particular.

Professor Reed postulates the possibility that from Bob checking Carol's certificate revocation list (CRL):[7]

> ... it might be possible for the courts to imply a contract from that communication. The relying party's message would be the offer, agreeing to rely on the certificate if in return the CA made promises about the accuracy of the information in the certificate. The CA's response that the certificate was still valid would be the acceptance.

It is not entirely clear what the implication is, but if it is that the courts would strive to imply an essentially fictitious contract from Bob's checking of the CRL then I would suggest that that is clearly incorrect. The courts have indicated that they will not imply fictitious contracts. In *The Aramis*, Bingham LJ took the view that:[8]

> it would, in my view, be contrary to principle to countenance the implication of a contract from conduct if the conduct relied upon is no more consistent with an intention to contract than with an intention not to contract. It must, surely, be necessary to identify

---

4   Reed, C, *Internet Law: Text and Materials*, 2nd edn, 2004, Cambridge: CUP, p 161.
5   We are here assuming an open system. In a closed system, there could be a contractual relationship between Carol and Bob; for example, in Bolero in section 6.3, Bolero itself acts as the CA and all parties contract with Bolero.
6   As described by Reed, *Internet Law: Text and Materials*, *op cit* fn 4, p 151.
7   *Ibid*, p 161. Hindelang, 'No remedy for disappointed trust?', *op cit* fn 1, section 4.1.1, postulates Bob being suspicious of the certificate.
8   [1989] 1 Lloyd's Rep 213, p 224.

conduct referable to the contract contended for or, at the very least, conduct inconsistent with there being no contract made between the parties to the effect contended for. Put another way, I think it must be fatal to the implication of a contract if the parties would or might have acted exactly as they did in the absence of a contract.

An even stronger statement can be found in *The Gudermes* three years later. Staughton LJ said that:[9]

> What [the parties] do must be consistent only with there being a new contract implied, and inconsistent with there being no such contract.

One could hardly argue that examination of the CRL was 'inconsistent with there being no such contract'. We are going to have to look for something that can reasonably be construed as a promise by one party (the offer), relied upon by the other party (the acceptance).

Of course, if Bob actually agreed to rely on the certificate if, in return, Carol made promises about the accuracy of the information in the certificate, and in response to this, in a subsequent communication, Carol did so, then of course there would be a contract. Carol's communication would have to come after Bob's interrogation of the CRL, since Bob's offer must surely precede Carol's acceptance. The scenario is possible, but surely unlikely. Usually all Carol will have done is publish the CRL in advance, and the idea that Bob positively undertakes to rely on the certificate (presumably exposing himself to a breach of contract action if he does not) is surely absurd.

At any rate, the following discussion assumes no direct communication, and hence no express contract between Carol and Bob.

7.1.2   Third party rights under express contract

A possibility, which would also depend upon details of the communication, is a contract between Carol and Eve, granting third party benefits to Bob.[10] Section 1(1) of the Contracts (Rights of Third Parties) Act 1999 allows Bob to enforce a term of the contract if either the contract expressly provides that he may, or the term purports to confer a benefit on him. Section 1(3) provides that:[11]

> The third party must be expressly identified in the contract by name, as a member of a class or as answering a particular description but need not be in existence when the contract is entered into.

Bob could be identified as a member of a class, for example of those relying on the certificate. Though there is no doubt that this is possible in principle, it depends on the terms of the contract between Carol and Eve (the applicant for the certificate). It also depends on the validity of that contract. If Eve were a minor, or an enemy in time of war, there would be no contract. More generally, however, since Carol believes she is contracting with Alice, rather than the impersonator Eve, there may not be a contract between Carol and Eve.[12] Even if Eve is present in person, the identity of the

---

9   *Mitsui & Co Ltd v Novorossiysk Shipping Co (The Gudermes)* [1993] 1 Lloyd's Rep 311, p 320.
10   See Reed, *Internet Law: Text and Materials*, op cit fn 4, p 162.
11   Note that this Act does not apply in Scotland.
12   The relevant authorities are referenced at Chapter 9, fn 64.

contracting party is surely crucial, and arguments for the validity of the contract from cases such as *Lewis v Averay* ought not to apply.[13]

7.1.3   Implied contract

Even in the absence of direct communication between Carol and Bob, it does not necessarily follow that there will be no contract between them. The issue of the certificate could still constitute an offer to Bob, accepted by his reliance upon it. The position is similar to the well known case of *Carlill v Carbolic Smoke Ball Co*,[14] although it is not on all fours. There, the defendants, who produced a medical preparation called 'The Carbolic Smoke Ball', issued an advertisement in which they offered to pay £100 to any person who contracted influenza after having used one of their smoke balls in a specified manner and for a specified period. The plaintiff, on the faith of the advertisement, bought one of the balls, used it in the manner and for the period specified, but nevertheless contracted influenza, and the Court of Appeal held that she was entitled to sue for the £100 in contract. The advertisement constituted the offer, accepted by the plaintiff's use of the smoke ball. The condition being triggered, she was entitled to the money offered.

The case shares with the present scenario that there was no direct communication between defendant and plaintiff. There was an open communication to anyone who read the advertisement, whereas Carol may communicate only with the applicant for the certificate. However, if Carol places the certificate on her own website, the communication position is essentially the same as in *Carlill*. The case also establishes that there is no need for the receiver to communicate his acceptance of any offer made to Carol.[15] There, however, the similarities end. In *Carlill*, the advertisement contained a precise offer and specified a mode of performance. Lindley LJ treated it as 'an express promise to pay £100 in certain events'. He also observed that it must have been a serious offer, and not a mere puff, on the basis of the statement that '£1,000 is deposited with the Alliance Bank, shewing our sincerity in the matter'.[16] Albeit that this was an unusual contract because the offer was unilateral, nonetheless this had all the makings of an express, rather than an implied contract. The situation was not really equivalent even to Carol placing a certificate on its own website, which merely states a fact and asks nothing of anybody reading it. There was no consideration difficulty in *Carlill*, the taking of the smoke ball being requested, and constituting sufficient detriment:[17] 'Inconvenience sustained by one party at the request of the other is enough to create a consideration.' By contrast, Carol does not request anything of Bob.

The decision of Mocatta J in *V/O Rasnoimport v Guthrie & Co Ltd* is, however, a much closer analogy[18] and, if applicable, suggests that there would be a contract

---

13   [1972] 1 QB 198.

14   [1893] 1 QB 256. See also Reed, *Internet Law: Text and Materials, op cit* fn 4, p 161.

15   See Lindley LJ [1893] 1 QB 256, at p 262, Bowen LJ, at p 269, but in any case, this is part of the *ratio* of *Carlill*. Whether communication of acceptance is required depends on the terms of the offer, however: see Bowen LJ, at p 270.

16   [1893] 1 QB 256, p 261. Also Bowen LJ, at p 268.

17   Bowen LJ, at p 271.

18   [1966] 1 Lloyd's Rep 1.

between Bob and Carol, whether or not Carol published the certificate on her own website. The defendants (loading brokers, who were acting in the same capacity as a ship's master) had issued a bill of lading for 225 bales of rubber loaded on board a ship, whereas only 90 bales had actually been loaded. The bill of lading was issued to the shipper, who then sent it to the plaintiffs, who paid against it. The situation is very similar to our own example. All that was expressly communicated was the fact of shipment; unlike *Carlill*, there was no express promise. Moreover, the communication was not to the plaintiffs directly, but to the shippers, but in the expectation that the bill of lading would be transferred and relied upon by someone in the position of the plaintiffs. This in fact happened. The plaintiffs took up and paid for a bill of lading representing that 225 bales had been loaded, when in fact only 90 were on board the vessel, the remainder having been stolen, prior to loading, by third parties, unbeknown to the defendants. The plaintiffs' loss was, of course, the value of the 135 bales of rubber for which they had been paid, but which had not been loaded.

On analogy with (among other authorities) *Carlill v Carbolic Smoke Ball Co*,[19] Mocatta J held the defendants liable to the plaintiffs in contract. The problem was implying a warranty, or promise, from a statement of fact that the bales had been loaded. There was, however, longstanding authority that a ship's master, or loading broker, has the shipowner's authority to sign bills only in respect of goods loaded on board the ship.[20] The defendants, by issuing a bill of lading for 225 bales of rubber, impliedly warranted that they had the authority to sign for them (because they would have had authority to sign for them, had 225 bales been loaded), whereas they actually had authority to sign only for the 90 bales which were loaded. The warranty of authority was made, not only to the shipper, to whom the bill of lading was issued, but to all persons who, in the ordinary course of business, might be expected to act and rely upon the representation therein that 225 bales had been shipped. It was an offer to enter into a contract, accepted by an indorsee taking the bill of lading in reliance upon the representation therein. In *Rasnoimport*, like *Carlill*, the offer was made by the defendant, an open offer to anyone who relied upon it. Thus, the plaintiffs became entitled, if their reliance had caused them detriment, to recover damages for breach of warranty of authority, a species of contractual claim.

Rasnoimport is analogous to Carol making an open offer by issuing the certificate to Eve, which is accepted by Bob's reliance upon it. Carol expects the certificate to be circulated, just as the defendants in *Rasnoimport* expected the bill of lading to be negotiated. It was possible to imply a warranty in *Rasnoimport*. It might also be possible to imply a warranty in our own scenario, since Carol, by issuing the certificate, surely represents that she has Alice's authority to do so. Equally clearly, there is a breach of this warranty of authority, since it is Eve, not Alice, who has applied for the certificate.

The reasoning in *Rasnoimport* supports the existence of a contract between Carol and Bob. The problem is to imply a promise from a statement of fact, but the case suggests that at least a warranty of authority may be implied from a statement of fact

---

19 Though the case is clearly a significant extension of *Carlill*.
20 *Grant v Norway* (1851) 10 CB 665.

alone, even when that statement of fact is simply in the form of certifying the accuracy of a statement made by somebody else. It is a one-off, first instance decision, however, and very much at the limits of implication of contracts. It might be a mistake to rely too heavily on the case.

7.1.4   Extent of liability

In principle, liability in contract is strict (there was no negligence in *Rasnoimport*).[21] However, if there is a contract, it will surely be on the terms of the representation. Carol will typically state the steps it has taken to identify Alice and should only be liable for failure to carry out those steps. In the manner of carrying out the steps, a due diligence obligation would probably be implied. Limits on liability would be subject to the usual control over contractual exemption clauses in the Unfair Contract Terms Act 1977 and the Unfair Terms in Consumer Contracts Regulations 1999.

7.2   CAROL'S LIABILITY TO BOB IN TORT

If Carol's certificate had been issued fraudulently, there would be liability in deceit on the principles of *Derry v Peek*.[22] Fraud by Carol alone will surely be rare, a more likely scenario being a collusive fraud between Eva and Carol. It is far more likely for Carol to be merely negligent, in which case the main problem is that Bob's loss will normally be economic only, for which traditionally there is no recovery in negligence.[23] If Carol is not negligent, there will be no liability at all, the burden of proof being on the claimant.

It is possible that Carol's position can be brought within the principles of *Hedley Byrne & Co Ltd v Heller & Partners Ltd*,[24] a view strongly supported by Martin Hogg, on the grounds that 'the whole purpose of a certificate is for third party reliance',[25] but the extent of *Hedley Byrne*'s application is by no means certain and the case is not on all fours with Carol's situation. In *Hedley Byrne*, the defendant bank was aware that the negligent misstatement, about the financial stability of one of its customers, would be relied upon by the plaintiffs, who wanted to know if they could safely extend credit to the bank's customer in a substantial sum. In other words, the defendants had in mind reliance by the particular plaintiffs, to whom the statement was made directly, for a specific transaction. Our situation is very different; Carol makes no statement directly to Bob; Bob is merely one of many people who might foreseeably rely on the certificate, and Carol typically has in mind no particular transaction.

---

21 See paras 4–8 of the statement of facts: [1966] 1 Lloyd's Rep 1, pp 3–4.
22 (1889) 14 App Cas 337.
23 *Weller & Co v Foot and Mouth Disease Research Institute* [1966] 1 QB 569, affirmed by the House of Lords in *The Aliakmon* [1986] AC 785.
24 [1964] AC 465.
25 Hogg, M, 'Secrecy and signatures', in Edwards, L and Waelde, C (eds), *Law and the Internet: A Framework for Electronic Commerce*, 2nd edn, 2000, Oxford: Hart, p 49, note 65.

Hedley Byrne liability has been extended beyond its original very narrow limit, however.[26] In *Smith v Eric S Bush*,[27] the House of Lords held a duty of care to be owed by a valuer to a purchaser of property even though the valuation was made for the mortgagee, because the valuer was aware that the prospective purchaser (the particular purchaser, not just any purchaser) would use that valuation to decide whether to purchase that particular property. Also, ultimately the purchaser had paid for the valuation, albeit through the intermediary of the mortgagee. In *Smith v Eric S Bush*,[28] Lord Griffiths required there to be an assumption of responsibility by the maker of the statement, not merely in general, but to the person who acted upon it.

By contrast, it is by no means certain that merely to issue a certificate identifying Alice, which will foreseeably be relied upon not only by Bob but by anyone to whom Eve (masquerading as Alice) shows it, in relation not to any particular transaction but to transactions in general, will give rise to *Hedley Byrne* liability. Indeed, the House of Lords held there to be no liability in *Caparo Industries plc v Dickman*,[29] though it was foreseeable that the plaintiffs, in deciding whether to purchase more shares in a public limited company, would rely on the defendant chartered accountants' audit of the company. The House of Lords expressly rejected the notion that economic loss could be recoverable merely because it was the foreseeable consequence of a negligent misstatement,[30] considering also proximity of relationship and the reasonableness or otherwise of imposing a duty.[31] In *Caparo*, no duty of care was owed, the relationship being insufficiently proximate, even if it was foreseeable that the certified accounts would be relied upon by those among whom they were circulated. Lord Bridge distinguished *Caparo* from *Smith v Eric Bush* as follows:[32]

> The situation is entirely different where a statement is put into more or less general circulation and may foreseeably be relied on by strangers to the maker of the statement for any one of a variety of different purposes which the maker of the statement has no specific reason to anticipate. To hold the maker of the statement to be under a duty of care in respect of the accuracy of the statement to all and sundry for any purpose for which they may choose to rely on it is not only to subject him, in the classic words of Cardozo CJ to 'liability in an indeterminate amount for an indeterminate time to an indeterminate class';[33] it is also to confer on the world at large a quite unwarranted entitlement to appropriate for their own purposes the benefit of the expert knowledge or professional expertise attributed to the maker of the statement.

---

26 Indeed, there are *dicta* (in *Hedley Byrne* itself, *per* Lord Devlin at p 532) suggesting that today, tort liability might be an alternative in the *Rasnoimport* situation. The case referred to is *Heskell v Continental Express Ltd* [1950] 1 All ER 1033, the facts of which are similar to *Rasnoimport*.

27 [1990] 1 AC 831. There were in fact two conjoined appeals, raising essentially similar issues, *Smith v Eric S Bush* and *Harris v Wyre Forest District Council*.

28 [1990] 1 AC 831, p 862.

29 [1990] 2 AC 605.

30 In the light of this decision, it is very difficult to justify the negligence reasoning in *Ministry of Housing and Local Government v Sharp* [1970] 2 QB 223.

31 In this regard, *Caparo* was distinguished, and a duty of care owed to the plaintiff, in *Spring v Guardian Assurance Ltd* [1995] 2 AC 296. The relationship between the parties was very close in *Spring*, however, and there is nothing in the case to suggest that foreseeability of economic loss is itself sufficient to found an action for negligent misstatement.

32 In *Caparo* [1990] 2 AC 605, p 621.

33 Here Lord Bridge notes see *Ultramares Corp v Touche* (1931) 174 NE 441, p 444.

Carol's position will normally be more akin to *Caparo* than *Bush*, although the criticism at the end of Lord Bridge's quote would not apply to Bob, since he is clearly intended to rely on Carol's professional expertise.

A similar distinction between limited and general circulation was also adopted by Lord Oliver, although the test he actually adopted might allow Bob to recover from Carol:[34]

> (1) the advice is required for a purpose, whether particularly specified or generally described, which is made known, either actually or inferentially, to the adviser at the time when the advice is given; (2) the adviser knows, either actually or inferentially, that his advice will be communicated to the advisee, either specifically or as a member of an ascertainable class, in order that it should be used by the advisee for that purpose; (3) it is known either actually or inferentially, that the advice so communicated is likely to be acted upon by the advisee for that purpose without independent inquiry, and (4) it is so acted upon by the advisee to his detriment.

Ultimately, the question is whether there is an assumption of responsibility by Carol towards Bob.[35] If Bob is no more than simply one of a class of people who might foreseeably be expected to rely on the certificate, then this question is likely to be answered in the negative. On the other hand, if Bob is known particularly, or perhaps if Carol is aware of the particular transaction, then tortious liability might attach. In *Bush*, the plaintiff was really the only foreseeable third party. By contrast, Carol's certificate is typically put into more or less general circulation, more general even than the bill of lading in *Rasnoimport*. It is true that it is envisaged, indeed intended, that someone in Bob's position will rely on it, but *Caparo* suggests that will not of itself be enough.

In *Niru Battery Manufacturing Co v Milestone Trading Ltd*,[36] SGS (an independent surveyor) were held liable to Niru (purchasers), on the basis of *Hedley Byrne v Heller*,[37] for falsely and negligently certifying that goods (lead ingots to be used in batteries) had been loaded. The facts are similar to our own situation in that SGS issued the certificate to the sellers rather than to the claimants and had no contractual relationship with the claimants. The relationship between the parties was, however, quite close; SGS knew the identity of the purchaser, that the purchaser was an Iranian company and that the certificate was required in order to satisfy the Iranian authorities.[38] It should not necessarily be assumed that liability would attach where the certificate was simply issued for general circulation. Arguably, this case is closely analogous to *Smith v Eric S Bush*, SGS being aware of the identity of the particular purchaser, and the reason he required their certificate.

This review of the authorities suggests that Carol will not normally be liable to Bob. It is, however, possible that the law would be extended, to fill a lacuna. The law is not set in stone and it has been said that categories of negligence can increase

---

34 [1990] 2 AC 605, p 638.
35 See also *Henderson v Merrett Syndicates* [1995] 2 AC 145.
36 [2002] EWHC 1425 (Comm), affirmed [2004] 1 Lloyd's Rep 344. The case is also reported at [2004] QB 985, but these aspects of the decision are omitted from the QB reports.
37 [1964] AC 465.
38 See paras 66–67 of the first instance judgment.

'incrementally and by analogy with established categories'.[39] There is a case for doing that here, since if Bob has no action against Carol, he will probably have no action against anybody.[40]

We might reasonably conclude, then, that *Hedley Byrne* liability is possible, but in the normal case unlikely.

7.2.1   Extent of liability

Assuming liability at all, Carol is liable only if she is negligent, the burden of proof being on Bob. She is also liable only in respect of the responsibility she has assumed. Therefore, any qualifications in the certificate ought, in principle, to be capable of protecting her.

This, however, is subject to a qualification. Section 2 of the Unfair Contract Terms Act 1977 provides, at any rate for this type of loss, that: 'A person cannot by reference to any contract term or to a notice ... exclude or restrict his liability for negligence except in so far as the term or notice satisfies the requirement of reasonableness.' In *Smith v Bush*, the House of Lords held that this provision applied to a disclaimer which otherwise might have prevented the duty from arising in the first place. Presumably this would apply were Carol to state something like 'No responsibility is accepted for any statements implied by the issue of this certificate'. However, if Carol clearly stated the steps she had undertaken to ascertain Alice's identity, it is difficult to see how she has assumed any responsibility apart from as to the accuracy of that statement. She should therefore surely only be liable if she has failed to take those steps. Similarly, if Carol states that the certificate is to be relied upon only for transactions up to £X, there should be no liability should Bob rely on it for a higher value transaction, not because this amounts to a disclaimer, but because his reliance has not been reasonable. It must be said, however, that *Smith v Bush* has left the matter rather unclear.

7.3   ALICE'S LIABILITY

Suppose Alice has been negligent in the use of her private key, allowing Eve to impersonate her. There is no question of contractual liability, except perhaps in a closed system such as the Bolero scheme, considered in section 6.3, where all the parties can be in a contractual relationship with each other. There might, in principle, be negligence liability, but *Caparo* almost certainly precludes this. The case is indeed weaker than that against Carol, because there will typically have been no communication of any kind between Alice and Bob.

7.4   CONCLUSION ON COMMON LAW LIABILITY

In the absence of legislation, Carol's liability to Bob is far from certain, yet Bob foreseeably suffers loss as a result of her negligence. Moreover, it is difficult to see how

---

39   *Caparo Industries plc v Dickman* [1990] 2 AC 605, at pp 618 and 634, *per* Lords Bridge and Oliver.
40   One of the grounds for extending liability (by a 3:2 majority) in *White v Jones* [1995] 2 AC 207.

Bob can protect himself. If there is no liability, there is at least an arguable lacuna, and negligence on the part of Alice, in particular, creates a clear lacuna. The common law might fill lacunae, but the process is uncertain and unreliable. Quite apart from the position adopted by the EU, which is examined below at section 7.5.4, there is a strong case for legislation in the UK if e-commerce is to prosper.

7.5   LEGISLATION: SOME GENERAL PRINCIPLES

Many of the states which have enacted legislation on electronic signatures have also created liability regimes to deal with the problems considered here. No clear international consensus appears yet to have emerged. The liability of CAs is limited, however, either to due diligence (EU), or by reference to legislative requirements (for example, Utah, now superseded), or statements in the certificate (Singapore).

If a particular regime is to apply to one area of commercial activity, then there is a case at least for allowing parties to choose whether they make themselves subject to it. It would be quite unreasonable to impose a special regime, for example, on an informal certifier (for example, in a chain of trust as used by Burmese freedom fighters). Where the legislation requires licensing, this is not a problem but, as we have seen, under the EC Directive, compulsory licensing is expressly ruled out. However, by virtue of Annex I, 'Qualified certificates must contain: ... an indication that the certificate is issued as a qualified certificate', and liability is imposed only on issuers of qualified certificates, so liability can only be imposed on a CA which has chosen to take the benefit of the legislation.

Utah and Singapore, but not the EU and the UK, also provide for subscriber liability (effectively, Alice's liability for the compromise of her private key).

7.5.1   Utah

The now-superseded Utah legislation limited CA liability by reference to legislative requirements; § 303(3) provided:

> (3) By issuing a certificate, a licensed certification authority certifies to all who reasonably rely on the information contained in the certificate that:
>
>   ...
>
>   (d) the licensed certification authority has complied with all applicable laws of this state governing issuance of the certificate.

Complying with the relevant laws provided a complete immunity, § 309(2) providing that:

> (2) Unless a licensed certification authority waives application of this subsection, a licensed certification authority is:
>
>   (a) not liable for any loss caused by reliance on a false or forged digital signature of a subscriber, if, with respect to the false or forged digital signature, the certification authority complied with all material requirements of this chapter.

The section went on to limit liability in excess of the amount specified in the certificate as its recommended reliance limit.

7.5.2   Singapore

The principle adopted in Singapore is that CAs can issue a certification practice statement, in which case their liability is defined by it (see s 30(1), below); otherwise, it is defined by general requirements (which effectively provide for strict liability: see s 30(2)). Section 30 of the Singapore Electronic Transactions Act 1998 provides:

> 30. (1) By issuing a certificate, a certification authority represents to any person who reasonably relies on the certificate or a digital signature verifiable by the public key listed in the certificate that the certification authority has issued the certificate in accordance with any applicable certification practice statement incorporated by reference in the certificate, or of which the relying person has notice.
>
> (2) In the absence of such certification practice statement, the certification authority represents that it has confirmed that—
>
> (a) the certification authority has complied with all applicable requirements of this Act in issuing the certificate, and if the certification authority has published the certificate or otherwise made it available to such relying person, that the subscriber listed in the certificate has accepted it;
>
> (b) the subscriber identified in the certificate holds the private key corresponding to the public key listed in the certificate;
>
> (c) the subscriber's public key and private key constitute a functioning key pair;
>
> (d) all information in the certificate is accurate, unless the certification authority has stated in the certificate or incorporated by reference in the certificate a statement that the accuracy of specified information is not confirmed; and
>
> (e) the certification authority has no knowledge of any material fact which if it had been included in the certificate would adversely affect the reliability of the representations in paragraphs (a) to (d).
>
> (3) Where there is an applicable certification practice statement which has been incorporated by reference in the certificate, or of which the relying person has notice, subsection (2) shall apply to the extent that the representations are not inconsistent with the certification practice statement.

Duties are also imposed on subscribers whose key pairs have been certified. Under s 38(2):

> (2) By accepting a certificate issued by himself or a certification authority, the subscriber listed in the certificate certifies to all who reasonably rely on the information contained in the certificate that—
>
> (a) the subscriber rightfully holds the private key corresponding to the public key listed in the certificate;
>
> (b) all representations made by the subscriber to the certification authority and material to the information listed in the certificate are true; and
>
> (c) all information in the certificate that is within the knowledge of the subscriber is true.

Under s 39:

> 39. (1) By accepting a certificate issued by a certification authority, the subscriber identified in the certificate assumes a duty to exercise reasonable care to retain control of the private key corresponding to the public key listed in such certificate and prevent its disclosure to a person not authorised to create the subscriber's digital signature.
>
> (2)   Such duty shall continue during the operational period of the certificate and during any period of suspension of the certificate.

It is not made clear to whom the duty is owed, but presumably it must be someone such as Bob, who is likely to rely on any identity certificate issued to the subscriber. This would impose liability, for example, on Alice, were she to lose her private key, allowing Eve to impersonate her.

7.5.3 UNCITRAL *Model Law on Electronic Signatures* 2001

As in the Singapore legislation, provision is made for both signatory and CA liability (Alice and Carol respectively), in Arts 8–10:

Article 8. Conduct of the signatory

1. Where signature creation data can be used to create a signature that has legal effect, each signatory shall:

   (a) Exercise reasonable care to avoid unauthorized use of its signature creation data;

   (b) Without undue delay, utilize means made available by the certification service provider pursuant to article 9 of this Law, or otherwise use reasonable efforts, to notify any person that may reasonably be expected by the signatory to rely on or to provide services in support of the electronic signature if:

      (i) The signatory knows that the signature creation data have been compromised; or

      (ii) The circumstances known to the signatory give rise to a substantial risk that the signature creation data may have been compromised;

   (c) Where a certificate is used to support the electronic signature, exercise reasonable care to ensure the accuracy and completeness of all material representations made by the signatory that are relevant to the certificate throughout its life cycle or that are to be included in the certificate.

2. A signatory shall bear the legal consequences of its failure to satisfy the requirements of paragraph 1.

Article 9. Conduct of the certification service provider

1. Where a certification service provider provides services to support an electronic signature that may be used for legal effect as a signature, that certification service provider shall:

   (a) Act in accordance with representations made by it with respect to its policies and practices;

   (b) Exercise reasonable care to ensure the accuracy and completeness of all material representations made by it that are relevant to the certificate throughout its life cycle or that are included in the certificate;

   (c) Provide reasonably accessible means that enable a relying party to ascertain from the certificate:

      (i) The identity of the certification service provider;

      (ii) That the signatory that is identified in the certificate had control of the signature creation data at the time when the certificate was issued;

      (iii) That signature creation data were valid at or before the time when the certificate was issued;

   (d) Provide reasonably accessible means that enable a relying party to ascertain, where relevant, from the certificate or otherwise:

       (i) The method used to identify the signatory;

      (ii) Any limitation on the purpose or value for which the signature creation data or the certificate may be used;

     (iii) That the signature creation data are valid and have not been compromised;

     (iv) Any limitation on the scope or extent of liability stipulated by the certification service provider;

      (v) Whether means exist for the signatory to give notice pursuant to article 8, paragraph 1 (b), of this Law;

     (vi) Whether a timely revocation service is offered;

  (e) Where services under subparagraph (d) (v) are offered, provide a means for a signatory to give notice pursuant to article 8, paragraph 1 (b), of this Law and, where services under subparagraph (d) (vi) are offered, ensure the availability of a timely revocation service;

  (f) Utilize trustworthy systems, procedures and human resources in performing its services.

2. A certification service provider shall bear the legal consequences of its failure to satisfy the requirements of paragraph 1.

Though the certification service provider (CSP) is required to act 'in accordance with representations made by it with respect to its policies and practices', the bulk of this provision is concerned with reasonable care to follow procedures. Article 9(1)(f) is filled out by Art 10:

Article 10. Trustworthiness

For the purposes of article 9, paragraph 1 (f), of this Law in determining whether, or to what extent, any systems, procedures and human resources utilized by a certification service provider are trustworthy, regard may be had to the following factors:

(a) Financial and human resources, including existence of assets;

(b) Quality of hardware and software systems;

(c) Procedures for processing of certificates and applications for certificates and retention of records;

(d) Availability of information to signatories identified in certificates and to potential relying parties;

(e) Regularity and extent of audit by an independent body;

(f) The existence of a declaration by the State, an accreditation body or the certification service provider regarding compliance with or existence of the foregoing; or

(g) Any other relevant factor.

Even the conduct of the relying party is controlled, under Art 11:

Article 11. Conduct of the relying party

A relying party shall bear the legal consequences of its failure:

(a) To take reasonable steps to verify the reliability of an electronic signature; or

(b) Where an electronic signature is supported by a certificate, to take reasonable steps:

    (i) To verify the validity, suspension or revocation of the certificate; and

   (ii) To observe any limitation with respect to the certificate.

What UNCITRAL have done, in effect, in order to maintain a position of technological neutrality, is to define closely the responsibilities of each of the parties. This is a very comprehensive piece of model legislation.

7.5.4 The EU

Article 6 of the EC Directive (1999/93/EC) on a Community framework for electronic signatures imposes minimum liability standards, but only for issuers of 'qualified' certificates, with a defence if 'the certification-service-provider proves that he has not acted negligently'. Article 6 provides:

1. As a minimum, Member States shall ensure that by issuing a certificate as a qualified certificate to the public or by guaranteeing such a certificate to the public a certification-service-provider is liable for damage caused to any entity or legal or natural person who reasonably relies on that certificate:

   (a) as regards the accuracy at the time of issuance of all information contained in the qualified certificate and as regards the fact that the certificate contains all the details prescribed for a qualified certificate;

   (b) for assurance that at the time of the issuance of the certificate, the signatory identified in the qualified certificate held the signature-creation data corresponding to the signature-verification data given or identified in the certificate;

   (c) for assurance that the signature-creation data and the signature-verification data can be used in a complementary manner in cases where the certification-service-provider generates them both;

   unless the certification-service-provider proves that he has not acted negligently.

2. As a minimum Member States shall ensure that a certification-service-provider who has issued a certificate as a qualified certificate to the public is liable for damage caused to any entity or legal or natural person who reasonably relies on the certificate for failure to register revocation of the certificate unless the certification-service-provider proves that he has not acted negligently.

This is concerned primarily with the accuracy of the information itself, rather than conformity with procedures. Note that it is for the certification-service-provider to prove that he has not acted negligently, not the other way round, as under UK common law.

CSPs are also entitled to limit their liability by reference to the use to which the certificate should be put, and the value of any transaction for which it is used. Article 6 continues:

3. Member States shall ensure that a certification-service-provider may indicate in a qualified certificate limitations on the use of that certificate, provided that the limitations are recognisable to third parties. The certification-service-provider shall not be liable for damage arising from use of a qualified certificate which exceeds the limitations placed on it.

4. Member States shall ensure that a certification-service-provider may indicate in the qualified certificate a limit on the value of transactions for which the certificate can be used, provided that the limit is recognisable to third parties. The certification-service-provider shall not be liable for damage resulting from this maximum limit being exceeded.

5. The provisions of paragraphs 1 to 4 shall be without prejudice to Council Directive 93/13/EEC of 5 April 1993 on unfair terms in consumer contracts.

The EU legislation is silent on subscriber liability and, unlike UNCITRAL, there is also nothing on the conduct of the relying party.

7.6 THE UK POSITION

There is as yet no UK legislation, though the government recognises it has probably not fully implemented the EC Directive in this regard.[41] Of course, the general law applies but, as we saw above, it is by no means clear that it adequately protects relying parties. For tort actions, the burden of proof is on the claimant, whereas the EC Directive requires it to be on the defendant.

It is also not clear that UK law is consistent with Art 6(3)–(5), above. As we saw in section 7.2.1, s 2 of the Unfair Contract Terms Act 1977 provides that: 'A person cannot by reference to any contract term or to a notice … exclude or restrict his liability for negligence except in so far as the term or notice satisfies the requirement of reasonableness.'[42] However, Art 6(5) of the Directive provides that 'The provisions of paragraphs 1 to 4 shall be without prejudice to Council Directive 93/13/EEC of 5 April 1993 on unfair terms in consumer contracts'.[43] These also import a concept of reasonableness, and were implemented as part of UK law by the Unfair Terms in Consumer Contracts Regulations 1999.[44] It seems, then, that control of terms is effectively the same in the UK as in the EU, at any rate where the relying party is a consumer. If the relying party is a business, however, an exclusion might possibly be struck down by the UK Unfair Contract Terms Act which would be valid under the EC Directive.

It might be argued that, since the UK has made no provision for a qualified certificate (given that the Law Commission deems them unnecessary), the attendant liability regime is technically unnecessary also. However, it seems likely that the UK will eventually have to implement Arts 5(1) and 6 of the Directive. That means that a special set of legal principles will apply just to this one area of activity. Can this be justified? There is perhaps an argument that if qualified certificates enjoy advantages, for example in terms of formal validity, and a CSP chooses to take these advantages, there is at least no unfairness in subjecting him to a particular liability regime. Another point is that, in the absence of liability, someone in the position of Bob has no obvious means of protecting himself.

Even if the UK brings into force the remainder of the EC Directive, it may be presumed that the common law liability will continue to survive alongside the new liability regime. Contractual liability is strict, so there could potentially be liability at

---

41 Department of Trade and Industry, *Consultation on EC Directive 1999/93/EC of the European Parliament and Council on a Community Framework for Electronic Signatures*, 2001, paras 39–42, available from www.minstrel.org.uk/papers/1999-93-ec/1999-93-ec-dti-consult.txt.

42 Note that there does not have to be a contract between the parties for this term to apply.

43 Full text can be found at http://europa.eu.int/smartapi/cgi/sga_doc?smartapi!celexplus! prod!DocNumber&lg=en&type_doc=Directive&an_doc=1993&nu_doc=13.

44 Available at www.opsi.gov.uk/si/si1999/19992083.htm, with commentary and links at www.oft.gov.uk/Business/Legal/default.htm.

common law, even where a qualified certificate is issued, where there is no liability under the Directive. Also, of course, if a CA issues an unqualified certificate, it will continue to be governed by the common law.

PRIVACY ISSUES

The first part of this chapter follows on naturally from the last two. State law enforcement authorities have an interest in controlling encryption. There is also, however, a state interest in promoting e-commerce, which depends on the free availability of strong encryption. There are also privacy issues which, though not directly relevant to e-commerce, nonetheless impact on the general issue of state control.

The second part of this chapter is also about privacy, but is not particularly connected with encryption (except in relation to transmission security). In the course of e-commerce transactions, much personal data can (indeed must) be taken, which can then be stored and processed by unaccountable private concerns. There are obvious privacy implications, and the law imposes controls on the storage and use of this information.

8.1 STATE CONTROL OF ENCRYPTION

8.1.1 The arguments

It is obvious from the last three chapters that e-commerce demands strong encryption, to determine identity and authenticity in the case of digital signatures, but also to hide content, not only of trade secrets, but also of consumers' details. I would be very unhappy about making purchases over the Web using a credit card, or using an online banking service, if I thought my transmissions were insecure. Indeed, as we shall see in section 8.2, data protection concerns positively require personal information to be stored in a secure, that is, encrypted manner.

There are also issues of privacy, nowadays regarded as a fundamental human right to be protected. These arguments relate primarily, but not exclusively, to e-mail. One argument is that e-mail is inherently less secure than other types of communication, especially where a satellite transmission is used, since, in effect, it is broadcast to the world. Moreover, all e-mail is likely to be routed via servers, into which it is possible to hack. To obtain a degree of privacy similar to that of sending a letter in an envelope, rather than leaving it for the world to read as in a postcard, it is necessary, so the argument goes, to encrypt it.[1]

The state law enforcement authorities see matters differently, at a period in history, after 11 September 2001, when security arguments are more likely to convince than they did previously. Law enforcement agencies are accustomed to having powers to intercept communications and, in particular, to tap telephones, but they would be powerless against strong encryption in the hands of terrorists and other criminals. Strong encryption in the hands of private individuals changes the status quo,

---

1 See generally, eg, the discussion in Singh, S, *The Code Book*, 1999, London: Fourth Estate, Chapter 7.

therefore, and it is not surprising that law enforcement agencies feel threatened by it, arguing that it jeopardises their ability to fight crime, including terrorism.

There is therefore a legitimate state interest in controlling encryption. On the other hand, it is not in the interest of any government to discourage e-commerce, which depends on strong encryption for digital signatures, storage and (perhaps) communication of sensitive (valuable) information. E-businesses would not wish this information be available to government employees who could be bribed or careless. If the Government is to control encryption, therefore, and even if it is prepared to override civil libertarian arguments, it must do so in a way that keeps the e-commerce lobby happy.

8.1.2   Options for control

Maintaining a balance between law enforcement agencies, civil libertarians and the needs of e-commerce is not the only difficulty facing state interests in controlling encryption. Another is that it is almost impossible to achieve the status quo *ante*. To allow, without restriction, strongly encrypted communication is certainly to shift the balance in favour of criminals and terrorists. On the other hand, to prohibit encryption, quite apart from the disastrous consequences this would have on e-commerce, would also shift the balance away from civil libertarians. E-mail is much easier to intercept than a telephone conversation[2] and satellite communication, in particular, requires no special equipment. Word searches make surveillance much easier than it is with the telephone. It is easy to significantly shift the balance one way or the other, therefore, but far more difficult to maintain it as it was, before digital communication became commonplace.

Another problem is that while legal measures taken against encryption will be obeyed by the law-abiding, they are unlikely to be obeyed by the very people about whom the law enforcement agencies worry: terrorists and other criminals. Indeed, it has been said that:[3]

> ... an old argument comes to mind: When guns are outlawed, only outlaws will have guns. The same will likely be true if we outlaw encryption by private citizens or corporations.

Another commentator commented that if strong encryption were banned:[4]

> Of course criminals are by definition not respectful of the law and will be the only individuals able to continue to use strong encryption.

There are also ways for criminals to hide the fact that a document or file has been encrypted. For example, it is certainly possible to send encrypted messages by altering a few bits in a large picture or sound file; if the file is sufficiently large the alterations will be undetectable, except to someone looking for them.[5]

---

2   Telephone tapping is usually performed at the exchange, and requires a warrant.
3   Atkinson, F, *Network Security*, www.mishmash.com/fredspgp/pgp.html.
4   Meryl, D, *Eyes Only*, April 1998, http://gizmonaut.net/soapflakes/EXE-199804.html. Similar sentiments have often been expressed.
5   To hide the very existence of a message is to engage in steganography, not cryptography. There is some historical discussion in Singh, *The Code Book, op cit* fn 1, Chapter 1.

Prohibiting encryption would probably not work, therefore, quite apart from being very unpopular with both civil libertarians and promoters of e-commerce. It is not the only option available to the law makers, but most of the others suffer from precisely the same problem. In the 1990s, the US government considered requiring the use of Clipper and Capstone chips, which provided encryption – Clipper for digital telephones and Capstone for computers. However, state authorities were able, subject to safeguards, to obtain private keys. This was compulsory key escrow, with escrowed keys being available to the authorities. Clipper and Capstone were abandoned in 1999, however, when it was realised that the idea was unworkable. By 1999, Pretty Good Privacy (PGP) was in the public domain, being widely (and freely) available throughout the world. Criminals were hardly going to use Clipper or Capstone. On the other hand, compulsory key escrow would have reduced, or perhaps even destroyed, the trust in the secure communication necessary for e-commerce, for commerce, unlike criminals and terrorists, would no doubt have obeyed the law.[6]

It might be thought that another possibility for state authorities is to target certification authorities (CAs), but there is no reason why CAs should keep records of anything but public keys, which are known to everyone anyway. In Bolero, for example, described in sections 5.1 and 6.3, private keys will be known only by the individual traders, and the message only by sender and recipient. No doubt, a CA could, if it wished, offer a key recovery system, in which case it would need also to keep private keys, but it would obviously constitute a significant security risk for private keys to be stored in one place. Even if they retained private keys, control of CAs could only work if they were licensed, in which case retention of private keys could, in principle, be a condition of the licence. As we have already seen, however, the EU is against compulsory licensing, favouring free competition.[7] Criminals could, in any case, easily avoid any such control by using an unlicensed CA, or more likely no CA at all.

Probably the only effective option is therefore for the state to put pressure on the people who know the keys, or the plaintext. In a properly run system these will only be the parties themselves to the communication. They will presumably be reluctant to disclose them, unless they are coerced. The UK has therefore provided for such coercion, subject, of course, to appropriate safeguards.[8]

8.1.3   The law

8.1.3.1   Disclosure of keys

The main part of the UK control on encryption can be found in the Regulation of Investigatory Powers Act 2000.[9] Powers to obtain keys for encrypted data are provided for in Part III, beginning at s 49, the persons being entitled to obtain them being set out

---

6   Again, there is a general discussion in Singh, *ibid*.
7   See section 6.5.7.
8   For the views of a frustrated law enforcer, prior to the enactment of the relevant UK legislation, see, eg, Barrett, N, *Traces of Guilt*, 2004, London: Bantam Press, Chapter 4.
9   Full text can be found at www.opsi.gov.uk/acts/acts2000/20000023.htm.

in Sched 2. Essentially, s 49(2) allows for disclosure orders requiring delivery up of keys, from any person (or persons) in possession of them. Section 49(3) provides that:

(3) A disclosure requirement in respect of any protected information is necessary on grounds falling within this subsection if it is necessary—

(a) in the interests of national security;

(b) for the purpose of preventing or detecting crime; or

(c) in the interests of the economic well-being of the United Kingdom.

Section 49(2) is limited, however, by the following:

(c) that the imposition of such a requirement [disclosure order] is proportionate to what is sought to be achieved by its imposition, and

(d) that it is not reasonably practicable for the person with the appropriate permission [as defined in Schedule 2] to obtain possession of the protected information in an intelligible form without the giving of a notice ...

The person against whom the disclosure order could be made could include the sender or recipient of the message, who would, in a criminal investigation, often be the only persons in possession of the key.

Schedule 2 defines the persons entitled to a disclosure order, or 'having the appropriate permission'. These include persons with the written permission of a judge, those who have obtained a warrant, and members of the intelligence services or others with statutory powers.

Civil libertarians argue that this goes further than necessary: disclosure of the plaintext ought to be sufficient; there is no need additionally to require disclosure of the key. Disclosure of the key does, however, allow future messages to be decrypted, and also allows the plaintext disclosed to be verified as genuine. In any case, where messages (perhaps stretching over several months) or other information are stored on a large hard disk in encrypted form, obtaining the key may be the only practicable method of obtaining the plaintext.

8.1.3.2   List of cryptography providers

The Secretary of State is also required, under s 1 of the Electronic Communications Act 2000,[10] to establish and maintain a register of approved providers of cryptography support services. Section 4 protects individuals against disclosure of information by approved providers, but there are exceptions in s 4(2), including:

any disclosure of information which is made ... in connection with the investigation of any criminal offence or for the purposes of any criminal proceedings.

Such a register could no doubt, in principle anyway, be used for a key escrow system. For the present, however, registration remains voluntary, and although there are wide powers given to the Minister to alter the legislation under s 8, this is unlikely to change and, indeed, is in line with EU policy. It seems unlikely, therefore, that powers under the Electronic Communications Act 2000 will significantly affect the security issue.

---

10 The full text of the Electronic Communications Act 2000 can be found at www.opsi.gov.uk/acts/acts2000/20000007.htm.

Any legal control of encryption must balance conflicting interests and concentrate on what is possible. It is possible that the UK legislation strikes the right balance, but the nature of the beast ensures that the efficacy of such powers, in a crime prevention context, must surely be open to doubt.

8.1.4   Human rights aspects

Privacy issues also raise human rights concerns. The Human Rights Act 1998 gives effect to some[11] but not all of the provisions of the European Convention on Human Rights (ECHR), which is set out in Sched 1 to the Act. Section 3(1) of the 1998 Act states:

> So far as it is possible to do so, primary legislation and subordinate legislation must be read and given effect in a way which is compatible with Convention rights.

It follows that the Regulation of Investigatory Powers Act 2000 and the Electronic Communications Act 2000 must both be read so as to be compatible with Convention rights.

Article 8 of the Convention (which is brought within the regime of the 1998 Act) provides for a right to respect for private and family life (which might perhaps include privacy of communications), and that there shall be no interference by a public authority with the exercise of this right, but:

> except such as in accordance with the law and is necessary in a democratic society in the interests of national security, public safety or the economic well-being of the country, for the prevention of disorder or crime, for the protection of health or morals, or for the protection of the rights and freedoms of others.

Section 6 of the 1998 Act makes it unlawful for a public authority to act in a way which is incompatible with a Convention right, but s 6(2) provides an exemption where the authority is acting in accordance with primary legislation.

I would suggest, therefore, that the Human Rights Act 1998 has no effect on the Regulation of Investigatory Powers Act 2000, as long as the authorities do not act outside its provisions. If they do, they will fall foul of the 1998 Act, unless they continue to fall within the Art 8 exemption and, additionally, unlawful interception can be an offence under s 1 of the Regulation of Investigatory Powers Act 2000 itself.

8.2   DATA PROTECTION ISSUES

For a supplier to process any World Wide Web (WWW) transaction, some information must necessarily be collected. The operation of the WWW itself requires knowledge of the Internet Protocol (IP) address of the customer. Billing and delivery details must also be collected. Whether or not it is necessary, however, a form on the WWW can collect from the customer any information the supplier wishes to request, and the supplier can, in principle at least, make processing the transaction conditional on the provision of the information. Moreover, since the information is supplied in a digital

---

11   Full text is at www.opsi.gov.uk/acts/acts1998/19980042.htm.

form, the format of which can be determined by the supplier, it can easily be processed into mailing lists, or any other form the supplier desires.

It is also possible for customer preferences to be stored, either collecting them using a similar type of form, or using cookies, which are stored on the customer's own computer.

There is nothing wrong, in principle, with information of this type being stored and processed, and indeed its retention by the supplier may be used positively to benefit the customer. There are, however, obvious privacy issues where the customer does not wish the information to be retained, so the law needs to provide safeguards where the customer does not consent.

In the EU, the general framework for data protection is Directive 95/46/EC,[12] implemented in the UK by the Data Protection Act 1998.[13] Directive 95/46/EC has been filled out for particular areas of activity and, in particular for our purposes, by Directive 2002/58/EC,[14] implemented in the UK by the Privacy and Electronic Communications (EC Directive) Regulations 2003.[15] I will refer to the directives respectively as 'the 1995 directive' and 'the 2002 directive'.

The data protection scheme applies only to personal data. Data is defined, essentially, as information that is processed or kept for processing, automatically or as part of a filing system, and personal data is capable of identifying an individual, either from the data itself or from the data 'and other information which is in the possession of, or is likely to come into the possession of, the data controller'. It 'includes any expression of opinion about the individual and any indication of the intentions of the data controller or any other person in respect of the individual'.[16] Processing of such data is allowed only in the circumstances identified in Sched 2 to the Human Rights Act 1998, which, apart from obvious compliance with legal obligations, administration of justice, and so on, include the consent of the subject, protection of the vital interests of the data subject, and where:[17]

> The processing is necessary for the purposes of legitimate interests pursued by the data controller or by the third party or parties to whom the data are disclosed, except where the processing is unwarranted in any particular case by reason of prejudice to the rights and freedoms or legitimate interests of the data subject.

This last will be a common situation in e-commerce, and involves balancing the interests of the data controller and the subject.

There are also general principles about the processing of personal data, elaborated in Sched 1 to the 1998 Act, with regard to its accuracy, access by the subject, etc.

---

12 Directive 95/46/EC of the European Parliament and of the Council of 24 October 1995 on the protection of individuals with regard to the processing of personal data and on the free movement of such data. There is a fully linked version at www.cdt.org/privacy/eudirective/EU_Directive_.html.

13 www.opsi.gov.uk/acts/acts1998/19980029.htm.

14 Directive 2002/58/EC of the European Parliament and of the Council of 12 July 2002 concerning the processing of personal data and the protection of privacy in the electronic communications sector (Directive on privacy and electronic communications), at http://europa.eu.int/eur-lex/pri/en/oj/dat/2002/l_201/l_20120020731en00370047.pdf. This updates and replaces Directive 97/66/EC on telecommunication services.

15 SI 2003/2426, at www.opsi.gov.uk/si/si2003/20032426.htm.

16 Data Protection Act 1998, s 1.

17 Paragraph 6(1).

The UK provisions specific to e-commerce are, however, contained in the 2003 privacy and electronic communications regulations, implementing the 2002 directive. These regulations add to, and elaborate on, any obligations under the 1998 Act. They replace and revoke the Telecommunications (Data Protection and Privacy) Regulations 1999 and the Telecommunications (Data Protection and Privacy) (Amendment) Regulations 2000, effectively to update them by including Internet communication, so that they are now combined telecommunications and Internet regulations. The origins of the Directive remain evident; many of the regulations are directed at mobile telephones, etc, rather than the Internet, and only those of importance to e-commerce are described here.

Regulation 5 requires service providers to 'take appropriate technical and organisational measures to safeguard the security of that service', and to inform the subject of any significant remaining risks and of possible measures to guard against them. This is an obvious problem where personal data is sent over insecure channels, such as analogue mobile phones, but Internet communication can also be insecure. In the recital to the 2002 directive is the following paragraph:

(20) Service providers should take appropriate measures to safeguard the security of their services, if necessary in conjunction with the provider of the network, and inform subscribers of any special risks of a breach of the security of the network. Such risks may especially occur for electronic communications services over an open network such as the Internet or analogue mobile telephony. It is particularly important for subscribers and users of such services to be fully informed by their service provider of the existing security risks which lie outside the scope of possible remedies by the service provider. Service providers who offer publicly available electronic communications services over the Internet should inform users and subscribers of measures they can take to protect the security of their communications for instance by using specific types of software or encryption technologies. The requirement to inform subscribers of particular security risks does not discharge a service provider from the obligation to take, at its own costs, appropriate and immediate measures to remedy any new, unforeseen security risks and restore the normal security level of the service. The provision of information about security risks to the subscriber should be free of charge except for any nominal costs which the subscriber may incur while receiving or collecting the information, for instance by downloading an electronic mail message. Security is appraised in the light of Article 17 of Directive 95/46/EC.

Security is often a matter that requires co-operation between service provider and subscriber, and in the UK legislation, a service provider is obliged only to take measures which are appropriate. By reg 5(4):

a measure shall only be taken to be appropriate if, having regard to—

(a)   the state of technological developments, and

(b)   the cost of implementing it,

it is proportionate to the risks against which it would safeguard.

Regulation 6 prevents accessing or storing information on a subject's computer terminal except with consent, except for technical storage or access:

(a) for the sole purpose of carrying out or facilitating the transmission of a communication over an electronic communications network; or

(b) where such storage or access is strictly necessary for the provision of an information society service requested by the subscriber or user.

It might be perfectly rational for a consumer to consent, for example, to cookies which can facilitate or optimise his or her use of the WWW. In the recital to the 2002 directive is the following passage:

(24) Terminal equipment of users of electronic communications networks and any information stored on such equipment are part of the private sphere of the users requiring protection under the European Convention for the Protection of Human Rights and Fundamental Freedoms. So-called spyware, web bugs, hidden identifiers and other similar devices can enter the user's terminal without their knowledge in order to gain access to information, to store hidden information or to trace the activities of the user and may seriously intrude upon the privacy of these users. The use of such devices should be allowed only for legitimate purposes, with the knowledge of the users concerned.

(25) However, such devices, for instance so-called 'cookies', can be a legitimate and useful tool, for example, in analysing the effectiveness of website design and advertising, and in verifying the identity of users engaged in on-line transactions. Where such devices, for instance cookies, are intended for a legitimate purpose, such as to facilitate the provision of information society services, their use should be allowed on condition that users are provided with clear and precise information in accordance with Directive 95/46/EC about the purposes of cookies or similar devices so as to ensure that users are made aware of information being placed on the terminal equipment they are using. Users should have the opportunity to refuse to have a cookie or similar device stored on their terminal equipment. This is particularly important where users other than the original user have access to the terminal equipment and thereby to any data containing privacy-sensitive information stored on such equipment. Information and the right to refuse may be offered once for the use of various devices to be installed on the user's terminal equipment during the same connection and also covering any further use that may be made of those devices during subsequent connections. The methods for giving information, offering a right to refuse or requesting consent should be made as user-friendly as possible. Access to specific website content may still be made conditional on the well-informed acceptance of a cookie or similar device, if it is used for a legitimate purpose.

Thus, cookies are acceptable, subject to appropriate safeguards. However, for example, using a network to search for illicit copies of software or music on a computer are prohibited.

Some data must be retained, simply in order to continue a communication, and for billing, etc, but storage of such information should be temporary, only for as long as the information is needed. Regulation 7 requires traffic data, 'when no longer required for the purpose of the transmission of a communication', to be either erased or 'modified so that they cease to constitute personal data of that subscriber or user'. 'Traffic data' is defined as:[18]

... any data processed for the purpose of the conveyance of a communication on an electronic communications network or for the billing in respect of that communication and includes data relating to the routing, duration or time of a communication.

---

18   In the interpretation section, reg 2.

Billing information, however, may be retained until:[19]

> the end of the period during which legal proceedings may be brought in respect of payments due or alleged to be due or, where such proceedings are brought within that period, the time when those proceedings are finally determined.

There are similar provisions for the prevention or detection of fraud, and a list of other purposes set out in reg 8(3).

It might be objected that to require the erasure of personal traffic data might deprive law enforcement authorities of a useful tool, especially in the detection of cybercrime.[20] Against that is the protection of privacy under Art 8 of the ECHR. There is always a question of balance, and this particular regulation comes down on the side of the civil libertarians. In any case, however, mandatory retention of traffic data could have proved very expensive for service providers.

Regulation 22 is aimed at spam or junk mail, and prohibits:

> unsolicited communications for the purposes of direct marketing by means of electronic mail unless the recipient of the electronic mail has previously notified the sender that he consents for the time being to such communications being sent by, or at the instigation of, the sender.

This is a direct opt-in provision, there being a limited exception in reg 22(3):

> (3) A person may send or instigate the sending of electronic mail for the purposes of direct marketing where—
>
> (a) that person has obtained the contact details of the recipient of that electronic mail in the course of the sale or negotiations for the sale of a product or service to that recipient;
>
> (b) the direct marketing is in respect of that person's similar products and services only; and
>
> (c) the recipient has been given a simple means of refusing (free of charge except for the costs of the transmission of the refusal) the use of his contact details for the purposes of such direct marketing, at the time that the details were initially collected, and, where he did not initially refuse the use of the details, at the time of each subsequent communication.

Regulation 23 prohibits the sending of anonymous e-mail, for direct marketing purposes.

Regulations 28 and 29 provide exceptions for national security and law enforcement.

---

19 Regulation 7(5).
20 Lodder, A and Kaspersen, H (eds), *eDirectives: Guide to European Union Law on E-Commerce*, 2002, The Hague: Kluwer Law International, p 137.

PART 4

CONTRACTUAL ISSUES

CONTRACT FORMATION AND RELATED ISSUES

The general law of contract operates in the same way on the Internet as elsewhere, but in its application there are issues that are peculiar to e-commerce. Some of these issues relate to conflict of laws (and, in particular, jurisdiction), some to payment, and some to consumer protection,[1] but it is also necessary to examine contract formation. It is necessary to determine whether a contract has been made and, if so, where and when. It may be necessary also to determine who are the parties to the contract, and what its terms are. All of these issues relate, to some extent at least, to contract formation. It is therefore useful to start by analysing e-commerce transactions in terms of offer and acceptance, which are necessary to the formation of any contract.

9.1   OFFER AND ACCEPTANCE

9.1.1   General principles

The process of making any contract usually involves some kind of negotiation, or at least a period before the parties have finally made up their minds. There comes a point, however, when the negotiations are over, and a deal is finalised. This is the point at which the contract is concluded. The conclusion of the contract irrevocably alters the position of the parties; they are now bound to perform their bargain, and legal consequences flow from non-performance, or partial or defective performance, by either side. The parties cannot, at least without a fresh agreement, simply revert to the position they were in before the contract was concluded.

It is sometimes said that a meeting of minds is necessary for the conclusion of a contract, but this has been formalised, in English law, into the idea of an offer by one of the contracting parties, which is accepted by the other contracting party. Once an offer has been accepted, an irrevocable step has been taken, and the parties are contractually bound. This contrasts with earlier stages of negotiation (including the making of invitations to treat), during which either party can withdraw from the negotiations without legal consequence.

It follows that both the offer and the acceptance assume an irrevocable commitment, the acceptance for obvious reasons, but the offer too, because if the other party accepts it, there will be a binding contract. It is often difficult to determine precisely at which stage of the negotiations this occurs. The acceptance must always be the final act, though. If there is anything else left to be done, there can have been no acceptance.

9.1.2   Why does it matter?

Despite the difficulty involved, it can be important to analyse negotiations in terms of offer and acceptance, since only after acceptance is there a contract at all. This clearly

---

1   These are covered in Chapters 10 and 11.

matters if one party wants to avoid, whereas the other wants to enforce the bargain. In a consumer context, this is most likely to determine the liability of the consumer to pay the price. In a commercial context, there can also be issues with volatile markets, such as has happened in the past with shipping markets after the closure of the Suez Canal in 1956, with crude oil markets after a major war in the Middle East (such as that which occurred in 1973–74, and again in 1979) and, more recently, with dotcom shares markets. Suppose we have an electronic trade on a rapidly rising market. Sellers will want to minimise existing commitments to enable them to take advantage of the price rise, whereas buyers will try to enforce bargains.[2] Disputes could revolve around whether negotiations have been finalised or, in effect, whether there has been a valid offer and acceptance.

The timing of acceptance determines not only whether, but also when and where a contract is made. When the contract is made is primarily relevant to incorporation of terms (see further section 9.4 below). The timing of the acceptance could, however, also affect whether there is a concluded contact at all if, for example, withdrawal of the offer and acceptance cross in the post; only if there has been a valid acceptance prior to a valid withdrawal of the offer will there be a contract.

Where acceptance takes place, and hence where the contract is made, is not generally relevant for choice of law, but it can be relevant to jurisdiction. It was relevant for service outside the jurisdiction in both *Entores* and *Brinkibon* (considered in detail below),[3] and still will be where the Rules of the Supreme Court have not been superseded.[4]

If the postal rule applies to contractual acceptances (below),[5] we need further to analyse who makes the offer and who makes the acceptance.

9.1.3   Offer and acceptance in the physical world

Where contracts are made by e-mail, it is difficult to see why the electronic context makes any difference; the analysis should be precisely the same as where communication is by letter.

With web-based contracts, the issue depends, to some extent, on whether the website is seen as analogous to a high street shop, or to an automatic machine such as a ticket machine. In most transactions, the high street shop analogy is probably closer, but this will not always be true and it is worth examining both analogies.

9.1.3.1   High street shops

It has long been accepted that a shop display is not an offer, but only an invitation to treat.[6] It is the customer, not the shop, who makes the offer, and this is accepted at the payment till. This view, which would originally have been developed in the context of

---

2   Obviously, the reverse is true on a falling market.
3   See section 9.2.2.
4   Ie, for states outside the Brussels Convention (EC or EFTA). See further the discussion of jurisdictional issues in section 10.2.2.
5   Section 9.2.
6   Invitations to treat occur earlier in the negotiating process, and are not offers.

shops where the customer asked the proprietor for the goods, was extended to a self-service store in *PSGB v Boots*.[7] The issue was whether the sale of medicine was supervised by a pharmacist. This depended on where the sale occurred; if at the counter then it was supervised, whereas if the customer accepted on picking the goods up at the shelves then it was not. Finding that the sale was supervised, Lord Goddard CJ reasoned that:[8]

> Ordinary principles of common sense and of commerce must be applied in this matter, and to hold that in the case of self-service shops the exposure of an article is an offer to sell, and that a person can accept the offer by picking up the article, would be contrary to those principles and might entail serious results. On the customer picking up the article the property would forthwith pass to him and he would be able to insist upon the shopkeeper allowing him to take it away, though in some particular cases the shopkeeper might think that very undesirable. On the other hand, if a customer had picked up an article, he would never be able to change his mind and to put it back; the shopkeeper could say, 'Oh no, the property has passed and you must pay the price'.

> It seems to me, therefore, that the transaction is in no way different from the normal transaction in a shop in which there is no self-service scheme. I am quite satisfied it would be wrong to say that the shopkeeper is making an offer to sell every article in the shop to any person who might come in and that that person can insist on buying any article by saying 'I accept your offer'. I agree with the illustration put forward during the case of a person who might go into a shop where books are displayed. In most book-shops customers are invited to go in and pick up books and look at them even if they do not actually buy them. There is no contract by the shopkeeper to sell until the customer has taken the book to the shopkeeper or his assistant and said 'I want to buy this book' and the shopkeeper says 'Yes'. That would not prevent the shopkeeper, seeing the book picked up, saying: 'I am sorry I cannot let you have that book; it is the only copy I have got and I have already promised it to another customer.' Therefore, in my opinion, the mere fact that a customer picks up a bottle of medicine from the shelves in this case does not amount to an acceptance of an offer to sell. It is an offer by the customer to buy and there is no sale effected until the buyer's offer to buy is accepted by the acceptance of the price. The offer, the acceptance of the price, and therefore the sale, take place under the supervision of the pharmacist.

The two reasons against the display being an offer, then, are to avoid the customer being bound before he or she has truly decided to buy, and to allow the shopkeeper the option of refusing to sell, for lack of stock or whatever other reason.

9.1.3.2 Ticket cases

However, there are a number of cases involving railway or other ticket sales, which are analysed in terms of offer by the trader and acceptance by the customer.[9] The principle in these cases applies where the seller simply issues a standard form document or a document incorporating standard terms, the buyer being asked simply to take it or leave it. In these cases, the railway company has in reality lost its opportunity to refuse the sale, and the final decision is actually made by the customer choosing whether or

---

7   *Pharmaceutical Society of Great Britain v Boots Cash Chemists (Southern) Ltd* [1952] 2 QB 795.
8   *Ibid*, p 802. This reasoning was approved in the CA [1953] 1 QB 401.
9   See the cases cited by Lord Denning MR in *Thornton v Shoe Lane Parking Ltd* [1971] 2 QB 163, p 169; also *Nunan v Southern Railway Co* [1923] 2 KB 703, p 707.

not to purchase the ticket. The acceptance does not occur until the customer has made up his or her mind, however, by which time the conditions can, in principle at least, have been read. The customer also accepted the offer in *Carlill v Carbolic Smoke Ball Co*[10] where, again, the placing of the advertisement had effectively deprived the trader of his right to refuse. In these cases, however, though the trader had deprived himself of the decision whether to enter into a contract, the customer had not; his or her acceptance remained a voluntary act.[11] The question therefore arises whether a similar analysis is appropriate where the trader has automated his side of the exchange, whereas the customer has not. This is, after all, a possible analysis of web-based dealings, where the customer is, in effect, dealing with a machine.

9.1.3.3   Automation of one side of the process

In fact, the main case on automation, *Thornton v Shoe Lane Parking Ltd*,[12] turns out to be of very little assistance. It was the plaintiff's first visit to an automatic car park where, upon driving up to the barrier, a ticket was issued by a machine, which the customer paid for by putting money into the slot, and then took the ticket. The ticket was said to be 'issued subject to conditions ... displayed on the premises'. These conditions, which were not then visible to the customer, purported to exclude liability for personal injury, but the Court of Appeal unanimously held them ineffective to do so. Lord Denning MR thought that the contract had been made before the conditions had been incorporated, whereas terms cannot be added to a contract once made.[13] He distinguished the railway cases, saying, with regard to a ticket which is issued by an automatic machine, that in general:[14]

> The customer pays his money and gets a ticket. He cannot refuse it. He cannot get his money back. He may protest to the machine, even swear at it. But it will remain unmoved. He is committed beyond recall. He was committed at the very moment when he put his money into the machine. The contract was concluded at that time. It can be translated into offer and acceptance in this way: the offer is made when the proprietor of the machine holds it out as being ready to receive the money. The acceptance takes place when the customer puts his money into the slot.

On this analysis, then, the offer is made by the company and the acceptance by the customer. He also said,[15] of the particular case before him:

> ... the offer was contained in the notice at the entrance giving the charges for garaging and saying 'at owner's risk,' that is, at the risk of the owner so far as damage to the car was concerned. The offer was accepted when Mr Thornton drove up to the entrance and, by the movement of his car, turned the light from red to green, and the ticket was thrust at him.

---

10 See the extensive discussion of this case, in a different context, in section 7.1.3. *Carlill* was distinguished in *Boots* [1952] 2 QB 795, p 801.

11 As will appear from the discussion below, I am not suggesting that acceptance need always be voluntary, at any rate in the sense of a human being making a conscious choice in the particular case.

12 [1971] 2 QB 163.

13 Lord Denning MR (*ibid*, p 169) cited *Olley v Marlborough Court Ltd* [1949] 1 KB 532.

14 [1971] 2 QB 163, p 169.

15 *Ibid*, p 169.

Thus, the offer and acceptance came at an earlier point than in the railway ticket cases, because the customer had no chance to inspect the ticket before he or she was committed. The contract was therefore made before the customer had had the opportunity to read the conditions on, or incorporated by, the ticket.

The issue is the extent to which, if at all, this reasoning can also apply to other automated dealings, such as a purchase on a website. I would suggest not at all. In the first place, Lord Denning's reasoning was not central to the decision. Megaw LJ made no comment on the timing of the contract, instead deciding the case only on the issue of sufficiency of notice.[16] It is true that Sir Gordon Willmer said that '... any attempt to introduce conditions after the irrevocable step has been taken of causing the machine to operate must be doomed to failure', perhaps implying that the contract must have been made by then, but he made no detailed analysis in terms of offer and acceptance. He also said 'I do not propose to say any more upon the difficult question which has been raised as to the precise moment when a contract was concluded in this case'. Thus, *Thornton* is not a very strong authority on the analysis in terms of offer and acceptance, or indeed the timing issue as a whole.

In fact, the automation aspect of *Thornton* was a red herring. The case would have been exactly the same as the railway ticket cases except for the physical impossibility of the customer withdrawing by the time he reached the ticket barrier. The customer is never put into a similar position in an Internet-contracting situation, so the decision turns out to be of no assistance.

This seems, in any case, to have been a very unsophisticated automatic process by today's standards. The company appears to have retained no discretion at all, the movement of the car necessarily triggering the change of the lights and the issue of the ticket. In *Thornton* itself, in the railway cases and, indeed, in *Carlill*, it is the lack of discretion retained by the company that determines that it makes the offer and the customer the acceptance. There is no reason to apply similar reasoning to a more sophisticated automatic process, where the machine reserves a discretion, for example not to admit cars when the car park is full, or indeed in most web-based contracts.

9.1.4 Application to e-commerce

For contracts made by e-mail, actively by the persons communicating, there seems to be no good reason to depart from the usual rules that apply to letters in the physical world.

With a web-based supplier communicating automatically with a consumer who is present at the terminal, normal contractual principles determine that the initial web page will be an invitation to treat; there is surely no reason to depart from the analogy of the display of goods in a shop. The reasoning in *PSGB v Boots* surely remains applicable,[17] especially in the normal situation, where there will be a dialogue establishing the customer's identity and financial details, and perhaps links to further and better particulars about the product, before the sale is concluded.

---

16 This aspect of the case is discussed further below, sections 9.4.2 and 9.4.3.
17 [1953] 1 QB 401.

Also, part of the *Boots* reasoning was that if the shop front constituted the offer, a *possible* conclusion would be that the company could exercise no control over with whom it did business, and would be in difficulty if it ran out of the product. This is equally true of a web page. There is also a good argument that, in a web context just as with a normal shop, the customer should normally make the offer and the trader the acceptance, to enable (for example) stocks to be checked before agreement is reached.

The question is whether the cases where the trader makes the offer should displace these arguments. In all the cases where acceptance is by the customer, the trader has simply issued terms on a take it or leave it basis, the trader himself then withdrawing from the transaction. No doubt, web commerce could be carried out on this basis, for example where an advertisement, similar to that in *Carlill*, is posted on the web, but obviously this will not be the normal case. Normally, I would suggest, the *Boots* reasoning should prevail.

Nonetheless, even accepting that a website is an invitation to treat, a web transaction might still differ, in some respects, from that in *Boots*. The acceptance is the last act of commitment. In most web-based contracts, the server asks for customer details and credit card information, unless already stored, and then asks the customer to confirm the order. It is fairly clear that the confirmation commits the customer. If the intention is that the customer's confirmation also commits the company, it must be the acceptance of the company's offer, any later confirmation by the company being post-contractual. If this is the correct inference to draw, it is the company which makes the offer, which the customer accepts. However, it is probably not correct to infer that the customer's confirmation also binds the trader. The inference might better be drawn that final acceptance is reserved to the company, either by the confirmation of receipt of order or, in theory at least, by shipping the product, and of course, the website could explicitly so reserve anyway. This would make the customer the offeror.

This has implications for the next section, at least if the postal rule applies to contractual acceptances, and only to acceptances, and also for section 9.2.5 because it is impossible for the customer to control the terms of an offer to an automated process. It also has implications for the discussion later in the chapter on electronic agents[18] because, if the argument is correct, it is possible to use a programmed automated process to accept an offer.

The common law must now be read in the light of the EC Council Directive (2000/31/EC) on Electronic Commerce, which applies to information society service providers (but not generally to other traders). To the extent that it applies, it supports the conclusion reached here. This Directive is considered briefly in section 9.3 and in detail in the next chapter.[19]

9.2   ACCEPTANCE OF CONTRACT: APPLICABILITY OF POSTAL RULE?

The Internet shares with snailmail the fact that it is not 100% reliable. Communications to a web server, or by e-mail, can get lost, delayed, or fail to reach their destination.

---

18   Section 9.7.
19   Section 10.1.5.

Moreover, there is no way of being 100% sure whether they have arrived or not.[20] For snailmail, which shares these features, the courts have decided that acceptance is complete when posted, whenever it arrives, or indeed whether it arrives at all. The issue is whether the same rule holds for electronic communications. This requires us to examine the rationale for the rule in the physical world.

9.2.1   Justifications for the postal rule

It is well known that the postal rule originated in *Adams v Lindsell*.[21] It has only been held to apply to acceptances and, while it does not follow that it cannot apply to other communications, it is clear that an offer, to be effective, has to reach the offeree. There are two main justifications for the postal rule: commercial convenience, and that delivery of a message to an agent of the offeror is to be construed as delivery to the offeror, both of which, I would suggest, are independently convincing arguments for the application of the rule, albeit applying in different circumstances. A third argument is essentially moral, putting the risk of communication delay or failure on the party choosing the communication method. This is unlikely to apply convincingly in an Internet context, where the choice is likely to be consensual.

9.2.1.1   *Commercial convenience*

The commercial convenience argument is that the offeree is unaware of whether his or her acceptance has been received. In *Harris' Case*,[22] Harris sent a postal application for shares in a company and the directors posted their acceptance of his application. However, before he received the acceptance, Harris wrote, purporting to decline to accept any shares. The Court of Appeal, applying the postal rule, held the contract complete when the acceptance was posted, Mellish LJ observing:[23]

> Now throughout the argument I have been forcibly struck with the extraordinary and very mischievous consequences which would follow if it were held that an offer might be revoked at any time until the letter accepting it had been actually received. No mercantile man who has received a letter making him an offer, and has accepted the offer, could safely act on that acceptance after he has put it into the post until he knew that it had been received. Every day, I presume, there must be a large number of mercantile letters received which require to be acted upon immediately. A person, for instance, sends an order to a merchant in London offering to pay a certain price for so many goods. The merchant writes an answer accepting the offer, and goes that instant into the market and purchases the goods in order to enable him to fulfil the contract. But according to the argument presented to us, if the person who has sent the offer finds that the market is falling, and that it will be a bad bargain for him, he may at any time, before he has received the answer, revoke his offer. The consequences might be very serious to

---

20   Remember that confirmation of receipt messages can themselves get lost, and therefore do not solve the problem.

21   (1818) 1 B & A 681, approved by the House of Lords in *Dunlop v Higgins* (1848) 1 HLC 381. In the early cases the message arrived eventually, but in *Household Fire and Carriage Accident Insurance Co Ltd v Grant* (1879) 4 Ex D 216 the Court of Appeal was prepared to extend the principle to cases where the message was entirely lost.

22   *Imperial Land Co of Marseilles, In re (Harris' Case)* (1872) LR 7 Ch App 587.

23   *Ibid*, p 594.

the merchant, and might be much more serious when the parties are in distant countries. Suppose that a dealer in Liverpool writes to a dealer in New York and offers to buy so many quarters of corn or so many bales of cotton at a certain price, and the dealer in New York, finding that he can make a favourable bargain, writes an answer accepting the offer. Then, according to the argument that has been presented to us to-day, during the whole time that the letter accepting the offer is on the Atlantic, the dealer who is to receive it in Liverpool, if he finds that the market has fallen, may send a message by telegraph and revoke his offer.

Both the uncertainty as to whether the message has arrived and the length of the delay are regarded as relevant in this passage. Clearly, the length of the delay is likely to be much shorter with Internet communications, but the uncertainty might be just as great. However, the length of the delay appears to be considered relevant only on volatile markets. Surely the crucial factor is the uncertainty as to whether the message has arrived.[24] If that is correct, then the principle in the case ought to apply to all Internet communications, whether by e-mail or over the WWW. If it is objected to that you can set up your e-mail client to confirm receipt or confirm reading, a negative response could equally mean that the confirmation itself, rather than your original message, has got lost. Similarly, if you get no response from a website, you have no way of knowing whether your original communication has been received.

If commercial convenience is a convincing argument in a snailmail context, therefore, it remains convincing in an Internet context.

9.2.1.2 Communication to offeror's agent

The other main argument that has been advanced, for the application of the postal rule, is that communication to the agent of the offeror is regarded as communication to the offeror himself or herself. *Household Fire and Carriage Accident Insurance Co Ltd v Grant*[25] was similar to *Harris' Case*, except that the acceptance, though posted by the secretary of the company, never arrived. The analysis of Thesiger LJ was in terms of the post office being a common agent of the parties, so that:[26]

> as soon as the letter of acceptance is delivered to the post office, the contract is made as complete and final and absolutely binding as if the acceptor had put his letter into the hands of a messenger sent by the offeror himself as his agent to deliver the offer and receive the acceptance.

Therefore, there was a contract binding the offeror, even though the acceptance never arrived. In fact, it is only necessary for the messenger to be the agent of the offeror for this argument to be convincing. Of course, the offeree would also have needed to constitute the post office his or her agent if the principle were to apply to a withdrawal of an offer, or any other message to be received by the offeree. Lindley J held that he had not done so in *Byrne v Van Tienhoven*,[27] where an offer and revocation were both

---

24 Cf Lord Brandon's view in *Brinkibon*, at p 48, where he emphasised the need, for the postal rule to apply, for 'a substantial interval between the time when the acceptance is sent and the time when it is received'. This seems to be a solitary voice, however.

25 (1879) 4 Ex D 216.

26 *Ibid*, p 221.

27 *Byrne & Co v Leon Van Tienhoven & Co* (1880) 5 CPD 344, p 348.

posted before being received by the offeree, but where the offeree, immediately on receipt of the offer, posted his acceptance. The acceptance was held to have taken place before the revocation of the offer, and the contract was held to have been concluded.

There can be no doubt that the principle that delivery to an agent is regarded as equivalent to delivery to the person has ramifications in an Internet context. The most obvious, at the very least, is that communication to the offeror's server must count as communication to the offeror.

9.2.1.3   Who chooses the communication method bears the risk

A third possible argument is that since it is the offeror, not the offeree, who has chosen the communication method, the offeror should bear the risk of loss of, or delay in, the communication. To put it another way, having chosen an insecure means of communication, he has impliedly waived the requirement for actual notification of the acceptance. In *Entores Ltd v Miles Far East Corp*,[28] Parker LJ observed that the general rule is that an acceptance of an offer made ought to be notified to the person who makes the offer.[29] However, in the case of the postal rule:[30]

> Since, however, the requirement as to actual notification of the acceptance is for the benefit of the offeror, he may waive it and agree to the substitution for that requirement of some other conduct by the acceptor. He may do so expressly, as in the advertisement cases,[31] by intimating that he is content with the performance of a condition. Again, he may do so impliedly by indicating a contemplated method of acceptance, for example, by post or telegram. In such a case he does not expressly dispense with actual notification, but he is held to have done so impliedly on grounds of expediency. Thus, in *Adams v Lindsell*, the court pointed out that unless this were so 'no contract could ever be completed by the post ...'

Though this argument could also conceivably apply in an Internet context, for example where an offer is made by e-mail, in most Internet transactions the choice as to the medium is likely to be consensual. If, for example, I decide to purchase a book from Amazon.com, it is not at all obvious which of us has chosen the communication method.

Nonetheless, there remains the commercial convenience argument for applying the postal rule to e-commerce transactions. There is, however, a principle that 'instantaneous communications' are not covered by the rule.

9.2.2   Instantaneous communications

The issue in *Entores Ltd v Miles Far East Corp* was *where* the contract had been made.[32] Communication was by telex and acceptance had been telexed in Holland and received in London. The Court of Appeal held that the postal rule did not apply and

---

28   [1955] 2 QB 327.
29   *Ibid*, p 336, citing Bowen LJ in *Carlill v Carbolic Smoke Ball Co* [1893] 1 QB 256, p 269.
30   *Ibid*.
31   Parker LJ clearly has *Carlill* in mind.
32   [1955] 2 QB 327.

that the contract had been made in England. Hence, this was a proper case for service on the defendant outside the jurisdiction.[33]

The case is often cited for the proposition that the postal rule does not apply to communications which are instantaneous, or more or less instantaneous. This might be seen as a reason for excluding it also from Internet communications. However, quite apart from the fact that neither e-mail nor WWW communications are instantaneous in the way that a telex is, it is clear that the real reason for the decision in *Entores* was that the parties would know immediately if there had been a break in communication. Perhaps the telex was still unfamiliar technology at the time of *Entores*, since it seems to have been envisaged that there would be a clerk present at each teleprinter at the time of the communication:[34]

> Lastly, take the Telex. Suppose a clerk in a London office taps out on the teleprinter an offer which is immediately recorded on a teleprinter in a Manchester office, and a clerk at that end taps out an acceptance. If the line goes dead in the middle of the sentence of acceptance, the teleprinter motor will stop. There is then obviously no contract. The clerk at Manchester must get through again and send his complete sentence. But it may happen that the line does not go dead, yet the message does not get through to London. Thus the clerk at Manchester may tap out his message of acceptance and it will not be recorded in London because the ink at the London end fails, or something of that kind. In that case, the Manchester clerk will not know of the failure but the London clerk will know of it and will immediately send back a message 'not receiving'. Then, when the fault is rectified, the Manchester clerk will repeat his message. Only then is there a contract. If he does not repeat it, there is no contract. It is not until his message is received that the contract is complete.

Denning LJ immediately continues: 'In all the instances I have taken so far [of instantaneous communication], the man who sends the message of acceptance knows that it has not been received or he has reason to know it. So he must repeat it.' Surely this is the crucial factor. This is what distinguishes spoken and telephone communication, and also the early telex communication in *Entores*, from the post. But it also distinguishes 'instantaneous communication' from Internet communication since, with Internet communication, it cannot be known whether a communication has succeeded or failed.

In *Brinkibon v Stahag Stahl Und Stahlwarenhandels-Gesellschaft mbH*,[35] the House of Lords affirmed *Entores*, again in the context of a telex communication (though this time where the telex had been sent in England and received outside the jurisdiction). However, the House refused to lay down a rule for all telex communications, Lord Wilberforce observing that:

> Since 1955 [when *Entores* was decided] the use of telex communication has been greatly expanded, and there are many variants on it. The senders and recipients may not be the principals to the contemplated contract. They may be servants or agents with limited authority. The message may not reach, or be intended to reach, the designated recipient immediately: messages may be sent out of office hours, or at night, with the intention, or upon the assumption, that they will be read at a later time. There may be some error or default at the recipient's end which prevents receipt at the time contemplated and

---

33   RSC Ord 11: see further section 10.2.2.
34   [1955] 2 QB 327, *per* Denning LJ, p 333.
35   [1983] 2 AC 34.

believed in by the sender. The message may have been sent and/or received through machines operated by third persons. And many other variations may occur. No universal rule can cover all such cases: they must be resolved by reference to the intentions of the parties, by sound business practice and in some cases by a judgment where the risks should lie.[36]

The present case is, as *Entores Ltd v Miles Far East Corporation* itself, the simple case of instantaneous communication between principals, and, in accordance with the general rule, involves that the contract (if any) was made when and where the acceptance was received.

Lord Fraser's view also did not extend to all forms of telex communication. He was prepared to hold only that[37] 'an acceptance sent by telex directly from the acceptor's office to the offeror's office should be treated as if it were an instantaneous communication between principals, like a telephone conversation'. One of his reasons was that:[38]

a party (the acceptor) who tries to send a message by telex can generally tell if his message has not been received on the other party's (the offeror's) machine, whereas the offeror, of course, will not know if an unsuccessful attempt has been made to send an acceptance to him. It is therefore convenient that the acceptor, being in the better position, should have the responsibility of ensuring that his message is received.

The risk of failure of communication, in other words, is placed on the acceptor, precisely because it is the acceptor, rather than the offeror, who is more likely to be aware of it.

Internet communications are generally (in that respect at least) unlike those in *Entores* and *Brinkibon*, however, and the postal rule ought therefore to apply to them.

9.2.3   Application of postal rule to e-commerce

Over some matters there can probably be little controversy. Each party must, at least, take the risks of his or her own equipment and set up. In *Entores*, Denning LJ envisaged the following:

But, suppose that [the offeree] does not know that his message did not get home. He thinks it has. This may happen if the listener on the telephone does not catch the words of acceptance, but nevertheless does not trouble to ask for them to be repeated: or the ink on the teleprinter fails at the receiving end, but the clerk does not ask for the message to be repeated: so that the man who sends an acceptance reasonably believes that his message has been received. The offeror in such circumstances is clearly bound, because he will be estopped from saying that he did not receive the message of acceptance.

There is no requirement, then, for the offeror actually to read the acceptance if, for example, there is a problem with his or her computer screen or printer, or with the connection to the Internet. Moreover, if it is accepted (as surely it must be) that

---

36 Lord Wilberforce cites *Household Fire and Carriage Accident Insurance Co Ltd v Grant* (1879) 4 Ex D 216, p 227 *per* Baggallay LJ, and *Henthorn v Fraser* [1892] 2 Ch 27, *per* Lord Herschell.
37 [1983] 2 AC 34, p 43.
38 *Ibid.*

communication to a person's agent is treated as communication to the person, then communication to the recipient's Internet Service Provider (ISP) is all that is required.

But surely it is possible to go further than this. Internet communication, whether e-mail or WWW, shares with its snailmail counterpart the feature that it is not possible to tell whether it has been received.[39] Surely, if the commercial convenience arguments that applied in *Harris' Case* are convincing at all, they apply just as forcibly in the Internet context. No doubt, the length of the delay is likely to be less, but that does not seem to be the crucial factor, no general rule having been laid down even for 'instantaneous communications'. Internet communications, especially over the WWW, are simply not like communications between two clerks, both present at their teleprinters and on the end of the telephone, the situation considered in *Entores*. If it is a good reason at all, the commercial convenience justification that has been advanced for the rule also argues for applying the postal rule to most Internet communications.

One situation which might be different is where the parties are on the same network, for example where each has a workstation connected to the same mainframe computer. There is no need now for messages physically to move anywhere at all and that transmission can, at least in principle, be literally instantaneous. Moreover, it should be possible instantly to obtain a confirmation of receipt into the recipient's mailbox. Now suppose that the mainframe itself, or at least the information in the recipient's mailbox, is destroyed before the recipient has the chance to read it. But here the parties really have entrusted their communication to a common agent, that is to say the mainframe computer.[40] This is also equivalent to receipt by the recipient's ISP. There is still every reason to apply the postal rule, to deem delivery of the message to be complete.

In conclusion, then, I would argue that the postal rule applies generally to e-commerce communications. Whether this is always a good thing is considered in section 9.2.6.

9.2.4   Withdrawals of offers

The postal rule has only been held to apply to contractual acceptances. There is no doubt, I think, that the offer must reach the offeree, since otherwise there is no clear basis for acceptance. In *Byrne v Van Tienhoven*, as we have seen, Lindley J held that the postal rule did not apply to a revocation of the offer.[41] In an Internet context, suppose the customer makes the offer to purchase goods over the Internet, for example having visited the trader's website. Before the trader accepts, the customer changes his or her mind and attempts to communicate revocation. The revocation does not reach the trader. *Byrne v Van Tienhoven* suggests that the trader may accept the original offer.

---

39 Being interactive, web-based communications are arguably equivalent to instantaneous communication, but although the sender might immediately be aware of non-delivery (because the browser will show an error message), he or she will not know the situation if the message reaches the recipient but the returned web page is lost; if the browser times out, the sender will simply not know whether the communication has been successful.

40 Davies, L, 'Contract formation on the internet: shattering a few myths', in Edwards, L and Waelde, C (eds), *Law and the Internet: Regulating Cyberspace*, 1st edn, 1997, Oxford: Hart, pp 112–13.

41 (1880) 5 CPD 344. See section 9.2.1.2.

I would suggest, however, that Internet contracting, whether by e-mail or over the WWW, is entirely different from the trading that was under consideration in *Byrne v Van Tienhoven*. In that case, the report does not mention any communications between the parties prior to the original posted offer, so there was no basis for inferring that the offeree had made the post office his agent to receive communications on his behalf. The offeror may have made the post office his agent, but the offeree had not. Lindley J says:[42]

> It may be taken as now settled that where an offer is made and accepted by letters sent through the post, the contract is completed the moment the letter accepting the offer is posted, even although it never reaches its destination.[43] When, however, these authorities are looked at, it will be seen that they are based upon the principle that the writer of the offer has expressly or impliedly assented to treat an answer to him by a letter duly posted as a sufficient acceptance and notification to himself, or, in other words, he has made the post office his agent to receive the acceptance and notification of it. But this principle appears to me to be inapplicable to the case of the withdrawal of an offer.

Of course, the offeror should not be able to enforce acceptance of the agency on the offeree. Nor (on essentially an extension of the same reasoning), simply because the offeror accepts the risks of postal delay or loss, should he or she be able to impose that acceptance of risk on the offeree.

Most Internet purchases are entirely different. If we imagine, for the moment, a web-based sale; there will typically have been many communications, choosing the product, identifying the customer, confirming financial and delivery details, and so on, before the offer is finally made by the customer. It must be clear, by this stage, that both parties have accepted the risks of Internet communication. There would seem to be as much reason to apply the postal rule to withdrawal of the offer as there is to apply it to its acceptance.

9.2.5   Offeror can stipulate

There is no doubt that the offeror can stipulate a mode of acceptance and, for example, that acceptance must reach him or her. In *Household Fire and Carriage v Grant*, Thesiger LJ said:[44]

> I am not prepared to admit that [this decision] will lead to any great or general inconvenience or hardship. An offeror, if he chooses, may always make the formation of the contract which he proposes dependent upon the actual communication to himself of the acceptance.

Obviously, this is only viable in a web context if the company is the offeror, for example in a *Carlill* situation. If the customer is the offeror, he or she is in no position to stipulate. However, where contracts are made by e-mail, it remains open for the offeror so to stipulate.

---

42   (1880) 5 CPD 344, p 348.
43   Lindley J refers to, among others, *Harris' Case*.
44   (1879) 4 Ex D 216, p 223. See also *Manchester Diocesan Council For Education v Commercial and General Investments Ltd* [1970] 1 WLR 241 (where the offeror stipulates, but does not make the mode exclusive, any other mode which is no less advantageous to him will also suffice).

9.2.6   Postal rule and consumer contracts

Though, in terms of the justifications that have been advanced for it, the postal rule should apply to Internet communications, it is not ideal in web-based consumer contracts, at least on the assumption that it is the customer who makes the offer. Suppose the customer clicks on 'I confirm' and then hears nothing. Perhaps the browser times out. The customer has no way of knowing whether his or her confirmation of the transaction has reached the server and, if so, whether the trader has accepted his or her offer, since an acceptance from the server may have failed to reach his or her ISP. If, however, the postal rule did not apply, the customer would not be bound unless the trader's acceptance reached his or her ISP.

Any moral argument based on the offeror choosing the medium of communication is wholly inappropriate here, since the choice is as much that of the trader as the customer. Nor can the offeror, who is after all dealing with a machine, specify a mode of acceptance.

It is surely undesirable for the consumer to be unaware whether he or she is contractually bound or not. If ordinary contractual principles lead to the conclusion that the postal rule applies, there is surely a case for legislation protecting consumers in this situation against its operation.

9.3   E-COMMERCE DIRECTIVE AND REGULATIONS

We will investigate later the effect of the EC Council Directive (2000/31/EC) on Electronic Commerce, which applies to information society service providers.[45] This Directive does not apply generally to e-commerce transactions, but only to suppliers of information society services – in effect, ISPs and online service providers, such as online newspapers, online databases, online financial services, online professional services (doctors, lawyers, estate agents, etc), online entertainment services (video on demand, advertising, etc). Article 11 requires these suppliers to acknowledge receipt of the customer's order, the order and acknowledgment of receipt being deemed to be received when the parties to whom they are addressed are able to access them. This, by itself, does not affect the present debate.[46]

However, the Regulations bringing the E-commerce Directive into effect in the UK are somewhat more detailed.[47] Regulation 9(1) provides:

9. (1) Unless parties who are not consumers have agreed otherwise, where a contract is to be concluded by electronic means a service provider shall, prior to an order being placed by the recipient of a service, provide to that recipient in a clear, comprehensible and unambiguous manner the information set out in (a) to (d) below—

---

45   See generally section 10.1.5.
46   Reed's conclusion (Reed, C, *Internet Law: Text and Materials*, 2nd edn, 2004, Cambridge: CUP, p 206) that this 'will make it more likely that the customer's final communication with the trader amounts to the offer' is surely too strong, since the acknowledgment could be simply that, rather than an acceptance. Note also that this Article does not in terms affect the postal rule, because that does not require receipt, when the rule operates.
47   Electronic Commerce (EC Directive) Regulations 2002, SI 2002/2013, at www.opsi.uk/si/si2002/20022013.htm.

(a)   the different technical steps to follow to conclude the contract;

(b)   whether or not the concluded contract will be filed by the service provider and whether it will be accessible;

(c)   the technical means for identifying and correcting input errors prior to the placing of the order; and

(d)   the languages offered for the conclusion of the contract.

This does not apply to contracts made by e-mail,[48] so we are talking about web-based contracts. By reg 11:

11. (1) Unless parties who are not consumers have agreed otherwise, where the recipient of the service places his order through technological means, a service provider shall—

(a) acknowledge receipt of the order to the recipient of the service without undue delay and by electronic means; and

(b) make available to the recipient of the service appropriate, effective and accessible technical means allowing him to identify and correct input errors prior to the placing of the order.

(2) For the purposes of paragraph (1)(a) above—

(a) the order and the acknowledgement of receipt will be deemed to be received when the parties to whom they are addressed are able to access them; and

(b) he acknowledgement of receipt may take the form of the provision of the service paid for where that service is an information society service.

(3) The requirements of paragraph (1) above shall not apply to contracts concluded exclusively by exchange of electronic mail or by equivalent individual communications.

These are obviously important consumer protection provisions and are considered in more detail later. What is interesting for present purposes, though, is reg 12:

12. Except in relation to regulation 9(1)(c) and regulation 11(1)(b) where 'order' shall be the contractual offer, 'order' may be but need not be the contractual offer for the purposes of regulations 9 and 11.

This clearly assumes that the customer makes the contractual offer under regs 9(1)(c) and 11(1)(b). Also, reg 11(2)(a) appears explicitly to replace the postal rule in contracts to which the Directive applies. Since these measures are intended clearly for the protection of the customer, this is perhaps justified.

9.4   INCORPORATION OF TERMS

In the physical world, traders like to incorporate their standard terms into contracts. The terms may be very lengthy, however, and may not fit within the documentation provided, for example, a ticket. In such cases, the ticket will often refer to another document containing the terms. Even if all the terms are in one document or otherwise easily accessible, there is no guarantee that the other party will read them.

---

48   See reg 9(4).

Similar problems exist in e-commerce. Although it is probably easier to make standard terms available, they may not fit easily on a screen, still less some of the devices, such as mobile phones, now being used to access the WWW. In any case, the home page is likely to be used as a shop window, rather than a display of terms, so it is likely that a terms page will be via a link.

The law on incorporation appears to be based almost entirely on form. An attempt to find any real meeting of minds is pretty well entirely absent. This may be inevitable, in order to achieve at least a reasonable degree of certainty as to what the terms are.

Even if terms are incorporated, they may be unenforceable, especially in consumer contracts, by virtue of the Unfair Contract Terms Act 1977 or the Unfair Terms in Consumer Contracts Regulations 1999 (enacting Council Directive (93/13/EEC)). Many web-based contracts are consumer contracts, so it is necessary to be aware of these, but they do not appear to give rise to any e-commerce specific issues.

9.4.1   Signed terms

If terms are signed, then they are incorporated into the contract, whether or not they have been read. The leading case is probably that of the Court of Appeal in *L'Estrange v Graucob*,[49] where the purchaser of a machine signed a document under which 'any express or implied condition, statement, or warranty, statutory or otherwise not stated herein is hereby excluded'. Though the purchaser had not read the document, the signature was held sufficient to exclude any implied warranty that the machine (which did not work satisfactorily) was fit for the purpose for which it was sold.

Conversely, if the document is not signed, perhaps through some oversight or error, then the terms will not form part of the contract. In *McCutcheon v David MacBrayne Ltd*,[50] the customer, who had shipped his car aboard a ferry, failed to sign the freight receipt the terms of which would have exempted the company from liability when the ferry sank, the customer's car becoming a total loss. He had signed the receipt on previous occasions and knew that it contained conditions, but on the particular occasion (probably because of oversight by the shipping company) it was unsigned. In consequence, the company was held unable to rely on the terms of the freight receipt. This also seems like a very technical decision, but as Lord Hodson observed:[51]

> The law as it stands appears hard on the holders of tickets who, unless they are exceptional persons, will not take pains to make an examination of a ticket offered to them to see if any conditions are imposed. It would be scarcely tolerable to take the further step of treating a contracting party as if he had signed and so bound himself by the terms of a document with conditions embodied in it, when, as here, he has done no such thing but may be supposed, having regard to his previous experience, to have been willing to sign what was put before him if he had been asked.

This is really a wholly objective view of the formation of contract. You are bound to terms not because of your actual intention, but because you have acted in a way that suggests you are so bound. Conversely, if you have not so acted, you are not bound.

---

49   [1934] 2 KB 394.
50   [1964] 1 WLR 125.
51   [1964] 1 WLR 125, p 130. Similar sentiments were adopted by Lord Devlin, pp 136–37.

This wholly objective view of contract formation has been criticised,[52] but is probably necessary to achieve reasonable certainty in commercial transactions.

In e-commerce, of course, documents are not signed physically, but a customer may well, by mouse click, expressly agree to a page of conditions. There seems no obvious reason why the fact that the signing process is electronic should make any difference. The nature of the signature, its physical form, is unimportant. As Lord Devlin observed in *McCutcheon*,[53] the 'signature is in truth about as significant as a handshake that marks the formal conclusion of a bargain'. It says, on an objective view of behaviour, 'I agree to these terms'. It does not say 'I have read these terms' or 'I have understood them'. It should not matter whether it is in the form of a pen mark or a mouse click.

9.4.2   Incorporation of terms by reference to another document

Written terms can also be incorporated by reference to another document, again whether or not that document is actually read. If the customer has read the terms then they will be incorporated. However, if, in the more usual case, it cannot be shown that the customer has read the terms, reasonable steps must be taken to have brought them to the customer's notice. This will depend, among other things, on whether the customer expects to see terms in a particular place. In the railway ticket cases, the following appear to have been accepted as the relevant questions:[54]

> (1) Did the passenger know that there was printing on the railway ticket? (2) Did he know that the ticket contained or referred to conditions? and (3) Did the railway company do what was reasonable in the way of notifying prospective passengers of the existence of conditions and where their terms might be considered?

To some extent, this will depend on whether contractual terms would normally be found in a particular document. If so, the customer would be expected to look.

However, there is also authority that the degree of notice depends on the term, a very clear signal being required for very onerous terms.[55] As Megaw LJ observed in *Thornton v Shoe Lane Parking*:[56]

> When the conditions sought to be attached all constitute, in Lord Dunedin's words,[57] 'the sort of restriction ... that is usual', it may not be necessary for a defendant to prove more than that the intention to attach *some* conditions has been fairly brought to the notice of the other party. But at least where the particular condition relied on involves a sort of restriction that is not shown to be usual in that class of contract, a defendant must show that his intention to attach an unusual condition *of that particular nature* was fairly brought to the notice of the other party. How much is required as being, in the words of

---

52 Eg, Spencer, JR, 'The rule in *L'Estrange v Graucob*' [1973] CLJ 104.
53 [1964] 1 WLR 125, p 133.
54 *Parker v South Eastern Railway* (1877) 2 CPD 416, but this quote is actually taken from Lord Hodson in *McCutcheon v David MacBrayne Ltd* [1964] 1 WLR 125, at 129, quoted again by Megaw LJ in *Thornton v Shoe Lane Parking* [1971] 2 QB 163, pp 171–72.
55 *Spurling (J) Ltd v Bradshaw* [1956] 1 WLR 461. Unusual terms require a greater degree of notice. See also *Interfoto Picture Library Ltd v Stiletto Visual Programmes Ltd* [1989] QB 433 (onerous contingent price term).
56 [1971] 2 QB 163, pp 172–173 (the emphasis is that of Megaw LJ).
57 In *Hood v Anchor Line (Henderson Bros) Ltd* [1918] AC 837, pp 846–47.

Mellish LJ,[58] 'reasonably sufficient to give the plaintiff notice of the condition', depends upon the nature of the restrictive condition.

In *Thornton*, the condition, excluding liability for personal injury, was unusual and onerous, and the company was held to have given insufficient notice of it, whenever the contract was concluded in the case. Indeed, Lord Denning MR said:[59]

> All I say is that it is so wide and so destructive of rights that the court should not hold any man bound by it unless it is drawn to his attention in the most explicit way. ... In order to give sufficient notice, it would need to be printed in red ink with a red hand pointing to it – or something equally startling.

It is reasonable to suppose that similar principles will apply in e-commerce. For a web transaction, the small size of the screen (especially with mobile phone devices) ensures that many terms will be incorporated via a link from the, or a, main page. Unlike tickets, there is probably not yet among customers an expectation of reference to terms. Traders ought ideally to make links very obvious, perhaps even taking up Lord Denning's red hand suggestion.

9.4.3   Terms cannot be incorporated once the contract is concluded

Lord Denning MR would have been prepared to decide *Thornton* on the alternative basis, that contractual terms cannot be incorporated once the contract is concluded.[60]

9.4.4   Effect of course of dealing

This was Mr Thornton's first visit to the car park. Had he been a regular visitor, he would have known of the notices and it would have been easier to argue that he had assented to the terms, even by Lord Denning's view of the time of conclusion of the contract. A previous course of dealing can make it easier for the company to show the requisite notice and that the customer has notice by the time the contract is concluded.[61] The principle upon which it could work in an incorporation case was explained by Lord Devlin in *McCutcheon v David MacBrayne Ltd*:[62]

> Previous dealings are relevant only if they prove knowledge of the terms, actual and not constructive, and assent to them. If a term is not expressed in a contract, there is only one other way in which it can come into it and that is by implication. No implication can be made against a party of a term which was unknown to him. If previous dealings show that a man knew of and agreed to a term on 99 occasions there is a basis for saying that it can be imported into the hundredth contract without an express statement. It may or may not be sufficient to justify the importation – that depends on the circumstances; but at least by proving knowledge the essential beginning is made. Without knowledge there is nothing.

There is no reason to suppose other than that this would also be true in e-commerce.

---

58   In *Parker v South Eastern Railway* (1877) 2 CPD 416, p 424.
59   [1971] 2 QB 163, p 170.
60   Above, section 9.1.3.3. He cited *Olley v Marlborough Court Ltd* [1949] 1 KB 532.
61   See, eg, the not particularly incisive discussion in *Mendelssohn v Normand Ltd* [1970] 1 QB 177, where, however, the company was unable to rely on the exemption clause for an entirely different reason. The course of dealing has to be sufficiently long, and consistent.
62   [1964] 1 WLR 125, p 134.

However, a previous course of dealing was held irrelevant in *McCutcheon* itself and, indeed, given Lord Devlin's view, it is difficult to see how it can ever cure the problem there, where on this particular occasion the document was unsigned. Immediately before the above passage he said:

> The fact that a man has made a contract in the same form 99 times (let alone three or four times which are here alleged) will not of itself affect the hundredth contract in which the form is not used.

It surely follows that where the problem is that a document has not been signed, the fact that it has been signed on many previous occasions is irrelevant; this is a different transaction from its predecessors.

9.5 IDENTITY OF CONTRACTING PARTIES: SHOPPING MALLS – WHO CONTRACTS WITH WHOM?

Shopping malls pose a problem as to the identity of the party contracting with the customer. Typically, the mall contains links to individual stores, but always displayed within the mall frame. It may not be at all clear to the visitor whether the page being visited is that of the mall or the merchant. Fortunately, malls appear to be getting wise to the potential legal problems their sites might create and this type of confusion now seems less prevalent than previously.[63]

Presumably, the shopping malls prefer any contracts to be made only with individual merchants, and not with themselves. The issue is the extent to which they succeed in this regard. This is basically an ostensible authority and notice problem and the principles are relatively straightforward.

9.5.1 Liability of the mall

In general, an offer made to X cannot be accepted by Y. In the particular case, on the assumption that the offer is made by the customer, an offer made to the mall can be accepted only by the mall. The mall cannot force upon the customer a contract with the individual trader if no offer was made to the trader.[64] Even if it is the trader who makes the offer, his identity should be crucial to the offer the customer accepts.

The issue is, then, whether the customer reasonably thinks he or she is making an offer to the mall or the trader. If the frame and URL remain that of the mall then surely, *prima facie* at least, the offer is made to the mall. No doubt, it is different if there is a clear statement on the mall's page that the contract is made only with the trader. No doubt, it would also be different if there were just a link from the mall to the trader's

---

63 Eg, Professor Reed (*Internet Law: Text and Materials, op cit* fn 46, pp 207–10) considered a shopping mall that operated in October 2000. Part of the site included T3's page, owned by Future Publishing, at www.t3.co.uk. When I visited this site early in 2004, I thought it would have been very difficult for a customer to know whether he or she was buying from T3 or from an individual merchant, and I felt that T3 were laying themselves open to potential litigation. Happily, T3 have revised their layout and this is no longer the case.

64 The authorities, beginning with *Cundy v Lindsay* (1878) 3 App Cas 459, are discussed and reviewed in *Ingram v Little* [1961] 1 QB 31, but the complications there, and in the later case of *Lewis v Averay* [1972] 1 QB 198, where the offeree was present in person, do not arise here.

site without the site coming up in the mall's frame; after all, one would not expect (for example) a Google link to a trader to lead to the implication that Google is the contracting party.

If the correct inference, though, is that the customer has contracted with the mall, this is unaffected by arrangements made between the commercial parties themselves. Moreover, the Court of Appeal has held that there is no constructive notice doctrine relieving from liability the party with whom, on the face of it, the contract is made, even if the customer ought to have known that there might be arrangements between the merchants purporting to alter the *prima facie* position.[65] If the mall is *prima facie* the contracting party, then only notice directly to the customer, prior to the conclusion of the contract, will affect that position.[66]

9.5.2   Liability of the individual trader

The individual trader can be liable directly from his own website to which the mall links. Alternatively, he may be liable if the mall has actual or apparent authority to make contracts on his behalf.

In most cases, there are unlikely to be any problems in this regard; the mall will have at least a general authority to act on behalf of the trader and, even if it exceeds its actual authority, it will probably have ostensible authority.[67] Thus, as long as the mall had general authority, the trader would probably be bound if an unauthorised link were made to an out-of-date mirror site, advertising old products or out of date prices. If the mall does not, in fact, have even the general authority of the individual trader to contract on his behalf, nothing the mall does unilaterally can give it that authority even if it appears to have authority,[68] although no doubt, even if the mall has no authority, the trader's own site, to which a link is made, will usually hold out offers to consumers directly. However, an individual trader would probably not be bound where a link is made by a mall without general authority to an imitation site (for example, a fraudster posing as the trader, perhaps in order to obtain credit card details).[69] He would also not be bound if, for example, the link were made to an out-of-date mirror site.

Even if the trader is the contracting party, the mall might still be liable in respect of any collateral promises made.[70] Malls should therefore be very careful not to appear to be the contracting party, and in respect of any promises that they make.

---

65 *Manchester Trust v Furness* [1895] 2 QB 539 (CA), where shipowners unsuccessfully attempted to defend an action for non-delivery by cargo-owners by claiming that the charterers, rather than themselves, were the contracting party. This well known authority has been affirmed many times.

66 Professor Reed (*Internet Law: Text and Materials, op cit* fn 46, pp 207–10) thought that T3 had not given sufficient notice, and this was also my own view when I visited the site in early 2004, but now I think there would be no reason to suppose T3 to be the contracting party at all.

67 If the link were to an old site with (eg) out-of-date prices, the mall would be liable to the trader for exceeding its authority.

68 *Armagas Ltd v Mundogas SA (The Ocean Frost)* [1986] 1 AC 717.

69 One of the relatively common frauds, discussed in section 11.2. Presumably, the trader could find himself bound were the mall to have general authority.

70 Eg, Reed's analysis of BarclaySquare, *Internet Law: Text and Materials, op cit* fn 46, p 209.

9.6 INTERNET CONTRACTS: HOW MUCH DETAIL IS NEEDED?

This is not specifically an Internet problem, but there seems little doubt that e-commerce will follow, and probably exacerbate, practices initially started with phone, telex and fax, where fixtures are made in general terms with details to be fixed later. This is especially likely on fluctuating markets where speed is of the essence, but the details of the contracts are quite complex (albeit often on standard forms).

A good example might be a charter of a ship. Charterparties are usually complex documents, although most or all of the terms will be on a standard form. Fixtures need to be made quickly, and today, of course, the Internet is often used. A typical firm offer for a voyage charter, for example, from a shipowner, might offer just the fundamentals of the fixture, it being understood that a standard form would later be used or adapted.[71] If the charterer suggests modifications, these will take effect as a counter-offer, but if he agrees, an enforceable agreement will be taken to have been concluded, even though it is only later that the other (less important) details will be formalised and the written form drawn up and signed. The fact that the parties intend later to record their agreement in a written form does not prevent the agreement being enforceable earlier.[72]

On fluctuating markets, there is always the temptation for one of the parties later to try to get out of it if the market has moved against him or her. The simplest argument is that no valid contract has been made in the first place. It is therefore necessary to decide when there is a binding contract in principle and, if so, the effect of a qualification such as 'subject details'.

Though the case law in this area is quite difficult to reconcile, there appear at least to be a number of general principles that the courts have adopted.

9.6.1 General principle in favour of giving effect to the intentions of the parties

The general position is that, as long as the parties clearly intend to be bound and have agreed enough to make the contract workable, the courts will fill in remaining terms. They do not set out to frustrate the parties' intentions. In the case of a contract for the sale of land, little (if any) more needs to be agreed than the identity of the land, the parties and the price. For goods and services, even the price need not be agreed; the courts will imply a reasonableness term. *Hillas v Arcos* is perhaps the leading case, where an option to purchase was enforced in spite of silence as to both quality and price.[73] Generally, then, the courts are prepared to fill in details, where the parties

---

71 For the sorts of details, see, eg, para 129 of the United Nations Conference on Trade and Development (UNCTAD) report by the secretariat on on Charter Parties, 1974. UNCTAD's website is at www.unctad.org. See also generally, paras 125–35 (on fixing a voyage charter) and paras 136–40 (on fixing a time charter).

72 *WJ Rossiter v Miller* (1878) 3 App Cas 1124; *The Blankenstein* [1985] 1 All ER 475 (valid contract sale of ship, although memorandum of agreement not signed and deposit not paid). See also Debattista, C, 'Charter-party fixtures "subject details" – further reflections' [1985] LMCLQ 241, p 243.

73 [1932] 43 LlL Rep 359. Perhaps it was easier than normal to imply terms, the parties already being in a business relationship, albeit for the previous year.

apparently intend to be bound, as long as there is sufficient certainty to determine the fundamentals of an agreement. Implied terms can fill in the details.

However, there are limits to this principle. In a charterparty context, Debattista observed that:[74]

(a) where the parties leave something unmentioned, it is easier to find that there is a contract;

(b) where the parties mention an issue which they leave unresolved, it is easier to find that there is no contract.

Indeed, it seems generally to be true that problems are more likely to arise with what the parties put in than what they leave out.

9.6.2 Uncertain terms cannot be enforced

If the parties say nothing, the courts can nearly always imply a term to fill the gap. It is a different matter where they say something, but it is meaningless. In *Scammell v Ouston*,[75] for example, an agreement for the sale of a van stated that:

> this order is given on the understanding that the balance of the purchase price can be had on hire-purchase terms over a period of two years.

There were, however, no usual terms, and many different hire-purchase arrangements. The House of Lords held this term to be too vague. It was not even clear whether finance was to be provided by the vendors or a finance house. Since the term was obviously fundamental, there was no enforceable contract.

Had the term been less fundamental, it would simply have been ignored and there would have been a binding contract.[76]

9.6.3 Agreement to agree is unenforceable

It is also a fundamental principle that the courts will not enforce an agreement to agree.[77] In *Foley v Classique Coaches*, Maugham LJ said:[78]

> It is indisputable that unless all the material terms of the contract are agreed there is no binding obligation. An agreement to agree in the future is not a contract; nor is there a contract if a material term is neither settled nor implied by law and the document contains no machinery for ascertaining it.

Phrases like 'subject to contract' are known to negate an intention to be bound,[79] although 'subject to' is only fatal if it negates an intention to be bound. For

---

74 Debattista, 'Charter-party fixtures "subject details" – further reflections', *op cit* fn 72, p 245. This is quite a comprehensive analysis, and though the article is now quite old, later authorities largely support his conclusions.

75 [1941] AC 251.

76 *Nicolene v Simmonds* [1953] 1 QB 543, where a contract was said to be subject to the 'usual conditions of acceptance'. No such conditions existed, but the CA, distinguishing *Scammell*, held the contract enforceable.

77 See *May & Butcher v R* [1934] 2 KB 17, where there was an agreement that the price for the goods should be subsequently fixed between the parties.

78 [1934] 2 KB 1, p 13. However, the agreement was saved: see sections 9.6.4 and 9.6.5.

79 *Chillingworth v Esche* [1924] 1 Ch 97 (CA).

example, an agreement to hold a fete, subject to the weather, could in principle be binding.

However, if the parties expressly make the contract 'subject to' something which is not yet agreed, the courts will infer a lack of agreement at this stage, even if the terms yet to be agreed are not fundamental. In *The Solholt*,[80] for example, Staughton J said (of a contract for the sale of a ship) that:

> She is described as having on that day been 'fixed subject to details'. That means that the main terms were agreed, but until the subsidiary terms and the details had also been agreed no contract existed.

This was *obiter*, but other authorities point in the same direction. In *The Samah*,[81] Parker J refused to hold a charterparty agreement concluded at the recap telex stage, where agreement still had to be reached on modifications to the vessel:

> At this time very little was known at all about the proposed modifications.[82] The telex specifically provides that the details are to be agreed and that the modification of plans, other than the water ballast tanks, is to be discussed with the owners. The owners had not then seen the charterers' *proforma*. It is undoubtedly possible to contract when much is left outstanding and for a party to commit himself to the acceptance of certain conditions which he has not seen. The present case is, however, not one of certain matters merely being left unmentioned. The parties have specifically stated that the details of the main modifications are to be agreed and the possible modification of other tanks is to be discussed. Furthermore, when Hellenic Seaways Overseas Corporation, the agents in Piraeus for the plaintiffs [would-be charterers], sent forward to Mr Maris the *proforma* charterparty, they stated:
>
> > ... you can add or alter clauses considering the special trading in which above mentioned vessels will be employed.
>
> This recognizes that the fixture was an unusual one for which special clauses would be required, as indeed they ultimately were. Mr Rokison [for the charterers] submits that the introduction of the special clauses later was merely a variation of an already binding fixture of the terms of the charterers' NYPE *proforma*.[83] But I cannot accept this. The reality of the situation is that both parties recognized that special provisions would have to be made. The charterers indeed set about drafting them. In my judgment neither party intended the final telexes to constitute a binding contract and neither party considered at the time that they had done so. Furthermore, even if they had so intended or considered, they would not have succeeded. The parties having expressly stated that certain further matters were to be agreed or discussed, the court cannot fill the gap. I therefore reject the plaintiffs' claim that a binding charter was made on Jan 3 [date of telex exchange].

Later cases are to the same effect.[84] If the parties expressly use terminology such as 'subject to details', which clearly indicates an intention not yet to be bound, the courts will give effect to that intention.

---

80 *Sotiros Shipping Inc v Sameiet Solholt (The Solholt)* [1981] 2 Lloyd's Rep 574, affirmed on other grounds [1983] 1 Lloyd's Rep 605.
81 *Mmecen SA v Inter Ro-Ro SA (The Samah and Lina V)* [1981] 1 Lloyd's Rep 40.
82 It seems that a Ro-Ro vessel was to be adapted for the import of bagged cement into Nigeria (my footnote).
83 NYPE is New York Produce Exchange, a widely used standard form time charterparty.
84 Eg, *The Nissos Samos* [1985] 1 Lloyd's Rep 378, *Granit SA v Benship International Inc* [1994] 1 Lloyd's Rep 526 (where, in the absence of the words 'subject to details', a contract was held to have been concluded), *Ignazio Messina & Co v Polskie Linie Oceaniczne* [1995] 2 Lloyd's Rep 566.

Agreements to negotiate also give rise to difficulties. An agreement to negotiate in good faith is too uncertain.[85] However, a lock-out clause was held valid in *Pitt v PHH Management*,[86] and there is some authority that a best endeavours undertaking could be valid.[87]

9.6.4   Mechanism to reach agreement

If the parties leave something to be later agreed by themselves, there is no contract. However, assuming agreement on fundamentals, it is possible for there to be a valid contract if there is a mechanism to agree other terms. This seems to be the effect of the House of Lords decision in *Sudbrook Trading Estate v Eggleton*,[88] where the price (of an option, given to a lessee, to purchase a reversion) was to be fixed by two valuers and, in default of agreement by them, an umpire appointed by the valuers.

On the same principle, an arbitration clause can be regarded as a mechanism to reach agreement. Debattista suggests that even where matters remain explicitly to be agreed, the inclusion of an arbitration clause as a mechanism to resolve any outstanding uncertainties might still save the contract.[89] This helped to save the contract in *Foley v Classique Coaches*, even though the petrol was to be sold 'at a price to be agreed by the parties in writing and from time to time'. Even where matters remain explicitly to be agreed, there can still be an enforceable contract if the agreement contains machinery for ascertaining them, such as the arbitration clause in the case itself, which covered 'any dispute or difference ... on the subject matter or construction of this agreement'.

However, in *May & Butcher v R*,[90] there was held to be no concluded agreement in spite of an arbitration clause, where the price for goods was to be subsequently fixed between the parties. But, in *May*, there was insufficient agreement, even on the fundamentals, so the problem was not simply that some terms remained to be agreed. The arbitration clause covered 'disputes with reference to or arising out of the agreement', and the House of Lords held that this did not cover failure to agree at all.[91]

By contrast, in *Foley*, there was arguably sufficient reason, even apart from the arbitration clause, to infer agreement to something, in which case arbitration could resolve the rest. *Foley* concerned a sale of land, with a subsidiary agreement to sell petrol[92] 'at a price to be agreed by the parties in writing and from time to time', and

---

85 *Walford v Miles* [1992] AC 128.

86 [1994] 1 WLR 327. In a negotiation for the sale of land, the lock-out clause precluded the vendor from negotiating with other potential purchasers as long as contracts were exchanged within a fortnight.

87 The authorities are set out in, eg, Smith, Sir JC and Thomas, JAC, *Casebook on Contract*, 11th edn, London: Sweet & Maxwell, pp 97 *et seq*.

88 [1983] 1 AC 444.

89 Debattista, 'Charter-party fixtures "subject details" – further reflections', *op cit* fn 72. He cites Lord Denning MR in *F & G Sykes (Wessex) v Fine Fare Ltd* [1967] 1 Lloyd's Rep 53, at 57–58.

90 [1934] 2 KB 17.

91 See especially, for example, the speech of Viscount Dunedin.

92 The vendors of the land retained a filling station on other land and the purchasers were coach operators.

the agreement was held by the Court of Appeal to be enforceable, in spite of the principles in section 9.6.3. One possibility, discussed in section 9.6.5, is that the agreement had been acted upon, so that it could easily be inferred at least that the parties had agreed something. Also, at least the price for the land had been agreed (and paid), the petrol sale being subsidiary.[93] Each of these is sufficient ground for distinguishing the case from *May*, where there was insufficient agreement to infer any contract at all, so that even the arbitration clause would not have been agreed. In *Foley*, there was clearly a contract, albeit with important matters remaining to be agreed, but the arbitration clause could resolve how to agree those matters.

9.6.5 Parties acting on agreement

Foley concerned an agreement for the supply of petrol (which was a subsidiary part of a contract for the sale of land) 'at a price to be agreed by the parties in writing and from time to time' and, despite lack of precise agreement as to price, the Court of Appeal held that there was an enforceable contract. Scrutton LJ said:[94]

> In the present case the parties obviously believed they had a contract and they acted for three years as if they had; they had an arbitration clause which relates to the subject-matter of the agreement as to the supply of petrol, and it seems to me that this arbitration clause applies to any failure to agree as to the price. By analogy to the case of a tied house there is to be implied in this contract a term that the petrol shall be supplied at a reasonable price and shall be of reasonable quality. For these reasons I think the Lord Chief Justice was right in holding that there was an effective and enforceable contract, although as to the future no definite price had been agreed with regard to the petrol.

Here, the parties had acted on the assumption of a valid contract for three years. They had clearly agreed to something, therefore.

As we saw in section 9.6.4, the arbitration clause was sufficient to resolve the details of the subsidiary agreement, but even in the absence of an arbitration clause, Scrutton LJ thought that the courts would have implied reasonableness terms. The fact that the parties had acted on the agreement for so long a time was clearly a crucial factor. This seems reasonable for a contract with ongoing commitments. After all, long term solus agreements rarely fix the price of, for example, petrol over the whole term, and variable rate mortgages are also valid.[95] Surely it should be sufficient that the parties have agreed the initial price, or alternatively, by acting on the agreement, given the courts sufficient information to determine what the initial price is.

9.6.6 Summary

The law was recently summed up in *Mamidoil-Jetoil Greek Petroleum Co SA v Okta Crude Oil Refinery AD*, as follows:[96]

---

93 See also *Hillas v Arcos* (1932) 147 LT 503, which decides the same as *Foley*.
94 [1934] 2 KB 1, p 10.
95 *Lombard Tricity Finance v Paton* [1989] 1 All ER 918. The parties had also acted on the agreement in *F & G Sykes (Wessex) v Fine Fare Ltd.*
96 [2001] EWCA Civ 406; [2001] 2 Lloyd's Rep 76 (CA).

Each case must be decided on its own facts and on the construction of its own agreement. Subject to that:

Where no contract exists, the use of an expression such as 'to be agreed' in relation to an essential term is likely to prevent any contract coming into existence, on the ground of uncertainty. This may be summed up by the principle that 'you cannot agree to agree'.

Similarly, where no contract exists, the absence of agreement on essential terms of the agreement may prevent any contract coming into existence, again on the ground of uncertainty.

However, particularly in commercial dealings between parties who are familiar with the trade in question, and particularly where the parties have acted in the belief that they had a binding contract, the courts are willing to imply terms, where that is possible, to enable the contract to be carried out.

Where a contract has once come into existence, even the expression 'to be agreed' in relation to future executory obligations is not necessarily fatal to its continued existence.

Particularly in the case of contracts for future performance over a period, where the parties may desire or need to leave matters to be adjusted in the working out of their contract, the courts will assist the parties to do so, so as to preserve rather than destroy bargains, on the basis that what can be made certain is itself certain. *Certum est quod certum reddi potest.*

This is particularly the case where one party has either already had the advantage of some performance which reflects the parties' agreement on a long term relationship, or has had to make an investment premised on that agreement.

For these purposes, an express stipulation for a reasonable or fair measure or price will be a sufficient criterion for the courts to act on. But even in the absence of express language, the courts are prepared to imply an obligation in terms of what is reasonable.

There, a long-term agreement was upheld, even though the price had not been agreed for the whole term.

9.7   CONTRACTING THROUGH ELECTRONIC AGENTS

At the time of writing, contracting through agents remains at the research stage, though no doubt the time will come when individuals and companies alike send electronic agents on to the Internet, programmed to do business on their behalf. Initially, one would expect to see experimentation to be confined to closed systems over which software can be standardised, but in the longer term it is reasonable to suppose that robotic agents will roam freely over the Internet.[97]

In the US, s 14 of the Uniform Electronic Transactions Act 1999 provides for automated transactions, at least in principle. In the EU, Art 9(1) of the E-commerce Directive provides that:

---

97   When I started using computers, well over 20 years ago, if I wanted to send someone a word processed file, we had to agree in advance the word processing program used, because one program would not read another's file. Nowadays, most of the common programs can read each other's files and, in any case, Microsoft Office seems to have become a *de facto* standard. We would no doubt see a similar standardisation evolving among electronic agents, allowing them freely to communicate with each other, even on open networks.

1. Member States shall ensure that their legal system allows contracts to be concluded by electronic means. Member States shall in particular ensure that the legal requirements applicable to the contractual process neither create obstacles for the use of electronic contracts nor result in such contracts being deprived of legal effectiveness and validity on account of their having been made by electronic means.

Arguably, at least, this provision includes fully automated contracts. However, there is nothing equivalent in the UK regulations bringing the Directive into force. Indeed, there is no provision for electronic agents in the UK, and English agency law does not (at least explicitly) recognise non-human agents.

It does not follow, however, that the UK is deficient in this respect. Although Professor Reed argues that contracting via electronic agents might be difficult, because of the difficulty of establishing a meeting of minds,[98] it is not easy to see what the difficulties are. To send a robot on to the Internet with negotiating powers would surely be akin to making an offer to all the world, as in *Carlill v Carbolic Smoke Ball Co*. We know from *Thornton v Shoe Lane Parking* that machines can make offers on behalf of their owners[99] and, if (as I argued in section 9.1.4) the customer makes the contractual offer, it seems also that programmed websites can accept offers from customers. Reed observes that the machine in *Thornton* had no negotiating ability, but it is difficult to see why this should matter as long as it has been programmed. After all, a website can at least carry on a dialogue, and surely make a contract, with a customer. It is true that genuine negotiation is another stage of development, but even there, ultimately at least, the machine is simply following the instructions programmed into it, those instructions being the evidence of the intentions of the parties.[100] Though it is too early to say for certain, if automated contracts become common features of e-commerce, then I would argue that English law has the conceptual tools to deal with this development.

Reed argues that agency concepts, such as ostensible authority, should be expanded to cover robots trawling the Internet and making decisions on their owners' behalf,[101] the choices and actions of the machine being attributed to the owner, but this may not be necessary. Even if the English law of agency explicitly applies only to human agents, the principles underlying it can surely apply more generally. If the robot is properly programmed, then it should not be possible for it to exceed its actual authority, and an intention to do what is within its actual authority should easily be attributed to the mind of the owner. Suppose, however, there is a problem with the software, so that the robot exceeds its authority and enters into contracts not intended by its owner. Clearly, there will be a contractual issue between the robot owner and the software writer. But, as far as third parties are concerned, the contracts entered into ought to be valid. The principles behind ostensible authority were stated as follows by Lord Keith in *The Ocean Frost*:[102]

---

98 Reed, *Internet Law: Text and Materials*, *op cit* fn 46, pp 210–12.
99 Section 9.1.3.3.
100 We are moving into the realms of artificial intelligence and a different type of programming, but, ultimately, the robot still acts on the instructions of its human user.
101 Reed, *Internet Law: Text and Materials*, *op cit* fn 46, p 211.
102 [1986] AC 717, p 777.

Ostensible authority comes about where the principal, by words or conduct, has represented that the agent has the requisite actual authority, and the party dealing with the agent has entered into a contract with him in reliance on that representation. The principal in these circumstances is estopped from denying that actual authority existed. In the commonly encountered case, the ostensible authority is general in character, arising when the principal has placed the agent in a position which in the outside world is generally regarded as carrying authority to enter into transactions of the kind in question.

This principle would seem just as apposite in the context of a robot agent as with a human. Obviously, given the seriousness of the potential consequences of the robot exceeding its authority, it will be very important to ensure that the software is correct.

10

OTHER CONTRACTUAL ISSUES

10.1 CONSUMER PROTECTION ISSUES

B2C e-commerce can cause particular problems for consumers, because of their ignorance of the other party, and because they are unable to examine the product as easily as they can in over-the-counter sales. These features are not unique to e-commerce, but nonetheless there are consumer protection provisions which affect B2C e-commerce, albeit that they might affect other consumer contracts also.

10.1.1 Application of general legislation on sale of goods and supply of services

Much domestic consumer protection legislation will apply in exactly the same way in an e-commerce as in a physical environment. Thus, for example, the general provisions of the Unfair Contract Terms Act 1977 and the Unfair Terms in Consumer Contracts Regulations 1999 apply to e-commerce, just as to any other contracts.[1]

There are also, however, provisions applying only to the sale or supply of goods or services. For example, ss 12–15 of the Sale of Goods Act 1979 imply into contracts for the sale of goods terms relating respectively to title, description, merchantable quality and fitness for purpose. Section 6 of the Unfair Contract Terms Act 1977 prohibits contracting out of the implied undertaking as to title and, in consumer contracts, the other implied undertakings also. In business contracts, contracting out of the implied terms (apart from title) is allowed, but subject to a test of reasonableness. There are also terms implied into contracts for the supply of services by ss 13–16 of the Supply of Goods and Services Act 1982, together with restrictions on contracting out. Much e-commerce involves the sale or supply of goods or services, in which case again there will be no problem; these provisions will apply, just as to any other such sale or supply.

It seems, however, that online deliveries (for example, of music files, computer programs online, films, etc) will not be regarded as goods and it seems unlikely that they will often be regarded as services either. In that case, obviously, any provisions which apply only to the sale or supply of goods or services will not apply to them. The following views were expressed by Glidewell LJ, in *St Albans City and District Council v International Computers Ltd*, on the definition of goods for the purposes of the Sale of Goods Act 1979:[2]

> In both the Sale of Goods Act 1979, s 61, and the Supply of Goods and Services Act 1982, s 18, the definition of goods includes 'all personal chattels other than things in action and money'. Clearly, a disk is within this definition. Equally clearly, a program, of itself, is not ...

---

1   The regulations, bringing into force Council Directive (93/13/EEC) of 5 April 1993 on unfair terms in consumer contracts, can be found at www.opsi.gov.uk/si/si1999/19992083.htm. There are also the Unfair Terms in Consumer Contracts (Amendment) Regulations 2001, at www.opsi.gov.uk/si/si2001/20011186.htm.

2   [1996] 4 All ER 481, p 492.

> Suppose I buy an instruction manual on the maintenance and repair of a particular make of car. The instructions are wrong in an important respect. Anybody who follows them is likely to cause serious damage to the engine of his car. In my view, the instructions are an integral part of the manual. The manual including the instructions, whether in a book or a video cassette, would in my opinion be 'goods' within the meaning of the 1979 Act, and the defective instructions would result in a breach of the implied terms in s 14.
>
> If this is correct, I can see no logical reason why it should not also be correct in relation to a computer disk onto which a program designed and intended to instruct or enable a computer to achieve particular functions has been encoded. If the disk is sold or hired by the computer manufacturer, but the program is defective, in my opinion there would *prima facie* be a breach of the terms as to quality and fitness for purpose implied by the 1979 Act or the 1982 Act.

Thus, on this reasoning, a program supplied on disk is 'goods', but a pure program is not, at least within the 1979 and 1982 definitions. If this reasoning is correct, it must surely also exclude all online deliveries from the definition of goods within the EC Directive on Distance Selling (on which see further section 10.1.2 below).

Supply of software could still possibly be a supply of services, at least if it is bespoke software, prepared specifically for the particular consumer. It would surely not be apposite, however, to describe an off the peg electronic supply as a supply of services, for example where music files are downloaded, or perhaps a standard program.

To conclude, most online deliveries will not involve a contract concerning goods or services, and hence will fall outside the UK provisions and also the Distance Selling Directive considered below. It seems certain, at any rate, that they will not be regarded as sales of goods. Most would not properly be described as supplies of services, though probably the delivery of a bespoke application could be so described. Another possibility might be an ongoing supply, for example where an anti-virus program is periodically updated.

St Albans involved the supply of faulty software to a local authority and, since the software was not goods, neither the statutorily implied terms of merchantable quality nor fitness for purpose applied. However, the supplier was in any case liable for breach of either express terms or common law implied terms, and it follows that the reasoning in the passages quoted was not part of the *ratio* of *St Albans*. It seems that the software was supplied on disk and the program installed by ICL, the supplier, on the local authority's computers, the local authority having no more than a licence to use the program. Glidewell LJ did not think there had been a sale or hire of the program, or a sale of goods by the transfer of the program in this way.[3] It does not appear to have been argued that there was a supply of services.

In the case itself, then, nothing ultimately turned on whether the software was goods or not. The common law will imply terms which are similar to the statutory terms:[4]

---

3   *Ibid*, p 492.
4   *Ibid*, p 493.

The terms implied by the 1979 Act and the 1982 Act were originally evolved by the courts of common law and have since by analogy been implied by the courts into other types of contract.

What the common law will not do, however, is place any restrictions on contracting out of the implied obligation. This is likely significantly to weaken the protection, particularly of consumers, in respect of online deliveries.

There are also localisation issues as to where the contract is performed, where delivery takes place, etc. This is not relevant to the present discussion, but has ramifications for proper law and jurisdiction (see further section 10.2 below).

10.1.2   EC Directive on Distance Selling

Though not all distance selling involves e-commerce, all e-commerce involves at least some of the features of distance selling. It would be surprising, therefore, if at least some aspects of the Council Directive (97/7/EC) on Distance Selling did not apply to e-commerce.[5] The provisions of the Directive are incorporated into UK law by the Consumer Protection (Distance Selling) Regulations 2000.[6] Though the UK has really done no more than implement the Directive in the most limited way it can, the Directive itself leaves quite a lot for Member States to fill out. The regulations are therefore somewhat more detailed than the Directive.

The basic idea behind the Directive is to require the provision of information, essentially to ensure transparency ('to ensure that the consumer makes a well informed purchasing decision, which is in the interests of both consumer protection and competition policy').[7] The consumer would generally have this information in a face-to-face transaction, and the Directive attempts to put him or her into a similar position, as far as possible, though the transaction be at a distance.

10.1.2.1   Introduction

Council Directive (97/7/EC) on Distance Selling predates widespread use of the Internet and consequently does not apply to e-commerce in a particularly satisfactory fashion. The 1997 date is quite misleading. In fact, the original Commission proposal dates back to 1992, and that was a response to a Council resolution of 1989.[8] Since the World Wide Web (WWW) did not become public until 1991, it is probable that at this time teleshopping and videophones ('telephone with screen') were predicted to take off and the WWW was not predicted at all. Consequently, the Directive makes poor provision for web-based commerce.

---

5   The full text of the Directive can be found at www.spamlaws.com/docs/97-7-ec.pdf.
6   Full text can be found at www.opsi.gov.uk/si/si2000/20002334.htm.
7   Lodder, A and Kaspersen, H (eds), *eDirectives: Guide to European Union Law on E-Commerce*, 2002, The Hague: Kluwer Law International, p 14.
8   *Ibid*, p 12.

10.1.2.2   Definitions and application

The directive is about distance selling which, in principle, would embrace most e-commerce. In reality, quite substantial sectors of e-commerce are excluded and it is not entirely clear what is included. A distance contract is defined in Art 2(1) (reg 3 of the Regulations) as follows:

(1) 'distance contract' means any contract concerning goods or services concluded between a supplier and a consumer under an organised distance sales or service provision scheme run by the supplier who, for the purpose of the contract, makes exclusive use of one or more means of distance communication up to and including the moment at which the contract is concluded.

Note the requirement that the contract be between a supplier and a consumer. This is nakedly a consumer protection provision, therefore, and has no relevance to B2B transactions. There are, however, many other gaps in the legislation, which we must now consider.

10.1.2.3   Online deliveries excluded?

The definition also requires that the contract concerns goods or services. Neither goods nor services are defined for the purposes of the Directive. It seems likely, however, that the definition will be similar to that considered above in relation to UK legislation. In that case, most online deliveries will be excluded from the scope of the Directive.

10.1.2.4   Other exclusions

The definition above requires the supplier to make 'exclusive use of one or more means of distance communication'. Article 2(4) expands this:[9]

(4) 'means of distance communication' means any means which, without the simultaneous physical presence of the supplier and the consumer, may be used for the conclusion of a contract between those parties. An indicative list of the means covered by this Directive is contained in Annex I.

This would appear to include Internet communications but, though electronic mail is included within the examples in Annex I, the WWW, unsurprisingly, is not. Nonetheless, the list in Annex 1 is non-exhaustive, or indeed indicative, and surely it would be nonsense to argue that the Directive does not apply to web-communications.

There is, however, a substantial list of exemptions in Art 3(1):

1. This Directive shall not apply to contracts:
    -   relating to financial services, a non-exhaustive list of which is given in Annex II,[10]
    -   concluded by means of automatic vending machines or automated commercial premises,
    -   concluded with telecommunications operators through the use of public payphones,

---

9   The relevant UK provisions are reg 3 and Sched 1.
10   These are now covered by Council Directive (2002/65/EC) concerning the distance marketing of consumer financial services. For views of the UK government on its implementation, see www.hm-treasury.gov.uk/media//E4F28/DMD%20Final_268.pdf.

- concluded for the construction and sale of immovable property or relating to other immovable property rights, except for rental,
- concluded at an auction.

It is perhaps arguable that automated commercial premises could include a website but, in any case, a truly noteworthy exclusion is auctions. With companies such as eBay becoming serious players in the e-commerce marketplace, this is certainly a significant exclusion.

Moreover, the UK reg 6(2) (enacting Art 3(2)) excludes from regs 7–19 (Arts 4 and 5 (see section 10.1.3.1), 6 (see section 10.1.3.2) and 7(1) (see section 10.1.3.5)) 'contracts for the supply of food, beverages or other goods intended for everyday consumption supplied to the consumer's residence or to his workplace by regular roundsmen'. Presumably, this was intended to exclude milk and bread deliveries, and so on, but its effect may be that, for example, Tesco Direct (Internet) food deliveries are excluded from everything except fraud protection.[11] This would again be a significant exclusion for which a logical basis is hard to find, but in fact it is by no means clear, the regulation being literally ambiguous. It could be read as either 'supplied to the consumer's residence or to his workplace by regular roundsmen', or 'supplied to the consumer's residence (or to his workplace by regular roundsmen)'. The former interpretation would not exclude Tesco Direct since the supply to the residence would not be by regular roundsmen, whereas the latter definitely would.

Also exempted are contracts for the sale of land or the construction of a building.

The Directive, as observed then, was conceived prior to the development of modern e-commerce and, though it applies to much e-commerce, there are some really substantial exclusions from it. Moreover, it is by no means clear exactly what is excluded, and what is not.

10.1.3   Substance of the Directive

The main point of this Directive is to require traders to provide information and allow for a cooling off period. The sanction for failure to provide the relevant information is to extend the cooling off period. The notice requirements do not appear to be contractual terms and the sanction from the consumer's viewpoint is cancellation. In that case, any card payment is also cancelled. Contractual terms are void insofar as they are inconsistent with the Directive/regulations.[12]

10.1.3.1   Information

Articles 4 and 5 require the provision of information, essentially, as we have seen, to ensure transparency.[13] They include matters like the identity and address of the supplier, which may not be obvious in an Internet environment. Article 4 applies in

---

11 Fraud protection being provided by Art 8. This is considered in greater detail in the following chapter.

12 Regulation 25.

13 The equivalent UK regs are 7 and 8.

'good time prior to the conclusion of any distance contract'. The information is quite basic and not at all onerous. The full list, from Art 4(1), is as follows:[14]

(a) the identity of the supplier and, in the case of contracts requiring payment in advance, his address;

(b) the main characteristics of the goods or services;

(c) the price of the goods or services including all taxes;

(d) delivery costs, where appropriate;

(e) the arrangements for payment, delivery or performance;

(f) the existence of a right of withdrawal, except in the cases referred to in Article 6(3);[15]

(g) the cost of using the means of distance communication, where it is calculated other than at the basic rate;

(h) the period for which the offer or the price remains valid;

(i) where appropriate, the minimum duration of the contract in the case of contracts for the supply of products or services to be performed permanently or recurrently.

By Art 4(2), the information 'shall be provided in a clear and comprehensible manner in any way appropriate to the means of distance communication used'. Recital 8 provides that 'the languages used for distance contracts are a matter for the Member States'. The requirements can reasonably be criticised for being weak.[16]

Article 4 (reg 7) applies prior to the conclusion of the contract. Article 5 (reg 8) requires a later written confirmation. Much of the information to be provided is the same as that in Art 4, but there are additional requirements concerning returns and rights of cancellation. The information must be confirmed, by Art 5(1), 'in another durable medium available and accessible to' the consumer:

> The consumer must receive written confirmation or confirmation in another durable medium available and accessible to him of the information referred to in Article 4(1)(a) to (f), in good time during the performance of the contract ...

This probably includes an e-mail communication, but perhaps not a web page confirmation. In the view of the UK government:[17]

> We consider that confirmation by electronic mail would meet the definition of confirmation in 'another durable medium available and accessible to [the consumer]', where the order has been made by means of e-mail. We have not however specified this in the Draft regulations since the Directive is not specific on the point, and only a court can determine the meaning of the wording.

A web page confirmation might be different because, although in principle it can be as permanent as e-mail, this is so only if the consumer downloads it (or at least the

---

14 See also reg 7(a).

15 These are exemptions from the withdrawal right: see further below.

16 Eg, Brownsword, R and Howells, G, 'When surfers start to shop: Internet commerce and contract law' (1999) 19 LS 287, p 301.

17 Department of Trade and Industry Publication, *Distance Selling Directive – Implementation in the UK*, November 1999, para 3.9. In an earlier paper, this was qualified by 'the consumer being the owner of the facilities (ie, the computer from which the electronic mail has been generated)': see Brownsword and Howells, *op cit* fn 16, p 303, note 69. The obvious problem is that the supplier would have no means of knowing whether the qualification had been met.

information on it). There might be good grounds, then, for including e-mail but excluding web confirmations.

Note that these requirements are additional to other information that might be required by Council Directive (2000/31/EC) on electronic commerce, considered below.[18] The E-commerce Directive applies only to a limited range of e-commerce transactions; unlike the provisions here, it imposes no particular formal requirements.

10.1.3.2   Withdrawal: the basic right

Article 6 (reg 10) provides a right of withdrawal, according to Recital 14 on the grounds that 'the consumer is not able actually to see the product or ascertain the nature of the service provided before concluding the contract'. This effectively places at least some of the risks of this type of transaction on the supplier, rather than the consumer:[19]

> Retailers of many ... consumer products remain unable to take full advantage of electronic commerce methods as potential purchasers are reluctant to buy without first inspecting the product, especially if it is a new product or service and/or the company offering the same is not one with which the customer is familiar. A right of withdrawal, however, means that a potential customer can take full advantage of the benefits of shopping online (lower price, home delivery, etc) knowing that if the product or service is not to his liking, he can withdraw from the contract without penalty or need of any justification.

The right of withdrawal can perhaps therefore be seen as putting the consumer back into a position equivalent to a face-to-face customer. It is also ultimately a sanction, an important aspect of the enforcement of the Directive. For example, Art 6(1) provides for a right of withdrawal for any reason, of at least seven days from the date of the confirmation of information under Art 5. If the supplier fails to fulfil the obligations laid down in Art 5, then three months is allowed. One of the consequences of the withdrawal right, therefore, is to encourage the supplier to comply with his obligations to provide information.

However, withdrawal rights are inappropriate for some types of contract, and there are exceptions in Art 6(3):[20]

> ... contracts:
>
> – for the provision of services if performance has begun, with the consumer's agreement, before the end of the seven working day period referred to in paragraph 1,
> – for the supply of goods or services the price of which is dependent on fluctuations in the financial market which cannot be controlled by the supplier,
> – for the supply of goods made to the consumer's specifications or clearly personalized or which, by reason of their nature, cannot be returned or are liable to deteriorate or expire rapidly,
> – for the supply of audio or video recordings or computer software which were unsealed by the consumer,
> – or the supply of newspapers, periodicals and magazines,
> – for gaming and lottery services.

---

18   Section 10.1.5.
19   Lodder and Kaspersen, *eDirectives: Guide to European Union Law on E-Commerce, op cit* fn 7, p 17.
20   The equivalent UK legislation is reg 13.

Obviously, in most of these cases, a right of withdrawal would operate unfairly against the supplier.

Article 6(3) does not address the issue of delivery of online material, were it otherwise covered by the regulations. They should arguably be exempted. It is possible that 'by reason of their nature [they] cannot be returned' and, of course, the newspapers, periodicals and magazines exception will cut out some online sales. It is probable, however, that computer software delivered online, or audio or video material, is not exempted, since the exemption clearly envisages delivery of a physical medium, which is sealed. This may well be academic, because it seems unlikely that most of these online sales come within the Directive in any event.[21]

An important exception is goods which, by reason of their nature, cannot be returned or are liable to deteriorate or expire rapidly. This will include much food, again quite a large area of Internet activity (and again assuming food deliveries fall within the Directive anyway).[22]

10.1.3.3   The cancellation period

The period is calculated in such a way as to encourage the supplier to perform his Art 5 (reg 8) obligations. The UK regulations approximately mirror Art 6(1) but, since they differ in detail, it is the regulation that is set out here. This is reg 11:

Cancellation period in the case of contracts for the supply of goods

11.(1) For the purposes of regulation 10,[23] the cancellation period in the case of contracts for the supply of goods begins with the day on which the contract is concluded and ends as provided in paragraphs (2) to (5).

(2) Where the supplier complies with regulation 8,[24] the cancellation period ends on the expiry of the period of seven working days beginning with the day after the day on which the consumer receives the goods.

(3) Where a supplier who has not complied with regulation 8 provides to the consumer the information referred to in regulation 8(2), and does so in writing or in another durable medium available and accessible to the consumer, within the period of three months beginning with the day after the day on which the consumer receives the goods, the cancellation period ends on the expiry of the period of seven working days beginning with the day after the day on which the consumer receives the information.

(4) Where neither paragraph (2) nor (3) applies, the cancellation period ends on the expiry of the period of three months and seven working days beginning with the day after the day on which the consumer receives the goods.

(5) In the case of contracts for goods for delivery to third parties, paragraphs (2) to (4) shall apply as if the consumer had received the goods on the day on which they were received by the third party.

Obviously, the effect of paras (2)–(4) is to encourage the supplier to comply with reg 8, or at least to provide the information as quickly as possible. As the explanatory note to the regulations says:

---

21 Not being sales or supplies of goods or services: see section 10.1.1.
22 See section 10.1.2.4.
23 Which provides for the right to cancel.
24 The UK equivalent of Art 5.

> Where the supplier fails to comply with the information requirement at all, the cooling-off period is extended by 3 months.
>
> Where the supplier complies with the information requirement later than he should have done but within 3 months the cooling-off begins from the date he provided the information (regulations 10–12).

Regulation 12 provides something similar for services, except that 'the cancellation period in the case of contracts for the supply of services begins with the day on which the contract is concluded', presumably because there is no single delivery date, unlike for supplies of goods.

Apart from the sanction element, there is no obvious reason for linking information and withdrawal rights, their functions being wholly different. However, Art 5 includes information about withdrawal and, arguably therefore, the information needs to precede the actual withdrawal right.

10.1.3.4   The actual process of cancellation

There are detailed provisions on how the withdrawal rights work in practice, for example reimbursement, return of goods and cancellation of credit card payment. Article 6(4) leaves these to the Member States to implement. Accordingly, reg 14 requires the supplier to reimburse the customer within 30 days; regs 15 and 16 deal with cancellation of any related credit agreements; reg 17 places a duty on the consumer to take reasonable care of the goods and restore them to the supplier; and reg 18 deals with part-exchange goods, allowing (where appropriate) 'the consumer ... to recover from the supplier a sum equal to the part-exchange allowance', the point being that it might not be possible to return the part-exchanged goods themselves.

The general idea, as stated in the explanatory note to the regulations, is that '[t]he effect of giving notice of cancellation under the regulations is that the contract is treated as if it had not been made'.

10.1.3.5   Performance

Performance issues, or at least the time of performance are dealt with under Art 7 (regs 19 and 20). There is nothing about defective performance as such, equivalent to s 75 of the UK Consumer Credit Act 1974 in the next chapter,[25] but arguably it is not needed as the right of withdrawal can provide redress in any case for defective performance (except that the period is rather short).

The basic obligation is that 'the supplier shall perform the contract within a maximum of 30 days beginning with the day after the day the consumer sent his order to the supplier', the sanction being again withdrawal and cancellation of any card payment. Note that there are no exceptions to the withdrawal right this time (and, of course, there should not be, given non-performance by the supplier).

---

25   Section 11.4.

10.1.3.6 *Fraud*

Fraud is essentially a payment issue, and we will consider it in detail in the next chapter.[26]

10.1.4 Enforcement

The enforcement provisions considered so far are rather weak. Contractual terms are void insofar that they are inconsistent with the Directive/regulations (reg 25). However, there is nothing in the regulations positively to incorporate into the contract any of the obligations considered, and there are no criminal sanctions (with the exception of inertia sales).

Moreover, others apart from the consumer might have an interest in enforcing the regulations, for example consumer organisations and competitors. The preamble to the Directive notes that:[27]

> ... non-compliance with this Directive may harm not only consumers but also competitors; ... provisions may therefore be laid down enabling public bodies or their representatives, or consumer organizations which, under national legislation, have a legitimate interest in consumer protection, or professional organizations which have a legitimate interest in taking action, to monitor the application thereof.

Accordingly, Art 11 provides:

Article 11. Judicial or administrative redress

1. Member States shall ensure that adequate and effective means exist to ensure compliance with this Directive in the interests of consumers.

2. The means referred to in paragraph 1 shall include provisions whereby one or more of the following bodies, as determined by national law, may take action under national law before the courts or before the competent administrative bodies to ensure that the national provisions for the implementation of this Directive are applied:

    (a) public bodies or their representatives;

    (b) consumer organizations having a legitimate interest in protecting consumers;

    (c) professional organizations having a legitimate interest in acting.

3. (a) Member States may stipulate that the burden of proof concerning the existence of prior information, written confirmation, compliance with time-limits or consumer consent can be placed on the supplier.

    (b) Member States shall take the measures needed to ensure that suppliers and operators of means of communication, where they are able to do so, cease practices which do not comply with measures adopted pursuant to this Directive.

4. Member States may provide for voluntary supervision by self-regulatory bodies of compliance with the provisions of this Directive and recourse to such bodies for the settlement of disputes to be added to the means which Member States must provided to ensure compliance with the provisions of this Directive.

---

26 Section 11.3.2.
27 Paragraph 20.

In the UK, the Office of Fair Trading and Local Authority Trading Standards have a duty to consider complaints, and can apply to the courts for an injunction.[28]

10.1.5   E-commerce Directive

The E-commerce Directive is largely covered in Chapter 12, in the Internet Service Provider (ISP) liability chapter. However, the parts of the Directive that require the provision of information are also relevant to this chapter.[29]

The E-commerce Directive is a diverse provision, covering many aspects of information society service providers, the establishment of their communication, conclusion of contracts and liability; this is said to reflect the life cycle of e-commerce activities. It covers only a limited range of e-commerce transactions and is not primarily a consumer protection provision (although there are consumer protection provisions within it), being intended instead to ensure a level playing field for such service providers within the Single Market. Unlike the Distance Selling Directive, therefore, it includes B2B as well as B2C transactions, including for example the provision of online newspapers, databases, financial services, video on demand, etc.

Nonetheless, in the UK at least, enforcement is primarily by the recipient of the service.[30] This rather assumes that it is the recipient of the service who will be primarily aggrieved.

10.1.5.1   What transactions are covered

The Directive is about provision of electronic services, such as those provided by ISPs. However, coverage is much wider than that, extending effectively to any commercial provision of electronic information. There are definitions and examples in Recitals 17 and 18. Recital 17 refers back to definitions in previous Directives, but adds 'this definition covers any service normally provided for remuneration, at a distance, by means of electronic equipment for the processing (including digital compression) and storage of data, and at the individual request of a recipient of a service …'. So we are talking about commercial providers (not, for example, non-profit organisations), at a distance, providing information or data in response to individual requests (but this last requirement, which is intended to exclude general broadcasting, will always be satisfied by a website). Recital 18 provides:

> (18) Information society services span a wide range of economic activities which take place on-line; these activities can, in particular, consist of selling goods on-line; activities such as the delivery of goods as such or the provision of services off-line are not covered; information society services are not solely restricted to services

---

28 Regulations 26 and 27 (general enforcement provisions).
29 Council Directive (2000/31/EC) of the European Parliament and of the Council of 8 June 2000 on certain legal aspects of information society services, in particular electronic commerce, in the Internal Market ('Directive on electronic commerce'). Full text is at http://europa.eu.int/eur-lex/pri/en/oj/dat/2000/l_178/l_17820000717en00010016.pdf. The UK regulations giving effect to the Directive, the Electronic Commerce (EC Directive) Regulations 2002 SI 2002/2013, are at: www.ipso.gov.uk/si/si2002/20022013.htm.
30 Regulations 13–15 make provision for breach of statutory duty actions, injunctions on application to a court, and rescission of contract.

giving rise to on-line contracting but also, in so far as they represent an economic activity, extend to services which are not remunerated by those who receive them, such as those offering on-line information or commercial communications, or those providing tools allowing for search, access and retrieval of data; information society services also include services consisting of the transmission of information via a communication network, in providing access to a communication network or in hosting information provided by a recipient of the service; television broadcasting within the meaning of Directive EEC/89/552 and radio broadcasting are not information society services because they are not provided at individual request; by contrast, services which are transmitted point to point, such as video-on-demand or the provision of commercial communications by electronic mail are information society services; the use of electronic mail or equivalent individual communications for instance by natural persons acting outside their trade, business or profession including their use for the conclusion of contracts between such persons is not an information society service; the contractual relationship between an employee and his employer is not an information society service; activities which by their very nature cannot be carried out at a distance and by electronic means, such as the statutory auditing of company accounts or medical advice requiring the physical examination of a patient are not information society services.

However, the Directive has nothing to do with physical goods, there being the following restrictions in Recital 21:[31]

... the coordinated field covers only requirements relating to on-line activities such as on-line information, on-line advertising, on-line shopping, on-line contracting and does not concern Member States' legal requirements relating to goods such as safety standards, labelling obligations, or liability for goods, or Member States' requirements relating to the delivery or the transport of goods ...

Although the legislation is intended for a wholly different purpose, the information provisions will no doubt fill some of the gaps in the Distance Selling Directive.

10.1.5.2   Establishment

Article 4(1) requires that the taking up and pursuit of the activity of an information society service provider may not be made subject to prior authorisation or any other requirement having equivalent effect. We have seen a similar position taken for certification service providers and digital signatures,[32] and this is, of course, consistent with Single Market principles.

10.1.5.3   Communication

There are requirements for the provision of information in Art 6. These overlap with the Distance Selling Directive, though there are other requirements, such as details of professional bodies and the like, where appropriate. In the UK, reg 7 requires all communications to be clearly identifiable as a commercial communication, together with other requirements, and reg 8 is intended to prevent spam.

---

31   There are also public policy/security exemptions in Art 3.
32   See section 6.5.7.

10.1.5.4   Contracts

These have, to some extent, already been covered in section 9.3, on the formation of contacts. We have also already come across (in the context of contracting via electronic agents) Art 9(1):

> Member States shall ensure that their legal system allows contracts to be concluded by electronic means. Member States shall in particular ensure that the legal requirements applicable to the contractual process neither create obstacles for the use of electronic contracts nor result in such contracts being deprived of legal effectiveness and validity on account of their having been made by electronic means.

This provision is clearly intended to promote e-commerce. There is no equivalent regulation, or other provision giving effect to this Article but, as we have seen, it seems likely that the UK already complies.[33]

Article 10 (information provisions) again overlaps with the Distance Selling Directive. Article 11 requires a trader to acknowledge receipt of order. We have already seen (in Chapter 9) the assumption that the customer makes the offer,[34] and that the postal rule does not apply to acceptance.

10.2   LAW AND JURISDICTION

E-commerce is clearly a global activity and it is quite likely that the contracting parties will be in different countries. Obviously, this can lead to potential for disputes about which country's law applies, and also as to jurisdiction over the defendant. A full review of the principles of choice of law and jurisdiction is, however, well beyond the scope of this book. We will concentrate instead on concerns that are e-commerce specific and, in particular, issues of localisation, it often being difficult in e-commerce disputes to determine precisely where something has happened. Principles of localisation will be discussed later, at section 10.2.3.

10.2.1   Whose law applies?

In the UK, contract proper law issues are determined by the Rome Convention, which was brought into force in the UK by the Contracts (Applicable Law) Act 1990.[35] In an Internet context, there are a number of 'when and where' issues. The most important provisions are these:

(1) A contract shall be governed by the law chosen by the parties. The choice must be expressed or demonstrated with reasonable certainty by the terms of the contract or the circumstances of the case. By their choice the parties can select the law applicable to the whole or a part only of the contract.

---

33 Eg, section 6.5.10.
34 Section 9.1.4.
35 Full text of the EC Convention on the Law Applicable to Contractual Obligations (1980) (the Rome Convention), which is also set out in Sched 1 to the 1990 Act, is available at: www.jus.uio.no/lm/ec.applicable.law.contracts.1980/doc.html. The Act itself is at www.ipso.gov.uk/acts/acts1990/Ukpga_19900036_en_1.htm.

The safest way to resolve any possible dispute about whose law applies is expressly to provide for it. This is quite straightforward but in reality, of course, in a web-based transaction, only the web operator can use this provision, not a customer. Article 3 is also subject to Art 3(3):

(3) The fact that the parties have chosen a foreign law, whether or not accompanied by the choice of a foreign tribunal, shall not, where all the other elements relevant to the situation at the time of the choice are connected with one country only, prejudice the application of rules of the law of that country which cannot be derogated from by contract, hereinafter called 'mandatory rules'.

The point of a provision such as this is to ensure that the parties do not, for example, in what is clearly an English contract, choose a foreign law in order to avoid, for example, the Unfair Contract Terms Act 1977, which would almost certainly be regarded as 'mandatory rules'. The provision does not seem to cause any Internet-specific problems, except that it is clearly necessary to localise 'all the other elements relevant to the situation at the time of the choice'.

If the parties do not expressly choose a proper law, Art 4 applies:

(1) To the extent that the law applicable to the contract has not been chosen in accordance with Article 3, the contract shall be governed by the law of the country with which it is most closely connected. ...

(2) Subject to the provisions of paragraph 5 of this Article, it shall be presumed that the contract is most closely connected with the country where the party who is to effect the performance which is characteristic of the contract has, at the time of conclusion of the contract, his habitual residence, or, in the case of a body corporate or unincorporate, its central administration. However, if the contract is entered into in the course of that party's trade or profession, that country shall be the country in which the principal place of business is situated or, where under the terms of the contract the performance is to be effected through a place of business other than the principal place of business, the country in which that other place of business is situated.

...

(5) Paragraph 2 shall not apply if the characteristic performance cannot be determined ...

Article 4 in general does not seem to create many Internet-specific issues. However, there are then specific consumer provisions in Art 5:

(1) This Article applies to a contract the object of which is the supply of goods or services to a person ('the consumer') for a purpose which can be regarded as being outside his trade or profession, or a contract for the provision of credit for that object.

(2) Notwithstanding the provisions of Article 3, a choice of law made by the parties shall not have the result of depriving the consumer of the protection afforded to him by the mandatory rules of the law of the country in which he has his habitual residence:

  – if in that country the conclusion of the contract was preceded by a specific invitation addressed to him or by advertising, and he had taken in that country all the steps necessary on his part for the conclusion of the contract, or

  – if the other party or his agent received the consumer's order in that country, or

  – if the contract is for the sale of goods and the consumer travelled from that country to another country and there gave his order, provided that the consumer's journey was arranged by the seller for the purpose of inducing the consumer to buy.

(3) Notwithstanding the provisions of Article 4, a contract to which this Article applies shall, in the absence of choice in accordance with Article 3, be governed by the law of the country in which the consumer has his habitual residence if it is entered into in the circumstances described in paragraph 2 of this Article.

This is intended to prevent sellers, by inducing consumers to leave their habitual country of residence, to contract by the law of a country that is less beneficial to them. To operate Art 5(2), however, we need to know in which country a web advertisement is addressed, where an order is received, and where an order is made, and perhaps also what is meant by 'all the steps necessary on his part for the conclusion of the contract'. The last could create problems, for example, if the consumer is roaming cybercafés throughout the world, or even perhaps staying at home but using an overseas ISP. Note also that the requirement applies only to a contract for the sale of goods which, as we have seen, would not include electronic material delivered over the Internet, nor licences to use software.[36]

Principles upon which localisation disputes might be resolved are considered later (see section 10.2.3).

10.2.2   Jurisdiction

Whether jurisdiction can be asserted against a defendant who does not submit to it depends on where the defendant has his domicile.[37]

If the defendant is not domiciled in an EU or EFTA state,[38] then RSC Ord 11 applies.[39] Among the criteria are that the contract was made within the jurisdiction or that there is a breach of contract within the jurisdiction.[40] In order to determine whether the contract was made within the jurisdiction, we have already seen that the place of acceptance is the crucial factor.[41]

Where the defendant is domiciled in the EU, the Brussels Convention applies, and if he is domiciled in an EFTA state, the Lugano Convention. The Conventions are quite similar and are Schedules to the Civil Judgments and Jurisdiction Act 1982, as subsequently amended.[42]

---

36   Section 10.1.1.
37   On jurisdiction in general, see, eg, D'Arcy, L, Murray, C and Cleave, B, *Schmitthoff's Export Trade: The Law and Practice of International Trade*, 10th edn, 2000, London: Stevens, Chapter 22.
38   The only members of EFTA today are Iceland, Liechtenstein, Norway and Switzerland. On EFTA generally, see www.efta.int.
39   These can be found at www.hrothgar.co.uk/YAWS/rsc/rsc-11.htm#rh-rsc-1(1). The Rules are periodically updated.
40   RSC Ord 11 rr 1(1)(d)(i) and 1(1)(e), respectively.
41   *Entores Ltd v Miles Far East Corp* [1955] 2 QB 327 and *Brinkibon v Stahag Stahl Und Stahlwarenhandels-Gesellschaft mbH* [1983] 2 AC 34, in section 9.2.2.
42   Scheds 1 and 3C respectively. Full text of the Brussels Convention on the Jurisdiction and the Enforcement of Judgments in Civil and Commercial Matters (27 September 1968) is at www.curia.eu.int/common/recdoc/convention/en/c-textes/brux-idx.htm, and the Lugano Convention (16 September 1988) at www.curia.eu.int/common/recdoc/convention/en/ctextes/_lug-textes.htm. The Brussels Convention is also set out in Sched 3 to the Contracts (Applicable Law) Act 1990: www.opsi.gov.uk/acts/acts1990/Ukpga_ 19900036_en_5.htm.

Article 5(1) of the Brussels Convention allows a person domiciled in a Contracting State to be sued in the courts of another Contracting State in matters relating to the performance of the contract there. This requires localisation of the performance, perhaps problematic with electronic material itself sent over the Internet (see below).[43] Article 13 applies to consumer contracts, the criteria in Art 13(3) being basically the same as the first criterion in Art 5(2) of the Rome Convention (above).

We can see, then, that where things happen can be important for the purposes of determining the law that governs the contract and, to a greater extent, the issue of jurisdiction. Professor Reed observes that tort rules are much simpler:[44] 'Jurisdiction is normally available in every jurisdiction where damage occurred as a result of the tort ... [Brussels, Article 5(3)], and the applicable law will normally be that of the jurisdiction in which the tort was committed.' However, this could give rise, in principle at least, to worldwide jurisdiction in a defamation action. This issue is considered fully in Chapter 12.

10.2.3   Where things happen on the Internet

If we start by considering where a delivery of electronic data such as music, software or a film takes place, this may at first sight seem to be analogous to acceptance in contract,[45] but in fact the issues are different in principle. The problem of not knowing whether the communication has arrived is likely to be less serious because, if it does not arrive, the intended recipient can simply request a resend. There are none of the problems of potential revocation of the offer in the meantime, or fluctuating markets.

On the other hand, delivery to the recipient's agent being delivery to the recipient is a principle of general application[46] and it would be difficult to justify departing from that principle here. That being so, delivery should take place at the recipient's server. This need not be in the country of the recipient's domicile. The problem is that this could be entirely capricious from the supplier's viewpoint, and hence arguably unfair in that jurisdictional rules could turn on it.

If the recipient collects the data from the supplier's website, there is a case for saying that delivery takes place there. Since there is no reason why this should necessarily be in the same country as the supplier's domicile, this could operate equally capriciously from the viewpoint of the recipient. There is also the problem that the website itself could straddle many jurisdictions but, unless the data itself is comprised of packets originating from several servers (by no means an impossibility), it ought at least to be possible to localise the server which actually sent the data.

It is far more difficult to determine where a consumer took steps towards contract formation. The logic of the legislation suggests that the physical location of the consumer should be the determining factor. From the supplier's viewpoint, of course, he may have no way of knowing where that is. For example, a travelling consumer

---

43 Section 10.2.3. These difficulties would, however, disappear were the UK to adopt the proposed Brussels Regulation on Jurisdiction: see further http://www2.warwick.ac.uk/fac/soc/law/elj/jilt/2001_1/gillies.

44 Reed, C, *Internet Law: Text and Materials*, 2nd edn, 2004, Cambridge: CUP, p 220.

45 Eg, Reed, *Internet Law: Text and Materials, op cit* fn 44, pp 223–24.

46 Eg, there is a somewhat similar principle relating to sale of goods, delivery to a carrier being regarded as delivery to the buyer, in the Sale of Goods Act 1979, s 32(1).

could easily access his server from a cybercafé anywhere in the world and the supplier would have no way of knowing where the consumer was.

This seems to be one of those areas where e-commerce is, in the absence of legislation to the contrary, governed by the existing law, which operates entirely haphazardly in an Internet context. There are good arguments for Internet-specific legislation. In Australia, for example, at least for the place of receipt of communications, the emphasis is on the normal physical location of the parties. This seems to be a reasonably sensible rule, and one which is likely to operate less capriciously than one which attempts to locate the server.[47]

---

47 Electronic Communications Act 1999, s 14(5) and 14(6). Curiously, a different approach is adopted for the time of delivery: s 14(3) and (4). The US Electronic Transactions Act 1999 is similar.

PAYMENT ISSUES

This chapter is primarily about payment, but the consumer protection issues from the previous chapter are also relevant. Ultimately, one of the sanctions the consumer can use is to withdraw from the transaction, and there are clear payment consequences in unravelling the transaction.

11.1   GENERAL ISSUES

Although it may be that there is nothing in principle that is special about e-commerce trading, there are risks which are far more likely to occur in a virtual than in a real environment. Although there is little legislation protecting business parties against the increased risks, consumers are protected, the risks being shifted to the banks or trading merchants,[1] the law determining to some extent which of these parties bears the loss.

Any sale at a distance involves risks which are not present in face to face sales, and these risks are probably increased in the electronic marketplace. Often the parties will be complete strangers and will have no reason to trust each other. From the seller's viewpoint, the obvious risk is that the buyer either cannot or will not pay. Commercial sellers usually avoid this risk by requiring payment, typically (in consumer sales at least) by credit or debit card, before despatching the goods, services or other product. Private sellers can also protect themselves by requiring payment in advance; eBay, for example, an auction house which describes itself as is 'The World's Online Marketplace', provides its own system of payment, PayPal, for sellers who have no arrangements with credit card companies, and who do not wish to wait many days for the buyer's personal cheque to clear.[2]

It is far more difficult to provide protection for buyers. The risks faced by buyers fall essentially into two categories: the fraudulent seller, and the incompetent seller (who provides defective goods or services). The elaborate forms of protection that originally developed in the 19th and early 20th centuries for international sales of goods are simply not available in today's e-commercial environment, at any rate in consumer sales.[3] eBay provides some protection for its buyers by setting up an elaborate feedback system to rate the reliability of traders, but this would provide no protection against, for example, a fraudster who took care to engage in a few honest transactions first, in order to build up a reputation (especially as these transactions might themselves not be genuine).[4] Very good levels of protection could, no doubt, be afforded in principle, for example by requiring sellers of goods to deposit them in a third party warehouse, which could also describe them and their apparent quality and condition, delivery being made from the warehouse only against payment by the

---

1   Usually the banks initially, who might then be able to shift them to the trading merchants.
2   See generally www.ebay.com.
3   In any case, even these measures were not designed to, and do not, protect against fraudulent traders.
4   It would be quite easy for two fraudsters, in collusion, to fake transactions and feedback.

buyer. However, such a system has not caught on and would probably be far too complicated and expensive for most e-commercial transactions, negating many of the advantages of speed and convenience. Moreover, it could only operate for sales of physical goods. The reality seems to be that, although technology can provide limited protection, particularly against risks of fraud, buyers must generally look to the law for such protection as they enjoy against the risks inherent in this type of trading.

11.2   FRAUD RISKS

There are three main types of fraud risk. One is interception of details, such as credit or debit card details, in transit, the fraudster then making use of the purchaser's credit card for unauthorised purchases of his or her own. Brownsword and Howells observe that interception risks might be limited by a more general adoption of digital cash,[5] discussed in section 11.7 below, but digital cash generally attracts no legal protection for the consumer.[6] Even with credit and debit cards, in principle, interception risks can be resolved by technical means of the type discussed in Chapter 5; the encryption techniques used for transferring credit card details are at least tolerably secure.[7] Of course, the card details must eventually be disclosed and, even if the disclosure is to a reputable firm, the particular employee might be dishonest. This is not specifically an e-commerce risk, however, since it applies equally to telephone sales, or indeed physical sales where the card is handed over to an employee of the trader (especially if it is taken out of site of the customer):[8] 'Credit card information is more likely to be intercepted at a restaurant or a store than online.'

The second type of fraud risk is the trader who has no intention of performing the contract and who simply disappears with the customer's money. It is probably quite difficult for a sham trader, posing on the web as a legitimate business, directly to obtain payment by credit card, but a well known problem is the fraudulent seller on an auction site, such as eBay, who takes the purchaser's money but simply fails to despatch any merchandise. This type of fraud is difficult to protect against by technological means and, as we will see, it is unlikely that the law will provide much assistance, since payment in such cases is unlikely to be by credit card.

The third type of risk is where a sham website is used, not directly to take money from purchasers, but to collect credit card details, since even if they are encrypted for transmission they are usually eventually disclosed in the clear to the seller. The fraudster will make purchases on his or her own account with legitimate traders, but using the stolen credit card details. The Web offers unique opportunities for the sham trader posing as a reputable business, by creating a web page looking like that of a

---

5   Brownsword, R and Howells, G, 'When surfers start to shop: Internet commerce and contract law' (1999) 19 LS 287, p 299. With digital cash, there is no reason for any details of the customer's financial arrangements to be disclosed to the merchant.

6   Card-based digital cash might attract the fraud protection of the EC Directive in section 11.3.2, and *The Banking Code* extends voluntary fraud protection to 'electronic purses' (see section 11.5), but there is no formal protection at all for other varieties of digital cash.

7   See section 5.5.2.

8   Heckman, CE, *Gateways to the Global Market: Consumers and Electronic Commerce*, 1998, OECD, p 55, quoted by Brownsword and Howells, 'When surfers start to shop: Internet commerce and contract law', *op cit* fn 5, p 299.

reputable company (rather as in the *Yahooindia* case discussed in section 3.7.4, though there was no evidence of any fraud there). Technology could counter this if both traders and consumers routinely used public keys as described in Chapter 5.

It is probably not necessary for the fraudulent trader to go as far as to pose as a well known legitimate company, however; he need do no more than pretend to be genuine. Technology can still be used to counter this type of fraud since, if SET encryption is used, the merchant cannot access the customer's payment details,[9] but by no means all credit card issuers support it. The more common SSL encryption simply encrypts the details that are sent to the merchant.[10]

The evidence suggests that Internet commerce is quite prone to fraud[11] but, apart from fraud, there is also the risk of poor (or non-) performance by the supplier, in the absence of fraud. The goods or services may not, for example, be of the quality stipulated in the contract or the trader may fail to perform due to insolvency.

With the exception of the second type of fraud risk discussed here, legislation provides quite a large degree of protection for consumers from the risks of Internet trading at the expense, initially, of the banks who finance the transaction, but often the banks can pass on the cost to the commercial trading parties. Businesses trading over the Internet, however, must generally look after themselves.

11.3   FRAUD PROTECTION

11.3.1   Consumer Credit Act 1974

The Consumer Credit Act 1974 was not, of course, aimed at Internet transactions. However, many Internet transactions involve some kind of credit, even if nothing more than a credit card. In such a case, the 1974 Act provides a certain amount of protection, effectively shifting the risks from the consumer to the financier.

Section 83 of the Consumer Credit Act 1974 applies to regulated consumer credit agreements, which are defined in s 8(2) as 'a personal credit agreement by which the creditor provides the debtor with credit not exceeding £25,000'. In the case of credit card sales, this implies that the credit limit is no more than £25,000,[12] but s 83 applies to other type of consumer credit and is not limited to credit card sales. Section 83(1) protects customers from fraudulent use of their credit cards in cases of unauthorised use:

---

9   Secure Electronic Transaction, which uses both the merchant's and the bank's public key, the bank's public key being used to encrypt the customer's payment details (which therefore cannot be read by the merchant). For a description, see, eg, http://whatis.techtarget.com/definition/0,289893,sid9_gci214194,00.html. See also generally section 5.5.2.

10 Secure Sockets Layer, recently succeeded by TLS (Transport Layer Security), described respectively at http://searchsecurity.techtarget.com/sDefinition/0,,sid14_gci343029,00.html and http://searchsecurity.techtarget.com/sDefinition/0,,sid14_gci557332,00.html.

11 Eg, Miller, S, in Edwards, L and Waelde, C (eds), *Law and the Internet: A Framework for Electronic Commerce*, 2nd edn, 2000, Oxford: Hart, p 58.

12 Note that, unlike s 75 in the next section, there is no lower limit.

> 83. (1) The debtor under a regulated consumer credit agreement shall not be liable to the creditor for any loss arising from use of the credit facility by another person not acting, or to be treated as acting, as the debtor's agent.

This appears wide enough to protect against the disappearing trader. However, it is subject to a £50 exception in s 84(1) if the card is not in the consumer's possession:

> 84. (1) Section 83 does not prevent the debtor under a credit-token agreement from being made liable to the extent of £50 (or the credit limit if lower) for loss to the creditor arising from use of the credit-token by other persons during a period beginning when the credit-token ceases to be in the possession of any authorised person and ending when the credit-token is once more in the possession of an authorised person.

Section 84(1) is no more likely to be triggered in Internet sales than in any other sales; indeed, less likely if the delivery address has to match the card address.

Section 83 does not just apply to credit cards, but to any regulated consumer credit agreement. Section 84 applies only where there is a credit token, implying either a credit card or (probably) a debit card, where the bank account is overdrawn.[13]

11.3.2   Distance Selling Directive

In the last chapter, we considered the Distance Selling Directive.[14] This is a consumer protection provision which applies to some but by no means all e-commerce transactions.[15] Unlike the UK Consumer Credit Act 1974, it applies generally to distance sales (that is, whether the transaction involves credit or not) but, as we saw in Chapter 10, there are wide-ranging exclusions from it. It is consumer protection legislation only and, as we saw in the last chapter, works rather formalistically, providing mostly for the provision of information. It may well not provide very strong protection in reality. It is noteworthy, for example, that it does not prohibit sellers requiring prepayment, a practice which obviously significantly increases the risks for buyers.[16]

However, like s 83 of the UK Consumer Credit Act, Art 8 of the Directive protects consumers against fraud by others, including the sham merchant. If the Directive applies at all to the transaction in question,[17] Art 8 provides:

> Article 8
>
> Payment by card
>
> Member States shall ensure that appropriate measures exist to allow a consumer:
>
> –   to request cancellation of a payment where fraudulent use has been made of his payment card in connection with distance contracts covered by this Directive,
>
> –   in the event of fraudulent use, to be recredited with the sums paid or have them returned.

---

13   There is a definition of a credit token in s 14 of the 1974 Act.
14   Council Directive (1997/7/EC) on distance selling. See section 10.1.2.2 for its application.
15   See further, on the application of the Directive, Brownsword and Howells, 'When surfers start to shop: Internet commerce and contract law', *op cit* fn 5, pp 300 *et seq*.
16   See, eg, the discussion by Brownsword and Howells, *ibid*, p 305.
17   See further section 10.1.2.2.

This is relatively cast-iron protection against fraud, including cancellation of any sums paid. Of particular note is that Art 8 covers payment cards, whether or not there is any credit involved, and that there is no equivalent of s 84(1) of the UK Consumer Credit Act.

The UK legislation bringing Art 8 into force is reg 21 of the Consumer Protection (Distance Selling) Regulations 2000,[18] which makes appropriate provision for transactions to which the Directive applies but the 1974 Act does not, and amends s 83 in cases to which the Directive also applies. The explanatory notes to the regulations explain that:

> The Regulations amend the Consumer Credit Act 1974 by removing the potential liability of the debtor under a regulated consumer credit agreement for the first £50 of loss to the creditor from misuse of a credit-token in connection with a distance contract.

In effect, therefore, in those cases to which the Directive applies, the entire risk of fraud is placed on the financiers, except to the extent that they may be able to use a charge back clause, considered below.[19]

11.4   BREACH OF CONTRACT BY MERCHANT

Though it provides a complete firewall against fraud, Art 8 protection provides no protection against poor performance by suppliers. In that respect, the UK domestic law is better.[20]

Section 75 of the Consumer Credit Act 1974 allows claims against the supplier in respect of misrepresentation or breach of contract also to be brought against the creditor. This section applies only to tripartite agreements or, in effect, credit card sales. It provides:

> 75. Liability of creditor for breaches by supplier.
>
> (1) If the debtor under a debtor-creditor-supplier agreement falling within section 12 (b) or (c) has, in relation to a transaction financed by the agreement, any claim against the supplier in respect of a misrepresentation or breach of contract, he shall have a like claim against the creditor, who, with the supplier, shall accordingly be jointly and severally liable to the debtor.
>
> (2) Subject to any agreement between them, the creditor shall be entitled to be indemnified by the supplier for loss suffered by the creditor in satisfying his liability under subsection (1), including costs reasonably incurred by him in defending proceedings instituted by the debtor.
>
> (3) Subsection (1) does not apply to a claim—
>
>   (a) under a non-commercial agreement, or
>
>   (b) so far as the claim relates to any single item to which the supplier has attached a cash price not exceeding £100 or more than £30,000.

---

18 SI 2000/2334. Full text can be found at www.ipso.gov.uk/si/si2000/20002334.htm.
19 Section 11.6.
20 See generally Brownsword and Howells, 'When surfers start to shop: Internet commerce and contract law', *op cit* fn 5, p 306. However, the withdrawal rights under the Directive, described in section 10.1.3, will provide an alternative form of protection against poor performance.

(4) This section applies notwithstanding that the debtor, in entering into the transaction, exceeded the credit limit or otherwise contravened any term of the agreement.

(5) In an action brought against the creditor under subsection (1) he shall be entitled, in accordance with rules of court, to have the supplier made a party to the proceedings.

Since any misrepresentation or breach of contract is covered, at any rate if it gives rise to an actionable claim against the merchant,[21] the section covers both insolvency and non- or poor performance, but it applies only to credit cards (tripartite credit arrangements), not to other forms of credit. The importance of this section is obviously increased with overseas sales, where remedies against the merchant are less likely to be effective.

A claim for misrepresentation or breach of contract can, of course, include consequential losses, so this section does not simply provide the purchaser with a refund of some or all of the purchase price of the product.

Note that the protection is lost with low value transactions. Section 75(3) limits the operation of the section to where the purchase price is between £100 and £30,000, and it seems likely that many Internet transactions will be below the lower figure.

Section 75(1) refers back to s 12(b) and (c), under both of which the purchase must be made under pre-existing arrangements between the card issuer (creditor) and the merchant (supplier). Until recently this was thought to be capable of excluding most overseas and many domestic sales, where the retailer was recruited to the network (eg, Visa) by a bank other than the card-holder's bank. For a time, card-issuers accepted voluntary liability in respect of overseas transactions, but in November 2004 the issue came before the High Court, and the argument that there must be a contract between the supplier and card-holder's bank was rejected by Gloster J in *Office of Fair Trading v Lloyds TSB Bank plc*.[22] In the same case, however, she also held that foreign transactions were excluded from the operation of s 75, at least where the contract between the consumer and supplier is governed by a foreign law; she declined, however, to define foreign transaction closely.

There was a Department of Trade and Industry threat in *Electronic Commerce*, 10th report, para 123:[23]

We recommend that, if any court was to decide that section 75 of the Consumer Credit Act 1974 did not apply to overseas transactions, then DTI speedily bring forward legislation to fill the gap.

The threat is clear; if the credit card companies attempt to rely on this loophole, the government will introduce legislation to close it. We should therefore await developments.

---

21 Section 75(1), though it is not necessary actually to sue the merchant.
22 [2004] EWHC 2600, available at www.bailii.org/ew/cases/EWHC/Comm/2004/2600.html. See also Brownsword, R and Howells, G, 'When surfers start to shop: Internet commerce and contract law', *op cit* fn 5, p 306. See also Miller, S in Edwards and Waelde, *Law and the Internet*, *op cit* fn 11, p 61.
23 At www.parliament.the-stationery-office.co.uk/pa/cm199899/cmselect/cmtrdind/648/64802.htm. The bold emphasis is in the original document.

11.5   CREDIT CARDS, DEBIT CARDS AND DIGITAL CASH COMPARED

It can be concluded that consumer protection is generally quite good where credit cards are used, providing effective protection against fraud, breach of contract and misrepresentation. Low value transactions are excluded, however, whereas micro-transactions might be expected to take off as a substantial part of e-commerce.

Section 83 protection extends to overdraft-bearing debit card holders, but (because there is no credit) not to debit cards in general. There is, however, a voluntary code of practice, *The Banking Code*,[24] under which banks agree effectively to extend s 83 protection to all debit cards. Section 75 does not apply to debit cards at all, even if overdraft-bearing; they are excluded by s 187(3A), as 'arrangements for the electronic transfer of funds from a current account'.

Digital cash (described in section 11.7) is similarly not a form of credit and does not therefore generally attract the assistance of the law, though *The Banking Code* extends what is effectively s 83 protection also to 'electronic purses'.[25] If digital cash is used for small value transactions, there is, of course, no legal protection in any event against misrepresentation by the merchant but, with the development of schemes like PayPal, it is by no means certain that its use will be so confined. Though digital cash also falls outside the formal protection of s 83, fraud risks are lessened in practice, since no financial information needs to be disclosed. However, digital cash always involves prepayment and pretty well removes all the risks to banks and traders.

11.6   CHARGE BACK ARRANGEMENTS

Section 75(2) expressly allows banks to require an indemnity from merchants in misrepresentation and breach of contract cases. It is difficult to object to this, given that the misrepresentation or breach was that of the merchant.

Credit card companies also use charge back clauses against retailers, where the consumer is not present,[26] the usual position of course with e-commerce sales. Effectively, this places on the retailer the risk of denial of order by the customer. It is difficult to see why these should not, in principle, be valid.[27] Of course, if a fraudulent trader simply disappears with the consumer's money, a charge back clause is not likely to be of use to the bank. Where, however, credit card details are obtained by a fraudster, perhaps by operating a sham (but apparently legitimate) website, the charge back clause will operate against the legitimate traders who later accept the

---

24 Available at www.bankingcode.org.uk/pdfdocs/bankcode.pdf. The problem described by Miller (see fn 22) in Edwards and Waelde, *Law and the Internet, op cit* fn 11, p 63, has been addressed in the latest (March 2003) version of the Code, para 12.10 (the earlier version, described by Miller, being more appropriate to lost or stolen cards than misuse of details).

25 Paragraphs 12.12–12.14.

26 These are discussed by Brownsword and Howells, 'When surfers start to shop: Internet commerce and contract law', *op cit* fn 5, pp 308 *et seq.*

27 Brownsword and Howells, *op cit* fn 5, pp 308 *et seq,* put forward, somewhat half-heartedly, a number of arguments why they might not be, but I would suggest that none is particularly convincing, given that the contracts are between two business parties.

fraudulently obtained card details. This could actually place quite a significant burden on legitimate e-commerce traders.

11.7   DIGITAL CASH

Many transactions on the World Wide Web (WWW) are of very low value and, indeed, one of the advantages of e-commerce, particularly for consumers, is the ability to make very small purchases without the need to package them with other unwanted purchases. In the physical world, for example, music is normally sold on CDs, with many songs being packaged on the same CD. It would not be economic, in the physical world, to sell the music in any other way, but it is inefficient from the viewpoint of the consumer, who might like only one track on the CD. By contrast, many of the online distributors, such as MSN and Napster (in its reincarnated legitimate form) allow downloads of single tracks, often for less than £1, and streaming (for listening just once), often for only £0.01. With increasing bandwidth, we can expect to see similar possibilities with other media, such as TV and film.

The problem with very low cost transactions is that, with conventional payment methods, the transaction costs can be disproportionately high. For example, at the time of writing, megabus.com offers bus fares, booked online, for as little as £1 from Swansea to London. Payment is by conventional credit card, however, and the shine of this excellent value is tarnished somewhat by a 50p booking fee. Fifty per cent is a high transaction cost indeed (although the percentage is more reasonable, of course, if a number of journeys are booked at the same time).[28]

MSN tackles the problem for its music sales by allowing purchase of block credit of up to £40, thereby minimising credit card transaction costs, but the credit can only be used with MSN. By demanding payment in advance it also, of course, negates one of the advantages to consumers of using credit cards, the interest-free period before repayment has to be made. What is ideally needed for e-commerce is digital cash, far better suited to small transactions than the traditional credit card.

There are digital cash systems ideally suited to micro-payments, but they have not enjoyed great success in the UK. Five years ago, Saul Miller described one of the most comprehensive, Mondex,[29] a smart card system which allows a card to be loaded with cash at, for example, an ATM, and either used as cash with participating merchants, or alternatively for pay for view TV or mobile phone airtime, or for transferring value over the Internet. Participating merchants can redeem their e-money at their own participating bank. Transaction costs, especially for low-value purchases, are very much lower than with a conventional credit card. Visa offers a similar type of smart card system, which appears, however, to be limited to a replacement for physical cash.[30]

---

28 Megabus is perhaps rather extreme, but it has been estimated that credit card costs can typically be up to 7.5% of the value of a transaction: Chissick, M and Kelman, A, *Electronic Commerce: Law and Practice*, 1999, London: Sweet & Maxwell, p 125, cited by Miller in Edwards and Waelde, *Law and the Internet, op cit* fn 11, p 75, note 87. Chissick and Kelman is now in its (2001) 3rd edn.

29 As far as I can tell, Mondex removed its website in January 2005. It has clearly not been a great success: eg, http://networks.silicon.com/webwatch/0,39024667,39126725,00.htm.

30 http://international.visa.com/ps/products/vcash/. Mondex is described by Miller in Edwards and Waelde, *Law and the Internet, op cit* fn 11, pp 64 *et seq*. See also www.ecash.com/online.

Another system which has caught on, even in the UK, is eBay's PayPal system.[31] This is not a card-based system, but is wholly virtual. PayPal accounts can be opened by anyone and loaded with money from credit cards, etc. When a sale is made, for example on eBay, the buyer e-mails value from his or her PayPal account to the account of the seller, who receives e-mail confirmation from PayPal. The money can either be retained in the seller's PayPal account or transferred to another bank account. Transaction costs are lower than with credit cards, but are better suited to larger transactions: with sellers paying 3.4% + 20p per transaction, the costs are too high for micro-sales, presumably because, ultimately, credit card costs have to be paid (to load up accounts).

11.7.1   Some legal implications

There is legal regulation of issuers of electronic money, intended in part, no doubt, to give consumers confidence. The heart of the regulation is Council Directive (2000/46/EC) (the E-Money Directive). Details of this Directive are beyond the scope of this book,[32] but the definition of electronic money in Art 1(3)(b) is perhaps instructive:

monetary value as represented by a claim on the issuer which is:

(i)   stored on an electronic device;

(ii)   issued on receipt of funds of an amount not less in value than the monetary value issued;

(iii)   accepted as a means of payment by undertakings other than the issuer.

It can be seen that all the schemes described above fall generally within this definition.

It is obvious that there is no credit element here, so none of the provisions of the Consumer Credit Act 1974 will apply (unless there is an overdraft facility).[33] Nor is digital cash legal tender, so nobody can insist on using it and no merchant is obliged to accept it. On the other hand, even a card-based system is safer than actual cash, because there can be a lock function on the card to guard against loss or theft. Because it is not currency, if a card is stolen and sold on, the purchaser would not get title.[34] In any case, a proper computer-based system, such as PayPal, would obviate both these problems.

Moreover, though with the lack of consumer credit protection the advantages of digital cash would seem to lie with commerce and the banks, the system is cheaper to operate than credit cards. In any case, for very small payments, fraud is not really a significant problem and there is no protection against misrepresentation in any event, even where payment is by conventional credit card.[35]

---

31 See http://pages.ebay.com/paypal/buyer/protection.html?ssPageName=MOPS123:PayPal. In the UK, the FSA has classified PayPal (Europe) Limited as an electronic money issuer: Kohlbach, M, 'Making sense of electronic money', http://www2.warwick.ac.uk/fac/soc/law/elj/jilt/2004_1/kohlbach.

32 See Kohlbach, *ibid*.

33 See, however, the reference to *The Banking Code* in section 11.5. Of course, s 75 of the 1974 Act does not apply in any event.

34 See also Miller in Edwards and Waelde, *Law and the Internet, op cit* fn 11, p 74.

35 See section 11.5.

PayPal is intended for larger purchases, which would, were a credit card used, attract protection under the 1974 Act. It offers its own protection scheme,[36] which only provides free coverage up to US$1,000, if, as a buyer '... you paid for an item and never received it or received an item that was significantly not as described'. In any case, a voluntary scheme, unbacked by legal regulation, is not ideal from the consumers' viewpoint. The advantage of PayPal is that it can be used even where neither seller nor purchaser have facilities for dealing with credit cards and, from the buyer's viewpoint, no financial details are disclosed (thereby significantly reducing fraud risk in practice). Digital cash can, in principle, hold multiple currencies,[37] and merchants need not fear charge back clauses. It would be surprising if digital cash really had no future for e-commerce.

11.7.2   Insolvency of participating parties

The regulation of electronic banking is intended, obviously, to reduce the risk of insolvency among issuers of such money. Nonetheless, bankruptcies will no doubt occur from time to time; this can obviously give rise to problems if the purchaser has paid using digital cash for which he or she has already paid, but the bankruptcy occurs before the vendor redeems it.

A lot will depend on the precise contractual arrangements made between the parties. Five years ago, Miller described various scenarios with the Mondex scheme, which had the noteworthy feature that the merchant's only express contract was with his own participating bank, there being no direct contractual relationship with the issuer (Mondex) at all.[38] This might be expected to weaken the position of the merchants but, in reality, issues of withdrawal from the scheme by, or the insolvency of, the issuer become straightforward issues of the contractual terms between the merchant and his bank. The bankruptcy of a participating merchant could obviously be problematic, because the merchant might no longer be able to redeem his digital cash, but he could still spend it with other participating merchants and would be unlikely, therefore, to lose the entirety of its value.

There is no need for the scheme to be as complex as that of Mondex. Much simpler is a direct contractual relationship between the issuer and participating buyers and sellers. In PayPal, for example, all sellers and buyers using the system open PayPal accounts, and PayPal makes arrangements with banks in various countries to allow withdrawal of PayPal funds electronically to their local bank account.[39] It seems that the only contractual relationships are likely to be directly between the participants and PayPal itself.

In such an arrangement, the problem arises if the issuer becomes bankrupt, unless the participating banks have agreed to redeem even in that event, surely an unlikely eventuality. Unless the issuer has set aside a separate fund for the e-money, in which

---

36   http://pages.ebay.com/paypal/buyer/protection.html?ssPageName=MOPS123:PayPal.

37   Avoiding exchange costs: eg, www.paypal.com/eBay/cgi-bin/webscr?cmd=p/sell/mc/mc_intro-outside.

38   In Edwards and Waelde, *Law and the Internet, op cit* fn 11, pp 64 *et seq*.

39   www.paypal.com/eBay/cgi-bin/webscr?cmd=_help-ext&eloc=958&loc=953&unique_id=4719&source_page=_home&flow=.

case it would be held on trust for those holding it, merchants holding e-money would simply be left as general creditors of the issuer. In effect, the e-money would be worthless.[40]

The question then would be whether a seller who had accepted the now useless e-money could require a second payment from the buyer or, if delivery had not been made, withdraw from the transaction. After all, the seller is now out of funds. On the other hand, the buyer has already paid for the e-money and, if he or she were now required to pay by cash or card, would have to pay twice. If the seller could withdraw from the transaction, the buyer would be left out of pocket, without the benefit of delivery of the product purchased.

In the physical world, if a buyer pays by cheque, he or she is required to pay again if the cheque is dishonoured. However, the bank is clearly the agent of the buyer, and 'it is not unreasonable to expect the customer to take responsibility for the default of his agent'.[41] It is usually also the case that a buyer who pays for goods by irrevocable documentary letter of credit is required to pay again, should the bank fail to pay.[42] However, the seller and buyer will be known to each other, the bank is again chosen (usually) by the buyer, and the 'sole purpose of the letter of credit is to provide security to the seller to replace that represented by the shipping documents which he gives up in exchange for the credit'.[43]

However, for credit card sales, the position has been held to be different and the buyer is not required to pay again in the event of the insolvency of the issuer of the card.[44] Many credit card sales are over the counter, between strangers where the seller would be unaware of the purchaser's address, and where the 'identity of the card-issuing company is necessarily a matter for agreement, since the card must be one which the customer is authorised to use and the supplier has the necessary equipment to accept'.[45]

Whether the use of digital cash is closer to credit card payments or to documentary credits may depend on precisely the nature of the arrangement entered into. However, a PayPal transaction looks much closer to the credit card than the documentary credit. Though delivery details will no doubt be exchanged, the parties will usually be

---

40 Kohlbach, 'Making sense of electronic money', *op cit* fn 31, makes interesting comparisons with PayPal as between the UK and the US. In the UK, '[t]he Service is an e-money payment service rather than a banking or escrow service, and we are not acting as a trustee with respect to balances that you choose to keep in your account', but in the US, 'PayPal acts as a facilitator to help you accept payments from and make payments to third parties. We act as your agent based upon your direction and your requests to use our Services that require us to perform tasks on your behalf. PayPal will at all times hold your funds separate from its corporate funds, will not use your funds for its operating expenses or any other corporate purposes, and will not voluntarily make funds available to its creditors in the event of bankruptcy or for any other purpose'. UK participants are unsecured, whereas those in the US are probably beneficiaries under a trust.

41 Millett J in *Re Charge Card Services Ltd* [1987] Ch 150, p 166.

42 The leading authority is *W J Alan & Co Ltd v El Nasr Export and Import Co* [1972] 2 QB 189, p 212, but see also *Maran Road Saw Mill v Austin Taylor Ltd* [1975] 1 Lloyd's Rep 156 and *ED & F Man Ltd v Nigerian Sweets & Confectionery Co Ltd* [1977] 2 Lloyd's Rep 50.

43 Millett J in *Re Charge Card Services Ltd* [1987] Ch 150, p 168.

44 *Re Charge Card Services* [1989] Ch 497 (CA), upholding Millett J, where the documentary credit cases were considered inapplicable.

45 Millett J in *Re Charge Card Services Ltd* [1987] Ch 150, p 168.

unknown to each other, and both must agree on the identity of the e-money issuer. I would suggest, therefore, that the seller takes the risk of the insolvency of the issuer, the purchaser not being required to pay again, if the insolvency occurs before the purchaser redeems the value of his e-cash.

PART 5

OTHER E-COMMERCE ISSUES

LIABILITY OF INTERMEDIARIES

We saw in Parts 1 and 2 of this book how the functioning of the Internet depends on intermediaries, who necessarily copy and, in some cases, store information; we considered the copyright consequences in Chapter 4. However, the publication of third party content can also expose intermediaries to liability in other respects, for example the criminal law in relation to obscene publications, blasphemy and sedition, and also the tort of defamation. This chapter concentrates on defamation, which is more likely to affect mainstream e-commerce than the criminal law areas mentioned. There is also a wealth of material on defamation. The immunities are general, however, and cover criminal law as well. In an e-commerce context, the criminal law is most likely to be relevant in areas such as control of advertising.

The immunities described here also apply to the breach of copyright actions described in Chapter 4.

12.1   SUBSTANTIVE TORT OF DEFAMATION

12.1.1   Definition of defamation

The tort of defamation focuses upon publications causing damage to reputation. It is a tort of strict liability, in the sense that a defendant may be liable even though no injury to reputation was intended and the defendant acted with reasonable care. There are, however, a number of defences, including that the statements were true, or that it was in the public interest to publish them, or that they were privileged statements.[1]

A distinction is traditionally drawn between libel and slander. Libel is written and is actionable *per se*, whereas slander generally requires proof of special damage.

Everyone who is involved in the publication of a libel is, in principle, liable. This includes not only the author, but also, for example, newspapers and, in an Internet context, hosts of websites where the defamatory material resides.

12.1.2   Defamation in other jurisdictions

The global nature of the Internet makes it necessary to be aware of the law elsewhere, but in any case there are many materials on the law of defamation and the Internet from outside the UK. The law throughout the English-speaking world was based originally on that of the UK and, in many countries (for example, Australia), it is still essentially the same, but materials from the US should be treated with caution. US law is far less protective of reputation than the UK, and there are a number of defences to a

---

1   A detailed discussion of the law of defamation is beyond the scope of this book, but see, eg, Collins, M, *The Law of Defamation and the Internet*, 2001, Oxford: OUP.

defamation action which do not exist in the UK, for example that the victim is a public figure.[2] Intermediaries are far less likely to be liable in the US than they are here.[3]

Also in the US, there are the implications arising from the First Amendment to the Constitution, giving free speech a constitutional status (this is certainly relevant to intermediary liability considered below). Indeed, we will see that much of the US Communication Decency Act 1996, which was aimed primarily at protecting children from Internet pornography, was struck down because it infringed the constitutional right to free speech in the First Amendment.[4]

It is unsurprising, then, that in *Godfrey v Demon Internet*, Morland J made the following general observations about US case law:[5]

> The United States was in the forefront of the early development of the Internet. Care has to be taken before American cases are applied in English defamation cases. The impact of the First Amendment of the United States Constitution has resulted in a substantial divergence of approach between American and English defamation law.

In the UK, liability for publishing defamatory material is strict, subject to defences (which are more limited than in the US). In *Godfrey v Demon Internet*, Morland J, commenting again on the American decisions cited before him, observed that:[6]

> in English law the defendant publisher has to establish his innocence whereas in American law the plaintiff who has been libelled has to prove that the publisher was not innocent.

Indeed, accidental innuendo can form the basis of a defamation action.[7] Conversely, some jurisdictions distinguish between intentional and negligent defamation.[8]

It is fair to conclude, therefore, that a defamation action is more likely to succeed in the UK than in the US and, indeed, in many other places in the world.

12.1.3   Defamation and the Internet: Internet-specific problems?

Subject to the limited immunities for intermediaries considered below in section 12.2.2.2, the law of defamation applies on the Internet exactly as it does everywhere else. There are, however, features of the Internet which affect the way it applies in practice. Some of these arise simply from the way the Internet is used. These include:[9]

---

2   At any rate in the absence of malice – Reed, C, *Internet Law: Text and Materials*, 2004, 2nd edn, Cambridge: CUP, p 113 cites *New York Times v Sullivan*, 376 US 254 (1964).
3   See section 12.2.1.2.
4   See further *ACLU v Reno*, Supreme Court of the US, 26 June 1997, fully reported at http://floridalawfirm.com/reno.html. The ISP immunities in the same Act remain in force, however. See further section 12.2.1.2.
5   [2001] QB 201, p 204.
6   *Ibid.*
7   As Reed points out: *Internet Law: Text and Materials, op cit* fn 2, p 117.
8   Reed, *op cit* fn 2, at p 113 cites Finland.
9   All these are mentioned in Edwards, L and Waelde, C (eds), *Law and the Internet: A Framework for Electronic Commerce*, 2nd edn, 2000, Oxford: Hart.

(a) e-mail mailing lists (it is easy to reply to the whole list, thinking you are replying only to one person);

(b) forwarding of e-mails;[10] and

(c) the Usenet culture of flaming, which (to a far greater extent than the World Wide Web (WWW)) predated the present commercial culture of the Internet.

Problems also arise from the international nature of the Internet. These can include forum shopping, but also, in principle at least, the prospect of being sued for defamation anywhere in the world. The UK (and some other English-speaking jurisdictions, such as Australia) provides far better protection for victims against defamation than other jurisdictions and, in particular, the US. Since Internet publications have a world wide reach, even if their main target is local, there is always the possibility that any Internet publisher, anywhere in the world, can be sued in a UK court and be subject to UK defamation law.

It has been observed that the global reach of the Internet is not unique to it, although its nature can certainly exacerbate issues that have arisen elsewhere. In principle at least, however, the same issues could arise from newspapers and especially broadcasting. The following observation is taken from *Dow Jones v Gutnick*:[11]

> In the course of argument much emphasis was given to the fact that the advent of the World Wide Web is a considerable technological advance. So it is. But the problem of widely disseminated communications is much older than the Internet and the World Wide Web. The law has had to grapple with such cases ever since newspapers and magazines came to be distributed to large numbers of people over wide geographic areas. Radio and television presented the same kind of problem as was presented by widespread dissemination of printed material, although international transmission of material was made easier by the advent of electronic means of communication.

> It was suggested that the World Wide Web was different from radio and television because the radio or television broadcaster could decide how far the signal was to be broadcast. It must be recognised, however, that satellite broadcasting now permits very wide dissemination of radio and television and it may, therefore, be doubted that it is right to say that the World Wide Web has a uniquely broad reach. It is no more or less ubiquitous than some television services. In the end, pointing to the breadth or depth of reach of particular forms of communication may tend to obscure one basic fact. However broad may be the reach of any particular means of communication, those who make information accessible by a particular method do so knowing of the reach that their information may have. In particular, those who post information on the World Wide Web do so knowing that the information they make available is available to all and sundry without any geographic restriction.

Dow Jones, which is discussed fully below,[12] was an Australian Internet defamation case, but the earlier UK decision in *Berezovsky v Michaels*,[13] also below, involved a magazine publication which gave rise to problems similar to those in *Dow Jones*. So the Internet really does not create new legal problems in this area. Nonetheless, the ease of publication on a world wide scale, and even of setting up as an Internet Service

---

10   A complication would arise if an e-mail is forwarded by a virus or worm (perhaps this would be a good reason for invoking the innocent dissemination defence in section 12.2).

11   *Dow Jones & Co Inc v Gutnick* [2002] HCA 56, paras 38 *et seq*. The case is discussed fully below.

12   Section 12.1.5.1.

13   [2000] 1 WLR 1004.

Provider (ISP), and the difficulty of discovering where things happen on the Internet, tend to exacerbate such problems as previously existed. Also, although it is possible to control access to web-based material, it is difficult to do so on a jurisdiction basis. These remarks are also taken from *Dow Jones*:[14]

> The nature of the Web makes it impossible to ensure with complete effectiveness the isolation of any geographic area on the Earth's surface from access to a particular website. Visitors to a website automatically reveal their Internet Provider ('IP') address. This is a numerical code that identifies every computer that logs onto the Internet. The visitor may also disclose certain information about the type of browser and computer that the visitor uses. The IP addresses of users are generally assigned to them by an Internet Service Provider ('ISP'). The user's IP address will remain the same whenever and wherever the user 'surfs' the Web. But some ISPs do not assign a permanent IP address. Instead, they assign a new IP address every time a user logs onto the Web. Because of these features, there is presently no effective way for a website operator to determine, in every case, the geographic origin of the Internet user seeking access to the website.

> For similar reasons, with respect to subscription accounts, checking the issuing location of a credit card provided by a user would not afford a universally reliable means of ascertaining the geographic location of a user seeking access to a website. Thus, even assuming that a geographic restriction could be introduced isolating Australia (and hence Victoria) by reference to the origin of the visitor's credit card, a resident of Australia with a credit card issued by a United States bank, would be able to access sites that might be denied to an Australian resident with an Australian credit card, although both users were physically located in Australia.

> In addition to these difficulties of controlling access to a website by reference to geographic, national and subnational boundaries, the Internet has recently witnessed a rapid growth of technologies ('anonymising technologies') that enable Internet users to mask their identities (and locations). By reason of these developments, the provision of cost effective, practical and reliable identity verification systems, that could afford a universally reliable recognition of the point of origin of an Internet user, has not emerged. This is why the nature of Internet technology itself makes it virtually impossible, or prohibitively difficult, cumbersome and costly, to prevent the content of a given website from being accessed in specific legal jurisdictions when an Internet user in such jurisdictions seeks to do so. In effect, once information is posted on the Internet, it is usually accessible to all Internet users everywhere in the world. Even if the correct jurisdiction of an Internet user could be ascertained accurately, there is presently no adequate technology that would enable non-subscription content providers to isolate and exclude all access to all users in specified jurisdictions.

12.1.4   Libel or slander?

We have seen that, unlike slander, libel requires no proof of damage to the claimant. Libel is written. It might be thought that what should be regarded as written requires no more than a re-run of the arguments in Chapter 6, but the rationale for requiring writing here is different from there. In the present context, a possible justification is that 'written words have at least a fixed partial context'.[15] The issue, then, is one of

---

14   [2002] HCA 56, paras 84 *et seq*.
15   Weir, T, *A Casebook on Tort*, 10th edn, 2004, London: Sweet & Maxwell, p 526.

permanence. Clearly, the WWW and more permanent bulletin boards should reasonably count as writing, but arguably e-mail and Usenet are more like spoken speech. In *Rindos v Hardwick*,[16] Ipp J considered a bulletin board posting to be libellous. Commenting on this case, Francis Auburn observed that:[17]

> Unlike the bulletin boards described by Ipp J, messages posted on newsgroups are informal and more akin to conversation than to a conventional letter.

However, a Usenet posting was considered to be libellous in *Godfrey v Demon Internet Ltd*.[18]

Though the matter can hardly be considered settled beyond doubt, since in neither case was the distinction between libel and slander considered in detail, it seems likely that most internet publications will be regarded as being as written. This also seems correct in principle. While Auburn's view is clearly arguable, a conventionally written letter or memorandum can be libellous, even if it is likely to be thrown away immediately. E-mail and Usenet postings can be saved if desired, and are surely therefore more like a conventional letter than they are like speech.

12.1.5   Jurisdiction and applicable law

Defamation protects reputations, and is jurisdiction-dependent in that a defamation action in the UK protects only reputations in the UK. We have seen that US and UK law take quite different approaches to defamation, US law being far kinder to the publisher. However, a statement emanating from the US, for example, but promulgated on the Internet, might be repeated, or indeed originally published, by an ISP in the UK (and the person making the statement will not necessarily know where the ISP is located). Caches and mirror sites may exist anywhere in the world. Moreover, wherever the statement originated, if the victim suffers damage to reputation in the UK, even if not a UK national or domiciled in the UK, an action for defamation can be brought in the UK, which might also be subject to UK law. UK defamation law could, at least in principle therefore, apply to any statement on the Internet that can be read in the UK, by a UK citizen. Clearly, therefore, anyone publishing on the Internet, anywhere in the world, needs to be far more careful about defamation in other jurisdictions than (for example) in a newspaper with a local circulation.

12.1.5.1   Jurisdiction

If the defendant is in the UK, then UK courts can assert jurisdiction. The question becomes more interesting when the author, or ISP or other intermediary, is overseas. Where the Brussels or Lugano Conventions apply, a person may be sued:[19]

---

16   Western Australian Supreme Court, No 1994 of 1993, judgment delivered on 31 March 1994.
17   Auburn, F, 'Usenet news and the law', http://webjcli.ncl.ac.uk/articles1/auburn1.html.
18   [2001] QB 201; [1999] 4 All ER 342.
19   Article 5(3) (both Conventions are identical). See also Chapter 10, fn 42.

In matters relating to tort, delict or quasi-delict, in the courts for the place where the harmful event occurred.

Otherwise,[20] RSC Ord 11 allows:

service of a writ out of the jurisdiction … with the leave of the court if … the claim is founded on a tort and the damage was sustained, or resulted from an act committed, within the jurisdiction …

However, this is subject to r 4(2):

No such leave shall be granted unless it shall be made sufficiently to appear to the court that the case is a proper one for service out of the jurisdiction under this Order.

Clearly, however, a starting point is to decide where the tort or harmful event occurred. In fact, as we will see, if it occurred in the UK, this will nearly always give UK courts jurisdiction and make UK law applicable to the dispute.

Many states in the US have adopted the uniform publication rule, either judicially or by adopting the Uniform Single Publication Act 1952.[21] The rule provides, in effect, that in respect of a single publication, only one action for damages is maintainable. Moreover, for newspapers and magazines, the place of that single publication is the place where the newspaper or magazine is published.[22] By analogy, in an Internet context, the place of publication would be the server. Therefore, at least as far as US law is concerned, an author who posts material to a US server need consider only the law of the US, the place of publication.

However, there is no equivalent to the Uniform Single Publication Act in the UK, where publication is in any case not regarded as a unilateral event determined by the publisher, but a bilateral act, including also receipt of the communication by the recipient.[23] In the UK, and in most English-speaking jurisdictions, each communication is a separate defamation, and the place of publication is the communication to the recipient. Lord Steyn observed in *Berezovsky* that 'publication takes place where the words are heard or read'.[24] Thus, if a person in the UK reads a communication hosted on a US server, as far as UK law is concerned, publication takes place in the UK. This is normally sufficient to establish jurisdiction.

Moreover, defamation protects damage to reputation within the jurisdiction. Jurisdiction can be asserted in the UK even if both claimant and defendant are foreigners and the statement originated abroad, as long as the claimant had a reputation damaged in the UK.

It might be thought that, at least where RSC Ord 11 applies, r 4(2) ought to lead to a stay of action in such cases. Indeed, the principles of the stay were considered in *Spiliada Maritime Corp v Cansulex Ltd*,[25] where the House of Lords held that the burden

---

20 Ie, where the defendant is domiciled outside EU and EFTA States. See generally section 10.2.2.

21 In *Dow Jones* [2002] HCA 56, para 29, it was observed that the rule was applied in some 27 states. There is also there, and in the following paragraphs, a description of the rule, and its history and development.

22 *Ibid*, para 32.

23 See especially the discussion in *Dow Jones*, below.

24 [2000] 1 WLR 1004, p 1012. The case is discussed in detail later in the section.

25 [1987] AC 460.

is upon the claimant to show that England is clearly the appropriate forum in which the case should be tried in the interests of all the parties and the ends of justice. The effect of *Spiliada*, essentially, is that:[26]

> a stay will be granted where there is some other competent and appropriate forum where the case may be more suitably tried in the interests of the parties and the ends of justice.[27] The court will look for the natural forum with which the action has the most real and substantial connection.[28] Relevant factors include convenience, availability of witnesses, expense and residence of the parties.

However, notwithstanding *Spiliada*, no stay was granted in *Berezovsky v Michaels*,[29] in a similar type of case, albeit one the facts of which did not arise primarily from the use of the Internet. An American magazine (*Forbes*) claimed that a Russian politician (Boris Berezovsky) was a criminal, describing him as the 'Godfather of the Kremlin'. Nearly all sales of the magazine (approximately 800,000) were in the US, but a small number of copies of the magazine were also sold in the UK (approximately 2,000). Apparently, Berezovsky wished merely to clear his name and was not interested in financial compensation[30] but, as a public figure, presumably did not consider his chances of success high in the US. He also had reasons not to wish to sue in Russia. As Lord Hoffmann observed:[31]

> He does not want to sue in the United States because he considers ... it too likely that he will lose.[32] He does not want to sue in Russia for the unusual reason that other people might think it was too likely that he would win. He says that success in the Russian courts would not be adequate to vindicate his reputation because it might be attributed to his corrupt influence over the Russian judiciary.

However, Berezovsky visited the UK from time to time on business, and claimed that he had a reputation to protect here. The House of Lords held (albeit by a bare majority) that a writ could be served on the publishers outside the jurisdiction and that the UK was an appropriate forum, so that this was not an appropriate case for a stay.

At first sight, this might appear to be an exclusively Russian matter; all the facts were alleged to have occurred in Russia, and all the witnesses would have been Russian. However, as Lord Steyn observed,[33] only 19 copies of *Forbes* had been sold in Russia and, in any case, the Russian courts would not protect damage to reputation in England. America might also seem, at first sight, to be a more natural forum than the UK, but 'the connections of both plaintiffs with the United States are minimal. They cannot realistically claim to have reputations which need protection in the United States'.[34] This will always be a problem, of course, where the server and the reputation

---

26 The quote is from Auburn, *op cit* fn 17.
27 Auburn, *op cit* fn 17, notes *Spiliada Maritime Corp v Consulex Ltd* [1987] AC 460, p 476, *per* Lord Goff.
28 Auburn, *op cit* fn 17, notes *The Abidin Daver* [1984] AC 398, p 415, *per* Lord Keith.
29 [2000] 1 WLR 1004 (HL).
30 Berezovsky did not want damages, merely vindication, and felt most likely to get that in the UK courts (see the end of Lord Hoffmann's speech, *ibid*, p 1024).
31 *Ibid*.
32 Lord Hoffmann cites *New York Times v Sullivan* (1964) 376 US 254.
33 [2000] 1 WLR 1004, pp 1014–15.
34 Lord Steyn at p 1015. Though Berezovsky was the main player, *Forbes* had also made derogatory remarks about one Nikolai Glouchkov who was also party to the action.

to be protected are in different jurisdictions. Anyway, it is at least arguable that England had as much connection with the action as anywhere else.

As we have seen, this was not, except incidentally, an Internet case, but the ramifications of the decision for e-commerce are clear.

The dissenting judgments, Lords Hoffmann and Hope, were doubtful whether there was really a reputation to protect in the UK. It was based entirely on activities in Russia, and was only a reputation in the minds of those representing foreign banks and institutions in their dealings with the Russian companies. Had a reputation in the UK been more clearly established, though, there is no reason to suppose other than that they would have gone along with the majority. As it was, they felt that the judge had made correct factual inferences, and had not misdirected himself as to the law, so that an appellate court should not interfere.

In the Australian case, *Dow Jones & Co Inc v Gutnick*,[35] the issues were essentially similar to *Berezovsky*, but in an Internet context. The plaintiff,[36] who claimed he had been defamed, was a resident of the state of Victoria, and had a reputation to protect in Victoria. The publication to which he objected was in Barron's Online, which was owned by Dow Jones, a corporation registered in the US (which also published the Wall Street Journal). Barron's Online was hosted on Dow Jones' own server in New Jersey in the US, but was, of course, accessible to Internet users in Victoria. The High Court of Australia held that the plaintiff, whose reputation had been besmirched in Victoria, was able to sue in a court in Victoria.[37] One issue was where publication had occurred. It is possible to argue that the Internet is different from a traditional publication, because the recipient may be taken to collect the statement from the server, in which case, even on a bilateral view, publication will take place there.[38] This view has not been tested in the UK, but has been effectively rejected in Australia, and would seem unlikely to form part of the law of the UK.

The relevant provision, r 7.01(1) of the Victorian Rules provided that:

(1) Originating process may be served out of Australia without order of the court where—

    ...

    (i)   the proceeding is founded on a tort committed within Victoria

    (j)   the proceeding is brought in respect of damage suffered wholly or partly in Victoria and caused by a tortious act or omission wherever occurring.

Paragraph (j) was clearly satisfied since, wherever the tort was committed, Gutnick was complaining only about damage to his reputation in Victoria. It was not therefore necessary to satisfy para (i) as well, but the court nevertheless thought that para (i) was satisfied. Thus, the tort was committed in Victoria, causing damage to reputation in Victoria. Therefore, this was also an appropriate forum for the case to be heard.[39]

---

35   [2002] HCA 56, with full text at www.austlii.edu.au/au/cases/cth/high_ct/2002/56.html.
36   Victoria has not adopted the new style 'claimant'.
37   The issue was the jurisdiction of the Australian court, and also the applicable law (see para 69). Substantive defamation was alleged but there was no trial of the substantive action.
38   Reed's view, *Internet Law: Text and Materials*, op cit fn 2, p 114.
39   Eg, [2002] HCA 56, para 48.

In respect of the Brussels Convention, the European Court of Justice (ECJ) took the view in *Shevill v Presse Alliance SA* (Case C-68/93)[40] that its effect in defamation cases was 'to confer jurisdiction on any court in whose jurisdiction the damage occurred, such court having jurisdiction only in respect of the damage which occurred there'. It concluded that:[41]

> In the case of libel by a newspaper article published in several contracting states, where the plaintiff seeks relief in respect of the damage caused by the publication of the libel in one contracting state, article 5(3) of the Convention is to be interpreted in the sense that the plaintiff may bring proceedings for such relief against the publisher either in the place where the libel was first put into circulation or in the place in which the damage in respect of which the plaintiff seeks relief occurred, provided always that damage has occurred in that place under the proper law of the tort.

In an Internet context, this means either the location of the ISP, or the place where the damage to reputation occurred.[42]

It would seem to follow that, in general, jurisdiction will be asserted whenever the communication is received in the UK and damage to reputation occurs within the UK. Of course, only the claimant's reputation in the UK would be protected by action in the UK.

12.1.5.2   Applicable law

The UK adopts the so-called double actionability rule, under which a claimant can sue for torts in the UK if the tort is actionable both in the UK and in the country where the tort was committed.[43] If we assume that the UK has jurisdiction, this only mitigates against the stringency of UK law if it is assumed that the place of publication is abroad. However, as we have seen, under UK law publication occurs wherever the defamatory material is received. Therefore, in a case such as *Berezovsky v Michaels*, the tort is committed in the UK and the applicable law will be UK law.

In *Dow Jones* also, it was accepted that both the jurisdiction issue, and that of choice of law, turned on place of publication.[44]

The double actionability rule could become relevant if the UK court had jurisdiction, for example if the defendant was in the UK, but the publication and damage to reputation had occurred outside the UK. In this case, the tort would not necessarily have occurred within the UK, and the double actionability rule in *Boys v Chaplin* would apply.[45]

The position adopted in the UK and Australia implies, of course, that a web publisher may be subject in principle to the defamation laws of every country in the world, and cannot guarantee the application of the single law of the country in which

---

40 [1995] 2 AC 18, p 31.
41 *Ibid*, p 31.
42 In *Berezovsky*, Lord Hoffmann noted ([2000] 1 WLR 1004, p 1018) that there was no power under the Brussels Convention to decline jurisdiction on the ground of *forum non conveniens*.
43 *Boys v Chaplin* [1971] AC 356, defamation having been unaffected by the reforms of the Private Law (Miscellaneous Provisions) Act 1995.
44 [2002] HCA 56, para 47. Also paras 105 *et seq*.
45 See also *Red Sea Insurance v Bouyges SA* [1994] 3 All ER 749, and the discussion by Lilian Edwards in Edwards and Waelde, *Law and the Internet, op cit* fn 9, p 260.

the server is situated. It is objected that this can stifle the operation of the Internet. Dow Jones, for example 'submitted that it was preferable that the publisher of material on the World Wide Web be able to govern its conduct according only to the law of the place where it maintained its web servers, unless that place was merely adventitious or opportunistic'. The alternative view would be to require the publisher to take account of the law of every country on earth, from Afghanistan to Zimbabwe. On the other hand, to place material on the WWW is, for the most part, to publish it world wide and, if in the UK I make statements which amount to blasphemy in Afghanistan, I cannot really be surprised if her citizens object. On the same reasoning, it is difficult to see why citizens of the US should be entitled, with impunity, to besmirch the reputations of others within their own countries. From a claimant's viewpoint, the *Berezovsky* position is also advantageous, in that it may be difficult to locate the server, and there may in any case be servers in different jurisdictions involved, but if publication is within the UK in any event, this problem need not concern the claimant. In any case, the objection seems overstated, since (in a defamation context) a publisher need concern himself/herself only with jurisdictions where the victim suffers damage to reputation. More importantly perhaps, it depends on any judgment obtained being enforceable in practice (and bearing in mind the cost). It may be that I am prepared to take the risk of committing blasphemy in Afghanistan if I have no assets there, nor any plans to visit, and if the courts in the UK would not enforce the judgment of the overseas court. Similarly, as we will see, citizens of the US can be fairly confident in limiting their consideration of defamation to the law of the US, unless they have assets in, or intend to visit, the country concerned. In *Dow Jones*, this was thought to limit the consequences of the WWW on defamation actions.

12.1.6   Enforcement of UK actions

To sue and recover damages in the UK is only of value if either the defendant has assets here or if the courts in his own jurisdiction will enforce an English judgment. The defendant in *Dow Jones*, though being based in the US, was an international concern, and would undoubtedly have had assets in the state of Victoria. Berezovsky was apparently concerned only to clear his name and was not interested in pursuing a damages claim.

In cases of this type, though, suppose the claimant wants damages, or a freezing order, and the defendant is an ISP situated in the US with assets only in the US. Now, the claimant is dependent on the enforcement in the US of a UK judgment. However, freedom of speech has a constitutional status in the US and it is by no means certain that he or she will succeed.[46] ISPs situated in the US may therefore in practice enjoy immunity, should they be involved in the defamation of persons with reputations elsewhere.

12.2   POSITION OF ISPS

In the context of defamation, intermediary liability is important, not just because of the deep pocket syndrome, but also because the originator of the statement may be

---

46   Youm, KH, 'The interface between American and foreign libel law: US courts refuse to enforce English libel judgments' (2000) 49 ICLQ 131; also Edwards and Waelde, *op cit* fn 9, p 260.

unknown.[47] The deep pocket syndrome describes the choice of claimants to sue defendants who are in a position to pay substantial damages, but, of course, if the originator of the statement is unknown, the claimant would be without redress if he or she were unable to sue an intermediary.

We saw in Chapter 4 that mere conduits are properly immune from liability for content.[48] Their role can be considered analogous to that of phone companies, but this cannot be said of ISPs, who store information as well as merely transmit it, in the case of websites, on a more or less permanent basis. A better analogy there might be with a newspaper or publisher of a magazine, but it is far more difficult in practice for an ISP to control content than, for example, a newspaper.[49]

It cannot be said that the law in this area is very satisfactory. Two particular problems are that the more irresponsible an ISP is, the less likely it is to be held liable, and that complainants, however unmeritorious, are given encouragement by the law. The US addressed both of these issues in 1996, but the resulting legislation is unlikely to be regarded as a good solution, at any rate outside the US itself. What is needed is a solution which protects responsible but not irresponsible ISPs. No country in the world seems fully to have achieved this.

This chapter is about UK law, not only what it is but what it ought to be. In answering the second question, comparisons will be made with legislation elsewhere. While all the jurisdictions considered wish to promote e-commerce, however, different values in other respects are likely to prevent any global harmonisation of the law. For example, freedom of speech is highly valued in the United States, which also adopts a hands-off approach to the regulation of e-commerce. Singapore, by contrast, is more heavily regulated and appears to place a greater value on the protection of reputation. The UK and EU fall somewhere in between, with the EU disfavouring compulsory licensing, for example.

We begin with a review of US law. This is partly because it lies at one extreme end of the spectrum of approaches described above, partly because of the wealth of material in that jurisdiction, and partly because American cases have, to some extent at least, informed the content of the law of the UK.

It has long been held, both in the US and the UK, that libraries, book stores and newsstands are merely carriers of information and are not liable for defamatory content. They are entitled to rely on the defence of innocent dissemination. An early UK authority is that of the Court of Appeal in *Emmens v Pottle*,[50] where a vendor of a newspaper was held not liable for its defamatory content. Lord Esher MR said that:[51]

---

47 This was the position, eg, in *Godfrey v Demon Internet* [2001] QB 201; see below at section 12.2.2.1. The full report is also at www.bailii.org/ew/cases/EWHC/QB/1999/244.html. In the US, a Californian citizen has recently subpoenaed Yahoo! for the names, addresses and phone numbers of those behind messages alleged to be defamatory, and it will be interesting to follow the action: PC Pro Archive for 6 August 2004: www.pcpro.co.uk.

48 Section 4.3.1. Mere conduits are also protected from liability generally by Art 12 of the E-commerce Directive.

49 See, eg, Edwards and Waelde, *Law and the Internet, op cit* fn 9, p 261.

50 (1885) 16 QBD 354.

51 *Ibid*, p 357.

We must consider what the position of the defendants was. The proprietor of a newspaper, who publishes the paper by his servants, is the publisher of it, and he is liable for the acts of his servants. The printer of the paper prints it by his servants, and therefore he is liable for a libel contained in it. But the defendants did not compose the libel on the plaintiff, they did not write it or print it; they only disseminated that which contained the libel. The question is whether, as such disseminators, they published the libel? If they had known what was in the paper, whether they were paid for circulating it or not, they would have published the libel, and would have been liable for so doing. That, I think, cannot be doubted. But here, upon the findings of the jury, we must take it that the defendants did not know that the paper contained a libel. I am not prepared to say that it would be sufficient for them to shew that they did not know of the particular libel. But the findings of the jury make it clear that the defendants did not publish the libel. Taking the view of the jury to be right, that the defendants did not know that the paper was likely to contain a libel, and, still more, that they ought not to have known this, which must mean, that they ought not to have known it, having used reasonable care – the case is reduced to this, that the defendants were innocent disseminators of a thing which they were not bound to know was likely to contain a libel. That being so, I think the defendants are not liable for the libel.

Bowen LJ said:[52]

The jury have found as a fact that the defendants were innocent carriers of that which they did not know contained libellous matter, and which they had no reason to suppose was likely to contain libellous matter. A newspaper is not like a fire; a man may carry it about without being bound to suppose that it is likely to do an injury. It seems to me that the defendants are no more liable than any other innocent carrier of an article which he has no reason to suppose likely to be dangerous. But I by no means intend to say that the vendor of a newspaper will not be responsible for a libel contained in it, if he knows, or ought to know, that the paper is one which is likely to contain a libel.

A number of observations can be made about these passages from the case. First, the defence depends upon the defendants not composing the content (as we will see, the modern terminology is secondary publishers).[53] Secondly, the defendants must not have known, nor ought to have known, that the paper contained a libel. Thirdly, the way this defence works, at common law at least, is that innocent disseminators are not regarded as being publishers at all. This is clear from Lord Esher's judgment; liability depends on being regarded as a publisher, and the defendants in *Emmens* were not publishers. Secondary publishers who are not innocent disseminators are, however, publishers at common law, and are liable.[54]

Emmens was distinguished in *Vizetelly v Mudie's Select Library Ltd*,[55] where proprietors of a circulating library were held to be liable as publishers, where they did not know, but ought to have known, of the libellous content of a book. AL Smith LJ said:[56]

---

52   *Ibid*, p 358.
53   'Secondary publisher' is a modern term used for someone who (like an ISP) publishes but is not the originator of the material published.
54   Subject, of course, to defences such as that the published statement was true, or privileged.
55   [1900] 2 QB 170.
56   *Ibid*, pp 176–77.

It appears from the evidence of Mr Mudie, one of the defendants' directors, that there was no one in the establishment to exercise any supervision over the books besides himself and his co-director, and the books were too numerous for them to examine to see if they contained libels. He admitted that they had had books on one or two occasions which contained libels, but they had never before had an action brought against them for libel, and that they did not employ readers because it was cheaper for them to run the risk, i.e., of publishing libels and being sued for those libels, of having actions brought against them, than to do so. Is it surprising that, after admissions of this kind, a jury should come to the conclusion that the defendants did not exercise due care to see that the books circulated by them did not contain libels, and that they did not get from the jury findings such as those in *Emmens v Pottle*? It seems to me that out of the mouth of Mr Mudie there was sufficient evidence to justify the jury in coming to the conclusion that the defendants had failed to prove their defence, and that it was through negligence on their part that they did not find out that the book contained a libel on the plaintiff. That being so, they failed to do what the defendants in *Emmens v Pottle* succeeded in doing, namely, prove that they did not publish the libel.

Note that it was no defence that 'the books were too numerous for [the defendants] to examine to see if they contained libels'. They should have examined them, in which case they would have known of the libel. Notice also that the defendants here, unlike those in *Emmens*, were held to be publishers, and that is why they were liable.

It seems clear that, at least under the common law of the UK, ISPs are treated similarly to newsvendors and circulating libraries. That being so, it is probably no defence that it is, in practice, impossible for them to monitor the content because of its bulk. But we need to examine the case law.

12.2.1   US law

12.2.1.1   US law prior to 1996

The American cases, prior to 1996, were based, in part at least, on English common law and can thus be used, tentatively at least, as indicators of what the English common law is. However, US law has also been influenced by the First Amendment to the Constitution, providing for freedom of speech, so that the American cases will tend to be more favourable towards defendants than the UK common law.

The first ISP case to be litigated in the US was *Cubby Inc v CompuServe Inc*,[57] where statements about a computer database (called 'Skuttlebut') were made by a competitor ('Rumorville'), in a local online forum (the 'Journalism Forum'). CompuServe did not dispute, for the purposes of the case, that the statements were defamatory, but denied that it had published them.[58] The Journalism Forum, though hosted by CompuServe, was managed by a third party, Cameron Communications Inc (CCI), which exercised editorial control over the forum, but CompuServe neither commissioned nor paid for any of the material on the forum, nor was it paid anything by CCI. Its only financial interest was in the standard online time usage and membership fees charged to all

---

57   (1991) 776 F Supp 135 NY DC, available at www.bitlaw.com/source/cases/copyright/cubby.html.

58   Apart from defamation, there were also (unsuccessful) claims for business disparagement, unfair competition, and that CompuServe should be vicariously liable.

CompuServe subscribers, regardless of the information services they used. Moreover, CompuServe exercised no editorial control over the forum.

The approach taken by the New York District Court was to treat the ISP (CompuServe) as equivalent to a library, book store or newsstand, observing that 'CompuServe's ... product is in essence an electronic, for-profit library'. Accordingly, CompuServe was held to be merely a distributor, not a publisher.[59] The test applied was basically that of the English common law, since CompuServe 'neither knew nor had reason to know of the allegedly defamatory statements'. Moreover, the contractual arrangement between CompuServe and CCI might have prevented CompuServe exercising any supervision of content. At any rate, the court observed that the material would be accessible instantaneously on being uploaded, and CompuServe certainly had no editorial control prior to uploading. Moreover, 'CompuServe has ... delegated control over the assembly of the contents of the Journalism Forum to CCI'. This is therefore more than it simply being impractical to check, as in *Vizetelly v Mudie's Select Library Ltd*, and it seems likely that CompuServe would also not have been liable under English common law. However, it may be that, in general, the innocent dissemination test is applied more favourably in the US than under English common law, since the:

> requirement that a distributor must have knowledge of the contents of a publication before liability can be imposed for distributing that publication is deeply rooted in the First Amendment, made applicable to the states through the Fourteenth Amendment.

Thus, although American defamation law is based on the common law, it cannot necessarily be assumed to be identical, if liability is assumed also to have been limited by the US constitution. It would be expected that US law would be, if anything, more favourable to defendants.[60]

Cubby was distinguished in *Stratton Oakmont Inc v Prodigy Services Co*.[61] This was another commercial defamation case concerning an allegation of commercial fraud by a securities investment banking firm and its president, which had been posted on Prodigy's bulletin board. Prodigy's problem was that, far from delegating its editorial role to a third party, as CompuServe had done, it had been pro-active in controlling the activities on its site. Indeed, it advertised, and indeed made a business virtue of the fact that it offered a moderated family service:

> We make no apology for pursuing a value system that reflects the culture of the millions of American families we aspire to serve. Certainly no responsible newspaper does less when it carries the type of advertising it published, the letters it prints, the degree of nudity and unsupported gossip its editors tolerate.

Perhaps it is not surprising, then, that the court took the view that Prodigy had put itself into the position of a newspaper rather than a distributor, and that the editorial control it thereby exerted made it a publisher of the defamatory material:[62]

---

59 Publisher in the English common law sense, not in the sense of primary publisher, as publisher is effectively defined in the UK Defamation Act 1996 (see section 12.2.2.1).

60 *Cubby* would probably be decided in the same way under UK law today, however: see further section 12.2.2.2.

61 [1995] NY Misc Lexis 229, NY SC, 423 Media L Rep 1794 (NY Sup Ct, 25 May 1995). Also at www.law.uoregon.edu/faculty/kaoki/site/secure/cases/defamatory/stratton_oakmont_v_prodigy.php.

62 Publisher again being used in the common law sense, not the more restricted sense under the UK Defamation Act 1996.

The key distinction between CompuServe and PRODIGY is two fold. First, PRODIGY held itself out to the public and its members as controlling the content of its computer bulletin boards. Second, PRODIGY implemented this control through its automatic software screening program, and the Guidelines which Board Leaders are required to enforce. By actively utilizing technology and manpower to delete notes from its computer bulletin boards on the basis of offensiveness and 'bad taste', for example, PRODIGY is clearly making decisions as to content ...),[63] and such decisions constitute editorial control. ... That such control is not complete and is enforced both as early as the notes arrive and as late as a complaint is made, does not minimize or eviscerate the simple fact that PRODIGY has uniquely arrogated to itself the role of determining what is proper for its members to post and read on its bulletin boards. Based on the foregoing, this court is compelled to conclude that for the purposes of plaintiffs' claims in this action, PRODIGY is a publisher rather than a distributor.

The court also noted that Prodigy gained a market advantage from its conscious choice to monitor.

It was accepted that Prodigy had at least two million subscribers who communicated on the bulletin boards, that 60,000 messages a day were posted on Prodigy bulletin boards and, therefore, that a manual review of messages was not feasible. However, to take account of that would be to allow the defence that had failed in the UK case of *Vizetelly v Mudie's Select Library Ltd* but, in any case, Prodigy had positively asserted a measure of editorial control over the bulletin boards. There is no doubt whatever that Prodigy would have been liable under English common law.

Lilian Edwards points out that this position is very undesirable, in that it encourages ISPs not to moderate content, observing that the:[64]

most unfortunate aspect of the Prodigy and CompuServe decisions was that the ratio that could most easily be extracted from the two contrasting results was that to avoid liability, an ISP should do as little as possible to monitor and edit the content of the messages or other material it carries.

Indeed, the court in *Stratton Oakmont v Prodigy* seemed concerned positively to encourage a hands-off approach by ISPs, on freedom of speech grounds, observing that 'Prodigy's current system of automatic scanning, Guidelines and Board Leaders may have a chilling effect on freedom of communication in Cyberspace, and it appears that this chilling effect is exactly what PRODIGY wants, but for the legal liability that attaches to such censorship'.

Edwards also points out that *Stratton Oakmont* put an undesirable brake on the development of the Internet where commercial ISPs increasingly wish to provide more sanitised information. A further criticism that can be made of the innocent dissemination defence in general is that it depends on lack of knowledge of the defamatory material. However, unlike newspapers, ISPs will not generally have the resources to risk defending a defamation action, so the most rational response to any complaint is to remove the defamatory, or allegedly defamatory, material. If the material is not in fact defamatory, then debate which could lawfully have been pursued on the Internet will in reality be stifled.

---

63   The court noted *Miami Herald Publishing Co v Tornillo*, 418 US 241 (1974).
64   Edwards and Waelde, *Law and the Internet, op cit* fn 9, p 263.

Primarily out of a desire to promote the development of e-commerce, the American legislature moved quickly to overrule *Stratton Oakmont*. The pros and cons of the resulting legislation are discussed further below.

It is necessary also to consider *Lunney v Prodigy*.[65] Though this case was decided after the 1996 legislation considered below, the facts had occurred prior to 1996. The court felt that it was in any case unnecessary to apply the legislation to hold the defendants not liable,[66] simply taking the view that the ISP was not a publisher.[67] The case concerned an impostor who sent e-mails and also posted messages to a bulletin board posing as Lunney, a teenage boy scout. The messages were criminally offensive and Lunney was visited by the police, the messages being ascribed to him. This was considered to be defamation and, of course, the victim was a young teenager. Moreover, the identity of the impostor was not known, so that if Prodigy were not liable, there was no redress.

Because both the ISP and the court were the same as in *Stratton Oakmont* (that is, Prodigy and the Court of Appeals of New York), it has been suggested that the earlier case was overruled,[68] but that is not the case. As far as the e-mail was concerned, it was accepted that Prodigy was a mere conduit, the analogy of a telephone company being used. It was also observed that the 'public would not be well served by compelling an ISP to examine and screen millions of e-mail communications, on pain of liability for defamation'. It was recognised that bulletin boards should be treated differently, 'owing to the generally greater level of cognizance that their operators can have over them'. Yet Prodigy were held not to be liable, even in respect of the bulletin board, in spite of their reservation to themselves of the right of editorial control. Different factual inferences were drawn from the earlier case.[69] The court agreed with the Appellate Division that:

> even if Prodigy 'exercised the power to exclude certain vulgarities from the text of certain [bulletin board] messages', this would not alter its passive character in 'the millions of other messages in whose transmission it did not participate'.

As we will see, in *Godfrey v Demon Internet Ltd*, Morland J did not think *Lunney v Prodigy* would have been decided the same way in the UK,[70] though he made no similar comment about *Cubby v CompuServe*. Though it is not expressed explicitly, presumably the view of Morland J is confined to the bulletin board postings. We have already seen, from the study of *Vizetelly v Mudie's Select Library Ltd*, that it is the ability to exercise editorial control that is crucial in UK law, whether or not it is practicable to

---

65 *Alexander G Lunney v Prodigy Services Co* (1999) 94 NY 2d 242: www.law.cornell.edu/ ny/ctap/I99_0165.htm, and also http://legal.web.aol.com/decisions/dldefam/ lunneyappeal.html.
66 Thereby avoiding the retroactivity argument in *Zeran v AOL*, below.
67 The court chose to rely on the common law doctrine, created by *Anderson v New York Tel Co* 35 NY2d 746.
68 Eg, Edwards and Waelde, *Law and the Internet, op cit* fn 9, p 262.
69 It is quite possible, of course, that Prodigy had altered its practices between the two cases, since these things are not set in stone. At any rate now, Prodigy has 'recently joined forces with Yahoo!', and there is no hint of a family-friendly policy: http://myhome.prodigy.net.
70 Morland J's remarks were made prior to the coming into force of the E-Commerce Directive. See further section 12.2.2.2 on whether *Lunney* would be decided the same way in the UK today.

do so. *Cubby* was different, where CompuServe had delegated editorial control entirely to a third party and had not even retained the possibility of control. *Cubby* may well therefore have been decided the same way under UK common law, and would probably also be decided the same way in the UK today.

12.2.1.2   US law after 1996

Partly in response to *Stratton Oakmont*, and the negative effect it was thought likely to have on the growth of the Internet, Congress enacted the Communication Decency Act (CDA) 1996, s 230 of which provides pretty well blanket protection for ISPs. It is a long way from current UK law, but is worth examining briefly as a route down which the UK could go, if it were felt desirable.

The US legislature was concerned to deregulate the Internet, while still controlling content. The CDA 1996 accordingly strengthened enforcement against the primary publishers, those who originated in particular obscene material, while protecting ISPs, who merely hosted third party content. The legislative intent can be gleaned from the following passage, taken from *Zeran v AOL*:[71]

> The preamble and history both demonstrate that Congress enacted Section 230 to foster robust discourse over interactive computer services by ensuring that the intermediaries of such discourse – service providers such as AOL – are not held liable for harm caused by third-party content.

> Section 230's preamble announces a congressional finding that 'interactive computer services offer a forum for a true diversity of political discourse, unique opportunities for cultural development, and myriad avenues for intellectual activity' and that these services have 'flourished, to the benefit of all Americans, *with a minimum of government regulation*'. ... The preamble also declares that it is 'the policy of the United States ... to preserve the vibrant and competitive free market that presently exists for the Internet and other interactive computer services, *unfettered by Federal or State regulation*'. ... Viewed in the context of the whole of Section 230, these declarations reflect Congress's view that a legal regime under which interactive computer service providers could face tort liability for dissemination of content produced by others inevitably would hurt the development of an emerging communications medium that obviously holds great promise for the Nation.

> At the same time, Section 230's preamble reflects that Congress recognized the need to deter and punish truly harmful online speech and chose to do so by strengthening enforcement of federal criminal laws against the actual wrongdoers who originate such speech. The preamble declares that it is the 'policy of the United States ... to ensure vigorous enforcement of Federal criminal laws to deter and punish trafficking in obscenity, stalking, and harassment by means of computer'. ... Thus, Congress made the policy decision to deter tortious online speech not by punishing the intermediary, but by strengthening the enforcement of legal remedies against the culpable source of the unlawful content.

> The legislative history of Section 230 further confirms Congress's intent to immunize interactive computer services from liability for dissemination of third parties' tortious online speech. Debate on the bill on the House floor revealed a congressional understanding that interactive service providers should not be responsible for harmful

---

71   Available from AOL's own site: http://legal.web.aol.com/decisions/dldefam/zeranapb.html.

third-party content because the nature of the medium makes it impossible for them to review and edit third-party content:

> There is no way that any of those entities, like Prodigy, can take the responsibility to edit out information that is going to be coming in to them from all manner of sources onto their bulletin board. We are talking about something that is far larger than our daily newspaper. We are talking about something that is going to be thousands of pages of information every day, and to have that imposition imposed on them is wrong. [Section 230] will cure that problem ...

...

Accordingly, Section 230 was intended to provide online services 'a reasonable way to ... help them *self-regulate themselves without penalty of law*'. ...

Congress's intention to immunize interactive service providers from liability for third-party content is further demonstrated by the CDA's conference report, which states that one of the purposes of Section 230 was to overrule the *only* reported case in which an interactive service provider had ever been found potentially liable for tortious third-party content. ... In *Stratton Oakmont Inc v Prodigy Services Co* ... [the] court decided to treat Prodigy as a publisher of the message because Prodigy had held itself out to the public as a family-oriented service and attempted to exercise editorial control over third-party content ... As the Conference Report stated:

> One of the specific purposes of [Section 230] is to overrule *Stratton Oakmont v Prodigy* and any other similar decisions which have treated such providers and users as publishers or speakers of content that is not their own because they have restricted access to objectionable material. The conferees believe that such decisions create serious obstacles to the important federal policy of empowering parents to determine the content of communications their children receive through interactive computer services.

The main thrust of this recital is a legislative intent to promote growth of the Internet by reducing control over intermediaries. At the same time, enforcement against originators of obscene and other criminal content is strengthened. Ironically, this second prong of the legislation was rendered largely impotent by *ACLU v Reno*,[72] which struck down the provisions aimed primarily at protecting children from Internet pornography, because they infringed the constitutional right to free speech in the First Amendment. The ISP immunities in s 230 remain in force in the US, however. Section 230 provides that:[73]

> No provider of an interactive computer service shall be treated as the publisher or speaker of any information provided by another information content provider.

And further that:

> No cause of action may be brought and no liability may be imposed.

Unfortunately, the identity of the perpetrators is not always known, in which case victims of even very nasty defamations are left entirely without redress. In *Zeran v AOL*,[74] a 'currently unidentified person' posted on AOL's bulletin board 'grossly

---

72 Supreme Court of the US, 26 June 1997, fully reported at http://floridalawfirm.com/reno.html.

73 See also the discussion in Reed, *Internet Law: Text and Materials*, op cit fn 2, pp 130 *et seq*.

74 [1997] 129 F3d 327. Full text can be found at AOL's own site: http://legal.web.aol.com/decisions/dldefam/zeranapb.html.

offensive' messages, implicating Zeran in selling 'Naughty Oklahoma T-Shirts', and hence profiting from the bombing of the federal building in Oklahoma City. Zeran complained to AOL, informing them that the postings were a hoax and they were swiftly removed, but not before Zeran had received threatening phone calls, and even death threats. This was therefore a truly outrageous defamation, where the identity of the actual perpetrator was unknown.

Nevertheless, the United States Court of Appeals held that AOL was protected by s 230 and, indeed, that the section afforded pretty well blanket protection.[75] The reasoning was that AOL's liability depended on them being treated as publishers, which the section prevented, and at common law, of course, this would be true of any defamation claim:

> ... under well-settled common law principles, liability for harm flowing from the dissemination of defamatory or otherwise tortious material may be imposed only on a party who is deemed to have 'published' the material. Basic hornbook law provides that an entity may be liable for harm caused by a defamatory statement if and only if the entity 'published' the statement.

The logic of this is that a blanket immunity is provided where the information is provided by a third party.[76]

In *Blumenthal v Drudge*, it was assumed that the main thrust behind the legislation was a desire to overrule *Stratton Oakmont*:

> One of the specific purposes of this section is to overrule *Stratton Oakmont v Prodigy* and any other similar decisions which have treated such providers and users as publishers or speakers of content that is not their own because they have restricted access to objectionable material. The conferees believe that such decisions create serious obstacles to the important federal policy of empowering parents to determine the content of communications their children receive through interactive computer services.

However, as *Blumenthal v Drudge* itself shows,[77] the legislation goes further than this, providing blanket immunity for all third party content. The 'Drudge Report' made allegations of marital violence against 'White House recruit Sidney Blumenthal', which (it was alleged) had been covered up. Though the allegations were defamatory, AOL were protected by the CDA 1996, even though they had actually commissioned and paid for this third party gossip, presumably to increase their own attractiveness. The United States District Court for the District of Columbia was clearly not happy with the situation, observing that:

> Because it has the right to exercise editorial control over those with whom it contracts and whose words it disseminates, it would seem only fair to hold AOL to the liability standards applied to a publisher or, at least, like a book store owner or library, to the

---

75 Reed, *Internet Law: Text and Materials*, op cit fn 2, pp 137–38 thinks *Zeran* goes too far.

76 Zeran attempted an alternative negligent distribution claim, which failed as being in reality a defamation action in disguise: '"distributor liability" is simply a species of "publisher liability"', and 'under well-settled common law principles, liability for harm flowing from the dissemination of defamatory or otherwise tortious material may be imposed only on a party who is deemed to have "published" the material'. Another issue in the case was whether the Communication Decency Act 1996 could apply to facts that occurred before it came into force.

77 Full text is at www.techlawjournal.com/courts/drudge/80423opin.htm, and also at AOL's own site: http://legal.web.aol.com/decisions/dldefam/blumenmo.html. See also summaries in Reed, *Internet Law: Text and Materials*, op cit fn 2, p 132 and Edwards and Waelde, *Law and the Internet*, op cit fn 9, p 268.

liability standards applied to a distributor. But Congress has made a different policy choice by providing immunity even where the interactive service provider has an active, even aggressive role in making available content prepared by others. In some sort of tacit *quid pro quo* arrangement with the service provider community, Congress has conferred immunity from tort liability as an incentive to Internet service providers to self-police the Internet for obscenity and other offensive material, even where the self-policing is unsuccessful or not even attempted.

As we will see below, neither the UK nor the EU generally adopts the position of the American court in *Drudge*.

12.2.1.3   Advantages and disadvantages of blanket ISP immunity

The UK law is widely regarded as unsatisfactory and the American position has been arrived at by deliberate choice. If law reform is canvassed, it is therefore a possible model to consider. Its main advantage is that it does not impede development of the Internet;[78] moreover, since all ISPs are treated alike, it does not discourage ISPs from being responsible, as did the pre-1996 US law. *Zeran* illustrates the disadvantage: there was a serious defamation there, as a result of which the victim suffered death threats, with no alternative party being obviously liable.[79] With the ISP immune, there was therefore no redress available at all. The UK Law Commission took the view that 'the *Zeran* decision gives very little weight to the protection of reputation'.[80]

12.2.2   UK law

12.2.2.1   The common law and the Defamation Act 1996

We have seen how the UK common law developed the defence of innocent dissemination, which, in principle at least, could protect ISPs. The Defamation Act 1996 consolidates, and (perhaps) gives additional protection to intermediaries.[81] It is not clear whether the 1996 Act consolidated or amended the common law and, if the latter, whether the common law continues to survive alongside the Act, but for present purposes it is probably safe to assume that the Act merely consolidated the pre-existing law,[82] albeit (and rather confusingly) adopting a different definition of publisher. Article 1(1) provides that:

---

78   It was noted in *Zeran v AOL* that 'saddling interactive computer services with liability for harm caused by third-party communications would be inconsistent with the vigorous and vibrant development of this new and important medium of communication'.

79   As the Law Commission observed, *Defamation and the Internet, A Preliminary Investigation, Scoping Study No 2*, December 2002, para 2.52: 'In *Zeran* the claimant had suffered real damage.' See also para 2.54. The report is at www.lawcom.gov.uk/files/defamation2.pdf.

80   *Ibid*, para 2.54.

81   See, eg, *Rogers, Winfield and Jolowicz on Tort*, 16th edn, 2002, London: Sweet & Maxwell, p 427, fn 86.

82   In *Godfrey v Demon Internet*, Morland J was at least heavily influenced by pre-1996 UK decisions. He also quoted Lord Mackay LC, who said of s 1 of the 1996 Act, in moving rejection of an amendment of Lord Lester of Herne Hill QC (*Hansard*, House of Lords Debates, HL Deb, Cols 214–15, 2 April 1996): 'It is intended to provide a modern equivalent of the common law defence of innocent dissemination ...' ([2001] QB 201, quoted by Morland J at p 207).

(1) In defamation proceedings a person has a defence if he shows that—

    (a) he was not the author, editor or publisher of the statement complained of,

    (b) he took reasonable care in relation to its publication, and

    (c) he did not know, and had no reason to believe, that what he did caused or contributed to the publication of a defamatory statement.

Note that these are cumulative requirements. Section 1(3) fills out s 1(1)(a), providing that:

(3) A person shall not be considered the author, editor or publisher of a statement if he is only involved—

    (a) in printing, producing, distributing or selling printed material containing the statement;

    ...

    (c) in processing, making copies of, distributing or selling any electronic medium in or on which the statement is recorded, or in operating or providing any equipment, system or service by means of which the statement is retrieved, copied, distributed or made available in electronic form;

    ...

    (e) as the operator of or provider of access to a communications system by means of which the statement is transmitted, or made available, by a person over whom he has no effective control.

In a case not within paragraphs (a) to (e) the court may have regard to those provisions by way of analogy in deciding whether a person is to be considered the author, editor or publisher of a statement.

Note that paras (a)–(e) are alternatives. Section 1(3)(e) is appropriate to cover ISPs,[83] except perhaps in the *Blumenthal* situation (assuming AOL had some control over the content there). However, the only relevance of this section, for present purposes, is to define a publisher, for the purposes of s 1(1)(a), in such a way as effectively to exclude a secondary publisher, for example a distributor rather than an originator of the defamatory statement.[84] As we have seen, the common law, by contrast, treated all distributors as publishers, except innocent disseminators.

However, ISPs as secondary publishers do not have an automatic defence under s 1, since they must also satisfy s 1(1)(b) and (c), which effectively enacts the common law innocent dissemination defence.

The only English authority is *Godfrey v Demon Internet Ltd*.[85] Demon was held to have defamed Mr Godfrey (a lecturer in physics, mathematics and computer science) by subscribing to a Usenet Newsgroup (soc.culture.thai) containing material which

---

83 Edwards observes (Edwards and Waelde, *Law and the Internet*, *op cit* fn 9, p 265) that s 1(3)(e) was intended to give blanket protection to ISPs, but, of course, it would not apply if the ISP provided additional services.

84 'Although this term does not appear in the legislation, it is commonly used to describe those involved in disseminating a defamatory statement, other than the author, editor and commercial publisher.' (Law Commission, *op cit* fn 79, para 2.2.)

85 [2001] QB 201; [1999] 4 All ER 342; [1999] EWHC QB 244, with a full report also at www.bailii.org/ew/cases/EWHC/QB/1999/244.html, and noted by Akdeniz, Y, *Godfrey v Demon Internet* on Nominet's site at www.nic.uk/ReferenceDocuments/CaseLaw/GodfreyVDemonInternet.html.

purported to come from him, but which was 'squalid, obscene and defamatory'.[86] Godfrey complained to Demon, but Demon took no steps to remove the material until it expired in the ordinary course of events, about 10 days later.[87] The material had been posted by 'someone unknown' in the USA.[88] Demon were able to show that they were not a publisher within s 1(3), and hence satisfied s 1(1)(a),[89] but were caught by s 1(1)(b) and 1(1)(c),[90] because they did not remove the offending news posting even after being alerted to the possibility that it was defamatory. The case does not therefore establish any general liability of ISPs in the UK, since it depended on Demon being made aware of the content of the newsletters and not removing them.

Suppose Demon had not been informed of the potential defamatory nature of the material and had simply carried the news without enquiring into its content. Probably they would now be able to satisfy s 1(1)(c), but maybe not s 1(1)(b), which is qualified by s 1(5):

(5) In determining for the purposes of this section whether a person took reasonable care, or had reason to believe that what he did caused or contributed to the publication of a defamatory statement, regard shall be had to—

(a) the extent of his responsibility for the content of the statement or the decision to publish it,

(b) the nature or circumstances of the publication, and

(c) the previous conduct or character of the author, editor or publisher.

It is tempting to think that this simply enacts something similar to the pre-CDA 1996 American position (with its undesirable effects). We have seen, however, that the American cases, though based on UK common law, were also heavily influenced by the First Amendment and Morland J found them 'of only marginal assistance because of the different approach to defamation across the Atlantic'.[91] He also observed that the Defamation Act did not did not adopt the approach or have the purpose of the US CDA 1996,[92] and also that it did not enact *Lunney*, because Prodigy would have been

---

86 Paragraph 12 of the judgment.
87 Paragraph 14 of the judgment.
88 Paragraph 12 of the judgment.
89 Reed (*Internet Law: Text and Materials, op cit* fn 2, p 114) suggests that Demon were held to be a publisher *at common law*, but though Demon may well have been, they were actually held *not* to be a publisher *under the 1996 Act*: there is an express statement by Morland J [2001] QB 201, p 206. The two definitions of publisher confuse the issue.
90 Para 20 of the judgment (a defence succeeds only if all three sub-sections are satisfied). Morland J does not distinguish between s 1(1)(b) and (c), but the problem must surely have been s 1(1)(c). The Law Commission observed (*Defamation and the Internet, op cit* fn 79, para 2.9) that the case 'does not deal with the question of "reasonable care" in relation to an internet publication, and at present there is little case law on this point'. The Commission clearly considers this to be a s 1(1)(c) case then.
91 [2001] QB 201, p 209 (para 36 of the judgment).
92 Paragraph 45 of the judgment.

regarded as a publisher in the UK.[93] In effect he is saying, therefore, that the pre-1996 US position was more favourable to ISPs than the UK common law.[94]

12.2.2.2 UK law and the E-commerce Directive

Since the decision in *Godfrey v Demon Internet*, the UK has implemented (in August 2002) the E-commerce Directive,[95] the relevant regulations being the Electronic Commerce (EC Directive) Regulations 2002.[96] The regulations on intermediary liability are 17–20, bringing into force Arts 12–14 of the Directive.

ISP hosting liability is governed by reg 19, bringing into force Art 14:

Hosting

19. Where an information society service is provided which consists of the storage of information provided by a recipient of the service, the service provider (if he otherwise would) shall not be liable for damages or for any other pecuniary remedy or for any criminal sanction as a result of that storage where

(a) the service provider—

(i) does not have actual knowledge of unlawful activity or information and, where a claim for damages is made, is not aware of facts or circumstances from which it would have been apparent to the service provider that the activity or information was unlawful; or

(ii) upon obtaining such knowledge or awareness, acts expeditiously to remove or to disable access to the information, and

(b) the recipient of the service was not acting under the authority or the control of the service provider.

This is almost identical to the wording of Art 14.[97] It supplements any s 1 defence. Its application clearly encompasses websites and, perhaps, web-based e-mail, where the service provided 'consists of the storage of information provided by a recipient of the service'. The provision applies less clearly to a bulletin board or newsgroup, although it seems likely that postings would be regarded as being made by recipients of the service.

---

93 [2001] QB 201, p 212 (para 49 of the judgment). At first sight this is a somewhat puzzling conclusion, given the factual similarities he saw with Demon, and that he thought Demon were not a publisher. However, it is clear that he regarded Prodigy as a publisher *at common law*, whereas Demon were *not* a publisher *under the Defamation Act*. Demon were not a publisher under the Act because they was not a primary publisher. Prodigy was a publisher at common law, although a secondary publisher, because he was not, in Morland J's view, an innocent disseminator.

94 There is, however, no express criticism of *Cubby v CompuServe*, where there had been a complete delegation of editorial function to a third party.

95 Council Directive (2000/31/EC) of the European Parliament and of the Council of 8 June 2000 on certain legal aspects of information society services, in particular electronic commerce, in the Internal Market ('Directive on electronic commerce'), full text at http://europa.eu.int/eur-lex/pri/en/oj/dat/2000/l_178/l_17820000717en00010016.pdf.

96 SI 2002/2013, with full text at www.opsi.gov.uk/si/si2002/20022013.htm, and for background see www.dti.gov.uk/industries/ecommunications/electronic_commerce_directive_0031ec.html.

97 Article 14 uses the term 'illegal' rather than 'unlawful'. 'Unlawful' is a more appropriate term in UK law to include tortious activity.

Regulation 19 appears to provide greater protection for ISPs carrying third party content than the Defamation Act 1996, in that there is no equivalent to s 1(1)(b) of the 1996 Act. It may well be, therefore, that there would be no liability if the facts of *Cubby*, *Stratton Oakmont*, *Lunney* or even *Zeran* were to occur in the UK today (and assuming the regulation applies to newsgroups and bulletin boards).[98]

The notice and take-down provision is not unlike s 1(1)(c), though it may provide greater immunity in requiring an ISP to know that the material was 'unlawful', in other words, actually defamatory (that is, that there are no defences). It is also arguable, however, that the Directive is effectively identical to s 1(1)(c) of the 1996 Act, providing no greater protection.[99] Certainly, the decision in *Godfrey* would not be affected, since Demon did not act expeditiously to remove the material, following the complaint. In any event, it is an actual or constructive notice provision, with a defence if the offending material is expeditiously removed.

Protection is for third party content only, and reg 19(b) removes exemption where the recipient of the [hosting] service is acting under the authority or control of the provider, thereby providing for liability in the *Blumenthal v Drudge* situation.[100] The Law Commission has also observed:[101]

> Nor does the Directive apply to those who 'aggregate' information, by selecting and compiling information from other sources. An example would be Factiva.com, a Dow Jones and Reuters company, which provides its users with global news and business information. The content is derived from around 8,000 sources, including newspapers, magazines, and company reports.

It comments, however, that the scale of the operation makes it very difficult for the service provider to check the content of each item before it is placed on the site. It is not clear whether an aggregator is a publisher within s 1 of the Defamation Act, considered above.[102]

12.2.2.3   ISPs and their own subscribers

A criticism that can be made of the UK law is that, in reality, because ISPs are not really in a position to defend defamation actions, the innocent dissemination defence has created a complainer's charter:[103]

> We were told that some ISPs receive over a hundred complaints each year. Particular concerns were expressed about the number of solicitors' letters sent on behalf of companies complaining about websites set up by their disgruntled customers. Under the present law, the safest course is for the ISP to remove such material, whether or not the alleged defamatory material is in the public interest or true.

---

98   Assuming, in *Zeran*, that AOL could be regarded as removing the material expeditiously once notified of it. In *Lunney v Prodigy*, Prodigy removed the offending material within two days of notification.

99   Law Commission, *Defamation and the Internet, op cit* fn 79, paras 2.22–2.23.

100 See, in general, Edwards and Waelde, *Law and the Internet, op cit* fn 9, pp 268–70.

101 Law Commission, *Defamation and the Internet, op cit* fn 79, para 2.25.

102 Law Commission, *Defamation and the Internet, op cit* fn 79, para 2.26.

103 Law Commission, *Defamation and the Internet, op cit* fn 79, para 1.5. Full text can be found at www.lawcom.gov.uk/files/defamation2.pdf. See also para 1.12, on the position of 'tactical targets'.

Another concern is that this can stifle legitimate debate on the Internet:[104]

> If the ISPs become more cautious over what material they allow to be published – by screening submissions or suspending websites – they could inflame the debate over freedom of expression or damage internet-based businesses.

Another point that needs to be considered, however, is the contractual relationship between the ISP and its own customers, should it remove the content complained of or block subscribers' websites. Clearly, an ISP cannot be required to commit the tort of defamation, so if the content is actually defamatory the ISP should not be liable for breach of contract. However, the ISP may not be in any position to judge this and, if the content turns out not to be defamatory, this could, in principle, put the ISP in breach of contract with its subscriber. This might be resolved by contractual terms with subscribers, but they would have to be drafted to give ISPs a very considerable discretion. This may be unacceptable to business customers and, in consumer contracts, any such term would have to satisfy the reasonableness test in ss 3 and 11 of the Unfair Contract Terms Act 1977.

Alternatively or additionally, as Lilian Edwards points out, ISPs could require indemnities from subscribers, though these might be difficult to enforce in practice and might be unpopular with business subscribers.[105] Another alternative would be to take out liability insurance, and pass the cost on to all subscribers.

12.2.2.4 UK law reform

Whether or not UK law is the same as, or more or less favourable to defendants than the pre-1996 US law, it is open to the objection that Lilian Edwards made of the earlier American cases, that ISPs are penalised for being responsible.[106] Other problems are that it is difficult in practice for an ISP to control content,[107] and we have already seen the difficulties faced by an impecunious tactical target faced with a complaint, however unmeritorious that complaint may be.

ISP liability may also be somewhat fortuitous from a claimant's viewpoint. Suppose, for example, in *Godfrey v Demon*, the ISP had been situated outside the UK – Godfrey may have found it considerably more difficult to bring a defamation action, or at any rate to enforce his judgment.[108]

We have seen that one possibility is the American solution. However, one reason for suing the ISP in *Godfrey* was that the originator of the posting was unknown. The

---

104 Comment on the *Demon* case at http://news.bbc.co.uk/1/hi/sci/tech/695596.stm. There are also possible implications for Art 10 of the European Convention on Human Rights: Law Commission, *Defamation and the Internet, op cit* fn 79, paras 2.36 *et seq*.

105 Edwards and Waelde, *Law and the Internet, op cit* fn 9, p 267. Indemnities in consumer contracts are in any case subject to s 4 of the Unfair Contract Terms Act 1977.

106 Edwards and Waelde, *Law and the Internet, op cit* fn 9, p 263. The ISP who turns a blind eye is unlikely to be liable, in the light of reg 19.

107 As we have seen, Prodigy claimed that they had 60,000 postings a day. That was many years ago, and we can assume far greater numbers today.

108 Though Morland J thought that damages were unlikely to be very great, the eventual settlement was for £15,000, plus legal costs estimated at £200,000: http://news.bbc.co.uk/1/hi/sci/tech/695596.stm. There is also comment at http://news.zdnet.co.uk/internet/0,39020369,2078072,00.htm.

American solution could leave someone like Godfrey with no redress at all. We have also seen the view expressed that US law does not protect reputations very well.

The Law Commission considered extending s 1 protection to secondary publishers who believe that the material, although defamatory, was not libellous.[109] This would reduce the extent to which the law could be used as a complainant's charter. This would, however, require the ISP to form a judgment on the truth of the material, by no means a simple matter in practice.[110]

Another possibility, also considered by the Law Commission, is the use of codes of practice.[111] To be useful, a code of practice would have to be very clear and include a procedure for dispute resolution, especially if ISPs were expected to be able to adjudicate the truth of the content. Ideally, I would suggest, an ISP which followed the code of practice ought to be immune from liability. There are jurisdictions which have adopted a code, and we will consider Singapore, partly because its values are so different from those of the US, and partly because of the wealth of material that is available.

Ultimately, the Law Commission considered that it 'would not be appropriate, in a short project of this type, to reach a conclusion on the relative merits of the various proposals'.[112] Few would regard the present law as satisfactory, however, and it is to be hoped that this matter receives more detailed consideration in due course.

12.2.3   The Singapore approach: codes of practice

Singapore is one of the few jurisdictions to have adopted a code of practice which, as we have seen, is a possible way forward for UK law. However, the Singapore code does not offer particularly clear guidance, and leaves ISPs exposed to the general law, even when they follow the code.

Like the US, the government of Singapore is anxious to promote e-commerce and the development of the Internet. For example, para 3(a) of the Internet Industry Guidelines, issued by the Singapore Media Development Authority (MDA), states:[113]

> MDA fully supports the development of the Internet. The Internet is an important communication medium as well as a rich source of information, education and entertainment.

Section 3(b) of the Electronic Transactions Act 1998 states among the purposes of the Act:

> to facilitate electronic commerce ... and to promote the development of the legal and business infrastructure necessary to implement secure electronic commerce.

In other respects, however, their values are vastly different. There is no First Amendment in Singapore, where reputations, by contrast, are accorded greater protection than in the US. Although para 3(f) of the Internet Industry Guidelines states

---

109 Law Commission, *Defamation and the Internet, op cit* fn 79, para 2.55. The idea is to protect an ISP which believes, for example, that a defence might be available, such as truth, or that publication is otherwise justified.

110 Law Commission, *Defamation and the Internet, op cit* fn 79, para 2.59.

111 Law Commission, *Defamation and the Internet, op cit* fn 79, paras 2.62, *et seq.*

112 Law Commission, *Defamation and the Internet, op cit* fn 79, para 2.66.

113 At www.mda.gov.sg/wms.file/mobj/mobj.496.internet_industry_guide.pdf. See further below.

that 'MDA takes a light-touch approach in regulating services on the Internet', there is, in fact, a compulsory licensing scheme in operation in Singapore, and the Singapore government certainly does not share the repugnance of the US Congress towards regulating the Internet. Indeed, ISPs are seen as analogous to broadcasters (a far remove indeed from postal services, and interesting in the light of some of the discussion in Chapter 4),[114] and are subject to regulation accordingly.

The main concern in Singapore appears to be the 'broadcasting' of pornography to the citizens of Singapore, but the original Internet Code of Practice also included sections on 'Public Security and National Defence' and 'Racial and Religious Harmony'.[115] Singapore is a multi-racial society with many religions. There has been unrest in the past, and the Government is very anxious to maintain 'Singapore's racial and religious harmony'.[116]

There are two strands to the legislation in Singapore. First, there is limited immunity provision. As in the EU, there is, in Singapore, a general immunity for packet transmission and caching but, unlike the EU, probably not at all for hosting.[117] The problem is that the immunity is confined in s 10(3) of the Electronic Transactions Act 1998 to:[118]

> ... the provision of the necessary technical means by which third-party material may be accessed and includes the automatic and temporary storage of the third-party material for the purpose of providing access.

This does not include hosting, which involves more permanent storage. The liability is therefore that of the general law, which is common law based. ISPs are regarded as publishers, therefore, and seen as the equivalent, in this regard, of newspapers, rather than libraries or postal services.

Not only is there no general immunity for ISPs, but the second strand of the legislation provides for positive regulation. Section 10(2)(b) of the Singapore statute allows for additional regulation, over and above the general law:

> (2) Nothing in this section shall affect—
>
> ...
>
> (b) the obligation of a network service provider as such under a licensing or other regulatory regime established under any written law ...

There is in fact a compulsory registration scheme for ISPs under the Singapore Broadcasting Authority (Class Licence) Notification 1996.[119] Authority is also given to the Media Development Authority (successor to the Singapore Broadcasting Authority) to issue the Industry Internet Guidelines and Code of Practice.[120] The code of practice in Singapore does not so much protect ISPs as, effectively, to create an

---

114 Section 4.4.3.
115 Described at http://www2.warwick.ac.uk/fac/soc/law/elj/jilt/2001_2/anil. The original Code of Practice was replaced by one slightly more tightly drafted.
116 Internet Industry Guidelines, para 14.
117 Reed's view: *Internet Law: Text and Materials, op cit* fn 2, p 134.
118 Singapore statutes, including the ETA, can be found at http://agcvldb4.agc.gov.sg.
119 www.bild.net/singapore.htm.
120 The Industry Internet Guidelines are at www.mda.gov.sg/wms.file/mobj/mobj.496. internet_industry_guide.pdf. The full text of the Singapore Internet Code of Practice is at www.mda.gov.sg/wms.file/mobj/mobj.497.internet_code.pdf.

additional layer of regulation. An ISP who follows the code incurs no liability *under the code*,[121] but is not immune from liability under the general law, so the defamation issues discussed in relation to the UK are not resolved.[122] Thus, cl 7 of the Schedule (Conditions of Class Licence) provides that: 'A licensee shall at all times comply with the laws of Singapore.' This is reinforced by cl 16:

> Nothing in this Schedule shall exempt the licensee from complying with the requirements of any other written law relating to the provision of the licensee's service.

In a review of the Code, Anil observes that[123] 'all Singapore laws, insofar as they apply to the electronic medium, are fully effective and operative in respect of acts committed in cyberspace' and 'that the parties continue to be subject to all other Singapore laws whether or not the Code stipulates as such'.

Moreover, as Anil points out, nothing in the code affects contracts with customers, which could therefore be enforced even against an ISP which complies with the code.[124]

12.2.4   Conclusions on ISP hosting liability

The Singapore and US positions might be seen as the two extremes, the UK and EU positions being intermediate. In principle, there is a lot to be said for a clear code, which requires ISPs to be responsible, but such that ISPs can also be certain that if they follow the code they will not be subject to liability. No country in the world appears yet to have adopted this position.

12.2.5   Other ISP immunities

Regulations 17 and 18 enact into UK law Arts 12 and 13, the immunity provisions of the EC Directive respectively for mere conduits and caches. Regulation 17 provides a general immunity in respect of gateways and routers that simply carry traffic, without storing it for any longer than necessary to ensure that it is successfully forwarded. The immunity covers transmissions, rather than storage, and the requirements are that:

(1) ... the service provider—

(a) did not initiate the transmission;

(b) did not select the receiver of the transmission; and

(c) did not select or modify the information contained in the transmission.

(2) The acts of transmission and of provision of access referred to in paragraph (1) include the automatic, intermediate and transient storage of the information transmitted where:

---

121 See paras 3(1)–3(3) of the code.

122 For a general (but now slightly dated) discussion of the Singapore Code of Practice, see Anil, S, 'Re-visiting the Singapore Internet Code of Practice': http://www2.warwick.ac.uk/fac/soc/law/elj/jilt/2001_2/anil.

123 *Ibid*, section 7.

124 *Ibid*, section 4.1. Presumably there would be a defence if the ISP was reacting to a clear direction by the authority.

(a) this takes place for the sole purpose of carrying out the transmission in the communication network, and

(b) the information is not stored for any period longer than is reasonably necessary for the transmission.

Regulation 18 provides a general immunity in respect of temporary caches, where:

(a) the information is the subject of automatic, intermediate and temporary storage where that storage is for the sole purpose of making more efficient onward transmission of the information to other recipients of the service upon their request, and

(b) the service provider—

(i)   does not modify the information;

(ii) complies with conditions on access to the information;

(iii) complies with any rules regarding the updating of the information, specified in a manner widely recognised and used by industry;

(iv) does not interfere with the lawful use of technology, widely recognised and used by industry, to obtain data on the use of the information; and

(v) acts expeditiously to remove or to disable access to the information he has stored upon obtaining actual knowledge of the fact that the information at the initial source of the transmission has been removed from the network, or access to it has been disabled, or that a court or an administrative authority has ordered such removal or disablement.

(ii) implies, for example, that if the original page requires payment for a service, so must the cached page. (iv) relates to matters such as recording number of hits. (iii) and (v) require cached material to be kept up to date, so as not to publish, for example, out of date prices, withdrawn products, etc.

The immunities roughly mirror, but are not identical to, that provided under the Copyright Directive in section 4.3.1. As with the immunity considered there, the requirement that storage be temporary would not appear to cover more permanent mirror sites.

INDEX